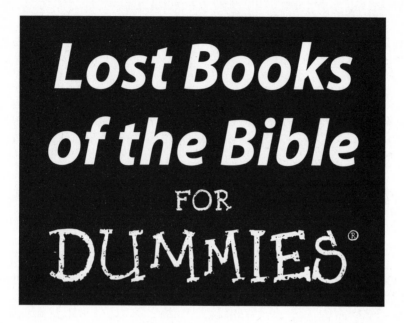

Lost Books of the Bible FOR DUMMIES®

by Dr. Daniel L. Smith-Christopher
and Stephen Spignesi

WILEY

Wiley Publishing, Inc.

Lost Books of the Bible For Dummies®

Published by
Wiley Publishing, Inc.
111 River St.
Hoboken, NJ 07030-5774
www.wiley.com

About the Authors

Dr. Daniel L. Smith-Christopher has taught Biblical Studies and Peace Studies at Loyola Marymount University in Los Angeles for 20 years. He received his Master of Divinity from Associated Mennonite Biblical Seminary in 1981 and his Doctor of Philosophy in Biblical Theology from Oxford University in 1986. He has published several books and articles in Biblical Studies and Peace Studies, including *Jonah, Jesus, and Other Good Coyotes: Speaking Peace to Power in the Bible; Introduction to the Old Testament: Our Call to Faith and Justice;* and *A Biblical Theology of Exile*. Dr. Smith-Christopher lectures widely in churches and parishes throughout the United States and abroad and also appears frequently on documentary television programs dealing with biblical themes on A&E, the History Channel, and the National Geographic Channel.

Dr. Smith-Christopher has the interesting job of being a Protestant (Quaker) Bible teacher at a Roman Catholic university, which means that he works across different Christian traditions. He enjoys diverse viewpoints and perspectives, and when it comes to "non-canonical" books, diversity is the name of the game!

Stephen Spignesi is a bestselling author, editor, screenwriter, and university instructor. He has written 42 nonfiction books and one novel, *Dialogues* (Random House). He is coauthor of several *For Dummies* books, including *Second Homes For Dummies* and *Native American History For Dummies*. He's also the author of the recent *George Washington's Leadership Lessons* (Wiley), which he co-wrote with the Executive Director of Mount Vernon, James Rees. He is a Practitioner in Residence at the University of New Haven where he teaches writing. He also has several original screenplays in submission to production companies and is the Founder and Editor-in-Chief of the small-press publishing company, The Stephen John Press. He lives in New Haven, Connecticut, with his wife Pam and their intelligent, asthmatic cat Carter.

Dedications

From Daniel: This book is dedicated to Zsa Zsa, whom I married in 1992 because I'm no dummy!

From Stephen: I dedicate this book to the memory of my father, with love.

Authors' Acknowledgments

From Daniel: This has been a very rewarding task, largely because of my talented cowriter Stephen, who transformed my often difficult (and occasionally just plain bad) writing into something understandable. If there are still problems in this text, it has nothing to do with him — he had plenty of heavy lifting with all the stuff he did catch! I would like to thank Chrissy Guthrie and Elizabeth Rea for their always valuable and insightful questions and clarifications in the writing process, and a special thanks to Mike Lewis for giving me the honor of writing this book. His insistence that I was the perfect author for this project was flattering and humbling. You have my heartfelt gratitude, Mike. Also, the entire editorial staff at Wiley have been tremendously helpful, and I appreciate them very much. Finally, I have two important sets of folks to mention: I feel deep appreciation to all my adult students in the Archdiocese of Los Angeles, the Diocese of San Bernardino, and the Diocese of Las Vegas (yes, you, Fr. Joe and St. Anthonys!) who always kept me on my toes and helped me to understand the importance of explaining things as clearly as I could — you are no dummies! And lastly I want to acknowledge the patience of my family as I worked on this project — love to Zsa Zsa, our son Jordan, and our daughter Sydney.

From Stephen: First and foremost, I'd like to thank my coauthor Daniel for his friendship, his good humor, and his talent and astonishing knowledge of biblical theology, which made working with him an absolute delight. Also, I must thank our Acquisitions Editor Mike Lewis for his . . . well, for just about everything. You're a real paesan, brother. Also, mucho gratitude to our Senior Project Editor Chrissy Guthrie and our Senior Copy Editor Elizabeth Rea for their keen sense of what this book needed to be, and for their counsel and questions that served to get it there! Also, personally, I'd like to thank my agent and great friend John White, my inordinately helpful Teaching Assistant Adrienne Candela, and my dearest friends Valerie, George, Jim, Charlie, and Bob for their support and strong shoulders on which I have been known to occasionally lean.

Publisher's Acknowledgments

We're proud of this book; please send us your comments through our Dummies online registration form located at www.dummies.com/register/.

Some of the people who helped bring this book to market include the following:

Acquisitions, Editorial, and Media Development

Senior Project Editor: Christina Guthrie

Acquisitions Editor: Mike Lewis

Senior Copy Editor: Elizabeth Rea

Editorial Program Coordinator: Erin Calligan Mooney

Technical Editor: Dr. Gary Allen Henecke

Editorial Manager: Christine Meloy Beck

Editorial Assistants: Joe Niesen, David Lutton

Cover Photo: Kenneth Garrett

Cartoons: Rich Tennant (www.the5thwave.com)

Composition Services

Project Coordinator: Katie Key

Layout and Graphics: Carl Byers, Reuben W. Davis, Andrea Hornberger, Stephanie D. Jumper, Christine Williams

Special Art: Interior images courtesy of Art Resource and Corbis

Proofreaders: Caitie Kelly, Bonnie Mikkelson

Indexer: Becky Hornyak

Special Help: Alicia South

Publishing and Editorial for Consumer Dummies

    Diane Graves Steele, Vice President and Publisher, Consumer Dummies

    Joyce Pepple, Acquisitions Director, Consumer Dummies

    Kristin A. Cocks, Product Development Director, Consumer Dummies

    Michael Spring, Vice President and Publisher, Travel

    Kelly Regan, Editorial Director, Travel

Publishing for Technology Dummies

    Andy Cummings, Vice President and Publisher, Dummies Technology/General User

Composition Services

    Gerry Fahey, Vice President of Production Services

    Debbie Stailey, Director of Composition Services

Contents at a Glance

Table of Contents

Introduction

The phrase "lost books of the Bible" is an oxymoron. If a book is really lost, then how does anyone know about it? Good question, right? In some cases, there are some genuinely "lost" books because historians and scholars know the title and maybe a quotation here and there from other ancient sources, but the writing itself isn't available because it didn't survive into the modern world. However, if that were the only kind of writing covered in *Lost Books of the Bible For Dummies,* it would be a very short book!

In most cases, of course, the lost books aren't really lost; they're simply rarely read, forgotten, or only recently rediscovered. That is, the main subject of this book is the ancient Jewish and Christian religious writings that didn't end up in the Hebrew Bible (what many Jews refer to as the "TaNaK," an acronym from the Hebrew words for "Torah, Prophets, and Writings"), the Christian Old Testament, or the Christian New Testament.

About This Book

If you're intrigued by the idea that the Bible was a "selection" of writings and that there were some writings "not selected," then this book is for you!

In this book, we attempt to summarize most, if not all, of the religious writings that have survived from ancient Jewish and ancient Christian writers. But if you want to know about those books not included in the Bible, then you clearly won't be satisfied with short summaries! So, this book is intended to be your *starting* point on your journey of discovery. From here, you can go to the various writings themselves (all available in English) and dig into them for yourself.

Here's what you can expect from this book:

- ✔ A basic introduction to the process that led to the formation of the Hebrew Bible, the Old Testament, and the New Testament
- ✔ A summary of most of the writings that are available for study and that aren't in the Bible

> ✔ An explanation of the differences among the available non-biblical writings, especially because some of them arguably came close to being included while others were definitely less popular
>
> ✔ Suggestions of ways to understand some of the more difficult-to-read writings
>
> ✔ Suggestions of how to start your own exploration of the world of non-canonical writings

In short, this book starts you on a journey of discovery of lost books that won't be so "lost" when you finish!

Conventions Used in This Book

In this book, we use the following general conventions that you should be aware of:

> ✔ When we introduce a new term in a chapter, we *italicize* it.
>
> ✔ Keywords appear in **boldface.**
>
> ✔ Web sites and e-mail addresses appear in `monofont` to help them stand out from the rest of the text.

As well, some terms, abbreviations, and other elements of this book may be confusing without some explanation, so the following sections clear up additional conventions used in this book.

"Canon" and "non-canonical"

The word "canon" comes from the Greek and typically refers to a set of measurements, like a "ruler" or "yardstick." But it also can refer to a set of measurements used to reproduce a copy of something. When the early Christians started using the term (sometime after 100 CE, it seems), it eventually came to mean the "set list" of writings that were to be included in the Bible. Problem is, people started using "canon" before lists were drawn up, so no one is absolutely certain what the early Christians thought was their "canon" until the first actual list of writings appeared around 367 CE.

All writings that didn't make it into the canon of the Old or New Testaments or the Hebrew Bible are therefore known as *non-canonical* writings. Bottom line: This entire book is all about non-canonical writings! For a terrific resource on the Bible itself, check out *The Bible For Dummies* by Jeffrey Geoghegan and Michael Homan (published by Wiley).

Dates: BCE and CE

Dates are always difficult to remember, but *ancient* dates can be downright confusing! In this book, we use the following designations when referring to the time before and after the beginning of Christianity.

- ✓ **BCE:** Before the Common Era (that is, before the beginning of Christianity)
- ✓ **CE:** The Common Era (after the beginning of Christianity)

These designations are the same as BC and AD, respectively, but BC and AD are specifically *Christian* forms, whereas BCE and CE are more inclusive of both Christians and Jews. What we today call Judaism was *also* taking shape at about the same time as Christianity — Judaism and Christianity are *both* descendants of ancient Hebrew religion, and they both went their own ways. To recognize this fact, we refer to the "Common Era" (common between Judaism and Christianity).

"Hebrew Bible" versus "Old Testament"

Although the Hebrew Bible and the Old Testament are the same group of writings, "Hebrew Bible" is the label Jews prefer to use when speaking of their Bible. The term "Old Testament" is the specifically Christian name for the first section of the Christian Bible. Christians, of course, added the New Testament writings to their Bible.

When we speak of the Old Testament in this book, we always keep in mind that Roman Catholic, Orthodox (Greek, Russian, Coptic, and so on), and Protestant Christians don't entirely agree on the specific writings to be included in their respective Old Testaments, but they do agree on the writings of the New Testament. You can find out more about these differences of opinion in Chapter 2.

Translations

In this book, we cite from the best translations of non-canonical writings that are available. In some cases, a few different translations are available, but we always go with the most recent, most scholarly translations available. The appendix provides you with a list of *all* the books and studies we cite.

What You're Not to Read

Believe it or not, this book does contain material that's entirely skippable. We don't mean to say that this material isn't useful or interesting; we simply mean that it isn't critical to your understanding of the material in the chapter. (Of course, we'd be flattered and honored if you read every single solitary word we've written in this book, but we both live in the real world, so no guilt if you don't!)

Anyway, information marked with a Technical Stuff icon is, well, technical. It's a tad arcane, but provided for those of you who are interested in the minutiae of ancient texts.

The sidebars, which appear in gray-shaded boxes, are full of interesting material (at least we think so; it is our book, after all) that you don't need to read to understand the chapter but that will serve to enhance your enjoyment of the chapter if you do.

So, to sum up, skip this stuff if you want, but a splendid time is guaranteed for all who don't!

Foolish Assumptions

In writing *Lost Books of the Bible For Dummies,* we made a number of assumptions about you, our reader. We assume that any or all of the following descriptors may be true for you.

- ✔ You're curious about ancient history.
- ✔ You're interested in making discoveries for yourself.
- ✔ You're fascinated with controversies in religious issues without being threatened by that controversy.
- ✔ You're willing to understand that not all ancient writings left out of the Bible are therefore bad or even wrong — some of them may surprise you with their beauty and wisdom!
- ✔ You're patient in understanding that summaries are always inherently unfair to the writing itself and serve only to whet your appetite and help you choose the ones you want to take the time to read.

How This Book Is Organized

We organize this book into parts so that you can jump around to the information you're looking for, but you also can read it from beginning to end if that suits your fancy. Here's a look at the different parts that comprise this book.

Part I: Setting the Stage

Most people are shocked (shocked, we say!) to discover that, for Jews and Christians both, the Bible didn't take its final shape until about the third or fourth century. What was the holdup? In this part, we examine how the Bible emerged in its current forms for Christians and Jews, the two religions that share major sections of the Bible. We also provide foundational information on the various categories of religious writing. Understanding these categories will help you to better understand the discussions that take place throughout the book.

Part II: Ancient Jewish Lost Books

In this part, we examine the pre-Christian Jewish writings that have survived but aren't in any of the Christian Old Testaments or the present Hebrew Bible. What are these strange writings, and where did they come from? We answer these questions, surveying lots of different writings, and we pay particular attention to the Dead Sea Scrolls, what's known as the Apocrypha, and to one very special lost book: the Book of Enoch.

Part III: Lost Books about Jesus

The Christian non-canonical writings that we cover in this part focus on the person of Jesus. These include gospels and other sayings of Jesus as well as some types of writings about Jesus that weren't included in the New Testament.

Part IV: Lost Early Christian Writings

The New Testament features four "Gospels" about Jesus but then proceeds to writings from and about the earliest followers of Jesus — the first Christians. Many writings about these early Christians weren't included in the New Testament. There are gems to be found, and discoveries to be made! In this part, we start by covering writings from a rather strange group called the "Gnostic Christians." We then follow with chapters on Christian books that almost made the cut, other apocalyptic writings, and legends about Paul and other early Apostles of Jesus.

Part V: The Part of Tens

In this traditional section of *For Dummies* books, we summarize some of the "bottom-line" issues. For example, if time is tight and you want to read about only the top ten Jewish and Christian books *not* in the Bible, start here at the back!

As a little bonus, we consider ten sayings of Jesus that don't appear in the New Testament and enjoy musing whether they're genuine words from Jesus. You also get our list of ten lost books that every student of the Bible *should* be familiar with.

Finally, we include an appendix of additional resources in which we provide the titles of most of the best English translations of the various non-canonical writings of the ancient Jews and Christians, as well as some key reference works. Enjoy!

Icons Used in This Book

All *For Dummies* books use graphic icons to call attention to key pieces of information that we like you to pay particular attention to as you read. Here's a quick rundown of the icons used in this book and what they mean.

This icon points out useful pieces of biblical or historical info that will aid in your understanding of the material being discussed.

This icon is attached to key themes, concepts, facts, or dates that you should keep in mind and that may crop up again.

When you see this icon, watch out for things to be wary of, such as making false assumptions about a topic or misinterpreting a commonly held belief in a way that confuses rather than clarifies an issue.

This icon highlights details on translations, linguistic anomalies, geographical specifics, and other nonthematic info that, nonetheless, is interesting and fun to know.

Where to Go from Here

This book is written so that you can read each chapter on its own. However, it makes sense to begin with Part I, which generally deals with questions about how the Bible was formed, before you decide to skip around in the chapters that summarize different kinds of writings. If you're mainly interested in Jewish writings that aren't in the Bible, then you want Part II. If you're interested in Christian books not in the Bible, then head to Parts III and IV. What about Part V? Well, we confess that we had some fun with that section because we got to create some unconventional lists.

Finally, if you find that you're really into all this lost books stuff and want to know more, you can check out some of the additional books and resources we list in the appendix.

Part I
Setting the Stage

The 5th Wave　　　　By Rich Tennant

"This is our family bible. It's truly a lamp to my feet, a light for my path, and a balance unto our bookshelf."

In this part . . .

This part starts by asking the obvious questions: How do books get "lost"? And if they're lost, how does anyone know anything about them? We provide some answers to these questions and discuss the very important issue of forming a "canon" of the Bible — an approved, "this is it, and no more" list. We also explore the important (and frankly, controversial) question about how the Bible came to be — both the Hebrew Bible (what Christians call the Old Testament); and the Christian Bible, which features both the Old Testament and the New Testament. Finally, we include a chapter in this part that gives you some tools to understand different styles of ancient Jewish and Christian religious writing so that you can better understand our discussions of various lost books.

Chapter 1

How to Lose Books of the Bible: A Hands-On Guide

*L*et's face it: the idea of "lost books" — no matter what the field — is tantalizing and exciting. And when you combine the appeal of arcane writings and "secret knowledge" with the Bible, well, the result is practically irresistible!

The idea of lost books suggests secrets to be discovered, information to be gained, and surprises ahead. It also calls up romantic images of archaeologists uncovering long-lost manuscripts, blowing off the dust, and reading the unexpected. (This is obviously one reason archaeologists are so romanticized, even though *most* archaeologists hardly have lives like Indiana Jones!)

In this chapter, we discuss the general idea of lost books in relation to the Bible and discuss some of the most spectacular discoveries of the 19th and 20th centuries in terms of ancient Jewish and Christian writings. We also talk about the debates and processes that finally led to the Bible that exists today, and the fact that most people think about two groups of writings when they should be thinking about *three*. What we mean is that most folks think of the writings that made it into the Bible and all the others that did not. But there's a *third* group that we call the "almost in" books. This is the especially fascinating group that *some* Jews and Christians deeply treasured but that still didn't make the final cut!

What Do We Mean By "Lost Books of the Bible"?

"Lost books of the Bible" is certainly an intriguing phrase and an even more intriguing concept. But what exactly does it mean? Are there really books out there that were supposed to be in the Bible, but somehow got "lost" along the way? Well, not really. By "lost books," we actually mean a few different things.

Books that were always around, just unknown by most people

Literally dozens and dozens of writings from the time *before* Jesus, written by different groups of ancient Jewish writers, weren't included in the standard collection of writings known as the Bible. But these writings were never actually lost. (For many people who don't know about them, however, they may seem like "lost books.") For example, most everyone has at least *heard* of the Dead Sea Scrolls, but most don't realize that in addition to the familiar books of the Hebrew Bible, these famous scrolls contain some *very* unusual writings from an unusual group of pre-Christian Jewish believers who lived in the desert near the Dead Sea.

Many people read the Bible but have no idea that ancient Jewish writings that weren't included in the Hebrew Bible (what the Christians call the *Old Testament*) even exist. Furthermore, many Christians who know their New Testament very well are unaware of the many early Christian writings that weren't included in the modern Christian New Testament.

Quite a few of these writings have long been available in English translation and gathered into collections, and biblical scholars read and study them very carefully as important historical sources — even if Christians in the churches don't read them or even know about them. For example, about a dozen writings now called the *Apostolic Fathers* (see Chapter 13) consist of writings that *some* early Christians *did* want in their New Testament! Other writings were written by factions or groups that had particular disagreements with what later emerged as Orthodox Christianity. It turns out that the first centuries of Christianity were quite a wild ride — lots of debates, meetings, arguments . . . and lots of writings! Sometimes the only reason historians even know about some writings that are *still* lost is because the writings are quoted in the arguments of early Christian theologians who try to show how *unacceptable* they are.

Books that were lost but found again

Some lost books have turned up over the centuries. Most of the time, these are writings that scholars knew existed but thought were lost. The famous *Book of 1 Enoch* (see Chapter 6) is one such example; it's not only well known from early Christian use but also is even quoted in the New Testament's Jude:

> *It was also about these that Enoch, in the seventh generation from Adam, prophesied, saying, "See, the Lord is coming with ten thousands of his holy ones, to execute judgment on all, and to convict everyone of all the deeds of ungodliness that they have committed in such an ungodly way, and of all the harsh things that ungodly sinners have spoken against him."*
>
> —Jude 1:14–15

Early Christian writers after the time of the New Testament also referred to 1 Enoch on occasion, so its existence was known. Then in the late 18th century, the Scottish explorer James Bruce was exploring in Ethiopia and found that the Ethiopic Christians had hand-copied editions of this book in the ancient Ethiopic language of Ge'ez. He brought some copies back to Europe, generating great excitement until it was finally published in English some 30 years later.

To Europeans, the Book of 1 Enoch was lost, but to Ethiopians (who probably wondered what all the fuss was about), it was not.

One way that lost books are found is in old libraries where they're gathering dust and ignored until someone realizes what they are and reveals them to the world. Many formerly lost books were discovered in this way — in the backs of ancient libraries or even in museums!

Books quoted in other works but never actually found

One category of lost books are those whose titles are known and that scholars have some general ideas about content-wise thanks to quotations and references in other ancient writings, such as early Christian theologians who are arguing about them. But they don't have actual copies of these books . . . yet. But in these cases, scholars and researchers definitely know what to look for!

The recent excitement about the rediscovery of the *Gospel of Judas* is similar. (We summarize this work in Chapter 11.) Scholars knew that such a writing existed, but it didn't turn up until the late 20th century. The discovery was announced to the world with great fanfare in 2005, with a rather significant campaign of books, television programs, and promotional activities.

Previously unknown books

We don't want to sound too cynical by suggesting that calling these works "lost" is always erroneous and an overstatement, because entirely unknown writings are occasionally discovered. It happened in 1948–1956, when the Dead Sea Scrolls were discovered. Included in the large number of texts found over a number of years in the caves by the Dead Sea in Israel/Palestine were ancient Hebrew versions of books in the Hebrew Bible. However, the collection also included a large number of writings entirely new, entirely unknown, and entirely unexpected by modern scholars and historians. These were unique writings written by the small group that once owned and produced these hand-written scrolls. So, sometimes unknown writings can turn up.

Three of the Greatest "Lost Books" Finds of All Time

To get an idea of how this "lost books" business works, take a look at three of the greatest finds of the 19th and 20th centuries that are directly related to the Bible:

- The discovery the Codex Siniaticus, one of the oldest complete New Testaments in Greek in possession today
- The discovery of the Nag Hammadi Library (1945)
- The discovery of the Dead Sea Scrolls (1947–1956)

Throughout this book, we discuss some of the results of these discoveries (and others), but here we focus on the stories of these three major discoveries and a bit about why they were so significant. Not every discovery is this dramatic, and, of course, we chose the best ones to get you, our reader, warmed up to the subject!

The Codex Siniaticus

Here's a great beginning to a story: There once was a German professor of the Bible named Constantin Tischendorff who was notable for his interest in recovering the earliest manuscripts of the Bible he could find. In 1844, he first visited the famous ancient Greek Orthodox monastery St. Catherine's, which sits at the base of a mountain in the Sinai desert traditionally thought to be *the* Mount Sinai where Moses received the law (a claim highly disputed by modern archaeologists and historians, by the way).

Although he was searching for old manuscripts, Tischendorff never could have dreamed that his travels would soon reveal one of the most important early manuscripts of the Bible. According to one version of the story, the visiting scholar spotted some Greek handwritten pages heading for the fire and recovered them, only to discover that they were ancient Christian manuscripts. In another version of the story, he saved actual pages of a Greek Bible that were headed for the trash, but either way, Tischendorff's inquiries led to his being shown what he thought *should* have been a treasured book from the monastery library (and, in still other versions of the story — it *was* already a treasured work): It was a Greek Bible from the fourth or fifth century CE! It had portions of the Greek Old Testament and a complete New Testament . . . and then some. (The "then some" included some of what was later called the Apostolic Fathers, books that eventually did *not* end up in the New Testament; see Chapter 13 for more on this collection of writings.)

Eventually, Tischendorff returned to the monastery in 1859 with funding from the Tsar of Russia and convinced the monks to lend (or sell, depending on whom you believe) the famous book to the Tsar. The monks today claim to have a letter from Tischendorff promising to return the manuscript, so they accuse him of stealing it!

Like a great murder mystery, the plot thickens. When the Russian Revolution occurred, Lenin needed cash and agreed to sell the ancient Bible manuscript to the British Museum in 1933. It remains on display at the museum to this very day. According to one story, a large crowd gathered when the book was delivered to the museum, and the entire crowd dropped to their knees as the book was slowly walked up the long stairway to the museum entrance. Great story. But why all the fuss?

This particular Bible, known today as *Codex Siniaticus* (which means *The Book from Sinai*), may well be one of the 50 Bibles commissioned by Emperor Constantine I, the first Christian Roman Emperor, who wanted Bibles produced for 50 churches in his new capital city, Constantinople (modern Istanbul). Furthermore, this New Testament contains the *Epistle of Barnabas* and the *Shepherd of Hermas,* which don't appear in the existing New Testament. The inclusion of these works in the Codex suggests to some scholars that *some* early Christians included them among New Testament books. Also, the *Gospel of Mark* that appears in the Codex differs slightly from the version in the existing New Testament — it has the famous "shorter ending" that follows the description of the empty tomb. (There are two disputed endings to the Gospel of Mark: the longer ending found in some early manuscripts, and the shorter ending found in Codex Siniaticus. Most English translations of the New Testament provide *both* endings so you can compare them.)

The discovery of the Nag Hammadi Library

In the Nag Hammadi region of southern Egypt, a couple of poor farmers were digging for some nitrates to fertilize their crops when they uncovered a jar. Hoping that it contained something valuable, they broke it only to discover a number of leather-bound papyrus pages and many fragments of written work. The farmers wrapped up the ancient writings and brought them home.

They recognized some of the ancient writing as Coptic (an ancient Egyptian language now used almost exclusively as a written language in the Coptic Christian churches in Egypt and Ethiopia), so they assumed that the writings had something to do with Christianity. Eventually, they gave the pages to the local Coptic Christian Priest. It wasn't long before the manuscripts made it to the Coptic Museum in Cairo.

The collection of writings turned out to be Coptic translations of older Greek manuscripts of Christian writings from the fourth century. Because ancient Christian monks once practiced solitary prayers in the local caves of the Nag Hammadi region, it was assumed that the writings were deposited in the caves for safekeeping and then forgotten. Some have suggested that, at one point, the discovered writings weren't considered acceptable for early Christians to read, and so instead of destroying them, some ancient Egyptian Christians decided to bury them.

Why do so many ancient manuscripts turn up in Egypt?

The answer to this question is easy: Ancient manuscripts survive really well in Egypt's very dry climate. Also, many ancient Egyptian writings are written on papyrus, which consists of flattened and interwoven long strips of leaves from the papyrus plant that grows wild up and down the Nile. Papyrus is very durable, and it likes dry climates!

Even moving the short distance north into modern Israel/Palestine and especially as far north as Lebanon increases the rainfall just enough to make the environment and atmosphere less friendly to ancient manuscripts. Unless these fragile writings are sealed in clay jars, they're unlikely to make it (even in Egypt, but it's where they have the best chance).

Of course, another important reason for so many discoveries in Egypt is that ancient Egypt was a major Jewish and Christian center — especially ancient Alexandria on the coast — and therefore many writings were produced there.

Most of the Nag Hammadi writings (collectively referred to as the Nag Hammadi Library) show signs of Gnostic influence, an ancient philosophy that influenced a large number of early Christians but led to serious quarrels from Christians who believed that Gnosticism introduced dangerous ideas into Christian theology (see the Gnosticism discussion in Chapter 12). No one knows for sure how these writings were first deposited or why, so the theories are pure speculation.

The discovery of the Dead Sea Scrolls

For biblical studies, easily the most spectacular find of the 20th century — and perhaps even the most spectacular find in the entire millennium — is the Dead Sea Scrolls.

The story is now rather famous: A Bedouin boy was trying to find a stray goat that had wandered into one of the dozens of caves in the hillsides by the shores of the Dead Sea (see Figure 1-1 for a photo of these caves). Apparently hoping to chase the goat out of the darkness in the back of the cave, he threw a rock to startle the goat, but the rock hit something and the boy heard the sound of breaking clay. The rest, as they say, is history.

Figure 1-1:
The caves where the Dead Sea Scrolls were found.

Erich Lessing / Art Resource, NY

Some of the scrolls were eventually sold to Professor Eleazar L. Sukenik at the Hebrew University; others were sold to clergy of the Syrian Orthodox Church, until they too were eventually purchased by representatives of Israel.

After it became clear where the original clay jars were discovered, all the remaining caves throughout the entire area were thoroughly searched, turning up more and more discoveries. All told, over 800 manuscripts and thousands of pieces and fragments were found, and other finds were discovered in later years. Most of the scrolls are now kept in Israel, but smaller pieces are in other museum collections.

The Dead Sea Scrolls contain two kinds of material:

- ✔ Copies of writings known from the Bible (the Bible, of course, was determined later than the time of the Scrolls)

- ✔ Copies of Jewish religious writings that were never seen before (some known, but some entirely unknown)

It's presumed that the community who originally produced these writings treasured both kinds of literature with equal reverence. The writings that only they knew and treasured most likely were writings that they composed, which is why they weren't known and quoted by other ancient Jewish writers (as far as scholars know) and also why there are multiple copies of these writings.

Portions — some more complete than others — of every book of the Hebrew Bible except Esther are represented in the Dead Sea Scrolls. The real significance of the "biblical" books (of course, there wasn't a Bible yet at the time) is that they're written in Hebrew and Aramaic and therefore are older than any other Hebrew versions that exist in modern times. Because of the tradition in Judaism of using scrolls that are only in very good condition, older scrolls were typically destroyed in favor of newer copies. Therefore, before the Hebrew manuscripts of the Dead Sea were discovered, the oldest Hebrew manuscripts were only as old as the ninth to tenth centuries CE.

Although scholars had old Greek translations of the biblical books (like *Codex Siniaticus*) prior to the discovery of the Dead Sea Scrolls, they didn't have very old Hebrew versions. So, when you look at a Dead Sea Scroll, you're looking at a Hebrew version of these writings that's virtually 1,000 years *older* than any Hebrew language copies of the Bible that had been seen for hundreds of years. It's like taking a giant step back in time to see how the Hebrew Bible looked back then. Of course, the discovery of these manuscripts revolutionized the study of the Hebrew Bible because it supplied much older manuscripts to work with and to compare with more recent versions.

The dates of the scrolls are estimated to be from about 300 BCE to 50–60 CE. Scholars assume that these scrolls were written by a community of Jews who were disappointed with the religious life in Jerusalem and may even have had some arguments with the people controlling the Temple there. It appears that the community left Jerusalem to set up a separate community somewhere near the Dead Sea and possibly at the ruins near Qumran. When the Jewish Revolt led to Roman military reprisals against Jewish towns and communities, one theory is that members of this community hid their library in hopes of coming back to retrieve it after things had settled down — but nobody survived who knew where the works were hidden. So, there they sat, in those caves, until the 20th century.

In, Almost In, and Out: Categorizing Ancient Religious Writing

Anyone who studies the formation of the Bible soon discovers that the process involved lots of discussion about various writings — especially among Christians. The Jewish scholars, interestingly enough, didn't talk much about the issue of a "set collection" of special writings even though they most certainly did make a final decision about their collection of religious writings — a collection that eventually became the Hebrew Bible. The Christians eventually had to decide what their Bible would contain, but they had to decide on contents for *both* their Old Testament *and* their New Testament. The Jewish tradition eventually decided what comprised their Hebrew Bible, but their decision process was quite different from the Christians' even though they were talking about some of the same writings!

To complicate matters even more, not only are we talking about three different processes (Christians working on *two* different collections and Jews working on *one*), but also there were never only two categories of religious writings: good and bad. That's far too simplistic, and furthermore, it's not true to the historical facts and the discussions that actually took place.

There are actually *three* categories of ancient religious writings in the lives of the ancient Jews and the ancient Christians:

- ✔ The books that *are* in the Bible.

- ✔ The books that were *almost in* the Bible. Lots of people like them, but in the end, they didn't make it.

- ✔ The books that were *rejected* for inclusion in the Bible. These books had no shot at being included.

Note: *Lost Books of the Bible For Dummies* doesn't focus on the first category, the books that are in the Bible. We briefly talk about them collectively, but if this is your real interest, then we recommend that you turn to *The Bible For Dummies,* by Jeffrey Geoghegan and Michael Homan (published by Wiley). Even though we speak about the Bible throughout this book, we're mainly interested in the second and third categories, the "almost in" and the "clearly out."

Complicating matters: Adding a fourth category

An early Christian historian named Eusebius of Caesarea (early fourth century) is often called the Father of Christian History Writing because he wrote a massive work (that we still have, usually published in two volumes) called the *History of the Church.*

In his work, Eusebius discusses some of the debates and discussions among Christians about the religious books that would eventually become part of the canon of the New Testament. Eusebius actually talks about dozens and dozens of early Christian writings, including the books that eventually did become part of the

New Testament. In his discussion, however, Eusebius divides these writings into no less than *four* categories:

- ✔ The writings that everyone agrees are centrally important

- ✔ The writings that people argue about but most everyone likes

- ✔ The writings that people argue about but only a few people like

- ✔ The writings that pretty much nobody likes

Questioning the Idea of Biblical Lost and Found

When you get past the initial excitement of the idea of lost books and especially lost books of the Bible, some questions start nagging: How does anyone lose a book of the Bible? In fact, how can anyone lose such an important writing? And how does anyone *find* such books? Do people know where to look, or are the discoveries simply fortuitous accidents?

How do books get lost?

The interest in discovering lost books isn't new, but you may be wondering how books that are so important get lost in the first place.

Well, the main problem is that we are modern persons who think like modern people! We have printing presses that produce *thousands* of copies of a book, and wonder how *anyone* could lose a book — even a bad book.

But in the ancient world, books were *rare.* They had to be produced by *hand,* and they were kept in libraries, sometimes far from population centers where the precious writings could be damaged, stolen, or destroyed. If you only have a few copies to begin with, you begin to understand how a writing could be "lost." If a tragedy occurs — disease, fire, conquest — precious manuscripts could be lost forever. Many discovered manuscripts appear to have been *hidden* precisely to prevent bad things happening to them. Furthermore, if the writings were produced by a small faction, a "group" within the larger Church, then perhaps only a few copies were *ever* made. And, last, we hate to admit it, but the early believers (bless them) were not above *destroying* books that they didn't like, either.

When you think about it, each and every discovery of an ancient manuscript from before the days of printing is an incredible gift to modern scholars, readers, and historians. The interesting thing is, finding rare writings was already something that *ancient* people loved to talk about. Of course *they* knew how rare writings were . . . so you know *they* knew how important it was to find something older! We can easily prove this with a story from the Bible itself.

Just because it's "found" doesn't make it important

Earlier in this section, we raise an important question: "How can such important writings ever be lost?" Part of the answer is already in the question: *Important* writings are rarely lost. For both the Jews and the Christians, the only books that became lost were books not considered important by very many people. Think about it — if a work is unknown and never quoted, or only rarely mentioned by other ancient writers . . . then the fact of the matter is that the work wasn't really missed. These writings are the work of a small group of people, and it's therefore very easy to *overestimate* their importance because of the romance of finding ancient writings!

Although it's *always* important to find ancient writings to add to the evidence for writing ancient history, it's another matter completely to try to determine how *important* a writing is. After all, somebody's ancient grocery list may be ancient, and it may tell historians something about ancient diets or family meals, but it hardly belongs in the Bible as a sacred discovery. In short, age is *not* the only issue here.

In fact, books of the Bible aren't really lost or found. The Bible emerged from a long process of using writings in the life of a religious tradition. The very fact that these writings weren't lost is important — you don't lose something that you use again and again, make copies of, and distribute all around. But if you're a small group whose writings don't appeal to very many folks, then when you die out, so does the interest in your writings . . . sometimes. The important point is this: Scholars actually have every single work that was quoted extensively and often by ancient Christians. They weren't lost. But what scholars don't have is *every* work that ancient Christians ever quoted. Some writings that weren't quoted very often (if at all) haven't survived. True, it would be nice to have them, but that's not the same as saying, "A book of the Bible is *missing!*" That would make a *great* headline, but it doesn't make sense. How could it be so important if it's lost?

Do Books Get Suppressed?

Another way to speak of lost books, however, has more to do with *modern* ideas than ancient ones. Some modern scholars, for example, have decided that they quite *like* some of the books that were excluded from the Bible. For one reason or another, they defend their interest in those books by suggesting that it was a "political" decision to exclude these writings.

However, the fact is that Christianity in the first few centuries was never so centrally and powerfully organized. Nobody paid much attention to "central leaders" until the Roman Empire became "Christian." So, most of the time, the early Christian leaders decided to endorse those writings that the Christians already were using for over 200 years and finding really positive and useful. Leaders weren't imposing books on people who didn't want them, just following along with the "group decision."

On the other hand, modern readers may wonder if there was some kind of agenda (religious or political) that led to some books being excluded. If you could make the historical case that a large number of people *liked* a particular writing that was excluded, then you may have a good argument that something is up — and you have reason to wonder what happened!

Although it doesn't happen anymore, books may have been suppressed, or even destroyed, among early Christians. In fact, some believe that the Nag Hammadi Library is a group of writings that some early Christian didn't have the heart to destroy, so he buried them (or hid them) instead, and the documents survived to the present.

The real question is whether there's any such thing as a modern conspiracy to hide some religious writings. The answer should be obvious to anyone who has visited a good university library! There they are in plain sight: English translations of everything that has been found so far.

It's traditional that historians or archaeologists have the right to be the first ones to publish their discoveries. But they're supposed to get to it in a reasonable amount of time. They're allowed a few years to do some research and carefully prepare a publication of what they've discovered, including a translation, but they aren't supposed to take lots of time to do it. Other scholars will get *very* impatient if the find isn't published fairly quickly.

For example, some of the Dead Sea Scrolls were held up for publication for decades, causing a great outcry among scholars until it was revealed that photographic copies of virtually all the main scrolls were available in libraries in different parts of the world. The Huntington Library in Los Angeles famously made the first announcement that they would make these previously secret photographs available for scholarly examination. Why were they kept from public view in the first place? We hesitate to answer this because it doesn't put scholars in a very good light! The scrolls weren't being suppressed because people were afraid of what they said; rather, it's now quite clear that the scrolls were being held by a handful of scholars who wanted the sole right to decide who could publish them and do research on them. Eventually, a public outcry against the scholars who kept these scrolls to themselves incited the Huntington Library to break the silence by announcing the availability of the photos.

What does this story reveal? Basically this: The scholarly world would never tolerate a suppressed discovery. No church, no museum, and no organization has the ability to keep discoveries from the public for long. The outcry eventually becomes intolerable (and rightly so!). Moreover, *most* scholars absolutely agree with full disclosure and staunchly resist the idea that anything should be suppressed. Although some people believe that some ancient writings may be suppressed to protect certain institutions or even whole religions, the simple fact is that many scholars have no particular religious interests, and so they certainly wouldn't go along with any religious-based attempt to suppress writings.

So, although "conspiracy to suppress evidence" sounds exciting, in the end it's really impossible to execute in the modern scholarly and academic world. Medical researchers wouldn't last long if they faked or withheld evidence . . . it's the same with ancient historians! The only lost books of the Bible that remain unknown are the *ones that are still lost.*

Chapter 2

Tracing the History of the Jewish and Christian Biblical Canons

. . . .

In This Chapter

▶ Defining a biblical canon and sorting out the differences based on religion

▶ Tracing the creation of the Jewish canon and the appearance of a written list

▶ Understanding the roots of the Christian canon in Jewish and Greek writings

▶ Debating what's in and what's out of the Christian canon

. . . .

*B*elieve it or not, the Bible as you know it didn't come into existence out of whole cloth or from any single unanimous decision by ancient scholars that also commanded widespread popular acceptance by the people. Furthermore, nobody sat down and consciously said, "Today I'm writing a book of the Bible." Instead, selected writings became well-known, well-loved, and passed around . . . and *that* led to the discussion of which collection or list of such writings were recommended to everyone.

Having said that, however, a good word to describe the period in which the decisions about the books of the Bible were made, as well as the process involved in such decisions, is *contentious*. While a core of writings seemed to always be at the center from as early as the second century CE, the fringes continued to be debated before lists were finally settled upon. In this chapter, we go through that process and look at what books and writings were considered, who did some of the considering, and who made the final decisions as to what the Holy Bible would actually look like.

But isn't this book about the books that *didn't* make it into the Bible as we know it today? Why does it matter how and when the biblical canon was assembled? And why should we even care? Glad you asked. There are very good answers to those questions . . . and that's why you're here.

The most obvious question about "lost books" is how they got, well, "lost" in the first place. That means revisiting how the canon was formed to see if we can figure out the basis for excluding some writings (it isn't always obvious). But more important, one discovers that this was a slow process that involved *lots* of debates and arguments, and was not a single decision imposed "from above" by any one leader in either the Jewish or Christian traditions. There is no "plot" here; it was a debate with lots of participants.

First Things First: Understanding a Biblical Canon

The word "canon" comes from a Greek term that originally meant "measuring stick," like a ruler or yardstick. The word was also used to refer to a set of measurements or even plans for proper construction of something, like a temple or a shrine.

When used in connection with collections of writings, the term "canon" refers to a widely recognized list of texts. For example, you may have heard of a canon of British literature, a canon of Greek poetry, and so on. These are simply the most popular works or the basics to get you started. In biblical studies, however — and this is important — "canon" means much more. A biblical canon refers to the actual approved list of scripture (meaning simply religious books) that became central to religious discussion and debate on matters of faith. If it isn't on the list and therefore part of the canon, it isn't considered a solid basis for the faith.

Keep in mind that when we talk about scripture, the term "canon" means "official and approved," not simply "suggested, recognized, or recommended." In other words, a canon of poetry is suggested writings, but a biblical canon is the approved list and no others! The latter is much more formal.

The notion of agreeing on a biblical canon is a very controversial idea because, for starters, there's a great difference between scripture and canon, and it's very important not to confuse the two. Many religious traditions have scriptures — written works that they consider to be very important for their religious traditions. Buddhism has a scripture, as does Hinduism. But not all these religious traditions have a canon — a limited list that was officially determined and which excludes some writings and includes others. Judaism, Christianity, and Islam fit the definition, so to speak, by having what can undeniably be called canons: lists of approved writings that intentionally exclude other writings.

Of course, a canon becomes important only when there are other books besides what's on the approved list. With lots of ancient writings available, the canon is a *selection* from the larger collection of material. When it comes to studying the biblical canon, the essential questions to ask are:

✔ Who determined this list?

✔ Why were the books that were excluded not chosen?

✔ Do these excluded books contain something interesting?

✔ Were they suppressed or hidden from people?

Curiosity is the name of the game. Whenever someone says, "These are the *good* books, the right books," we instantly want to know about the bad ones and the rejected ones! It's just human nature, we guess. After all, you did just buy a book on the *lost* books of the Bible, right?

Not Everyone's Biblical Canon Is the Same

The main reason biblical canons become a bit complicated is that no less than *four* different religious groups are involved in the discussion about the Bible. Start with Judaism: Judaism has a Bible that they usually call the *TaNaK* (an acronym for Torah, Prophets, and Writings) or sometimes the Hebrew Bible.

All three Christian groups — Catholic, Orthodox, and Protestants — adopted the Hebrew Bible as the first part of their Bible, and then all three added a New Testament composed of selected early Christian writings.

This is where things get a bit complicated. The three main Christian bodies all adopted the same New Testament (which is an impressive achievement, given everything they disagree on). However, they did *not* adopt the same version of the Old Testament. It's a fascinating story that's fairly straightforward:

✔ The Roman Catholic Church adopted the Hebrew Bible but added a few later Jewish writings commonly known as *The Apocrypha* or *Deutero-Canonical Books*. We discuss these books in Chapter 4.

✔ The Protestant churches, beginning with Martin Luther and John Calvin in the 16th century, excluded the Deutero-Canonical Books and decided to adopt the same list of books as the Jews. So, the Protestant Old Testament is the same list of books as the Hebrew Bible (but usually arranged in a different order).

✔ The various Orthodox churches (Russian, Greek, Ethiopic, and so on) added even a few *more* Jewish writings to their Old Testament, in addition to the Apocryphal books added by the Catholic Church.

The remaining sections in this chapter walk you through how the Jews formed their Hebrew Bible and how Christians formed their Old and New Testaments.

The Evolution of the Old Testament (Or Hebrew Bible)

Because the Hebrew biblical writings are much older than the Christian writings, most historians start discussions about the formation of the canon by talking about the origin of sacred writings among Jews. And this makes sense because these sacred writings were the basis for the Christian canon as well.

In this section, we take a look at how a "scripture" led to a "canon" for the Hebrew writings that became the Old Testament for Christians and the Hebrew Bible for Jews.

Transitioning from oral tradition to the written word

A very old Jewish tradition claims that the famous Hebrew scribe Ezra drew up the list of the books now known as the Hebrew Bible for Jews. It's a tradition that's really based on only a few verses from the book of Nehemiah, and when you actually look at those verses, you can see that it doesn't quite say that. The problem is that the Hebrew Bible rarely talks about sacred writings. This tradition arose among the early Rabbis, the first Jewish religious leaders of the kind of Judaism that survives to this day. In fact, the Bible itself doesn't really talk about *any* writings. Most communications — even from God — were oral and therefore passed on by *speaking*.

In the ancient world, very few people could read except for trained scribes. Even kings usually couldn't read and hired scribes to write for them, so references to kings "writing letters," for example, probably meant that they dictated the letters. If you read the famous stories about how God communicated to the people in the desert after the Exodus from Egypt, you quickly see that the tradition is that Moses and the people *heard* God — God didn't send a letter:

> *Then the Lord said to Moses, "I am going to come to you in a dense cloud, in order that the people may hear when I speak with you and so trust you ever after." When Moses had told the words of the people to the Lord . . .*

> —Exodus 19:9

"Hear," "told," "speak" . . . that was the means of communication. Practically speaking, even if someone like Moses *could* write, the people would have needed to have things read to them by someone literate.

Most historians think that the first major indication of scriptures (religiously important reference writings for the Jews) is during the time of King Josiah, who reigned in Jerusalem from 640–609 BCE. The book of 2 Kings says that King Josiah started a reform campaign to clean up the Temple and try to reform the religion of Israel to return to the teachings of Moses after a series of bad kings. While cleaning up the Temple, one of the Priests found a scroll.

What did the Priest find? What was this writing, this discovered scroll? The general consensus among historians is that it was the present book of Deuteronomy or at least the laws that appear in the book of Deuteronomy.

The discovery of the scroll is one of the oldest references in the Bible to important writings. But you should keep in mind that nobody is saying anything about "scriptures" or "holy writings" yet. The find in 2 Kings is just an important writing that was referred to as a "book of the covenant" (presumably a version of the laws of Moses, and most likely a version of the book of Deuteronomy). Still, it's a beginning.

Grouping writings together

When did religious writings become important for the Jewish community as a whole? The next important event in the evolution of the Jewish canon comes almost 200 years after King Josiah (but still about 450 years before Jesus) and involves Ezra.

Ezra and Nehemiah were both Jewish officials and descendents of the exiles that the Babylonians led away from the destroyed Jerusalem back in 587 BCE. After the Babylonians, the Persian Empire took over, and they allowed some of the Jewish captive exiles to return to the land of Palestine. Nehemiah and Ezra were allowed to visit back in Jerusalem. The Book of Nehemiah 8:1–6 says that the Priest who was also described as a "scribe," Ezra, brings some very special things with him on his visit back to Jerusalem:

> *All the people gathered together into the square before the Water Gate. They told the scribe Ezra to bring the book of the law of Moses, which the Lord had given to Israel. Accordingly, the priest Ezra brought the law before the assembly, both men and women and all who could hear with understanding.*
>
> —Nehemiah 8:1–2

As we mention earlier, this was 200 years later than King Josiah, and look how things were changing! "Reading the Law" was a big event — part of a religious service, even! People stood to listen to it. Clearly, the "book of the Law of Moses" was becoming a centrally important writing. In short, the people were now acting like they had a scripture that was important. No specific books are mentioned, and it's still too early to talk about a canon, but things were definitely progressing toward the importance of religious writings.

Clues of preferred writings in the book of Sirach

The Jewish writing called the book of Sirach (sometimes called Ecclesiasticus) was written by a famous Jewish scholar named Jesus ben Sira, who lived about 200–175 years before Jesus Christ. This book has some important passages that support interest in the formation of a list of Hebrew religious writings. In a long chapter about the heroes (and villains) of Hebrew history, Sirach eventually says something quite interesting:

> It was Ezekiel who saw the vision of glory, which God showed him above the chariot of the cherubim. For God also mentioned Job who held fast to all the ways of justice. May the bones of the Twelve Prophets send forth new life from where they lie, for they comforted the people of Jacob and delivered them with confident hope.
>
> —Sirach 49:8–10

This passage mentions the prophet Ezekiel . . . but not a book. It seems hard to believe, however, that author Jesus ben Sira is only referring to *oral* traditions considering that Ezekiel lived almost 400 years *before* Sirach! Even more interesting, however, is that this passage refers to "the Twelve Prophets." Clearly, some writings were being grouped into a kind of set already at this time, and the set was referred to as "The Twelve." It seems a bit unusual to talk about "the bones" of the prophets, but clearly what Sirach means is that their *writings* continue to inspire even though the speakers are long dead! Sounds like these writings are becoming highly valued in the community!

Furthermore, in a famous Prologue later attached to the book of Sirach, a writer who claims to be Jesus ben Sirach's grandson says something even more striking — and note that the timing is only about 135–120 years before the time of Jesus Christ:

> Many great teachings have been given to us through the Law and the Prophets and the others that followed them, and for these we should praise Israel for instruction and wisdom. Now, those who read the scriptures must not only themselves understand them, but must also as lovers of learning be able through the spoken and written word to help the outsiders. So my grandfather Jesus, who had devoted himself especially to the reading of the Law and the Prophets and the other books of our ancestors, and had acquired considerable proficiency in them, was himself also led to write something pertaining to instruction and wisdom, so that by becoming familiar also with his book those who love learning might make even greater progress in living according to the law.
>
> —Sirach Prologue 1:1

This Prologue seems to set up the three categories of important Jewish books:

- ✔ **Law:** The five books of the Torah — Genesis, Exodus, Leviticus, Numbers, and Deuteronomy

- ✔ **Prophets:** "The Twelve" plus Isaiah, Jeremiah, and Ezekiel

- ✔ **Other writings:** Probably including Psalms, Song of Songs, Esther, and eventually Daniel . . . and perhaps even other writings (including even Enoch for some Jewish readers at this early stage)

Rabbis and other experts weigh in

Soon after the time of Jesus, there's a fork in the road. Judaism develops down one road, and Christianity goes down a separate road. We focus on the Jewish path first. For Judaism, the authority of groups of rabbis in the Jewish community is enormously influential in the determination of canonical writings. So, we turn to their writings to follow the story of the canon in the Jewish tradition. (Later in this chapter, we backtrack and follow the Christian debates about their canon.)

Who is Josephus?

Josephus was a Jewish military leader who was part of the Jewish Revolt against the Roman occupation of Palestine between 66–70 CE. Josephus was captured by the Romans and eventually went (or was taken) to Rome. It seems that he became so impressed with the Roman Empire that he decided that the revolt was all just a big misunderstanding! He believed that if the Romans were to really understand who the Jews were and their important history, then the Romans would realize that the Jews would be better allies than enemies. In order to accomplish this reconciliation with Rome, Josephus took it upon himself to write a history of the Jewish people, in Greek, so that Roman citizens (and especially leaders) could read it and come to appreciate what swell people the Jews were.

Happily for us, most of Josephus's many volumes of writings have survived and have become a very important source of Jewish thought in the first century. However, it's important to always keep in mind that Josephus was writing to try to impress the Romans, and this intention may have influenced his reports. For example, when Josephus retold the stories of the Bible, he sort of smoothed over little bits that he thought might offend the Romans.

Josephus is an important source of historical information (whether biased or not!) for the centuries just before, and even during, the time of Jesus because he carried on his historical descriptions right up to his own time!

A rabbinic council at Yamnia?

One very common theory about the creation of a Jewish canon is that it started with a very special gathering of Jewish rabbinic students and scholars under the leadership of Rabbi Yohanon Ben Zakkai, one of the most important early Jewish Rabbinic leaders.

The rabbi led a gathering in his school in a town on the coast of Israel called Yamnia. So, some historians refer to a "Council at Yamnia" around 90 CE. It's thought that a canon may have started to emerge among Jewish leaders in Yamnia, but is there any evidence that they made a decision? Not really.

Other Jewish voices: Does Josephus write about the Jewish Scriptures?

With little evidence that any decisions were made at Yamnia regarding a canon of books, scholars often turn to a Jewish historian who was not a Rabbi, but a soldier-turned-historian named Josephus, for more clues to the story of the Jewish canon.

Josephus was a Jew writing in the first century CE, and lucky for everyone, he wrote about the Jewish Scriptures. Included in Josephus's writings are the following interesting passages:

> . . . we do not possess myriads of inconsistent books, conflicting with each other. Our books, those which are justly accredited, are but two and twenty, and contain the records of all time . . . which contain the records of all the past times; which are justly believed to be divine; and of them five belong to Moses . . . but as to the time from the death of Moses till the reign of Artaxerxes king of Persia, who reigned after Xerxes, the prophets, who were after Moses, wrote down what was done in their times in thirteen books. The remaining four books contain hymns to God, and precepts for the conduct of human life . . .

> We have given practical proof of our reverence for our own Scriptures. For although such long ages have now passed, no one has ventured either to add, or to remove, or to alter a syllable . . .

> —Against Apion, section 1:8

Looks great, but how helpful is this, really? Josephus gives a number, 22, suggesting pretty much the books now recognized in the Jewish canon (if you combine Ezra-Nehemiah, for example, and suggest that Esther was still being questioned) — but Josephus *does not make a list*. And it's not known what he means by "accredited." Josephus does suggest, however, three sections: Moses, Prophets, and the "remaining books." It seems clear that some kind of collection of books was emerging clearly in the first century CE, but a firm list remained out of reach. Furthermore, Josephus talks about different groups of Jews disagreeing over which scriptures are important and which ones aren't. So, if they were still debating the matter, clearly no central list had emerged just yet.

The rabbis discuss books that "defile the hands"

So, neither Yamnia nor Josephus provides a canon yet. The problem is, there's further evidence that the rabbis were still debating some of the books even after Yamnia!

Early Jewish rabbis debated about holy books by discussing books that "defile the hands." These are books that are so holy that they shouldn't be handled in an improper way.

The problem is these discussions in the early rabbinic writings we call The Talmud really only talk about three disputed books: Esther, Song of Songs, and Ecclesiastes. The debate is whether these three books "defile the hands" — and many historians interpret the debate as evidence that the issue of the canon was *still* being debated by the rabbis in the second to fourth centuries CE!

The Talmud: At last the list appears!

In modern Judaism, the generally acknowledged decision about the canon of the Hebrew Bible is identified in the Talmud (but not part of the "defile the hands" discussion; refer to the preceding section "The rabbis discuss books that 'defile the hands'"). The Talmud is a collection of authoritative rabbinic teachings compiled in the sixth century CE, but it also includes material from many centuries before and even some material from the time before Christianity (although not very much of it is *that* early). A section of the Talmud that many scholars date no later than 200 CE contains a discussion that includes the following:

> *Our Rabbis taught: The order of the Prophets is, Joshua, Judges, Samuel, Kings, Jeremiah, Ezekiel, Isaiah, and the Twelve Minor Prophets . . .*

> *. . . The order of the Hagiographa is Ruth, the Book of Psalms, Job, Prophets, Ecclesiastes, Song of Songs, Lamentations, Daniel and the Scroll of Esther, Ezra and Chronicles . . .*

> —Baba Bathra 14, Babylonian Talmud

Who wrote the scriptures referred to here? The Babylonian Talmud suggests some proposed authors:

> *Moses wrote his own book and the portion of Balaam and Job.*

> *Joshua wrote the book which bears his name and [the last] eight verses of the Pentateuch.*

> *Samuel wrote the book which bears his name and the Book of Judges and Ruth.*

> *David wrote the Book of Psalms.*

> —Baba Bathra, 14a–14b, Babylonian Talmud

Clearly, this is the elusive evidence that lists and titles of writings were clearly understood, and the Talmud comes about as close as possible to evidence for a Jewish canon, even though rabbinic leaders in Judaism didn't use the term "canon."

In fact, for Jewish history, there was no real debate about the importance of the first scrolls of Moses that made up the Torah, the first part of the Hebrew Bible, because older references establish its use. Even if there's no evidence of some final meeting among rabbis to decide the canon of the Jewish Hebrew Bible, by the sixth century CE and probably already by the second to third centuries CE, the Hebrew Bible was largely agreed and set (despite continued discussions about Esther).

Jewish scholars still debate what criteria were used for this list that finally appears in the Talmud, but it seems that one major criterion was that the books needed to be written in Hebrew and were thought to be written before the time of Ezra (450 BCE) because of the tradition in early Jewish teaching that "prophecy ceased" after the time of Ezra. These issues continue to be discussed to this day.

The Christian Old Testament: Translations of Jewish Writings into Greek

In the previous section, we follow the development of the Hebrew Bible for the Jews, but there was *also* a translation of the Jewish writings into Greek in the last two centuries before Jesus. This translated collection of Jewish writings ended up not being the same as the Hebrew Bible because later writings were included with the Greek translations of the older Hebrew works . . . and this difference becomes especially important for the Christian movement when it comes along.

In order to discuss how the Christians started to put together their Bible, we need to begin with the older work of the translation of the Jewish writings into Greek, because this leads us directly to the Christian Old Testament.

Sometime between 300 and 200 BCE, a massive project was started among those Jews who had been living for a few generations in Alexandria, the great Egyptian coastal city that served as a kind of headquarters for the Greek rulers over Egypt after Alexander the Great's conquests. Eventually, a large Jewish community resided in Alexandria, so it seems logical that it was the base for this great project of translating the Hebrew Scriptures into Greek so that Greek-speaking Jews could read their scriptures in the language that they were most comfortable using.

Yet another name for the Hebrew Bible/Old Testament!

In Australia, there's a growing tradition of referring to the Old Testament as the "First Testament" and the New Testament as the "Second Testament." Some university professors down under even identify themselves as a "Professor of the Second Testament" or "Lecturer in First Testament." It's an interesting idea that has one interesting side benefit: Some Australian Christians refer to modern life as the "Now Testament." Those clever Aussies!

Even though this project was largely completed before Christianity, the resulting Greek translations became centrally important for the Christian movement when it started. The Greek version of the Hebrew Bible, called the *Septuagint,* was quickly adopted by the first Christians as the "Old Testament Scriptures" even before the New Testament writings started to emerge.

This Greek version included *more* writings than the Jewish rabbis accepted for the Hebrew Bible, and those extra writings became part of the Christian Old Testament but *not* part of the Hebrew Bible.

Over 80 percent of the time the New Testament quotes the "scriptures," it prefers the *Greek* version of the Hebrew Bible over the *Hebrew*-language version. This speaks volumes, so to speak. (Sorry.) Christianity was becoming a religion spoken in Greek (and eventually also in Latin), and thus Christianity had a tendency to prefer the Greek translations of the old Jewish writings for the Old Testament.

One Last Push to the Christian Old Testament: The Influence of Marcion of Sinope

Christians adopted the Greek translations of the Jewish writings (plus a few extra writings), and that collection (called the Septuagint) became the Old Testament for Christians. But there was one last debate among Christians that really clarified the issue of even *having* a Christian Old Testament, and it was the debate around the *highly* controversial early Christian intellectual known as Marcion.

Marcion of Sinope (who died around 160 CE) was a very powerful personality and intellect, and as a wealthy ship owner, he had the money to back up his brains.

Marcion started a religious movement based on his ideas about Christianity. Basically, he was so repulsed by the violence and rituals of the Hebrew Bible that he came to believe that the God preached by Jesus must have had nothing to do with the god of the Jews!

Marcion therefore advocated that Christians should only use an edited version of the Gospel of Luke (*his* edited version, of course) and the writings of Paul (at least the ones he liked). Marcion thought that Paul taught that Christians were no longer connected to the laws and traditions of Moses and thus no longer connected to the Jews.

But Marcion went even farther and said that Christians should have *nothing* to do with the Hebrew Bible — and thus have no Old Testament at all!

So, did Marcion's little collection of writings spur other Christians into action? In other words, did the Christians start to decide their list as a *response* to Marcion's pressure? Clearly Marcion posed a major challenge, especially on the matter of the Hebrew Scriptures (Old Testament).

Historians know that many early Christian writers responded to Marcion — sometimes with fiery rhetoric. Particularly vocal was a North African Christian theologian named Tertullian (155–230 CE), who wrote responses to Marcion almost 50 years after Marcion began to get noticed. Tertullian and others worked furiously to reaffirm the Christian commitment to the Hebrew Scriptures and the use of other Christian gospels and letters. But it's also clear that the Christians were still in no hurry to set an official canon; they only wanted to reaffirm that they treasured the Hebrew Bible as scripture.

Two Nudges for Christians to Begin Forming Their Own "New" Testament

The adoption of the Greek translations of the Hebrew Scriptures and the debate with Marcion (both discussed previously in this chapter) clarified for early Christianity that it had an Old Testament. But what about a New Testament? When did the Christians finally decide on that part?

It seems that for the first century at least, the Christians were content to cite Hebrew Scriptures in their preaching and writing and also cite sayings of Jesus or even letters of Paul. But there was very little talk of a New Testament in the first century.

Why did Christians move in the direction of a second set of scriptures — a "New" Testament? Were Christian writers pushed to come up with one list? Why draw up a list at all? After all, even though Christians as early as Paul refer to the Jewish scriptures, many early Christians preferred the *oral* traditions about Jesus! They preferred preaching and knowing who taught the preacher so that they could trace the teachings back to Jesus through the Apostles. So why worry about a New Testament at all? Scholars typically debate the impact of two "nudges":

- ✔ The rise of the Montanists
- ✔ Gnosticism

The rise of the Montanists

If Marcion wanted to *cut* too much from inclusion in the Christian canon, arguably Montanism would have potentially *added* too much. Montanism's challenge was really more for a New Testament than an Old Testament, but when you start talking about lists, you find that the Christians talked about both parts.

Montanism was a fascinating early Christian movement founded by Montanus, who was from Phrygia (in modern Turkey). In 170 CE, he began to preach about the near return of Jesus. He seemed to have that certain something — a very attractive personality that apparently had a particularly strong impact on women (not that there's anything wrong with that, of course).

Montanus claimed to be a prophet and therefore able to add new messages and the possibility of new writings to the body of existing religious texts. Montanus defended his idea of "new revelations from God," but he also taught a strict regimen of self-control, fasting, and even seeking martyrdom. Some thought that the Montanists were crazy, but others were impressed; Tertullian became a "convert" to the Montanist perspective, perhaps because he was always rather a strict kind of guy and liked the Montanist rules of personal discipline!

The idea here is that, in Montanus, the Christian church faced someone who claimed to have more revelations (as opposed to Marcion arguing for *less* revelation) and therefore the idea that the Montanists could, in theory, *continue* to add more ideas to the Christian tradition. The creation of a canon raises two very important questions:

- ✔ Can someone or anyone add new books to the canon?
- ✔ Where does the adding of scriptures for the Christians stop?

What if Montanus had written books and claimed that they were "New Words" from Jesus? How could the Christians respond to him if they didn't have a set list of books? So, Montanism and the Christian response to it furthered the discussions about first locking into a canon and then protecting the teachings of Jesus and the Apostles from later "prophets" who would try to add things.

In addition to "new words" — what about *changed* words of Jesus? What happens when people start to write their own *versions* of the sayings of Jesus? This is the next challenge: Gnosticism.

Gnosticism

Sometime in the early third century, historians begin to see evidence of a new teaching spreading among some Christians. It was a movement of people who believed that they had secret knowledge about Christianity.

"Gnosticism" is derived from the Greek word "gnosis," meaning "knowledge." In the 19th century, a German ancient history scholar coined the term "Gnosticism" and applied it to this Christian movement, and the name stuck even though the ancient Gnostics had other names for themselves, like "ones with knowledge."

Gnosticism seems to have emerged from certain Greek, and especially Platonic, philosophical ideas about the importance of the spirit over the material or body. Central to Gnostic beliefs is the notion that the material world, the body, and all things one sees are ultimately not real or important. Rather, the spirit is real, and people must not let the "apparent" world distract them from that fact.

According to the Gnostics, this material world was created by a lesser god, not the "true God of spirit and light." This thinking, of course, is a direct challenge to the importance of the Hebrew Bible. (It's similar to Marcion's challenge but is more philosophically based.) Gnostics further believed that death liberated the spirit and therefore wasn't bad at all! Even more, some Gnostics also believed that Jesus wasn't a real physical person and only appeared that way because someone from the higher God of spirit and light could only be pure spirit, not involved in this dirty world. Gnostics were deeply offended at the idea that Jesus really suffered like a human would, and most important, Christian Gnostics believed that Jesus taught secret knowledge to only the select, the spiritual elite. Gnostics had very secretive groups and even wrote their own scriptures to defend their ideas (see Chapter 12 for more on Gnostic writings).

Truth be told, they were *not* above literally making up words of Jesus to defend their views! Regardless of the quality of the content, Gnostics wrote a lot, and thankfully many of their buried scriptures survived to be discovered in Egypt in 1945 (specifically the Nag Hammadi Library, which we explore in

Chapter 12). So, historians and scholars now understand a lot more about Gnostic Christianity (and non-Christian Gnosticism, which was an even larger movement) than they used to.

Obviously, Gnosticism presented a serious threat to early Christianity and its relationship to the Hebrew Scriptures. With the increase in Gnostic writings from the time, it seems clear that these writings eventually got the attention of Christian leaders who carefully argued against them, revealing the truth about them. There were even Gnostic writings that claimed to be "Gospels" — like the recently recovered Gospel of Judas (which we discuss in Chapter 11). We know it to be a Gnostic writing because of its ideas, like the fact that it denigrates the physical and praises death as a release from this world. The Gnostic philosophy is the reason Judas is seen in this work as a hero — because his actions released Jesus from his physical body! Weird? Absolutely. And many early Christians clearly thought so, too.

Second-Century Debates on the Christian Bible

Eventually the Christians got around to drawing up lists of what they felt should be considered their biblical canon. As we discuss in the previous section, this list making was in part a reaction to various fringe groups of Christians that began to crop up.

The formation of the Christian biblical canon really kicked into high gear in the second century when some early Christian writers — Melito and Origen, in particular — took a shot at it. The earlier discussions of particular books, and shorter lists, all seem to lead to a final decision at the time of Constantine and were followed by lots of final decisions from the different Christian churches.

Note: From this point on, the Christian debates about their canon of the Bible becomes difficult to separate between Old Testament debates and New Testament debates. So, to make matters a bit easier to follow, in this section, we discuss the Christian formation of their Bible as a whole: Old and New Testament.

Irenaeus and Clement of Alexandria defend the four Gospels

In addition to the highly controversial groups and movements that may have pushed Christians to think about their important writings, some early

Christian writers already in the second century (100–200 CE) were referring to many of the books that would become part of the Christian Bible.

For example, Irenaeus (living around 120–200 CE) makes an interesting argument about why the Christians use four Gospels: He points to the four directions (east, west, north, and south) as clear evidence for why there should be four Gospels! Okay, the argument seems silly, but at least he was defending *four* Gospels! We know that there were others, so mentioning "four" means that a list is clearly emerging; choices are being made.

Clement of Alexandria (150–around 216 CE) and Tertullian (155–230 CE) also referred to four Gospels, and a second section of the Christian writings was being based on a foundation of Paul's letters. Historians have second-century references to most of the writings that became part of the New Testament and evidence of heavy use of the Greek translations of the Old Testament.

Athanasius outlines the Christian Bible in use today . . . almost

Athanasius's *Festal Letter* of 367 CE is renowned as one of the clearest statements of the Christian canon in possession, and Athanasius even uses the word "canon" to boot! (A *festal letter* is a missive written on the occasion of important festivals.) The nearby sidebar offers a lengthy excerpt from the letter.

The Muratorian Fragment: The oldest list of New Testament books?

Sometime around 1740, an Italian scholar named Lodovico Antonio Muratori discovered leaves of an old Latin text in a seventh to eighth century CE *codex* (hand-written, bound book) in a library in Milan.

Scholars soon determined that a very important segment of this work was translated from Greek and probably dated to about 180–200 CE. The fragment includes a discussion of the books of the New Testament and mentions "four Gospels," but it only names Luke and John. It also mentions epistles of Paul, Peter, and John as well as Revelation. Thus, the Muratorian Fragment provides evidence of the existence of these New Testament writings.

Even more interesting, the Muratorian Fragment mentions "forged letters" of Paul, which the writer attributes to Marcion (refer to the earlier section "The influence of Marcion the Sinope"). Because the document refers to the Shepherd of Hermas as "written very recently" and scholars date the Shepherd of Hermas to the first half of the second century — Muratori's Fragment is dated *late* second century.

But not everyone agrees that the Fragment is that old, and some even say it's from the fifth century. If it's older, it suggests that the New Testament canon (it doesn't use that term, by the way) was forming at that time but still wasn't absolutely certain.

An excerpt from Athanasius's Festal Letter

"Since some few of the simple should be beguiled from their simplicity and purity, by the subtleties of certain men, and should henceforth read other books — those called *Apocryphal* — led astray by the similarity of their names with the true books; I beseech you to bear patiently, if I also write, by way of remembrance, of matters with which you are acquainted, influenced by the need and advantage of the Church.

In proceeding to make mention of these things . . . it seemed good to me also, having been urged thereto by true brethren, and having learned from the beginning, to set before you the books included in the Canon, and handed down, and accredited as Divine; to the end that any one who has fallen into error may condemn those who have led him astray; and that he who has continued steadfast in purity may again rejoice, having these things brought to his remembrance.

There are, then, of the Old Testament, twenty-two books in number; for, as I have heard, it is handed down that this is the number of the letters among the Hebrews; their respective order and names being as follows. The first is Genesis, then Exodus, next Leviticus, after that Numbers, and then Deuteronomy. Following these there is Joshua, the son of Nun, then Judges, then Ruth. And again, after these four books of Kings, the first and second being reckoned as one book, and so likewise the third and fourth as one book. And again, the first and second of the Chronicles are reckoned as one book. Again Ezra, the first and second [Ezra and Nehemiah] are similarly one book. After these there is the book of Psalms, then the Proverbs, next Ecclesiastes, and the Song of Songs. Job follows, then the Prophets, the twelve being reckoned as one book. Then Isaiah, one book, then Jeremiah with Baruch, Lamentations, Baruch, the epistle, one book; afterwards, Ezekiel and Daniel, each one book. Thus far constitutes the Old Testament.

Again it is not tedious to speak of the [books] of the New Testament. These are, the four Gospels, according to Matthew, Mark, Luke, and John. Afterwards, the Acts of the Apostles and Epistles (called Catholic), seven, viz. [namely] of James, one; of Peter, two; of John, three; after these, one of Jude. In addition, there are fourteen Epistles of Paul, written in this order. The first, to the Romans; then two to the Corinthians; after these, to the Galatians; next, to the Ephesians; then to the Philippians; then to the Colossians; after these, two to the Thessalonians, and that to the Hebrews; and again, two to Timothy; one to Titus; and lastly, that to Philemon. And besides, the Revelation of John.

These are fountains of salvation, that they who thirst may be satisfied with the living words they contain. In these alone is proclaimed the doctrine of godliness. Let no man add to these, neither let him take ought from these. For concerning these the Lord put to shame the Sadducees, and said, 'Ye do err, not knowing the Scriptures.' And He reproved the Jews, saying, 'Search the Scriptures, for these are they that testify of Me.'

But for greater exactness I add this also, writing of necessity; that there are other books besides these not indeed included in the Canon, but appointed by the Fathers to be read by those who newly join us, and who wish for instruction in the word of godliness. The Wisdom of Solomon, and the Wisdom of Sirach, and Esther, and Judith, and Tobit, and that which is called the Teaching of the Apostles, and the Shepherd. But the former, my brethren, are included in the Canon, the latter being [merely] read; nor is there in any place a mention of apocryphal writings. But they are an invention of heretics, who write them when they choose, bestowing upon them their approbation, and assigning to them a date, that so, using them as ancient writings, they may find occasion to lead astray the simple."

—Excerpt taken from the 39th Festal Letter

In his letter, Athanasius seems to have had an "A" list of books that he said were central to his list, and a "B" list of other books that he also liked and recommended, like Wisdom of Solomon, Sirach, Esther, Judith, Tobit, the Christian book the Didache, the famous Shepherd of Hermas, and also the book of Baruch in the Old Testament.

His famous Festal Letter is often quoted in debates about the emergence of the Christian biblical canon.

Constantine settles the matter (sort of) at the Council of Nicea

While debates regarding books of the Bible raged, bigger things were happening also. Huge changes came over Christianity and the entire Roman Empire in 313.

This was the time when Constantine, one of the most powerful warriors of ancient Rome, was trying to consolidate his rule over the entire Empire. When he tried to return to Rome to solidify his power as Caesar and Lord of all the Roman Empire, he faced a larger army already stationed in Rome. As he crossed the famous Malvern Bridge in 312 CE, Constantine apparently had a vision in which he was shown a symbol and assured that "with this symbol, you will be victorious." The symbol was apparently a form of the Christian cross, and Constantine painted it on the shields of his soldiers and created crosslike symbols for the soldiers to carry into battle. When Constantine was victorious, he came to believe that he had been called by the Christian God to rule Rome.

Christianity was gaining its most militarily powerful convert ever! As soon as Constantine came to power over the Roman Empire, he passed the "Edict of Toleration" in 313, making it illegal to persecute Christians. In short order, however, Christianity also received lots of royal favors — new buildings built at royal expense, protection for Christian leaders, and Roman power behind Christian gatherings to settle long-simmering issues. In short, Constantine worked to make Christianity the central religion of the Roman Empire.

Whether he was genuinely interested in the teachings of Jesus or not (and we'll try to resist being *too* cynical about this question), Constantine was definitely a good Roman soldier and thus was interested in what Roman Caesars were *always* interested in: absolute power and absolute stability of his Empire. It just wouldn't do to have the Christian leaders of his new "Imperial Religion" arguing with each other over trivial matters. He had an Empire to run! So, Constantine called an official Council of the Church at Nicea in 325 CE (see Figure 2-1 for an artist's rendering of this historic event).

Figure 2-1:
What the
Council
of Nicea
may have
looked like.

© Bettmann/Corbis

Part of the debates at this Council was over the Bible. Eusebius, who has supplied most of information about all these events in possession (including his highly favorable opinions of Constantine), records that Constantine appears to have imposed his power behind the present canon of the Bible that included the Apocryphal books in the Christian Old Testament. Thus, the results of Nicea are evident in the fact that, soon after, confident lists were written, such as the Festal Letter of Athanasius in 367 CE (refer to the preceding section).

In fact, when Constantine made the interesting decision to shift his capital to Constantinople (modern Istanbul), he decided to commission 50 copies of the Bible for the churches in his new capital city. Clearly the decision to commission these Bibles was part of Constantine's influence in finally settling the issue of the canon.

Modern churches follow with final statements of their own

By the end of the fourth century, the Christian canon was settled more or less for western Christians (for example, the "Roman" Catholic Church). Still,

Christians often gathered for great councils to debate and discuss important religious subjects, including the canon.

These councils are usually named for the city where they took place. The Council held in Laodicea (perhaps around 363 CE) discussed the books of the Bible, but the results probably resembled the Festal Letter of Athanasius. Finally, however, the Council at Hippo, influenced by the famous early Christian theologian St. Augustine, met in 393 and also determined a list and made a formal pronouncement. But did this pronouncement really settle the matter of the Christian canon? Apparently not, because *modern* churches have felt the need to *also* make final statements! Here's a rundown of more modern developments:

- The Roman Catholic Church didn't finally and officially set its canon of the Bible until 1546! It took place at the famous Council of Trent centuries after the time of Jesus. The Roman Catholic Church's canon, which remains in place today, includes the standard Jewish list of the Hebrew Bible, *plus* the Deutero-Canonical books and the standard list of the New Testament.

- The Greek Orthodox Church finally established its official canon in 1950 (yes, *1950*) and included 2 Ezra and 3 Maccabees, with 4 Maccabees printed in an appendix in the Bible.

- Protestantism is thought to have started with Martin Luther (1483–1546), so the various Protestant groups established their canons after his time. Martin Luther famously determined that his movement would adopt the Jewish canon, which is why the Jewish Hebrew Bible and Luther's Old Testament differ only slightly in arrangement, but contain the same writings.

- The Reform churches (for example, the churches emerging from John Calvin's traditions, such as Presbyterian churches and many Baptist churches) established their present canon in the late 16th century. Calvin endorses the same canon as Luther, which is why *all* Protestants in the modern world have the same books of their Bible.

In any case, it should be clear that if you want to understand the canon of the Christian Bible (both Old and New Testaments) and even the Jewish Hebrew Bible, you have to recognize that their creations were *slow processes*. Nobody's canon dropped from the sky ready-made!

Chapter 3

The Different Categories of Ancient Religious Writing

Ancient religious writings are commonly grouped into accepted "styles." When studying the "lost" writings, it's necessary to understand these various styles in order to use a common vocabulary and identify individual omitted texts by their type.

In this chapter, you discover the various styles and patterns that ancient Jewish and Christian religious writing tend to follow. This is very helpful information because it allows you to identify, classify, and better understand the other writings that weren't included in the Bible as you know it today.

We use these classifications throughout this book as we look at the lost books of the Bible, so you may want to check back in with this chapter as you read to refresh your memory of the classifications.

The Hows and Whys of Organizing Ancient Writings into Style Categories

Ancient religious texts are defined by the kind of writings they contain. These styles include poetry, gospels, apocalyptic writings, and more. Modern biblical scholars have not created these various styles and categories of religious writings out of whole cloth, but they've worked to refine the categories to make them more helpful for organizing ancient texts.

Scholars know with certainty that some stylistic structures and creation of categories of religious writing began in the ancient world. In the days before the Bible, and even in the days before Jesus, the Jews used important styles of religious writings over and over. As certain ancient writings among the Jews became increasingly popular, they began to be arranged together and increasingly mentioned together in groups.

For example, the Bible has more than one list of the "Laws of Moses" — one at Exodus 20, another at Deuteronomy 5 — which is why there are actually *two* versions of the iconic Ten Commandments. Books that contain laws in the Hebrew Bible were organized together. *All* the laws of ancient Israel, no matter *when* they became laws, are grouped together in the first five books of the Bible.

Similarly, the books of the various Prophets evolved into a collection as well. Over 150 years before the time of Jesus, the shorter Prophetic scrolls like *Amos, Hosea, Nahum,* and *Obadiah* are called simply *The Twelve.*

In the ancient period before the Bible became a set number of books, or a *canon,* these writings were already being sorted or organized by their style and content. Law books were kept together; prophetic books were kept together; and poetry books, including *Psalms,* the *Song of Solomon,* and others, also tended to be kept together. The Christian tradition even tended to sort all "history-sounding" writings together as well, which is why *Samuel, Kings, Chronicles, Ezra,* and *Nehemiah* are all together in the Christian Old Testament.

Fortunately for you and your understanding of all the different descriptions of lost books or other writings discussed in this book, modern scholars have fine-tuned the definitions of these styles.

How does one determine a style?

Styles of ancient Jewish and Christian works are determined by a variety of factors. The imagery used, the language used (sometimes right down to the specific words used), and the ideas expressed all contribute to assigning a specific writing to a particular style or genre of religious writing. In ancient Jewish writing, for example, laws are virtually impossible to confuse with stories or parables. In the New Testament, it's hard to confuse "Gospel" with "Epistle/Letter." Knowing these styles makes it much easier to assign lesser known works to a particular category.

Using style as a tool for studying the lost books

You may be thinking to yourself, "Okay, so biblical books fall into style categories. So what?"

Finding out about these various style forms of ancient Jewish and Christian religious writing is a tremendous help when it comes to reading books that *aren't* in the Bible. When you know the styles, you begin to recognize that these books most certainly do follow a style — often the same style as the books that *are* in the Bible. The styles place the writings within a context, both historical and literary, and provide insights into the minds of their creators.

Knowing the patterns and styles of biblical literature helps you sort out what a non-biblical book is *trying* to be. Here are some possibilities:

- ✔ Is it attempting to be a letter in the style of Paul's letters?
- ✔ Is it attempting to be a Gospel like Matthew or Luke?
- ✔ Is it attempting to be a Prophetic speech like Micah, Jeremiah, or Isaiah?

When trying to assess whether something is a valid piece of potential Scriptural writing, it helps to know what the writer was hoping to accomplish. For instance, suppose you're an early Christian (play along, okay?), and you believe that you have something important to say about Jesus. Odds are you'll want to write a Gospel — the typical kind of Christian writing about Jesus — because you'll know that the form will almost guarantee a readership, and your message, narrative, speculation, or advice will be heard.

In case you're wondering, these lost books were *not* rejected from the Bible because they broke the rules for ancient religious writing. They aren't "technically defective," so to speak. Rather, writings are rejected because of their content and ideas. The issue is "orthodoxy," not "fashion"!

Surveying Styles of Religious Writing in the Old Testament

The variety of Old Testament religious book styles is, in a sense, a response to the times and the needs of the people. When a culture is floundering, or at least searching for answers, books of laws, wisdom, and allegorical stories fill the void.

There was undeniable social, cultural, political, and religious instability in the days the Old Testament books were written — *especially* beginning in the late eighth century and continuing under the conquering armies of Assyria, Babylon, and Persia. The writings were an attempt to provide answers and balance.

In this section, we survey these various styles of writings in the Hebrew Bible, explaining each category and listing which books fall into which category.

Please keep in mind that even the following assignment of styles is not universally agreed upon in every detail by religious scholars and historians. The experts have disagreements regarding specific definitions of each style, as well as what should and should not be included in individual "lost" canons. But for purposes of our discussion, these categories are more than adequate.

Law

Typically, historians refer to law "codes" in the ancient world (a *code* in ancient writing is simply a body of laws). In order to be defined as a law code, the text must be a listing of laws, often (but not always) organized by subject and typically written in a set form in the ancient world.

In the Bible, laws are typically written in two forms, the *Apodictic* and *Casuistic* forms:

- **Apodictic laws:** These are laws written as if God is speaking directly, as in "You shall not. . . ."

- **Casuistic laws:** These follow the classic form of ancient law: "If (or "when") X, then Y." For example, Leviticus 6:1–5 contains the following casuistic law: "When any of you sin and commit a trespass against the Lord by deceiving a neighbor in a matter of a deposit or a pledge, or by robbery, or if you have defrauded a neighbor . . . you shall repay the principal amount and shall add one-fifth to it."

It's also common for explanations to follow the actual laws in the text. For example, Exodus 21:28 is a law about an ox that gores someone. But the verses that follow include more details that a judge or elder must examine in order to come to a decision about what to do about the ox (for example, has it done this before?).

Scholars don't have any lost books of the Laws of Moses — at least not yet. (They're still looking.) They do have the books of Exodus through Deuteronomy, which include all the known laws of Moses (far more than the famous Ten Commandments, of course). So, a newly discovered collection of *more* laws from the Jewish tradition would be quite interesting to find.

Words to the wise: The Wisdom Books

When we speak of "wisdom," we mean something different than book knowledge. Wisdom is the result of experience, which is why people tend to ask elders for advice that they hope is wise advice.

The Hebrew Bible has three classic books known as *Wisdom Books* that pass on knowledge gained from human experience. These are

- The Proverbs
- Ecclesiastes
- Job

The Greek translation of the Hebrew Bible (begun around 250–200 BC) adds two more Wisdom Books:

- Sirach
- The Wisdom of Solomon

The Wisdom Books have three specific characteristics that make identifying them as such quite simple. They are as follows:

- **The word "wisdom":** The word is used predominantly in these books to describe what they're talking about: wise advice designed to provide a life lesson. The word "wisdom" isn't used to describe laws, for example, or the speeches of prophets.

  In Hebrew, the word "wisdom" is *hokma.* This is the source of the popular Arabic name "Hakim" from the same Semitic language root.

- **The "compare and contrast" instructional adage:** In addition to the standard form of a *proverb,* which is a short saying intended to communicate brief but profound lessons for life, the Wisdom books also employ an Israelite wisdom technique known as the *comparison* or *contrast* that's pretty easy to spot. (Jesus used this teaching style occasionally as well.) Here are some examples:

- "The wise of heart will heed commandments, but a babbling fool will come to ruin." (Proverbs 10:8)

- "The wise are cautious and turn away from evil, but the fool throws off restraint and is careless." (Proverbs 14:16)

✔ **The illustrative parable:** *Parables* are model stories that praise the wisdom and foresight of the central character (for example, Ecclesiastes 9:13-16 is a short little tale of a wise man saving an entire city).

Incidentally, the parables of Jesus are often considered stories modeled on the ancient Hebrew form of wisdom stories used to teach people proper behavior and attitudes. In other words, when Jesus told these stories, his followers would have recognized the style of his storytelling from older books of wisdom and wisdom stories.

Back to the past: The historical narratives

Some examples of Old Testament historical books include:

✔ Joshua

✔ Judges

✔ The two books of Samuel

✔ The two books of Kings

✔ The two books of Chronicles

✔ Ezra

✔ Nehemiah

Reaching across style lines: The book of Daniel

The stories of the book of Daniel are often considered wisdom stories because, in the text, Daniel and his three friends are praised for their great acumen and because the words "wise" and "wisdom" are used throughout. Yet, Daniel isn't considered a Wisdom book and is usually grouped with the apocalyptic texts due to its dominant visionary content.

Daniel is an unusual book in that it has two radically different styles. Chapters 1–6 are the famous stories, including the story of Daniel in the lion's den. But Chapters 7–12 radically shift gears into apocalyptic visions. Most scholars question if they came from the same hand; it seems clear that the apocalyptic visions were added to the stories at a later date.

These books are all written in the form of a historical narrative, meaning that their main purpose seems to be a survey of events over a period of time.

In ancient Hebrew writing, historical writing isn't necessarily an objective recounting of historical events. Like *all* historical writing, the ancient Hebrews put a spin on their telling in order to teach profound ideas, pass judgment on bad characters and their behavior, and praise the exemplary behavior of their "good" characters.

For example, check out this basic fact, followed by a judgment:

> *In the third year of King Asa of Judah, Baasha son of Ahijah began to reign over all Israel at Tirzah; he reigned twenty-four years. He did what was evil in the sight of the Lord, walking in the way of Jeroboam and in the sin that he caused Israel to commit.*

> —1 Kings 15:33–34

The Prophets weigh in

Prophetic books in the Hebrew Bible consist of collections of the sayings of a Prophet. These sayings are typically gathered into speeches, or what biblical scholars refer to as *oracles.*

Prophetic books include larger writings such as Isaiah, Jeremiah, and Ezekiel, and shorter books such as Amos, Hosea, and even Obadiah, which is only one chapter long!

Typically, a Prophet speech begins with the all-important *messenger formula,* which may be expressed as "Thus Says the Lord," "God says," or something else along these lines. Then the Prophetic speech is written *as if God is speaking* because the Prophet is communicating to the people as literally a messenger from God. Check out this formula in Amos, where Amos speaks for God after the initial phrase:

> *Thus says the Lord:*
> *For three transgressions of Israel*
> *And for four, I will not revoke the punishment*

> —Amos 2:6

Some prophetic books consist mostly of sayings from the Prophet, like Amos or Hosea or even shorter books like Nahum or Habakkuk. But some prophetic books contain historical narrative also, even describing some aspects of the life of the Prophet.

Once upon a time: Stories and legends

Truth be told, stories and legends is a rather dangerous category. Why? Because for some people, the very idea that the Bible contains stories that aren't intended to be factual, literal history is troublesome, and many reject the notion completely.

But it's clear that some stories in the Bible are just that — stories. One example is *Jotham's Fable* in Chapter 9 of Judges, in which olive trees, fig trees, and grapevines talk and express a powerful message, which is the purpose of the story.

Although it's true that it's sometimes hard to see the line between what is *intended* to be a story and what's now *believed* to be a story, the fact remains that the Bible contains stories. Jesus told many stories with messages, and yet, for example, people don't worry about whether the Good Samaritan was real because they understand that it's part of a story intended to teach a message about generosity of spirit and treating others as you would like to be treated.

Writings often suggested as pious stories include the Joseph tales in Genesis 37–50, Daniel, Esther, Jonah, and Ruth. In the little story of Ruth, undoubtedly told to challenge certain negative attitudes toward Moabites, the opening line even *sounds* like a story: "In the days when the judges ruled, there was famine in the land, and a certain man of Bethlehem in Judah went to live in the country of Moab" (Ruth 1:1). There isn't much specificity here because it doesn't really matter to the point of the story.

Why is it important to acknowledge the fiction in the Bible?

When studying books not included in the New Testament, you come to writings that describe events in the lives of Jesus, Paul, or Peter. Sometimes, these writings have storylike elements, such as people flying through the air, a lion speaking to Paul, and so on, that raise the question of whether these were stories told by some early Christians as educational entertainment — like Christian folklore.

Accepting the idea of intentionally fictional biblical folklore is much easier than accepting the existence of false claims about what really happened. With writings with storylike elements, you have to decide if such stories were excluded from the Bible because they recount events that never really happened or because Church leaders didn't like the messages of the stories, even if the leaders *knew* that they were just stories. In any case, trying to decide what was originally intended to be a story is usually tricky business. Welcome to the world of biblical scholarship!

Poetry

The Hebrew Bible also contains poetry books. These poems can be deeply religious, like the famous *Book of Psalms,* or they can be entertaining and even erotic love poetry, like the *Song of Solomon.* (If the Song of Solomon were translated literally — as it rarely is — and if ratings were assigned to books, it would no doubt be rated "R."):

> *How fair and pleasant you are*
> *O loved one, delectable maiden!*
> *You are stately as a palm tree,*
> *And your breasts are like its clusters*
> *I say I will climb the palm tree*
> *And lay hold of its branches*
> *O may your breasts be like clusters of the vine*

—Song of Solomon 7:6–8

In the category of religious poetry like the Psalms, you find many kinds of poems — such as poems of great sadness or "laments" (Psalm 44), poems of celebration (Psalm 46), or even poems of learning history (like Psalms 105–106, a poetic history of Israel). But how does anyone know what Hebrew poetry *is?*

The key to recognizing Hebrew poetry is parallelism. The poetry doesn't always rhyme or have a set pattern, but typically the two (sometimes three) lines have a very close relationship called *parallelism.* Parallelism may be indicated by lines repeating the same idea in slightly different words or saying the opposite of each other. You also may notice an inherent "beat" as you read it aloud. Consider this example:

> *Why do the nations conspire,*
> *and the peoples plot in vain?*

—Psalm 2:1

The parallelism is seen in the fact that "nations" and "peoples" are the same, and "conspire" and "plot in vain" are also the same. In this case, virtually the same idea is stated in two different forms.

Most of the time, it's easy to spot parallelism in Hebrew poetry, allowing you to quickly identify it as poetry and not narrative or normal speech patterns.

Some poems were sung (it's possible that *most* were intended to be sung), but not all of them. Scholars believe that some poems had an educational purpose, and if they were sung, it was along the lines of an educational song like the ones commonly used on *Sesame Street* to teach children.

The New Testament Styles of Religious Writing

The styles of writing in the New Testament are simpler and somewhat more accessible than the types of books in the Old Testament. They break down into the three following categories:

- ✔ Gospels
- ✔ Acts
- ✔ Epistles

This section looks at all three of these styles and their identifying characteristics.

The Jesus tales: The Gospels

One of the most interesting questions that New Testament scholars often discuss is a deceptively simple one: What is a Gospel?

The word "gospel" is a translation of a Greek word meaning, simply, "good news." The question *seems* so simple because a few examples of Gospels are available, so one is tempted to point to one and say, "There, *that* is a Gospel."

But then the issue gets a bit more complicated with a follow-up question: How do you know a Gospel when you see one? If a writing tells stories about Jesus's life, and also includes his Teachings, it's a Gospel. The four examples from the Bible — Matthew, Mark, Luke, and John — exemplify perfectly the quintessential religious Gospel.

The discussion starts getting interesting when you consider where the early Christians got the idea for a Gospel. Many historians aren't certain that the Gospel form had any precedents. In fact, one prominent theory is that the earliest Christians quite simply invented it. Some modern historians suggest that the Gospels in the New Testament can be compared to the short biographies written by the Greek writer Diogenes in *The Lives of the Philosophers* in 200 CE. The problems with this theory are twofold: Diogenes came after the biblical Gospels, and his biographies didn't include the teachings of the philosophers, as the Gospels do. In the end, you don't really need to know where the concept of the Gospel came from in order to appreciate the form and recognize its important role in the New Testament.

In Chapter 13, we tell you about the few gospels written that were *not* included in the New Testament, and you discover that sometimes the term "gospel" is used for *any* book that purports to talk about Jesus or the sayings of Jesus.

Stories of early Christians: The Acts

The idea behind the Acts books is to show how the first followers of Jesus carry on what Jesus started. That's why Acts shows the Apostles doing miracles like Jesus and teaching about Jesus: *acting* and preaching like Jesus did.

So, any early Christian writings that claim to give more information about some of the first followers of Jesus are often called *Acts,* like *Acts of Peter* or *Acts of Paul.* They're modeled on the general idea of the Bible's *Acts of the Apostles.*

In general, the Acts-type literature of the early Christians is often compared to the historical section of the Hebrew Bible, although there are some important differences. Acts, nevertheless, is the main source of information about what happened to the very first followers of Jesus and how the Christian movement took root.

Not-so-breaking-news (although this may be new news to many): The book in the Bible known as Acts of the Apostles was written by the same guy who wrote the Gospel of Luke. In fact, Acts is the second part of a two-part project of which Luke was the first installment. It's notable that the early Christians located Acts right after the four Gospels. The early Christians had to intentionally break apart Luke and Acts in order to achieve the present arrangement. *Why* they broke it apart is anyone's guess — perhaps to emphasize the similarity of the Gospels? Or to model the New Testament after the Old Testament, with historical books following "Laws of Moses"?

As I write this letter: The Epistles

One of the most unique forms of literature used by the early Christians was the *Epistle,* or letter. This is an interesting form of writing in that it vividly depicts and reflects the lives and times of the first Christians. There are lots of Epistles, of course: Romans, 1 and 2 Corinthians, Colossians, Ephesians, Philippians, Thessalonians — all of which are called by the name of the addressee (for example, the church in Corinth, the church in Rome, and so on).

Christianity grew under the yoke of the Roman Empire. In addition to committing horrific acts of violence and taxing people nearly to death, Rome built roads and maintained communications along these roads. Letters were an obvious and important form of communication between the far-flung locations where Christianity grew in the empire.

The important thing about ancient letters is that they have a definite form that consists of three main parts:

1. The author

2. The persons to whom the author is speaking

3. A greeting

Consider the beginning of three different writings in the New Testament by the Apostle Paul:

- ✔ "Paul, an apostle of Christ Jesus by the will of God, To the saints who are in Ephesus and are faithful in Christ Jesus: Grace to you and peace from God our Father and the Lord Jesus Christ." (Ephesians 1:1–2)

- ✔ "Paul, called to be an apostle of Christ Jesus by the will of God, and our brother Sosthenes, To the church of God that is in Corinth, to those who are sanctified in Christ Jesus, called to be saints, together with all those who in every place call on the name of our Lord Jesus Christ, both their Lord and ours: Grace to you and peace from God our Father and the Lord Jesus Christ." (1 Corinthians 1:1–3)

- ✔ "Paul and Timothy, servants of Christ Jesus, To all the saints in Christ Jesus who are in Philippi, with the bishops and deacons: Grace to you and peace from God our Father and the Lord Jesus Christ." (Philippians 1:1–2)

Paul writes letters, which also all *end* with a similar pattern, too: Usually Paul finishes his letters with personal greetings to or from specific people if he knows someone, and gives a final blessing.

Paul is just one example of Epistles that follow the styles and rules for letter writing in the ancient world, and he rarely changes his style.

In a Class All Their Own: Apocalyptic Writings

The people living in the ancient lands of Palestine, Egypt, and Mesopotamia couldn't just flip on the TV set and watch *Star Trek* when they wanted to see what a possible future world may look like. But they most certainly did dream about the future, and they also wrote about it — *a lot!*

We can say this because great quantities of their writings have survived from the ancient world, including lots of visions of the future that were written by ancient Jewish writers. However, these visions weren't accepted into the Hebrew Bible, nor did the early Christians accept them as part of the Old Testament.

These ancient Jewish visions of the future are *apocalyptic writings*. This is arguably one of the most important styles of religious literature because so much non-biblical writing is apocalyptic visions. If Wisdom books look back to the experience of elders and the past (see the earlier section, "Words to the wise: The Wisdom Books," for an explanation), then one could say that apocalyptic books look to a revealed future for knowledge.

In this section, we look at what makes a work "apocalyptic," where such writings can be found in the Bible, and what are their characteristics.

What makes it apocalyptic?

"Apocalypse" is a Greek word that literally means "revelation." One of the most famous apocalyptic books in the Christian Bible is the New Testament book known as the book of Revelation. The real title of this book, however, is the Apocalypse of John.

Revelation begins with brief letters to seven churches in Asia Minor (all now in modern Turkey) but then launches into the visions of John, revealed to him (he says) by Jesus. The rest of the book consists of John's narration of these visions of judgment of the earth, leading up to a great spiritual battle between Jesus and Satan.

The other apocalyptic book that made it into the Bible isn't really a whole book, but part of one. The book of Daniel is divided into two sections: wisdom stories of Daniel and his friends in the first half, typically counted as Chapters 1–6; and a series of strange visions in Chapters 7–12.

But the category of apocalyptic books also can include a whole group of books that have a similar style and feel to Revelation and Daniel 7–12 but that weren't included in the Bible.

Some genuine, genuinely strange mysteries surround these apocalyptic writings, one of which is their abundance. Apocalyptic writing was clearly a very popular form of literature that interested many ancient people (many modern people, too, for that matter), and it's clear that a large number of people took it very seriously. Is there some kind of code to understanding apocalyptic writing? What did the ancients see in this stuff? The following sections pose some answers to these questions.

The apocalyptic writing in the Bible

Professor John J. Collins explains that there are really two different kinds of apocalyptic writing that one can identify among the dozens of examples:

- **Otherworldly journeys:** Descriptions of strange places in heaven or hell
- **Historic symbolism:** Descriptions of strange events and happenings that are intended to be symbolic of events that are going to occur in the real world

Both Revelation in the New Testament and Daniel 7–12 in the Old Testament are apocalyptic writings that fall under the historic symbolism category.

Characteristics of apocalyptic literature

Apocalyptic literature has personality traits, so to speak, and these common elements appear in the writings consistently and repeatedly. Here's a look at the eight most common facets of *apocalyptica,* to coin a term.

- **Turmoil:** Apocalyptic writings are written in a style emphasizing spiritual and social turmoil. Things aren't right in the world, and the writer expresses a great sense of unrest.
- **Urgency:** Apocalyptic writings have a sense of urgency, implying that the changes coming in the world (or the entire cosmos) are coming very soon. When you read these writings, try to imagine a *very* excited and agitated voice reading them aloud.
- **The end is coming!:** Apocalyptic writing writes as if history — the world the writer and readers know — is coming to an end and the present circumstances are going to change.
- **But it will be great!:** In many apocalyptic writings, the end that's coming will be followed by one more step: the new paradise. Beyond the coming catastrophes is a new reality.
- **Let me explain . . . :** One of the really interesting parts of apocalyptic writings is the presence of a heavenly being who is willing to explain the strange and frightening visions.

✔ **What is *that*?:** Typically, apocalyptic writings describe visions that are populated by strange and alarming beasts, such as multiheaded dragons and animals that combine features from different species.

✔ **We've seen this before, haven't we?:** It seems clear that apocalyptic writers read each other's work because many of the strange images and beasts appear in many different apocalyptic works.

✔ **Who wrote this!?:** Apocalyptic writings are typically written under a *pseudonym,* or false name. This is usually thought to be for two reasons: because apocalyptic writing is usually hotly political, often very critical of present regimes and governments; and because the naming of these books borrows the fame of older biblical characters.

Why did people write (and read) this stuff?

It's possible that the oldest apocalyptic writings, and maybe including Daniel 7–12 in the Bible, were actually based on strange visions that the writers experienced. But it's equally clear that many apocalyptic books seem to have been written intentionally — that is, *written in the style of apocalyptic litera-ture.* Thus, scholars can say that it became a literary style. But why? What is it about the apocalyptic style that appealed to Hebrews in the ancient world?

The appeal boils down to the mood and thinking of these books: The times are bad, God is going to bring about change, and the change is coming very soon (thank goodness!). It's clear that many of the apocalyptic writings arose in circumstances of oppression when Jews had to live under the brutal economic and political policies of the Persians, Greeks, or Romans.

Ultimately, scholars and historians think that most of these visionary stories were really hopeful reassurances that God is with the people, and especially that God wasn't losing control of world events that may have seemed out of control.

Part II
Ancient Jewish Lost Books

The 5th Wave
By Rich Tennant

Though many questioned its claim to be divinely inspired, The First Book of Gossip was a popular item at food stands across Jerusalem during the 1st century B.C.E.

"Not another St. Elvis sighting...?"

In this part . . .

We open this part with a survey of the writings called the "Apocryphal books." These books are the writings that Jews and Protestant Christians don't include in their Hebrew Bible/Old Testament, but that Catholics and Orthodox Christians do. Technically, they aren't "lost," but because most Protestants don't know much about them, we include them here.

In this part, we also cover some sacred writings from Jewish writers before and after Jesus that nobody included in their Bible. (Take note that we identify these books by the kinds of religious literature outlined in Part I.) The fact that they didn't make it into the Old Testament (or New Testament) doesn't mean that the books in this part are "bad books"; many of them have good, strong messages and were big hits in the early centuries. These are the books that hardly anyone knows about except historians who specialize in this kind of stuff. But why should they have all the fun? After all, most of these writings are in English and just waiting for you to read them.

Chapter 4

The Controversial Apocrypha

Most readers of the Bible don't take long to figure out that *some* Bibles have more books than others. What is going on here?

Put simply, the *canons* of different churches — that is, the authoritative lists of books that are endorsed by church officials as writings that can be used to determine faith and theology (see Chapter 2) — are, well, *different.*

In this chapter, we take a look at a group of writings that *did* make it into the Catholic and Orthodox Old Testament, but did not make it into the Hebrew Bible or Old Testament of Protestant Christians. (To this day, Catholic and Protestant Old Testaments are still different in this regard.) We also look at some reasons why some groups decided to include them, and why others did not.

Getting to Know the Apocryphal Books of Jewish History

After Alexander the Great started conquering throughout the ancient Near East in 333 BCE, Greek started to become the "language of the Empire." As Jews spread to different parts of Alexander's great conquests, they slowly began to adopt Greek as the language most people could understand outside the Jewish homeland. So, as they continued to write religious works, some of these writings were composed in Greek, but *all* of them are *now* known in only Greek editions. Some of them *may* have been written in Hebrew originally, but what's in possession today is mainly Greek. All these materials come from *later* Jewish history but are still before the time of Christianity.

In this section, we survey these important books that compose what's now called the *Apocrypha* (from the Greek word "hidden") but what the Catholic Church refers to as *Deutero-Canonical Books* ("Deutero" means "second," so the term probably suggests "Secondary Canonical").

What are these books and where did they come from?

The Apocryphal books include the following:

- ✔ Tobit
- ✔ Judith
- ✔ Additions to Esther (often cited as Esther 10:4–16:24)
- ✔ Wisdom
- ✔ Ben Sira, also called Sirach or Ecclesiasticus
- ✔ Baruch, including the Letter of Jeremiah
- ✔ Additions to Daniel:
    - Song of the Three Children
    - Story of Susanna
    - Bel and the Dragon
- ✔ 1 Maccabees
- ✔ 2 Maccabees
- ✔ 3 Maccabees
- ✔ 4 Maccabees
- ✔ 1 and 2 Esdras
- ✔ Psalm 151

These writings come from the Greek translations of the Hebrew Bible. In fact, these books originated in the Jewish project to translate the older Hebrew/Aramaic writings of their tradition into Greek, starting in the late third century BCE. But as they worked, they started to include writings written nearer to their own time, and some works continued to be written and added. (Remember, there wasn't a set canon yet, so why shouldn't they have kept adding more?) The result of their translation efforts is normally referred to as the *Septuagint* (pronounced sep-*two*-a-gint or *sep*-two-gint; see the nearby sidebar for what this means).

The Septuagint and the meaning behind the number 70

"Septuagint" literally means "70" in Greek. Why 70? One theory is based on an ancient legend recorded in a writing known as the *Letter of Aristeas* (from around 150–100 BCE). It tells the story that Ptolemy II of Egypt, one of the rulers who lived after Alexander the Great's conquests, wanted a copy of the Jewish scriptures for his great library in Alexandria. He commissioned six Jewish scholars from each of the Twelve Tribes of Israel to translate the Bible into Greek, and those 72 scribes were cut to 70, thus the Septuagint.

It's a good story, but most scholars and historians don't buy it. Regardless of the origin, the name stuck and is always used today. Furthermore, there seem to be different versions of the Greek translations as well, so there isn't just one single form of the Septuagint. Modern scholars have tried to combine all the versions into one "critical edition," which is the version used by students of the Greek Bible today.

A source of controversy

Christians appear to have routinely included the Septuagint among their sacred scriptures, and the New Testament quotes or alludes to some of these writings, suggesting that Christians were well aware of them and read them. In fact, when the early Christians eventually created the canon of the Old Testament, these Apocryphal books *were* included.

This is not to say, however, that early Christians weren't aware of the works' status as later writings. For example, Jerome (347–420 CE) was a famous early Christian who was responsible for producing a Latin translation of the Bible for Christians (known as the *Vulgate*). Although Jerome used both Hebrew and Greek originals to produce his Latin translation, he included the Apocryphal books, which he very consciously identified as "secondary," and he even used the term "Apocrypha" to describe them.

Christianity had always used and read these Apocryphal books, but the actual decisions about whether to consider them sacred scripture — that is, to include them in official canons — faced continued debate in Christian history. See the next section for more on how Jews, Protestants, Catholics, and Orthodox Christians view these books.

How different faiths view these works

What's the main difference between Catholic and Orthodox Christian readers on the one hand, and Protestant Christian and Jewish readers on the other hand? The difference is their opinion about the importance of this collection of these writings.

The Jewish view

Although all Jews read and knew these later writings in the century before Jesus and the first century CE (and they still know all about them), it appears clear that the Jewish communities never used these additional writings to the extent that the Christians did.

There's little evidence of much debate in Jewish sources about including the writings in any official list of scripture. However, even if these writings aren't part of the Jewish canon of the Hebrew Bible, there's widespread Jewish appreciation for the stories in the Apocryphal books as fine examples of Jewish storytelling, such as in Judith (seen as a heroine of the faith for her courage) and Tobit (deeply committed to his faith even in a foreign land).

Bottom line: The Jewish tradition has no significant religious use for these books because they're seen as, at best, pious stories with highly doubtful historical roots, and they're also long after the days of Ezra, who is seen as a traditional authority for bringing together sacred writings (see Chapter 2 for more on Ezra's role in the formation of the Hebrew Bible).

The Protestant view

If you want to say that Protestants all agree on anything, be prepared for a fight. After all, you're dealing with *Protest*ants: Protest is what they do.

Most Protestant Christians believe that Catholic and orthodox Christians should never have adopted these Apocryphal books in their Bible because Martin Luther felt that they had questionable religious value. Thus, Luther, noting that Jerome already referred to later Jewish writings as "Apocryphal," felt free to remove them from his suggested list of biblical books for his movement, which grew into the Protestant Reformation in Europe.

In fact, ol' Marty was rather cavalier about all previous official canons and muttered a number of unkind remarks about some of the New Testament books that he didn't much like, either (*James* comes to mind. Luther called it an "epistle of straw!" because he didn't like its very Jewish emphasis on doing acts of faith). But eventually his movement decided not to remove them from its canon. Conveniently, Luther then adopted the Jewish list of books, which is why the generally agreed-upon Protestant canon of the Christian Old Testament consists of precisely the same books as the Hebrew Bible — although in a somewhat different order.

Protestantism in general exists after the 16th century, but the dates of the official canonical lists of the Bible are obviously later. The Church of England (Episcopalians or Anglicans) affirmed their canon in 1563, and the Calvinist traditions (known as "Reformed" traditions, such as the Presbyterian and Baptist traditions) affirmed their canon in the Westminster Confession of 1647.

Bottom line: In general, Protestants assign canonical status only to those books that also appear in the Jewish canon of the Hebrew Bible, and Protestants reject the status assigned to the Apocryphal books in both Catholic and orthodox traditions.

The Catholic view

Basing their canonical decision on a variety of early Christian witnesses but definitely also on Jerome's Latin *Vulgate,* which quickly became the Bible of choice in the Western Catholic tradition, the Roman Catholic Church continued to produce Bibles over the centuries that included the Apocryphal books, often situated between the Old Testament and New Testament.

However, this list wasn't official until the stunningly recent date: 1545! This was the Nineteenth Ecumenical Council of the Catholic Church, usually referred to as the Council of Trent. Famously, Trent was the Council called to respond to the growing challenges of Protestantism in Christian Europe, and it was here that the Catholic Church made its final decision about the biblical Canon. This is when the Deutero-Canonical books were officially *in.*

It seems hard for some modern Christians to believe that the final decision was made so late in history, but it was merely a formality to officially stamp what writings the Church had been using in practice for literally centuries. The pressure of Protestant questions, however, forced the decision. It's interesting to speculate on whether the Catholic view would have hardened in this way *without* Protestant challenges, but that's a matter for another book!

Bottom line: The term "Apocrypha" should be used carefully. The Catholic and orthodox traditions prefer to dub the writings "Deutero-Canonical." For these Christians, these are definitely *not* considered lost books of the Bible but rather *list* books of the Bible! (Sorry for the bad joke, but coauthor Dan's a theologian, not a comedian!)

The Orthodox Christian view

Orthodox Christian churches take their canon a step further and have tended to include even more later writings in their Bible, such as 3 and 4 Maccabees, and an extra Psalm, numbered as Psalm 151, and sometimes the books of 1 and 2 Esdras, which closely resemble (and even partially reproduce) Ezra and Nehemiah and discuss roughly the same time period of Jewish history.

Each Orthodox Church (that is, Russian, Slavic, Ethiopic, Armenian, and so on) made independent decisions about the Canon of the Bible, of course, but the Greek Orthodox Church, for example, seems to have taken official action at the Jerusalem Synod of 1672, but others suggest that it wasn't "official" among Greek Orthodox throughout the world until 1950(!).

Bottom line: Those Christian churches where a great amount of doctrinal and liturgical tradition are central aspects of church life (for example, Catholic and Orthodox) felt less need to be absolutely clear on the approved list of scripture, those writings that had been used, commented upon, and studied for centuries. There was, in short, a trusted tradition of use.

A Survey of Apocryphal Books

Whether you consider them canonical or not, the Apocryphal writings certainly contain important history. After the Babylonian Exile of 587 BCE, the Hebrews lived under foreign occupation right through the era of the Roman Empire and the beginnings of Christianity. The Babylonians were conquered by the Persians in 539 and lived under Persian rule for 200 years, but precious little is known about what life was like under the Persian Empire.

The period of time that's better known is the time after the conquests of Alexander the Great and the following rule by Hellenistic (Greek) rulers who divided up his vast territories when he died in 323. It's *this* period of time, after Alexander's conquests, that most of the Apocryphal/Deutero-Canonical books talk about. One of the basic questions these writings (as well as writings universally accepted in the Bible) address is, "How shall we live in these times?"

On the one hand, some of the writings reflect stories that arose about Hebrew advisors to foreign rulers who seemed to get along (and even occasionally do very well) with the foreign monarchs. Stories like Daniel 1–6, Tobit, and Esther suggest that there were certainly dangers facing Hebrews living as minorities under vast Empires, but that survival and success were certainly possible with God's help.

Other writings, however, represent a much stronger assertiveness about Jewish independence from foreign rule. There were times when Jews in Israel even managed to live in semi-independence under Jewish leaders known as *Hasmoneans* (the descendants of the Maccabean Revolutions described in 1 and 2 Maccabees). In fact, it's possible to divide these Jewish writings before Christianity into two tendencies according to their attitudes toward foreign rule: hostile (for example, Judith and 1–4 Maccabees) and limited cooperation (for example, Tobit and the additional stories added to the book of Daniel in the Deutero-Canonical materials, which don't change its general tone of limited resistance).

As we summarize these later historical texts in the following sections, keep the following question in mind: Is a political as well as religious attitude reflected in these writings? Clearly, books like Maccabees and Judith carry a strong political message that even advocates violence against enemies, whereas books like Tobit and Wisdom of Solomon seem more pious and even, at times, conciliatory.

The Maccabean books preach the message of nationalism

The book of 1 Maccabees is a kind of history of the violent events that led to a temporary, semi-independent state of the Hebrews under the dominance of a strong Jewish family known as the Hasmoneans and their descendants. The other Maccabean books deal with slightly different parts of Greek period Jewish history. 2 Maccabees retells some of the story of 1 Maccabees, but then discusses famous martyrs. 3 Maccabees tells of Jewish resistance to oppression in Egypt. Finally, 4 Maccabees is a somewhat strange book dealing with the "reasonableness" of the martyrs of 2 Maccabees, suggesting that their actions did in fact pay attention to reason — a trait particularly valued among Greeks.

The attitude of most of the material of these books is combative and strong. The writers believed that many of the Jews were becoming corrupt by pagan rule in Jerusalem and advised that this rule must therefore be thrown off at all costs! The revolution (today you'd call it a guerilla war) that broke out is often called the Maccabean Revolution because it was initially led by a man named Judas who was nicknamed "the Maccabee" (meaning "the Hammer") because he was so successful as a military strategist. However, the books vary in their assessment of the tactics for successfully resisting foreign oppression. 1 Maccabees is definitely military, but 2 and 3 Maccabees also depend on God's miraculous intervention.

The history leading up to the Maccabean Revolt and the events that occurred right up to direct Roman rule in 63 BCE are somewhat complex. The principal sources for the Hellenistic period are the books of 1 and 2 Maccabees; scholars also have some information from the Jewish historian Josephus, but Josephus lived after the time of Jesus and sometimes his descriptions from a later time are considered questionable by modern historians.

Alexander's vast empire was divided among his generals on his death in 323 BCE. The fate of the Hebrew people was determined in the struggles between the ruling dynasties of the generals' descendants (the Ptolemys of Egypt and the Seleucids of Syria). There was considerable internal struggle in Palestine, and inevitably a violent struggle broke out among Jewish factions about the control of the Temple, its worship, and who would be the High Priest.

These internal debates, however, were made worse by the fact that a growing faction of Jews sought to be more Greek in attitude, practice, and outlook. This also meant becoming less and less scrupulous about the observation of traditional Jewish practice and rites. Such "modernist" attitudes inevitably drew a reaction from a more traditional population.

Now that you have a bit of background on the books in general, in the following sections, we examine the interesting similarities and differences between these four books that all now bear the name "Maccabee."

1 Maccabees: A soap opera with swords

The primary text of the group of books now called 1, 2, 3, and 4 Maccabees is clearly 1 Maccabees.

The book of 1 Maccabees can be summarized as the histories of the victories, setbacks, and eventual reign of the family descendants who ruled right up to the Roman occupation of Palestine in 63 BCE. In general, the book outlines two main points:

- ✔ How God used this family to provide leadership to engage in military and diplomatic maneuvering to successfully stay in power for several generations (and of course, these books presume that this is a good thing, despite the fact that the books admit that they had Jewish opposition)
- ✔ How the Priesthood of the Temple, the central institution of Jewish life at this time, passed into the control of this ruling family

The book follows the pattern of biblical history writing modeled after the historical books of the Bible such as 1 Samuel, 2 Samuel, 1 Kings, and 2 Kings, and therefore many modern readers consider it to be written as if it continues the story of the rulers of Israel.

The heroes of 1 Maccabees clearly stand in a biblical tradition of power and reassertion of Hebrew military identity mixed with some serious desire for vengeance for centuries of Jewish exile and foreign rule. Consider some of the last words of the elder Mattathias, the instigator of the revolt, as he passes the torch to his son, Judas:

> *Judas Maccabeus has been a mighty warrior from his youth; he shall command the army for you and fight the battle against the peoples. You shall rally around you all who observe the law, and avenge the wrong done to your people. Pay back the Gentiles in full, and obey the commands of the law.*
>
> —1 Maccabees 2:66–68

If you like soap opera intrigue, changing alliances, threats, and counterthreats, you'll love 1 Maccabees. It's a celebration of military prowess, strategy, and victory after setback.

2 Maccabees offers more support for the Maccabean Revolt

Somewhat oddly, the book known as 2 Maccabees backtracks to cover only *part* of the historical period addressed in 1 Maccabees.

2 Maccabees begins with a description of the reign of Seleucus IV (187–175 BCE), who reigned before the hated Antiochus IV (175–164 BCE). The book of 2 Maccabees doesn't go any farther than Judas Maccabeus's impressive defeat of a Greek General, Nicanor, whereas 1 Maccabees carries on much farther.

The oddity is perhaps best explained by the fact that 2 Maccabees claims to be a summarization of another work that's now lost but which was a history of the Maccabean Revolt written by Jason of Cyrene. 2 Maccabees also features two letters at the beginning, apparently directed to Jews in Egypt and Cyrene, imploring them to take up the celebration of Judah's impressive victories in Jerusalem (and also, it would seem, recognize Judah's claim to authority!).

It's normally thought that 2 Maccabees was composed finally in the late second century BCE, but others think it was later into the first century BCE.

Compared to 1 Maccabees, some scholars have argued that 2 Maccabees is just a more dramatic and emotional work in support of Judah's revolution, but others have wondered whether the introduction of more miraculous assistance and the theme of martyrdom was intended to introduce a more profoundly religious element into discussions of the Maccabean Revolt. After all, even though 1 Maccabees presents the warriors as pious, there's little doubt that they engage in decidedly worldly strategies, alliances, and tactics.

2 Maccabees, on the other hand, introduces much more of God's involvement by means of miracles and features extended descriptions and testimonies of non-warriors (the priest Eleazer, and most famously, a woman and her seven sons) who nevertheless die for the cause as martyrs rather than betray their faith.

3 Maccabees: Angels save the Jews

Although this book is called 3 Maccabees, it's a work with an entirely different character than 1 and 2 Maccabees except that it also narrates Jewish resistance to foreign rulers. 3 Maccabees takes place during the reign of Ptolemy IV (around 221–205 BCE).

The precise date of this work is impossible to pinpoint, and scholars argue that it may be a veiled reference to later persecutions of Jews, such as in the time of Roman Emperor Augustus, who started to register Jewish subjects and charge a poll tax around 24 BCE. However, persecutions were sadly all too common in the ancient world, so this amounts to guesswork.

Unlike 1 and 2 Maccabees, 3 Maccabees isn't generally considered an accurate historical account of real events but rather a dramatic series of stories intended to encourage readers to faithful resistance to foreign rulers who attempt to persecute Jews.

In 3 Maccabees, Ptolemy, one of the Greek rulers over Egypt in the days after Alexander the Great's death, has determined to exterminate the Jews of Alexandria because he's angry at his reception in Jerusalem when he tried to enter the Temple, which is forbidden to non-Jews! Back in Egypt, Ptolemy tries to get a listing of all the Jews in order to know who will abandon their faith or be executed, but the officials run out of ink and papyrus after 40 days of work and can't finish the job.

So, the King orders that the Jews be rounded up in a large coliseum and be trampled by elephants. But on the first try, the King oversleeps and can't give the actual order. The King completely forgets about his order and even acts surprised that he would suggest such a thing! When he recovers his anger, however, angels appear and drive the elephants back toward the King's officials. In the end, the King repents of his attempts and recognizes the loyalty of his Jewish subjects.

3 Maccabees almost has the air of dark comedy, but it also reminds the reader of the same kinds of threats of total annihilation that appear in the biblical book of Esther and stories like Daniel. 3 Maccabees reminds us that behind these stories is the reality of persecution of the Jews. Some have even suggested that 3 Maccabees contrasts a kind of nonviolent resistance to suggest alternative tactics from those advocated in the more militaristic resistance of 1 Maccabees. An interesting idea, to say the least.

4 Maccabees provides examples for martyrs

The only reason that 4 Maccabees is called a Maccabean book in the first place is because the subjects of this writing are the martyrs described in 2 Maccabees: Eleazar and the mother and her seven sons. But 4 Maccabees isn't a historical work at all; it's an argument defending the notion that these martyrs acted in a reasonable as well as pious manner. In deeply Greek style, the writer defends their actions as the expression of reason, which is able to control the passions and thus allow these martyrs to act in the courageous manner that they did:

> *The supremacy of the mind over these cannot be overlooked, for the brothers mastered both emotions and pains. How then can one fail to confess the sovereignty of right reason over emotion in those who were not turned back by fiery agonies?*

> —4 Maccabees 13:4–5

It appears that this work is intended to convince Greeks of the Jewish commitment to reason and rationality while at the same time affirming Jewish religious practice. Early Christian interest in 4 Maccabees, however, seems to be based on the examples provided for early Christian martyrs in both 2 Maccabees and this book, 4 Maccabees, which praises their sacrifice as both faithful *and* rational! Given the number of important Christian leaders who also faced martyrdom, the Jewish martyrs of the two Maccabean books would have been of obvious interest as examples of courageous faith.

Tales of Jewish heroes

Among the Apocryphal writings are a series of stories that focus on a central hero — male or female. These stories, although very likely legendary, often portray the central characters facing very real threats so that Jewish readers could relate quite closely to the dangers in the story — and the characters' wisdom in finding solutions to their dilemmas!

The book of Tobit and the book of Judith are the two best examples of Jewish hero stories from the Apocryphal collection. We give you a rundown of these stories in the following sections.

The charming Tobit

The book of Tobit introduces one of the most charming figures in later Jewish tradition. Tobit is introduced as a descendant of the exiles from the Assyrian Empire's conquest of the Northern State of Israel in 722. This claim about Tobit is highly doubtful, historically, because scholars know virtually nothing about any survivors of that deportation, and it's unlikely that a story such as this would surface over 600 years later!

Because the work appears to make no reference to the Maccabean Revolt (which surely would have been alluded to in some way if it had occurred at the time of writing), Tobit is presumed to have been written in the early second century BCE — in other words, *before* the Maccabean Revolt broke out. The book mentions honoring "the Prophets" (14:4–5) and tithing, both later Jewish traditions, so it can hardly be dated much earlier than this.

Tobit is a pious Jew who risks his life to give a proper burial to murdered Jews in the land of the Assyrian Empire. One day he's blinded and begins to ask God to end his life. Just before doing so, however, he remembers some unfinished business involving money he left in another town, and he sends his son Tobias to go and bring it back. Meanwhile, precisely when Tobit was asking for death, a young maiden named Sarah is in the town where Tobias is headed, and she's also asking for death because she was engaged to seven men who were all killed by an evil demon named Asmodeus.

God sends an angel to accompany young Tobias, who doesn't know that an angel is advising him, keeping him safe, eventually delivering him from the demon Asmodeus, and finally healing his father's blindness. There are some charming details in the story. For example, when Tobias falls in love with Sarah, Sarah's father Raguel starts digging his grave, telling his wife that they should expect the worst and try to keep dead fiancé number eight as quiet as possible!

But the book of Tobit also has some serious aspects. For example, the speech Tobit gives to his son before sending Tobias on his journey is a moving speech containing wise and pious advice about being a good person even when living in a foreign land. Following is an excerpt from this speech:

> *Revere the Lord all your days, my son, and refuse to sin or to transgress his commandments. Live uprightly all the days of your life, and do not walk in the ways of wrongdoing; for those who act in accordance with truth will prosper in all their activities. To all those who practice righteousness give alms from your possessions, and do not let your eye begrudge the gift when you make it. Do not turn your face away from anyone who is poor, and the face of God will not be turned away from you. If you have many possessions, make your gift from them in proportion; if few, do not be afraid to give according to the little you have.*

—Tobit 4:5-8

Judith makes Holofernes lose his head

In striking contrast to the book of Tobit is the story of the powerful Israelite woman, Judith. Although the book of Judith was probably written some time in the first century BCE, the setting of Judith is unclear: Judith is said to live in a town known as Bethulia, but the location of this city is somewhat disputed. It's accepted that Judith isn't intended as a historical source, so readers can overlook the setting and just appreciate the story and think about why it was considered so important.

Faced with threatening Assyrian troops, the town leaders of Bethulia are about to surrender. The very beautiful Judith, appalled at this lack of faith, decides to take matters into her own hands and use the oldest power in the world — feminine attraction. She pretends to switch her loyalty to the Assyrians and is quickly escorted to the General, Holofernes (a name unknown outside of the book of Judith). Holofernes, predictably, begins to think of ways to seduce Judith. Playing coy for a time, Judith insists that she be allowed to leave the Assyrian camp to engage in prayers and bathing, which she does for a few days. Then on the night that Holofernes thinks he is going to get lucky, Judith gets him drunk, cuts off his head, and walks out of the camp. (The Assyrian guards still think that she's innocently going into the wilderness to bathe and pray.) When Judith returns to Bethulia and presents the head of Holofernes, the people are emboldened to defeat the Assyrian army, now in disarray at the death of its leader. In the end, Judith is celebrated as a hero.

Judith's activism has sometimes been compared with that of the Maccabees and contrasted with the quiet piety of Tobit, who seems entirely nonthreatening in his dependence on God's assistance but also his quiet resistance to assimilation.

More Daniel stories

In the Greek translations of Daniel, four large sections were added to the book of Daniel. Of these, the first is a pious poem of praise, but the other three are additional stories of the central hero, Daniel. All three stories — Susanna, Bel, and the Dragon — reveal Daniel to be a wise and cunning man. These stories are sometimes referred to (with due apologies to Edgar Allan Poe's Inspector Dupin!) as the first genuine detective stories in history. Daniel examines evidence and produces information with all the skill of Sherlock Holmes himself. Like other Apocryphal writings, these stories clearly fit the times — pious stories of spiritual heroes in the days after Alexander's conquests of the East.

The Prayer of Azariah

A poem usually called "The Prayer of Azariah" but sometimes called "The Song of the Three" is attached to chapter 3 of the book of Daniel. Chapter 3 is where the three pious Jews (Mishael, Hananiah, and Azariah) are miraculously spared from death in the fiery furnace of the Babylonian ruler, Nebuchadnezzar.

The poem begins with a confession of sin and request for forgiveness as the three face death, and after the miracle of being spared from the fire, the section changes and goes into an extended praise of God, glorifying the power and majesty of the God who has saved the young Jews from their fiery death.

Susanna

The story of Susanna is about a pious Jewish woman who routinely bathes in her private backyard but is seen by two elderly Jewish men. They made a pact with each other to try and force Susanna to sleep with them, and when Susanna piously refuses, the two then publicly accuse her of committing adultery with someone else. They claimed to have seen the act firsthand. Because they're respected elders, the people believe the two men and prepare to execute Susanna for adultery as the law demands. All are in agreement with the punishment — except young Daniel. Daniel separates the two men and reveals their stories to be contradictory. Thanks to Daniel, Susanna's honor is restored (and the elders are executed)!

Bel

In the story of Bel, Daniel is shown a great handmade idol, called Bel, by King Nebuchadnezzar, who aims to prove to Daniel that it really is a god. The King believes that the idol actually comes to life and eats the food put before it every day. Rather strikingly, Daniel laughs at Nebuchadnezzar for his foolishness (a detail suggesting that this story comes long after the actual conditions of living under the cruel Babylonians!) and proposes a test. Daniel asks for ash to be spread around the food table, and when Daniel and the King return the next morning, Daniel points out to the King that there are footprints in the ashes, revealing that the Priests of Bel have emerged in the night and taken the food to fool the King into believing that Bel the idol had eaten.

The Dragon

The Dragon is a short story that features Daniel proving that an impressive animal (called a "dragon," but not of the Harry Potter variety!) is no god by concocting a potion that kills it.

An expanded book of Esther

The expansions of Esther are quite interesting because, in a direct sense, they restore God to the book of Esther. The original version of the book of Esther may be as old as the later part of the Persian Period (523–333 BCE). But in the Greek translations of biblical books, Esther actually *grew* in size with a number of significant additions to the story.

It has long been noted that God is never mentioned in the older (and shorter) Hebrew book of Esther, but God makes rather important appearances in the Greek additions to this book, which were most likely made in the first century BCE. The original was likely at least 200 years older than the more religious Greek additions (possibly even older). The sections of these Greek additions (some of which may have been written originally in Hebrew before they were translated into the Greek that we now have) are typically distinguished by letters; see the following list for explanations:

- ✔ **Addition A:** Mordecai's dream of the future and the way he discovers a plot against the Persian monarch
- ✔ **Addition B:** A text of the King's proclamation to kill all the Jews as his evil advisor Haman had intended; the text of this proclamation wasn't included in the older Hebrew version of the story

✔ **Addition C:** The extended texts of Mordecai and Esther's prayers to God for deliverance, especially for Esther as she prepares to beg the King to reverse Haman's evil plot against the Jews

✔ **Addition D:** Further details about the King's compassion for Esther and his sympathy for her emotional state

✔ **Addition E:** The text of the King's proclamation allowing the Jews to live and proclaiming their innocence and righteousness; the proclamation also allows the Jews to defend themselves if anyone tries to carry out the original evil order

These additions attest not only to the popularity of the Esther story — which obviously fits right in with the themes of 3 Maccabees, Tobit, and the additions to Daniel (see those sections earlier in the chapter) — but also the freedom to edit, supplement, and honor a story by, well, adding to it!

Later collections of Wisdom

Wisdom collections were a very popular form of Jewish literature (examples include Proverbs and Ecclesiastes), and it's clear that Jews just kept writing these accounts of folk wisdom and wise advice (a bit like Ben Franklin's wise advice). The cool thing about reading Wisdom books is that *most* of the advice sounds just as true today as it was then!

The Wisdom of Solomon

The *Wisdom of Solomon* is a collection of wise teachings gathered by someone who obviously was in serious conversation with Greek philosophy and ideas; a number of fascinating features in this writing show development of Jewish thought in the Greek period and development of classic Wisdom thought as well. (See Chapter 3 for an explanation of the different forms of Jewish religious writing, including Wisdom literature.) The Wisdom of Solomon is an example of a later book that nonetheless preserves the older Wisdom style and theme.

The Wisdom of Solomon features two unusual aspects that we think are especially worthy of comment. It carries on the tradition within Wisdom literature of actually personifying Wisdom as a special creation of God. In the book of Proverbs, the classic Wisdom book of the Bible, there's an interesting tendency to personify Wisdom as a beautiful woman. In addition to the rather racy way of talking about the seductions of foolishness (portrayed as a dangerous woman) as opposed to the wholesome love of wisdom (the other beautiful woman), there's also a further discussion of "lady wisdom" as a creation of God before God even created the cosmos (see Proverbs 8:22–31). The Wisdom of Solomon continues to speak in the feminine of this personified Wisdom:

> *Wisdom is radiant and unfading, and she is easily discerned by those who love her, and is found by those who seek her. She hastens to make herself known to those who desire her. One who rises early to seek her will have no difficulty, for she will be found sitting at the gate. To fix one's thought on her is perfect understanding, and one who is vigilant on her account will soon be free from care . . .*

—Wisdom 6:12–15

The Wisdom of Solomon also comments on violence in earlier Hebrew history. The writer talks about how God didn't originally intend to wipe out the Canaanites in the time of Joshua's entry in the land, but their stubbornness in refusing less lethal means was their downfall:

> *But even these you spared, since they were but mortals, and sent wasps as forerunners of your army to destroy them little by little, though you were not unable to give the ungodly into the hands of the righteous in battle, or to destroy them at one blow by dread wild animals or your stern word. But judging them little by little you gave them an opportunity to repent, though you were not unaware that their origin was evil and their wickedness inborn, and that their way of thinking would never change.*

—Wisdom 12:8–10

Does such a discussion represent the writer's attempt to explain God to foreigners who may wonder whether the destruction of the Canaanites in the days of Joshua wasn't a bit excessive? There are many such hints that Wisdom is a book intended as a dialogue with non-Jews and thus appeal to reasoned arguments, religious devotion, and especially Platonic forms of philosophical argument.

Sirach's words of wisdom

In the book bearing his name, *Jesus Ben Sira*, or just *Sirach*, this Jewish philosopher seems to return to the confident views of the older Wisdom book of Proverbs — confidence that it's possible to lead a wise and productive life even if one isn't among the wealthy or elite. Sirach is normally dated between 200–175 BCE because the Prologue, added by someone claiming to be Sirach's grandson, is fairly securely dated to about 132–120 BCE.

Although not much is known about either Grandpa Sirach or his grandson, the style of the writing is rather typical for Wisdom material, with the interesting exception that Sirach addresses more characters from Jewish history than Proverbs, Ecclesiastes, or Job — the three older Wisdom Books. For example, the Patriarchs (Abraham and Jacob) are discussed in Sirach but never make an appearance in the older material. Sirach, then, seems to presume the beginnings of a collection of writings that by his time are considered important already! He even refers to the 12 shorter books of the Prophets as simply "The Twelve" — in short, already a set as they now appear in the Old Testament.

Sirach offers a long series of sage advice — much of which seems as valid today as when the ink was still wet. For example:

> *Do not abandon old friends, for new ones cannot equal them. A new friend is like new wine; when it has aged, you can drink it with pleasure.*

> —Sirach 9:10

These writings of Sirach have an interesting social conscience as well; for example, "Stretch out your hand to the poor, so that your blessing may be complete" (Sirach 7:32). Like Proverbs, reading Sirach is a delight. Many of the sayings are wise pearls that a modern person can string on his or her own collection of helpful and enriching insights into the human condition.

Jeremiah-inspired literature

Two writings in the Apocryphal books focus on the importance and influence of the Prophet Jeremiah: a short document known as the Letter of Jeremiah and the book of Baruch.

The Letter of Jeremiah

The Letter of Jeremiah is an expansion of the letter that Jeremiah wrote to the Babylonian exiles in chapter 29 of the biblical book of Jeremiah. In that famous biblical letter, Jeremiah talks about the length of time that the exiles will be in captivity. In the Letter of Jeremiah, however, the subject changes to idol worship and the advice to resist the worship of idols no matter how impressive the idols look (referring to ones made of gold and silver, and so on).

It's likely that this Letter was recast at a later time to try to warn against the enticements of the Greek civilization and their gods given that their cultural achievements, monuments, temples, and rituals were otherwise so impressive. "Don't be fooled," says the Letter of Jeremiah!

The book of Baruch

Although based on a real historical character named Baruch who wrote the book of Jeremiah (as reported in Jeremiah 36:4), the book of Baruch is a late work only *attributed* to the famous Scribe of the Prophet Jeremiah.

Baruch features two main sections: a long prayer and a long, poetic hymn (or song) addressed to Israel. The writing is set in the time of Jeremiah, when the

Babylonian armies defeated and destroyed Jerusalem and forced the tragic exile of many Jews from Jerusalem and the surrounding countryside to Babylon.

Reflecting the ideas of the Prophet Jeremiah, Baruch reminds readers that Jerusalem was defeated because of the sins of the people. In the second part, however, the book turns to encouragement, especially teaching that the people should seek the knowledge of God. Yet the book also promises that those who so cruelly destroyed Jerusalem will be punished.

Baruch, therefore, uses the setting of the Babylonian destruction of Jerusalem in 587 BCE, and the exile of many Judeans right after that tragic event, to write about persecutions and trials faced by the Jewish people in later times. In a sense, it speaks in a historic "code." "Babylon" came to be used to symbolically speak of *all* oppressors of the Jews. (Note that the Roman Empire is called "Babylon" in the New Testament book of Revelation, and in 1 Peter 5:13.) It appears that Baruch, like many of the books of the Apocrypha, was written to encourage Jews in troubled times.

Sadly, books of encouragement in troubled times were always useful because troubled times kept coming. Probably one of the main reasons these writings survived is that they were relevant in the frequent difficult times of Jewish history from 587 BCE right down to the Roman Empire (and, of course, beyond).

In the Bible or Not, These Books Are of Great Value to Modern Readers

Whether Christians or Jews choose to "include" these books in their Bible as the Roman Catholic and Orthodox traditions have chosen to do, they are still valuable works that provide a great deal of information about Jewish thought and practice in the centuries leading up to the rise of Christianity, and the rise of Rabbinic (Modern) Judaism.

We hear about severe persecutions, we hear deeply moving calls to encouragement and reassurance, and we hear charming stories of Jewish "heroes," both violent and nonviolent, warriors and martyrs, who give us a profound sense of a religious tradition and a people struggling to survive the challenges of living under various world empires.

Chapter 5

The Dead Sea Scrolls

Most people have heard of the Dead Sea Scrolls, but not many really understand what that refers to. It's important to know about the once unknown writings of the Dead Sea Scrolls because they can help you understand the diversity of Jewish beliefs in the years leading up to the beginnings of Christianity; they also teach about the diverse backgrounds before the clear development of early Rabbinic Judaism.

No one claims that the Dead Sea Scrolls include "missing" or "lost" books of the Bible, but like some of the more unusual Christian writings we examine in later chapters, these writings show how wild some religious speculation can get. When you read the Dead Sea Scrolls in English, you may conclude: Interesting place to visit . . . but I wouldn't want to live there. In other words, although we're deeply grateful that the community kept copies of what later became the books of the Hebrew Bible (all except Esther), it's also clear that their *own* writings (which they may have treasured as equal in importance to the writings that later became Scripture) are typically rather strange, difficult to understand, or downright mean-spirited.

In this chapter, we give you an introduction to the Dead Sea Scrolls and the kind of literature that they contain. But half the fun is starting with the stories about how they were found in the first place! I mean, finding sacred scrolls in caves — you can't beat that, even in Hollywood.

Note: Throughout this chapter, we cite two different sources for each actual quote from a scroll. We use the standard, scholarly numbering system for *all* fragments and scrolls of the Dead Sea (used by all scholars in all publications about the scrolls), but we also refer to the page number of the English translation provided in the best edition currently available: *The Dead Sea Scrolls Translated: The Qumran Texts in English*, Second Edition, by Florentino Garcia Martinez (Eerdmans).

A Little Background on the Dead Sea Scrolls

The term "Dead Sea Scrolls" refers to a number of "collections" of ancient manuscripts that since about 1948 have been discovered over the years in the caves along the shores of the Dead Sea (the basin of the Jordan River, the border between modern Israel and modern Jordan).

The main collection that everyone thinks of as the Dead Sea Scrolls consists of scrolls found hidden in 11 caves on the shore of the Dead Sea. Unfortunately, these scrolls were in a very bad state (Figure 5-1 represents one of the more intact scrolls), and although they include known biblical books of the Hebrew Bible, most of the pieces are exactly that — frustratingly broken, torn, or deteriorated fragments. A few scrolls are nearly complete — such as the Prophet Isaiah — but virtually everything else has pieces missing.

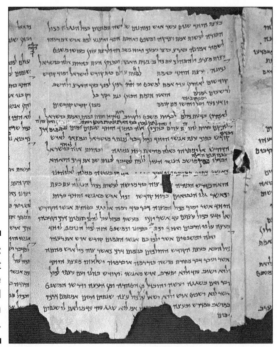

Figure 5-1: A fragment of one of the discovered Dead Sea Scrolls.

Most of these texts are on *papyrus,* a form of writing material made by weaving and flattening the leaves of the papyrus plant that grows along shorelines throughout the Middle East.

How they were found: Be careful where you throw rocks!

There's real romance to the legends of the finding of the Dead Sea Scrolls. However, as the modern Dead Sea Scroll scholar Florentino G. Martinez has written, the stories have conflicting versions.

The most famous version is that a young Bedouin boy named Mohammed ed-Dhib chased his goat into a cave, and when he threw a rock, it struck one of the sealed clay jars where some scrolls were placed all those centuries ago!

In another version of the story, it was *three* shepherds who found the scrolls. But regardless of the specifics of their discovery, the fact is that by 1947, the scrolls were coming to light.

Who wrote them

Even after the scrolls came to the public's attention, debates raged about how genuine and how old they really were. After decades of careful research on the pottery forms where some of the manuscripts were found, the kinds of writing used in the scrolls, and the chemistry and form of the scrolls themselves, it's clear today that the scrolls are Jewish writings written by a group of Jews with unusual religious ideas (often called *sectarians* or *separatists*). They lived apart from the rest of Jewish society because they believed that they were the "pure" Jews and that the others were corrupt — especially those Jewish officials running the Temple in Jerusalem. These strange ideas are represented by their own religious writings — writings different from the books that they also kept copies of that later became Jewish scripture. Remember, two bodies of texts make up the Dead Sea Scrolls: the texts that are copies of biblical books and the texts that are the separatists' own writings.

The scrolls were produced by a community living at Qumran, a site not far from the various caves on the edge of the Judean desert, where similar pottery was discovered. It seems obvious that all the various finds came from Qumran because copies of the same writings were found in various caves. This community composed these writings from the third century BCE right up to about 68 CE, when the site was used by the Romans as a garrison in preparations for their conquest of Masada (the last holdouts from the Jewish Revolt of 67–70 CE).

This Qumran community kept these writings until they hid them in the caves, probably as a result of Roman threats. What they kept were two different categories of writings: biblical writings (many of which may not have come from this community in the first place) and their own religious writings outlining their unique Jewish beliefs.

Patience pays off: Gaining access to the scrolls

Before 1991, access to even photographs of the various scrolls and pieces of scrolls was forbidden by the Israel Antiquities Authority, which appointed a group of scholars as the "guardians" of the scrolls. Obviously, this limitation created a huge outcry among scholars around the world, who protested that important discoveries should be available to *all* scholars as soon as possible.

On September 22, 1991, the Huntington Library of Pasadena, California, revealed that the Israeli government had quietly deposited a complete set of photographs of the scrolls (sets were also given to other international libraries) with the library and that it would make these photographs available for study. Since that time, other libraries have opened up their sets of photos, and research on the scrolls has increased dramatically.

Why the Discovery of the Scrolls Was Sensational for Biblical Scholarship

Before the discovery of the Dead Sea Scrolls, modern scholars didn't have *ancient* Hebrew texts of the Bible! Only copies of copies of copies . . . well, you get the idea. Although they had very old *Greek* fragments and biblical writings from as early as the fourth century (that is, Greek *translations* of the Hebrew writings), as well as pieces from as early as the second century, the oldest actual versions of the Hebrew Bible, also known as the Old Testament, *written in Hebrew* were from the ninth to tenth centuries CE.

Among the Dead Sea Scrolls discoveries were pieces — and sometimes large, almost complete sections — of every single book of the Hebrew Bible except Esther. To this day, you can visit "The Shrine of the Book" in Jerusalem and read the Hebrew manuscripts of biblical books like the Prophet Isaiah on display there. It's a real treat to watch visiting Israeli schoolchildren read these 2,000-year-old texts because they recognize much of the Hebrew!

With the discoveries of the Dead Sea Scrolls in the caves, scholars had Hebrew writings of biblical books that were sometimes 1,000 years *older* than what they had before 1947. Amazing! Now they were able to check their ideas of what the Hebrew versions of the old books must have been (based on those ninth- to tenth-century versions) by comparing *much* older manuscripts. The discovery really gave a boost to biblical scholarship.

The following sections discuss the areas of study that were broadened with the discovery of the Dead Sea Scrolls.

Different versions of biblical books

Particularly intriguing to scholars was the fact that some biblical books were present in the scrolls in more than one version! There appeared to be different arrangements of some books, for example, and a different chapter order for a copy of Psalms that even included a few Psalms not otherwise included in the later "canonical" version. These differences suggest that different versions of biblical books were circulating in the days before definite versions were agreed upon and definitely before final "lists" were drawn up! What's so interesting to modern biblical scholars is that the Qumran community clearly maintained different versions of the *same* books.

Did the Qumran community have a "canon"? Many of their writings quote from biblical books, but they also quote from books that weren't later accepted in the Jewish "canon" of the Hebrew Bible, such as Jubilees. It doesn't appear that they had an idea of a definitive "list."

Some possible lost fragments of biblical books

Are there "lost books" of the Bible among the Dead Sea Scrolls? Well, part of the answer to this question is obvious — the Bible didn't yet exist in the conventional sense when the Qumran community lived and wrote their materials. They obviously treasured their "biblical writings" as well as their own writings. But occasionally, there are some tantalizing hints of some materials that *may* have once been part of the biblical books we now have but that were in fact "lost."

Our favorite example of this is a fragment known as the "Prayer of Nabonidus." Nabonidus was a Babylonian Ruler who lived about 556–539 BCE. Many scholars believe that many of the stories in the book of Daniel that talk about Nebuchadnezzar originally must have been talking about Nabonidus. The name was probably changed to Nebuchadnezzar because he was the more famous Babylonian ruler and the destroyer of Jerusalem in 587 BCE.

The question is this: Is there a lost story of Daniel in the Dead Sea Scrolls? Here's the text (the [brackets] indicate missing parts, with educated guesses filled in):

> *Words of the prayer which Nabonidus, king of the land of Babylon, the great king, prayed when he was afflicted by a malignant inflammation, by decree of the God Most High, in Teiman. I, Nabonidus, was afflicted . . . for seven years, and was banished far [from men, until I prayed to God Most High] and an exorcist forgave my sin. He was a Jew from [exiles, who said to me]*

Make a proclamation in writing, so that glory, exaltation and honor be given to the name of the God Most High. And I wrote as follows: When I was afflicted by a malignant inflammation . . . I prayed for seven years [to all] the gods of silver and gold [of bronze and iron] of wood, of stone and of clay, because [I thought] that they were gods . . .

—4QPrNab (tr. Martinez, 289)

That's pretty much all we have. But it's intriguing and sounds so much like many of the elements of the famous Daniel stories in the book of Daniel 1–6! And, given that three more Daniel stories turned up in the Greek translation of the book of Daniel, is it too much to suppose that perhaps *other* Daniel stories once circulated and that this fragment from the Dead Sea Scrolls is yet another one? The problem is that "Daniel" isn't specifically mentioned; otherwise, the apparent similarities to the plots of the known Daniel stories seem pretty amazing.

Even though the Dead Sea Scrolls don't provide revolutionary lost books that will change everything about modern religion, they do provide lots of intriguing hints and suggestions.

"Interpretations" of biblical books

Another form of writing from the Dead Sea Scrolls that involves biblical material is works that interpret biblical books, including works known as *Pesherim* (the singular form is *Pesher*).

Pesherim are "interpretations" of biblical books, mostly the Prophets. But the style is quite strange and unfamiliar to modern readers. Often, the biblical Prophet (such as Habakkuk, one of the more famous scrolls) is quoted by a single verse and then the phrase "The Interpretation is . . ." appears followed by a very brief explanation. Consider an example from the Pesher on Micah; we indicate the direct quote from Micah in bold:

> **What are the High Places of Judah? Is it not Jerusalem? I will reduce Samaria to a country ruin, a plot of vines.** *The interpretation of this concerns the Spreader of Lies, since he has misdirected simpletons.* **What are the "high places" of Judah? Is it not Jerusalem?** *The interpretation of this concerns the Teacher of Righteousness who teaches the law to his council and to all those volunteering to join the chosen of God, carrying out the law in the council of the community . . .*

—4QpMic10 (tr. Martinez, 194)

Two things are worthy of note here because they're fairly typical of these Pesher interpretation writings:

- **The interpretation is rather loose.** In this example, the words of Micah about Jerusalem are considered positive (about the community) and the words about Samaria negative. In fact, in the actual passage in Micah, it seems clear that *both* places are being condemned by the Prophet Micah in the late eighth century BCE.

- **Individuals are named.** In this example, the "hero" is the "Teacher of Righteousness" (probably the founder of the community) and an enemy is named as "Spreader of Lies" (quite possibly the High Priest who was serving in Jerusalem at the time).

Reading these Pesher materials from the Dead Sea Scrolls reveals that the interpretation was almost always carefully applied to the time of the writer of the scroll itself and *not* the time of the biblical book being quoted. Some of these scrolls specifically mention events known to have occurred in the first century BCE, so the general idea seems to be that these interpretation scrolls are trying to apply the biblical teachings of various Prophets to their own time, paying no attention to the details of the biblical book's own time!

Possible new Mosaic laws revealed

Apparent rewritings of the Laws of Moses in the Torah, which consists of the first five books of the Bible, are among the more controversial kinds of literature discovered among the Dead Sea Scroll fragments.

This finding is surprising because one would think that the laws of Moses would have been pretty off-limits as far as change was concerned. Yet, even in the Dead Sea community, it seems that Moses material wasn't sacrosanct.

The Temple Scroll not only was the single longest scroll discovered (nearly nine meters long with 67 columns written on it) among all the Dead Sea Scrolls, but also many copies and fragments of the document were discovered in other locations.

This scroll reads very much like the laws of Moses in the biblical books of Leviticus, Exodus, and Deuteronomy, but in the Temple Scroll these laws have been rather freely mixed together with occasional materials that don't appear in the biblical books. Some scholars suggest that the Temple Scroll was considered part of the Torah in the Qumran Jewish community.

Some go further and suggest that the Temple Scroll *was* the Torah for this community, which used it instead of the more well-known books of Moses that ended up in the Bible. In other words, it's possible that the scroll had the same religious and "ethical" status as the laws of Moses, which according to Jewish tradition are the words of God as given to Moses. A rather large percentage of the Temple Scroll laws are written in the same style (God speaks to Moses directly in the first person) as the books of Moses in the Bible. Most of these laws have to do with ritual practices of the Priests, sacrifice, and other aspects of ritual (down to details like burial of the dead, for example). Often the practices are elaborated beyond the instructions given in the Bible.

Looking at Other Writings Commonly Referred to as Dead Sea Scrolls

Although the term "Dead Sea Scroll" is usually intended to refer to a limited number of scrolls (and hundreds of *fragments* of scrolls) found on the shores of the Dead Sea, other writings are sometimes included in the general term. It's important to understand the different kinds of literature, when and where they were found, and more important, when they're normally dated. Here's a rundown:

- **The Wadi Daliyeh Papyri:** This collection of papyrus writings, dated from the fourth century BCE, was discovered in caves north of Jericho. It was accompanied by many artifacts (seals and metal work in particular) which were considered just as important as the Wadi Daliyeh writings themselves. The writings appear to be mostly business documents, including a number of "bills of sale" for slaves written in ancient Aramaic (the language of the region in the fifth to fourth century BCE or toward the end of the Persian rule over Palestine). This collection doesn't appear to have any religious writings, but the writings are valuable sources for historians.

- **The Masada Manuscripts:** When the famous mountaintop fortress of Masada was excavated by archaeologists in the 1950s, they found several manuscripts. Among them were several biblical books, including Sirach (the late Wisdom book that appears in Catholic and Orthodox versions of the Old Testament), pieces of other biblical writings, and some non-biblical books known from fragments in the main collection of Dead Sea Scrolls. Most of the biblical manuscripts weren't different than our present versions, although pieces of Ezekiel apparently showed some interesting variations.

- **The Manuscripts of Murabba'at:** These texts were found at a *wadi* — a ravine created when water cuts into a mountainside — called Murabba'at. Several pieces of correspondence dealing with the Bar Kochba revolt of 132–135 CE were discovered along with small pieces of biblical texts.

- ✔ **The Manuscripts of Nahal Hever:** Most pieces of these religious writings are too small to identify, but this collection includes a great number of contracts and letters from the Bar Kochba era. These writings were discovered in 1960–1961.

- ✔ **The Manuscripts from Wadi Seiyal and Pieces of the Twelve Prophets:** These texts consist of several pieces of legal documents in various ancient languages. Some scholars suspect some of these documents to really be from the area of Nahal Hever.

Checking Out the Unusual Religious Writings from the Dead Sea Collection

Among the most spectacular finds of the Dead Sea Scrolls are the books that are *not* biblical books at all but rather are writings made by the Qumran Jewish community to defend their own religious ideas and encourage them in their life and in their ideals.

Most historians refer to the Qumran community as separatists or sectarians because the vast majority of their writings seem to either advise a form of purity and removal from others who aren't in the community or amount to angry dreams of future warfare and destruction of their enemies.

Scholars who work on these writings suggest dividing the "unusual" writings from the Dead Sea Scrolls into the following categories:

- ✔ Predictions of future spiritual battle
- ✔ Rules for community life
- ✔ Poetry
- ✔ Liturgy
- ✔ Astronomical texts

Predictions of future spiritual battle

Much of the non-biblical material in the Dead Sea Scrolls collection engages in contrasts between the good guys and the bad guys. The good guys (Sons of Light), obviously, are the members of the Qumran community, and the bad guys — well, this could be generic (all the rest of those people) *or* some have wondered if it was directed against specific enemies. Could it be, for example, that the bad guys were specifically the Jewish leaders back in Jerusalem? Some have speculated that the Qumran community was started by disenfranchised Priests who felt alienated (or even thrown out!) by the powerful Priests back in Jerusalem, and so they retreated to the desert to start their own purified community and wait for the day when God would lead them back to Jerusalem, and to power, in triumph!

Among the most important documents that suggest this interpretation is the famous War Scroll. Included in this fascinating (and often shockingly violent) set of documents are careful instructions for a "spiritual war" that's coming very soon. The opening lines set the stage:

> *For the Instructor: The Rule of the War. The first attack by the sons of light will be launched against the lot of the sons of Darkness, against the army of Belial, against the company of Edom and of Moab and of the sons of Ammon.*
>
> —1 QM 1:1 (tr. Martinez, 95)

Evil spiritual armies are aligned with foreign peoples (Edom, Moab, and so on) so that this battle is understood to be heavenly *and* earthly armies together. Frankly, it all begins to sound like some big Lord of the Rings-type battle with hordes of evil troops against the "sons of Light":

> *There will be infantry battalions to melt the heart, but God's might will strengthen the heart of the sons of light.*
>
> —1QM 1:14 (tr. Martinez)

Included in these many scrolls and portions of scrolls are even banners with messages written on them (the messages are provided), trumpets sounding, and even battle cries, such as:

> *For the battle is yours!*
> *With the might of your hand*
> *Their corpses have been torn to pieces*
> *With no-one to bury them!*
>
> —1 QM XI.1 (tr. Martinez, 103)

Also included in this category of writings are texts that set forth actual measurements for the rebuilding of Jerusalem. This seems to go along with the war, it seems, because plans are already established for the reconstruction of Jerusalem after the war. From these texts, it's understood that Jerusalem is the anticipated goal of the battle — not the community in the desert! The community is simply waiting there for the heavenly trumpets to sound the charge. Although the war extends for 40 years, much of the books centers on the last battle.

Rules and ethical instructions for the community

Two of the most famous writings in the Dead Sea Scrolls are the documents known now as the *Rule of the Community* and the *Damascus Document*. Both documents establish a kind of discipline, or set of rules, for the community. This fact becomes more obvious when you read lines like this one from the beginning of the Rule of the Community:

> *This is the rule for the men of the Community who freely volunteer to convert from all evil and to keep themselves steadfast in all he prescribes in compliance with his will. They should keep apart from men of sin in order to constitute a community in law and possessions, and acquiesce to the authority of the sons of Zadok . . .*
>
> —1 QS V:1–2 (tr. Martinez, 8)

Zadok is the famous founder of an order of Priests in the Bible, and it seems that the community saw themselves as inheritors of the "pure" line of the biblical Zadok. His name occurs frequently in Dead Sea documents.

Included in the Rule of the Community are all kinds of instructions for how people are supposed to relate to each other in this community as well as the ritual means of maintaining the "purity" of the individual and the group. Along the way are interesting discussions of the community in relation to "evil tendencies" that community members are warned about. Clearly, this group thought that their rules were part of what made them superior to outsiders — that is, all the rest of the Jews!

The rules can get rather strict, such as the rules against falling asleep during meetings of the community, where numbers of days of punishment are given:

> *Whoever utters with his mouth futile words, three months; for talking in the middle of the words of his fellow, ten days. And whoever lies down and goes to sleep in the session of the Many, thirty days . . .*
>
> —1 QS VII 11–13 (tr. Martinez, 11)

(Hmmm . . . maybe something to read to your kids. . . .) Part of the Rule contains some poetry — perhaps intended as rules to be "sung" to help people memorize them. Others think that that the community repeated the poetic phrases together during some kind of religious service.

On the other hand, the famous Damascus Document also has historical interest, and speculation surrounding this document is based on the fact that it may give a kind of history of the Qumran community. Typically, scholars turn to this document as a basis to suggest that the Qumran community was a breakaway group when the Hasmoneans (descendants of the Maccabees) took over the Priesthood in Jerusalem. In this writing, historical events can be interpreted in the symbolism. For example, when they talk about the evil ones — they mean those Jews who oppose them — they often interpret biblical passages to refer to their enemies literally. In the following example, the text quotes a passage from Deuteronomy 32:33:

> *"Their wine is serpents' venom and the head of cruel, harsh asps." The serpents are the kings of the peoples and the wine their paths and the asps' head is the head of the kings of Greece.*

> —Col. VIII (tr. Martinez, 38)

Poetry

Among the interesting non-biblical materials contained in the Dead Sea Scrolls collection are a number of poetic texts — often in pieces so small as to make it difficult to reconstruct entirely — that are very similar to the Psalms in the Bible. In fact, most scholars refer to these as *Apocryphal Psalms.*

Many of the fragments of these non-biblical Psalms seem entirely acceptable in content and probably weren't included only because they were written later than the collection that ended up as "canonical" in Jewish and Christian traditions. Some of these so-called other Psalms may well have been older than the Qumran community and simply were preserved among their biblical materials. In other words, many scholars believe that *some* of this Psalm-like poetry wasn't actually written by the community.

"Wisdom is a woman" poems

Other poems can be a bit, well, unusual. For example, one of the interesting traditions that's typical of ancient Jewish *wisdom literature* (literature that gives advice on wise ways of living and success in life) is that, on occasion, wisdom becomes "personified" as a beautiful woman. Learning wisdom is equated with falling in love with wisdom.

Most of the poetry isn't like this, though, and one of the clues of the late nature of many of these Psalms is surely the fact that many, if not most, of the themes play off light against dark, good against evil, and especially name an evil being (often "Belial") against the goodness of God. Finally, themes of God's ultimate judgment against evil are also common throughout.

Acrostic Psalms

A popular form among the Dead Sea poems is *acrostic* Psalms. These are Psalms arranged so that consecutive lines of poetry begin with the next letter of the Hebrew Alphabet (kind of like, "A is for . . ., B is for . . .," and so on). But, of course, it isn't possible to reflect and express this pattern in an English translation, so you just have to take our word for it!

These contrasts are further examples of the "us against them" feeling drawn from the vast majority of the Dead Sea materials that are not in the Bible. Much of the poetry is lovely, but then it takes a turn toward a nasty vindictiveness, and at that moment, you can breathe a little sigh: "Thank goodness *that* one wasn't included in the canon!"

Exorcism Poems

Among the Apocryphal Psalms are a few really spooky poems. These are called *Exorcism Poems,* and they're clearly intended to ward off evil spirits, or "Belial," a term used for the same spirit that later Christians would know as the Devil. These poems are written like a Psalm, as if David wrote them, but they advise certain ways to ward off evil. Here's an example, with missing parts filled in as best guesses:

> *Call on the heavens at any time, when Belial comes upon you, you shall say to him: Who are you, accursed amongst men and amongst the seed of the holy ones? Your face is a face of futility, and your horns are horns of a wretch. You are darkness and not light, sin and not justice . . .*

> —11 Q 11 IV (tr. Martinez, 377)

So, basically, insult him a lot and he goes away. Apparently it's that simple.

Liturgy

Included in this collection of materials are fragments that have been sorted together because they appear to suggest prayers for special occasions. The presumption is that these are prayers that were given for certain times of the year, on specifically numbered occasions or even every day, as evidenced by the opening, "When the sun rises, you shall say. . . ."

In this group, there's special interest in a group of texts named *Word of the Luminaries.* These writings are interesting because they seem so similar to a set form of prayer known from the Bible in Daniel Chapter 9, Nehemiah

Chapter 9, and the apocryphal book of Baruch. This form of prayer seems to have become popular among Jews after the disasters of the Babylonian conquest of Jerusalem in 587 BCE because examples of the prayers are in biblical books that come *after* that date.

Typical of these prayers are elements including

✔ Recounting God's deeds of mercy in the past

✔ Recounting people's mistakes in the past

✔ Admitting that people are suffering because they ignored God's warnings

✔ Asking God to forgive people one more time

Knowing this, you can recognize these themes in the following text, which begins with a discussion of God's just punishments in the past but nevertheless continues:

> *But in spite of all this you did not reject the descendants of Jacob and did not hurl Israel to destruction, breaking the covenant with them. For you are a living God, you alone, and there is no other apart from you. You remembered your covenant. . . .For you have poured your holy spirit upon us, to fill us with your blessings, so that we would look for you in our anguish, and whisper in the grief of your reproach . . .*

—4 Q 504 V (tr. Martinez, 415)

Another writing in this group is often called *Sons of the Sabbath Sacrifice*. This writing reflects the realm of angelic speculation and nearly apocalyptic-like imagery (see Chapter 3). For those who enjoy reading the strange imagery of books like the last book of the New Testament, John's Revelation, then this is the Dead Sea Scroll for you! Here's a sampling:

> *He will celebrate the God of the exalted angels seven times, with seven words of wonderful exaltations. Psalm of praise, on the tone of the fourth, to the Powerful One who is above all the gods with his seven wonderful powers. He will praise the God of the powers seven times, with seven words of wonderful praise . . .*

—4 Q 4031 (tr. Martinez, 421)

In this document, you see typical signs of this kind of literature — lots of repetition, use of numbers like seven (Hebrews loved to use number 7 and number 12 whenever possible, viewing them as numbers that were whole and complete), and imagery of angels and heavenly beings. You even get the idea that the very *reading* of these passages is supposed to induce some kind of altered state of consciousness. To be honest, this stuff alters *our* state into *un*consciousness (zzzzzz), but to each his own.

Astronomical texts

Saving the strangest for last, among the unusual religious writings in the Dead Sea Scrolls are elements of astronomical, perhaps even astrological, interest in the movements of the stars and planets. The reason for these documents seems obvious: When you're in the desert and the oil lamps go out and the sky opens up before you, it's hard *not* to be impressed. And if you're of a religious turn of mind (as the Qumran community most certainly was), you may start turning that religious mind toward making sense of what you're witnessing above you!

It's known from such books as the Book of 1 Enoch (see Chapter 6) that ancient Jews, like most ancient people, were fascinated with the skies and often sought to interpret information from their observations. When you stare long enough, you begin to see patterns in the stars and in the movement of the lights. The sun rises and sets, the moon changes shape, and the star patterns appear to move as well.

One of the practical uses of all this observation, of course, was setting the calendar of festivals, feasts, and holy days. So, the *main* reason for observing the sun, moon, and stars was to make sure that the community was doing things at the right time (like farmers have had to do from the beginning of human agriculture). But, their minds could have easily wandered to other things. If said farmer didn't understand basic astronomy, he could have drawn some, well, shall we say (ahem), *unusual* conclusions from all this.

In fact, most historians think that there may well be a close relationship between the speculation in 1 Enoch (see Chapter 6) and the pieces of astronomical texts that were found among the Dead Sea Scrolls. It seems that 1 Enoch was a summary of much wider speculation going on among ancient Jewish observers of the skies.

Most of the astronomical texts are long lists of numbers and calculations; because they're physically in such a fragmented state, it's difficult to make sense of the text. However, some pieces seem to suggest interest in horoscopes! Zodiac signs are actually mentioned in some fragments, and one fragment even seems to engage in a kind of prediction:

> *. . . And his thighs are long and slender, and the toes of his feet are slender and long. And he is in the second position. His spirit has six (parts) in the house of light and three in the pit of darkness. And this is the sign in which he was born: the foot of Taurus. He will be poor. And his animal is the bull . . .*
>
> —4 Q 186 (tr. Martinez, 456)

Who is this talking about? Is it a prediction about a person? Is it a description of a constellation? This excerpt is a good example of the problem with working with fragments of texts . . . tantalizing words, but incomplete.

Perhaps, in the end, one of the most fascinating aspects of working with Dead Sea materials is the detective work — poring over little pieces of papyrus in hopes of matching something up!

Chapter 6

The Strange Story of the Book of Enoch

*I*n 1773, Scottish explorer James Bruce (1730–1794) returned from Ethiopia with three copies of the *Book of Enoch*. (He was in Ethiopia searching for sources of the Nile River, which he found, by the way.) Before Bruce's discovery, scholars thought that it *had* existed at one point in pre-Christian times, but the Book of Enoch was believed to have been irretrievably lost. Bruce proved this notion wrong.

In 1821, an English translation of the book was produced and was a sensation. Had *The New York Times Book Review* been around in 1821, it's a safe bet that Enoch would have made the bestseller list (although numbers-wise, it probably wouldn't have beaten the *Harry Potter* series!). *Note:* The English translation used here is translated by Professor Isaac and is included in the volumes edited by Charlesworth, *Apocrypha and Pseudopigrapha of the Old Testament* (see appendix).

Arguably one of the most important lost books of the Bible — and a book that really was lost to most of the world for centuries — the Book of 1 Enoch is a book that both Jews and Christians really ought to know something about. It was widely read by Jews and Christians and was especially influential to early Christian thought. Even now, 1 Enoch is the subject of some full-scale commentaries — the ultimate indicator of an important writing in the modern academic world! Therefore, 1 Enoch has pride of place in this book as the *only* writing that has its very own chapter!

The Book of Enoch discussed in this chapter is 1 Enoch. There are two other Enoch books, called 2 and 3 Enoch; however, they're less influential and not well-known writings. Most people, therefore, refer to 1 Enoch simply as "The Book of Enoch." (You can check out Chapter 8 for a bit on the other Enoch books.)

Who the Heck is Enoch, Anyway?

You're probably wondering who this "Enoch" is and why we can justifiably consider "his" book a lost book of the Bible.

A better question may be who Enoch *isn't*. Enoch isn't the writer of the Book of 1 Enoch. The truth is, no one has any idea who wrote the Book of 1 Enoch because it was common for ancient writers of these kinds of books to give the book a famous name, like a pseudonym. Furthermore, there's great suspicion that other writers may have added material to 1 Enoch along the way. The first writer chose the name "Enoch," and later contributors added more material about this same Enoch as the central character of their stories. Why was this Enoch such a popular topic for writers of this kind of visionary book?

Although the Book of 1 Enoch isn't in the Bible, the person named Enoch is, and thus the book is worth looking at as a possible contender (OK, maybe a long shot) for Biblical inclusion — assuming it was widely available back when the final versions of the Old and New Testament were being compiled.

Enoch had Scripture cred, for lack of a better phrase. The Enoch we speak of is a descendant of Seth, the son of Adam and is also the father of Methuselah who lived (according to Genesis 5:23) for 969 years. He's mentioned by name in the Old Testament in Genesis and in the New Testament in Luke and Hebrews. As well, The Book of Enoch is actually quoted in Jude 1:14.

A famous verse about Enoch sets our stage for his being able to give us divine information:

> *Enoch walked with God; then he was no more, because God took him.*
>
> —Genesis 5:24

This verse is so intriguing that artists, such as Sebastiano Ricci, have re-created this experience (see Figure 6-1).

Figure 6-1:
Enoch being
carried up
into heaven.

God *took* him? What does *that* mean?

Centuries later, one writer in the New Testament book of Hebrews gives a pretty good idea of what ancient people thought this meant: "By faith Enoch was taken so that he did not experience death . . ." (Hebrews 11:5). Yes, the tradition emerged that Enoch was taken up into heaven instead of having died.

The many translations of Enoch

A fraction of the present Book of Enoch was discovered among the fragments found among the Dead Sea Scrolls, and about one-third of the book is preserved in various other Greek fragments. Also, chapters 1–32 were found bundled with the Christian works known as the *Gospel of Peter* and the *Apocalypse of Peter* in a Coptic grave discovered in 1886 in Akhmim, Egypt.

The full form of the Book of 1 Enoch as we now have it is from the Ethiopic language, which is technically known as Ge'ez. It's a Semitic language, which means it's related to biblical and modern Hebrew and also modern Arabic. James Bruce's copies came from the 15th century, but numerous clues suggest that this book was translated into Ge'ez centuries ago from Greek, and in turn, the Greek was translated from Aramaic originals. (Aramaic was an ancient language used by the Jews in the time before and after Jesus.)

Simply put, 1 Enoch is about what Enoch saw in heaven and was able to tell people upon his return to earth. In fact, all the books of Enoch are written with that premise, but 1 Enoch truly intended to be a message from the other side.

What Makes 1 Enoch So Important?

Lots of ancients read Enoch, lots of ancients knew Enoch, and lots of ancients quoted from Enoch.

Okay great. But why are *modern* people interested in this book? The answer is multifaceted:

- ✔ The Book of Enoch is the oldest form of visionary literature known as *apocalyptic writings* (refer to Chapter 3 for more on this and other styles of religious writing), and so it's studied as an early example of what will become an *explosion* of writings in the centuries after Enoch.

- ✔ Enoch proves that different Jewish writers were thinking quite different things in the centuries before and during early Christianity. In short, it proves that ancient Jewish thought was quite diverse.

- ✔ Enoch seems to have had some serious influence on early Christian ideas.

> ✔ Enoch presents a full form of the idea that Satan began as a fallen angel, and that this fall led directly to evil angels having sex with humans and producing a race of giants that God wipes out with the famous Flood. In short, Enoch provides a somewhat different version of why the famous Flood occurred!

These are mega-important issues for historians, so we look at each of them in turn in this section.

The ultimate example of apocalyptic literature

Enoch is written in the literary style of ancient religious writing that's called *apocalyptic.* ("Apocalypse" literally means "revelation," and thus apocalyptic literature claims to reveal something from an unusual vision or even from the author's personal visit to heaven.)

Apocalyptic literature is a form of symbolic and visionary writing that often uses bizarre imagery, sometimes features travels in heaven, and usually uses strange creatures to communicate a message about events that are about to unfold. It's clear that reading such speculative visionary literature was highly popular in the ancient world (among both Jews and Christians and beyond) because there are so many surviving examples of this type of ancient "sci-fi/ fantasy."

Enoch fits the literary style of apocalyptic literature because the central figure, Enoch, reveals to the reader what he sees during an extended visit into the heavens. Among the opening lines is this: "This is a holy vision from the heavens which the angels showed me: and I heard from them everything and I understood" (Enoch 1:2).

At the same time, the book is also written in highly symbolic and, at times, difficult to parse language. Some sections are more difficult to understand than others. For example, consider the extended observations about the movement of the sun and moon:

> *This is the first commandment of the luminaries: The sun is a luminary whose egress is an opening of heaven, which is located in the direction of the east, and whose ingress is another opening of heaven, located in the west. I saw six openings through which the sun rises and six openings through which it sets. The moon also rises and sets through the same openings, and they are guided by the stars together with those whom they lead.*

—1 Enoch 73:1–4

Okay, so maybe these are some kind of calculations based on ancient observation, but it gets weirder:

> *These are the names of the sun, the first Oryares, and the second Tomas. The moon has four names: Its first name is Asenya, its second Abla, the third Banase, and the fourth 'Era. These are the two great luminaries.*

1 Enoch 78:1–3

There have been attempts to interpret these various names (for example, based on Hebrew words, "Oryares" may break down into "or" = "light" combined with "heres" = "sun"), but they're guesses at best and are often read as corruptions of the suggested Hebrew terms.

In many parts, the visions of Enoch as described to his son Methuselah are classic examples of apocalyptic-style visions of coming destructions and calamities:

> *First I saw a scary vision regarding which I prayed to the Lord . . . I saw in a vision the sky being hurled down and snatched and falling upon the earth. When it fell upon the earth, I saw earth being swallowed up into the great abyss, the mountains being suspended upon mountains, the hills sinking down upon hills, and tall trees being uprooted and thrown and sinking into the deep abyss.*

—1 Enoch 83

For many centuries, it was widely believed that the six chapters of Daniel in the Hebrew Bible/Old Testament were the oldest example of apocalyptic literature. Now, however, scholars know that Enoch is much older than Daniel and may well be the oldest example of apocalyptic writing in possession. Fragments and pieces of the book of Enoch found among the Dead Sea Scrolls have been conclusively dated much earlier than Daniel.

Insight into the diversity of Jewish belief and thought

Enoch is a fascinating work because it's a large book that presents religious ideas that are quite different from those in the Hebrew Bible/Old Testament. For example, Enoch boasts much more speculation, more strange visions and images, more fascination with things like the movement of the stars and sun, and even an odd symbolic way of speaking of historical events.

And this is precisely why it's so interesting. Obviously *some* ancient Jews were interested in Enoch-type religious writing, and therefore — and this is important — Enoch proves that Jews believed, thought, and practiced their religious lives in a variety of ways.

Enoch's influence on Christianity

Did Enoch influence later Christian ideas? Many scholars answer a resounding yes. Enoch scholar Professor George Nickelsburg supplies a nice list of themes and ideas from the Enoch tradition that he thinks may have influenced some of the writers of the New Testament, including:

- ✔ **Early references to the "Son of Man":** The Gospels may reflect some of Enoch's use of the theme of the "Son of Man." Scholars had previously supposed that the Gospels drew this phrase and image mainly from Ezekiel and especially from Daniel 7, which the Christians then applied to Jesus. But it's now equally possible that 1 Enoch 62–63 may be even more influential on Matthew 25, which portrays Jesus teaching about the judgment of people who are being judged according to their treatment of the Son of Man. The Enoch connection is especially strong because the people being judged are the elite, wealthy, and powerful people who ignored the needs of others. This is very similar to the point being made in Matthew, but not similar to Daniel 7!

- ✔ **Direct quotes from Enoch in the Epistle of Jude, which deals especially with themes of judgment:** Consider this excerpt from the Epistle of Jude, verses 14–15:

  It was also about these that Enoch, in the seventh generation from Adam, prophesied, saying, "See, the Lord is coming with ten thousand of his holy ones, to execute judgment on all, and to convict everyone of all the deeds of ungodliness that they have committed in such an ungodly way, and of all the harsh things that ungodly sinners have spoken against him."

- ✔ **Quotes from Enoch about the angelic rebellion and references to the Flood in 2 Peter 2:4:** What's interesting is that this reference in 2 Peter specifically connects the angelic rebellion and the Flood — a connection not explicit in Genesis but clear in Enoch!

- ✔ **Many varied and prominent themes from Enoch in the book of Revelation:**

  - Both chronicle a seer's ascent into heaven.

  - Both record similar throne visions.

- Both are dominated by earthly and heavenly events related to judgment.

- Both use "Son of Man," "Suffering Servant," and Davidic Messiah — that is, the idea that a king will eventually arise from the line of David.

- Both mention the locking up of Satan for a period of years as part of the events of the coming judgment day.

An alternate explanation of the Great Flood

One of the enduring fascinations with the Book of Enoch is the fact that it greatly elaborates on the Flood narrative of Genesis. As it reads now, Genesis states that the flood was brought about by the sins of humanity, especially their horrific violence against one another (Genesis 6:11,13). Enoch, however, brings wider issues into play; the flood was brought about by God in order to put an end to the horrific mixing of evil, fallen angels with humans. When the two cohabitated — fallen angels and humans — they gave birth to creatures on the earth.

Did Enoch simply elaborate on the strange four verses in Genesis 6:1–4? Scholars have wondered what those verses are referring to for literally centuries, and the modern scholarly view is that these four verses are what's left of a tradition that has been lost. Whether Enoch actually supplies the missing information or, more likely, Enoch simply makes up an explanation for these verses at a much later time is a matter of continued debate.

Surveying the Sections of 1 Enoch

One of the most interesting and controversial aspects of the Book of Enoch is that it's clearly divided into five discreet and different sections. This isn't controversial because people disagree with the idea of five sections; rather, the controversy is over *dating* the five different sections. Did they all come at the same time? Or did the Book of Enoch grow over the years, which could suggest that a community of "believers" treasured these writings, added to them, and kept them? If this is the case, then what kind of community treasured this book?

Because Enoch places very little emphasis on obeying the laws of Moses, some historians have suggested that maybe it was a kind of "alternative Torah" with its own Five Books that contrast with or offer a different kind of spirituality than the older Torah (the Five Books of Moses with the traditional laws). Others think this idea is rubbish and argue that the number of sections isn't so clearly five, anyway.

This section provides a rough outline of the contents of this amazing book so that you can form your own opinion on this issue of five sections.

Scholars of Enoch (especially Professor George W. E. Nickelsburg, arguably the most important scholar working on 1 Enoch in the late 20th century and the present) suggest that the following ideas are expressed in the Book of Enoch as a whole:

✔ The authors live in bad times characterized by violence.

✔ The times are also characterized by perverse teaching.

✔ This state of affairs parallels the situation before the Flood.

✔ Divine judgment will sweep away sinners and their teachers, like the Flood did once before.

✔ Those who maintain this proper view do so by divine wisdom and teaching.

✔ The revelation of "watchers" or teachers and the judgment on evil teachers is part of God's plan for salvation of others. Readers are expected to learn by observing teachers of truth and falsehood!

✔ The wisdom of the book is Enoch's; what the book reveals is what he learned.

1. The Book of Watchers, Chapters 1–36: Hooking up with evil angels

The Book of Watchers is one of the oldest sections of Enoch, and it was probably already completed at least 200 years before the time of Jesus, and maybe even older than this. *Note:* Dating Enoch sections is, we should add, rather controversial business!

The heart of this section is chapters 6–11. This is the section that describes the revolt of "heavenly watchers" — angels — who do evil on earth and bring forth God's judgment. One of the horrible things they do is have sex with human women, subsequently creating horrendous evil beings. 1 Enoch 7 says that the human women gave birth to "great giants" who quickly turned cannibal when the people stopped feeding them. The angels' affairs bring on God's angry judgment in the Flood. The Book of 1 Enoch has a somewhat *different* explanation of the Flood than Genesis chapter 6.

It's interesting that Enoch associates certain kinds of magic with evil. This could be a reflection of the author's attitudes toward magical rites and practices. On the other hand, you just gotta love a book that says that two of the most horrible evils that the bad angels taught humans have to do with making weapons . . . and women's cosmetics.

> *And Azaz'el taught the people the art of making swords and knives, and shields and breastplates; and he showed to their chosen ones bracelets, decorations, shadowing of the eye with antimony, ornamentation, the beautifying of the eyelids, all kinds of precious stones, and all coloring tinctures and alchemy . . .*
>
> —1 Enoch 8

Weaponry and makeup in the same passage? Is Enoch comparing the two as equally effective tools of conquest? We'll leave that judgment to you, dear reader, because we won't touch that one with a 10-foot shepherd's staff.

11. The Book of Parables, Chapters 37–71: The one who is sent

The Book of Parables is usually dated to the first century BCE and therefore is considered the most recent part of the Book of 1 Enoch. This section is a detailed description of the judgment that God is preparing, and it introduces God's "vice-regent," the being who will serve as God's deputy over the judgment.

The vice-regent is really the center of attention for many scholars. The figure goes by many different names and titles, including

- The Elect One
- The Anointed One
- The Son of Man

Christians have long found this section of 1 Enoch very intriguing because it suggests that some Jews *before* the time of Jesus were talking about a second, important heavenly being — and this guy sounds an awful lot like later Christian descriptions of Jesus. This section is crucial, obviously, for those who seek a full and complete background to their New Testament study.

When you look at some specific parts of the Book of Parables, it's easy to see why some readers are so fascinated. Check out this passage in which Enoch watches events in front of him and then asks his angel friend who they're seeing:

> *And I asked . . . Who is this? . . . And he . . . said to me, "This is the Son of Man, to whom belongs righteousness, and with whom righteousness dwells. . . . for the Lord of the Spirits has chosen him, he is destined to be victorious before the Lord of the Spirits in eternal uprightness. This Son of Man whom you have seen is the One who would remove the kings and the mighty ones from their comfortable seats and the strong ones from their thrones. He shall loosen the reins of the strong and crush the teeth of the sinners. He shall depose the kings from their thrones and kingdoms."*
>
> —1 Enoch 46:2–5

This section drives some historians crazy. You can almost hear the frenzied outcry of academic voices shrieking, "Okay, time out!" (Do academics actually shriek?) Many of these folks suspect that some later Christian did some creative editing to this section, and they even have a likely scriptural source: the famous words of Mary known as the "Magnificat" in the first chapter of the Gospel of Luke:

> *He has shown strength with his arm; he has scattered the proud in the thoughts of their hearts. He has brought down the powerful from their thrones, and lifted up the lowly; he has filled the hungry with good things, and sent the rich away empty. He has helped his servant Israel, in remembrance of his mercy . . .*
>
> —Luke 1:51

But scholars don't jump to conclusions, and they also ask these questions: Isn't it *also* possible that there were Jews *before* the time of Jesus who were expecting God to send someone special to do precisely these kinds of things? Could Mary have been one of those Jews expecting God to do something soon? Is it too much to suggest, then, that Mary knew the discussions featured in the book of Enoch? As is the case with many ancient writings, instead of providing lots of answers, 1 Enoch tends to raise more interesting questions.

In any case, Enoch shows that there were all kinds of different ideas about who the "one sent by God" would be and what he would be like. This is precisely why so many New Testament readers find Enoch so fascinating. It shows the variety of views held by Jews in the centuries and decades just before the beginning of the Christian movement.

Keep in mind that the Son of Man described in Enoch presides over horrendous judgment and the bad people — the kings and rulers — aren't given a chance to repent because they find out about the truth too late. Passage 63 talks about these rulers begging for "a little breathing spell," but that idea's a non-starter, so to speak, and the text says that these guys have "no chance to become believers."

There's no denying that a real nasty streak of sadistic, hellfire-type punishment of the wicked runs through 1 Enoch and the Book of Parables in particular. Most Christians and Jews — then and now —quite rightly find this a bit disturbing.

III. The Book of the Heavenly Luminaries, Chapters 72–82: "So, what sign are you?"

The Book of the Heavenly Luminaries contains detailed astronomical and calendrical lore, including descriptions of movement of the moon, sun, and stars; the number of days in the year; and other celestial topics.

This section, sometimes called "Luminaries," probably has some roots in the Persian period ranging from 539–333 BCE, and so many experts consider it to almost certainly be the oldest, or among the oldest, section of the Book of 1 Enoch. It is, in any case, hardly ever dated after the second century BCE.

Among the more interesting aspects of this complex section is that it establishes the importance of the *solar* calendar against the older Jewish and Mesopotamian traditions of the *lunar* calendar. Why is this so important? Perhaps because calendars determine ritual observations, but another interesting reason is that 1 Enoch interprets the regular movements of the stars, moon, and sun as actually containing *moral* lessons. How'd the writers come up with this notion? Because they believed that the regular movements of the heavenly bodies are regular because they're *obedient to God*.

Obviously, the writers of this section didn't understand things like gravity and physics, so they concluded that the interesting regularity that they noticed was a lesson for life, and that lesson was something like: "Behave yourself and obey God. If the planets can do it, you can, too."

If you enjoy reading astrological charts, plotting hurricane movements on a map, and doodling the solar system, then you may find this section of 1 Enoch interesting. It's certainly an acquired taste.

IV. The Dream Visions, Chapters 83–90: Tales of sheep and goats

The Dream Visions is a shorter section that contains two visions that Enoch recounts to his son. The first is about the destruction of the world — not a surprising topic for a book of apocalyptic literature. But the second vision is really a zinger and one of the truly amazing bits of this truly amazing book.

The second vision is a long retelling of Jewish history but with all the people played by animals. It's known as the *Animal Allegory,* and it takes the story of Hebrew history from the beginning all the way to the time of Judas Maccabeus, around 167–164 BCE. The content of the vision helps scholars date this section of 1 Enoch.

The Israelites are sheep, the Egyptians are wolves (sounds a bit like Orwell's *Animal Farm,* doesn't it?), and all the action takes place in the form of a narrative about these animals wandering here and there, facing dangers, and getting new leaders (goats, rams, you get the idea). Here's a version of the rise of Judges to assist the Israelites in the days before the kings, when the Israelites were attacked by other tribes (the dogs, foxes, and boars in this account):

> *Now the dogs, foxes, and the wild boars began to devour those sheep till the Lord of the sheep raised up another sheep, one from among them — a ram which would lead them.*
>
> —1 Enoch 89:42

The section follows the story of the Bible right up to the time of the Maccabean Revolution against the Greek rulers over Palestine, stopping somewhere around 164 BCE.

The Dream Visions is a fascinating read and a good challenge of your Bible knowledge: see if you can guess what biblical characters are referred to as the story progresses.

V. The Epistle of Enoch, Chapters 91–105: Final words

The Epistle of Enoch is written as a letter to Enoch's son, and it was probably composed in the second century BCE.

Like other such letters in Enoch literature, this section is filled with instructions on living a good life and learning the lessons from Enoch. Of course, all the Enoch lessons, speeches, and letters were intended for everyone to read, not only Enoch's son, so the advice is general and comprehensive.

In Verse 91, the boy is told to "love righteousness," which isn't a bad suggestion when you come right down to it. Some other examples from Verse 94 include:

✔ Walk in the way of peace.

✔ Be worthy.

✔ Stay away from oppressors.

✔ Eschew injustice.

✔ Don't put your trust in wealth.

✔ Don't forget God.

In reading this section of 1 Enoch, it quickly becomes obvious that people held considerable resentment toward the powerful of their day — the ones the writers consider to be responsible for the times being so bad. (This sounds like a case of the more things change, the more they stay the same.)

Ironically, this theme is why the book of Enoch continued to be read in its day and remained popular: Blaming the rich and powerful is always in style and always a popular spectator sport.

Odds and ends

In addition to Enoch's five basic sections, most scholars conclude that there exists other material that ought to be considered additional content. These writings don't fit into the final (fifth) section but rather are add-ons of different kinds of shorter material. Here they are:

✔ **Chapters 106–107, the birth of Noah:** This short section is a version of the birth of Noah, an important figure in all the Enoch literature. In this section, Noah is praised as a wonderful, righteous man who will survive the coming judgment. Verse 106 describes Noah's Flood and reveals that Noah and his three sons will survive the deluge. (We say "will" because from Enoch's perspective, the flood hasn't happened yet!)

✔ **Chapter 108:** This chapter is a final warning about coming judgment, written as a letter to Enoch's son, Methuselah. It repeats themes already found in earlier portions of 1 Enoch and is a very short chapter at the end of the book.

The Major Religious Themes of the Book of 1 Enoch

Enoch claims to give you information that you need. It isn't so much that you're supposed to *do* something but that you're supposed to be *informed*. This, by the way, is one important reason many Christians and Jews didn't like the book of Enoch: To be blunt, it isn't a very moral book. There are few instructions for living a good life, caring for others, and knowing what that means. Enoch isn't like a prophet who instructs, or a Moses who teaches how to live, or even a wise teacher who provides proverbs of wise sayings. Enoch just gives information and descriptions that sometimes imply living a good life but rarely explain how to go about it. Having said that, the Book of Enoch *is* a very religious work.

In this section, we look at some of the major religious themes that stand out in this long work.

Judgment

Judgment is probably the most central and most important theme of the whole Book of Enoch. Using the Flood narrative as a kind of universal lesson about judgment, 1 Enoch condemns those who claim that they're correct and that they know that God isn't going to judge them. But at the same time, the book encourages those who may waver in their commitment to the way of truth.

Along the way, however, Enoch describes a very interesting aspect of that judgment: It will involve a vice-regent — Wisdom personified as an existent person, drawing on other themes from the Bible such as the fascinating image of the "Suffering Servant" of the Prophetic book of Isaiah (chapters 52–53), and even the archangel Michael as presented as "one like a Son of Man" (which probably simply meant that Michael looked like a person) in Daniel 7.

The ones who are particularly in danger of judgment are the rulers of the world — the kings and the powerful individuals. The judgment aspect of 1 Enoch raises all sorts of questions: Is Enoch, then, a statement that represents the anger of the oppressed? Is it a kind of apocalyptic religion of liberation? Or is it just vindictive literature written by people who love to sit around and talk about how the powerful will pay someday?

Why read this "judgmental" stuff?

An ancient book like Enoch discusses judgment on nearly every page. Final, harsh, and severe judgment for some, and wonderful paradise for others. These are rarely popular ideas in the modern world, so it's reasonable to wonder why people enjoy reading about judgment (both then and now).

Some people think that Enoch represents a group of people who consider themselves a persecuted minority, and that's why they're so interested in judgment. There certainly is a vindictive streak in Enoch, but there also are ways in which judgment has been a comforting theme close to the hearts of many people who have suffered from the hands of the powerful. Consider Negro spirituals that deal with the biblical Flood story. In one venerable old song, people are pounding on the Ark, trying to get Noah to let them in! Yet the Flood story in Genesis says nothing about people pleading

with Noah and nothing about knocking on doors. But this judgment theme is a focus of the old spirituals . . . and it isn't too difficult to figure out why!

Judgment *is* an attractive subject if you believe that you've suffered unjustly, that the rich and powerful have gotten away with murder and think that they'll continue to get away with it. In that case, judgment literature is strangely comforting because it reaffirms your belief that right is right and wrong is wrong, and if it looks like "right" isn't doing too well just now, these writings and songs reassure you that judgment is coming — for *all*.

Next time you wonder why ancient people loved reading judgment stories, think about how you feel when the criminal is led away in handcuffs at the end of *CSI*. Hmm. Maybe Horatio Caine, Perry Mason, and Judge Judy are simply modern versions of Enoch?

We think that the answer is all of the above. By reading about the judgment of the powerful and elite, you're not only warned not to behave like them but also assured that justice will be done — eventually, even if not in the present age.

The judgment theme is clear: Those who righteously die will be vindicated, and those who escape justice will be punished. In the end times described in Enoch, judgment will make injustice right again because the created order will be restored.

Sin as rebellion

According to Enoch, sin was brought into the world because of the fallen angels — a sort of heavenly revolt. (Note that Enoch pretty much blows off the whole Adam and Eve and the forbidden fruit story!)

But, the book cautions, sin is still also the responsibility of each human being. You can pay attention to the warnings of Enoch, or you can (and almost certainly will) suffer the consequences. The saved are those who respond well to the wisdom and warnings of Enoch; the others are the sinners. Thus there's little discussion of forgiveness because people tend to be divided into the good and the bad.

In fact, one of the main arguments that Enoch isn't a strongly Christian document is based precisely on the absence of the notions of repentance and change, which are major themes of the New Testament. In Enoch, there's little possibility of change: You're in, or you're out.

The elevation of Enoch and devaluation of Moses?

Some scholars of Enoch note that for a Jewish book, there's precious little about obeying the laws and commandments — that is, the laws of Moses.

If there's one thing that defines what it means to be a Jew in the ancient world, obeying the laws of Moses is right up there. Yet, hardly anything in Enoch talks about this. The book tells people to be "righteous" but doesn't really explain what that means. You get the idea that righteous means "Pay attention to Enoch's words." So, did the people who wrote Enoch have a lower opinion of Moses and the Mosaic laws? Some Enoch scholars place great credibility in this idea.

Forewarned is forearmed

The writers of 1 Enoch believed that they were informing everyone of the truth. Readers of Enoch believed that the book contained dire warnings of the consequences for those who ignore the book and its teachings and therefore aren't prepared for the coming judgment.

But how are readers supposed to know that these words and teachings are true? It's simple: Enoch went to heaven, so you can take what he says to the bank.

But in other sections, the book seems to suggest that you can also figure out the truth by thinking about Jewish history (the animal story in the Dream Visions section is a version of Jewish history; refer to the section "IV. The Dream Visions, Chapters 83–90: Tales of sheep and goats" earlier in this chapter for more). The book also suggests that you can figure out the truth by just being observant and watching how the planets, stars, sun, and moon move — which is the point, it seems, of the extended discussions in the sections on the Heavenly Luminaries.

So we would be remiss not to acknowledge the contradictions in Enoch and to suggest that its inconsistencies may be part of the reason Enoch never made it into the Old Testament.

Chapter 7

Plays, Poets, and Other Ideas Borrowed from the Greeks

The Jews and the Christians learned how to write different kinds of books and writings. Some of these writings have their roots deep in Jewish history (Prophetic books, for example, or Psalms and other poetry) while other writing styles were learned from other people. Modern biblical scholars, for example, are pretty sure that the ancient Hebrews learned how to write *Wisdom Literature* (that is, Proverbs, Ecclesiastes, and Sirach) from the ancient Egyptians because Egyptian "Wisdom" writing is so much older than Hebrew versions. Also, some of the Hebrew writings actually copy specific passages from older Egyptian writings. For example, compare Proverbs 22:17–23:11 with the ancient Egyptian "Wisdom of Amenemope"; the latter is historically dated well before the actual papyrus itself, which is from the seventh to sixth centuries BCE.

When Jews encountered another major literary civilization, the Greeks, there was bound to be some mutual influence and, in fact, some mutual admiration. Like the Roman civilization, which also deeply admired the Greeks, it's now perfectly obvious to historians that many ancient Jews were more than a little impressed with Greek ways of life, thought, and living — and some Jewish literature reflects the deep influence from the "classical" world of Greece and later Rome.

In this chapter, we survey some ancient writings that clearly reflect Jewish interest in the Greek world and the times after Alexander the Great conquered this region (333 BCE). Virtually all these writings are available in

English in various sources, but coauthor Daniel recommends the wonderful, two-volume book *The Old Testament Pseudopigrapha,* edited by James Charlesworth (see the appendix for full description). Charlesworth's edited volumes contain the entire text of the works that we now discuss in this chapter, and Charlesworth's volumes also provide scholarly comments by various experts and translators.

Writings from the Greek Period (333–64 BCE) were typically intended to defend the Jews and their religious beliefs and practices, but they usually weren't considered "inspired" — especially if they borrowed Greek literary forms! They were written to defend Jewish beliefs and sometimes used and cited the older writings that eventually did become part of the Bible. Still, you have to admit . . . it would have been cool to have had a play in the Bible, wouldn't it?

The Sibylline Oracles

In the ancient Greek world (and far beyond it!), there was commonly a legendary "seer" who was often described as an old woman. Purportedly, she could peer into the unknown and give reports, or *oracles,* of what she saw.

Sibyl is, by all accounts, the Queen of Prophecy, Miss Prediction, and the Oxford Dictionary of Anticipated Events. So widespread was the fame of the earliest "Sibyl" that she ended up multiplying, so to speak. At one time, many Sibyls were giving predictions and speeches all around the ancient world. So you got your "Nostradamus," your "Edgar Cayce," and your evening news weatherperson (okay, maybe that last one isn't so good at predictions). But in the ancient world *none* of these prognosticators had *anything* on "Sibyl"! Cities became famous for their own Sibyls, so it's hardly a surprise that some ancient chambers of commerce sat around saying, "What we need in *this* town is a *Sibyl!*"

Sibyl's influence on Jewish writers

No one knows if there ever was a real Sibyl back in history who started all this legendary stuff, but references to her start as early as the fifth century BCE! So, anything that claimed to be a message from a Sibyl commanded instant attention.

In fact, it appears that it wasn't long before some Jewish writers, and also Christian writers later on, decided they liked this Sibyl stuff (it sounded rather like other aspects of Jewish writing) and began using this style of writing. The result is the *Sibylline Oracles.*

The Oracles is a rather large collection of materials, now referred to as *Books 1–14,* although much of the collection is fragmented. The dates of this material begin as early as the third to second centuries BCE, and it continued to be produced and added to after the seventh to eighth centuries CE. Obviously, this chapter is particularly interested in those portions of the Sibylline Oracles that show earlier thought and influence. ***Note:*** One of the most important modern scholars to work on these writings is Professor John J. Collins, and it's his translation into English that we cite along the way (it's also in the collection that we recommend in the chapter's introduction).

Sibyl speaks: Portions of the Sibylline Oracles

Typical of all the Sibylline Oracles are somewhat vague "predictions" of the rise and fall of empires, individual rulers, and even palace intrigue. These details are often important for modern historians trying to identify a specific historic ruler so that modern readers have a better idea of the time period of the writing and the possibly historical information that is contained.

Tales of Jewish history and connections to biblical writings

The Jewish character of these adaptations of Sibylline literature is clear from the prophetic nature of judgment passages such as this:

> *Therefore the Immortal will inflict on all mortals*
> *Disaster and famine and woes and groans*
> *And war and pestilence and lamentable ills*
> *Because they were not willing to piously honor the immortal begetter of all men, but honored idols made by hand.*
>
> —Sibylline Oracles 3:600–605

The Jewish or Christian content is further apparent from specific passages that praise the history of the Jews, explicitly refer to the coming of Jesus, or call for repentance, like this one:

> *Ah, wretched mortals, change these things, and do not*
> *Lead the great God to all sorts of anger, but abandon*
> *daggers and groanings, murders and outrages,*
> *And wash your whole bodies in perennial rivers.*
> *Stretch out your hands to heaven and ask forgiveness*
> *For your previous deeds and make propitiation . . .*
>
> —Sibylline Oracles 4:160–165

In Book 1, for example, you see very early the influence of a Jewish writer who speaks of the Creation account with some interesting variations on the Genesis material. While describing Adam, for example, the writer states that he was alone but goes on to say this:

> *Behold another form like his own. God himself indeed took a bone from his flank and made Eve, a wonderful maidenly spouse, whom he gave to this man to live with him in the garden. And he, when he saw her, was suddenly greatly amazed in spirit.*

> —Sibylline Oracles 1:20–30

Connections to non-biblical Jewish writings

There are important connections in Sibylline thought to other non-biblical Jewish writings. For example, the Book of 1 Enoch refers to heavenly "watchers" that appear to be angels. In the Sibylline Oracles, their specific creation is mentioned.

The Oracles also provide delightful additions to biblical tradition, such as the notion that God told Noah to preach to the world so that the people might be saved before God determined to flood the earth:

> *Noah, embolden yourself and proclaim repentance to all the peoples, so that all may be saved . . .*

> —Sibylline Oracles 1:127–128

Brain teasers

Part of the fame and attraction of the Sibylline literature is the difficult and puzzling passages that lend themselves to multiple interpretations and meanings. Consider, for example, this "riddle" on the name for God, which still defies modern attempts to work out what the writer is getting at:

> *I am the one who is, but you consider in your heart . . .*
> *I have nine letters, I am of four syllables. Consider me.*
> *The first three have two letters each.*
> *The last has the rest, and five are consonants.*
> *The entire number is: twice eight*
> *Plus three hundred, three tens and seven. If you know who I am*
> *You will not be uninitiated in my wisdom.*

> —Sibylline Oracles 1:135–145

Even though we are talking about largely Jewish writings, occasionally it looks like a later Christian writer has inserted a few lines. This reminds us that it was often early Christians who preserved these writings — and just couldn't resist making a few comments as they recopied the texts! Check out this one that sounds as if the pagan Sibyl recognizes the significance of Jesus:

> *I speak from my heart of the famous son of the Immortal . . .*
> *He will walk the waves; he will undo the sickness of men;*
> *He will raise the dead. He will repel many woes.*
> *From one wallet men will have surfeit of bread*
> *When the house of David brings forth a shoot . . .*

> —Sibylline Oracles 6:1, 6:12–15

The Treatise of Shem: An Early Astrology Column

The Greeks loved watching the stars and making up stories to go with the shapes and forms they saw. In fact, they also rather liked the zodiac tradition. So, it seems, did some ancient Jews as well! The *Treatise of Shem* gives clear astrological guidance in the general terms familiar to those who are into this kind of stuff but vague enough to be impressive to all (for example, "You will walk through a door today" . . . that kind of thing . . .). Here's an example that refers to Hebrew letters:

> *And if the year begins in Taurus: Everyone whose name contains a Beth, or Yudh, or Kaph will become ill, or be wounded by an iron [weapon]. And there will be fighting . . .*

> —Treatise of Shem 2:1–2

Historians note that this work isn't very "Jewish" except for the occasional reference to Passover in the chapter on Virgo, for example, or references to prayers to the Living God in the chapter on Libra. Still, coauthor Daniel rather likes the end of the chapter on Pisces, which hopefully promises, "Then at the end of the year there will be peace and prosperity among men, and love and harmony among all the kinds who are on the entire earth. . . ." (On a personal note, I can't help but wonder as to when precisely such love and harmony is supposed to occur on our planet.)

This work, which is dated by historians to no later than 31–20 BCE, is quite significant for one essential reason: It proves Jewish interest in the zodiac signs and thus at least some Jewish interest in the entire realm of astrology. The interest is probably from Jews living in the dispersed Diaspora, where they would have had more contact with astrological lore.

One of the many reasons why this interest by some ancient Jews in zodiac lore is a bit of a surprise is that the Old Testament is clearly opposed to anything that smacks of "worshipping" the stars. Here are two passages as evidence:

> *And lest thou lift up thine eyes unto heaven, and when thou seest the sun, and the moon, and the stars, even all the host of heaven, shouldest be driven to worship them, and serve them, which the Lord thy God hath divided unto all nations under the whole heaven.*
>
> —Deuteronomy 4:19

> *And he put down the idolatrous priests, whom the kings of Judah had ordained to burn incense in the high places in the cities of Judah, and in the places round about Jerusalem; them also that burned incense unto Baal, to the sun, and to the moon, and to the planets, and to all the host of heaven.*
>
> —2 Kings 23:5

Most historians take these passages to be a not-too-subtle condemnation of any kind of astrological speculation.

On the other hand, there are subtle suggestions here and there that some kind of astrological interests remained a part of Jewish (and later Christian) interest. Note the astrological suggestions of young Joseph's dream: He had another dream and told it to his brothers, saying, "Look, I have had another dream: the sun, the moon, and eleven stars were bowing down to me" (Genesis 37:9). Furthermore, New Testament historians often point out that the famous "wise men" must have been referring to some kind of astrological knowledge when they came to find the young Jesus:

> *In the time of King Herod, after Jesus was born in Bethlehem of Judea, wise men from the East came to Jerusalem, asking, "Where is the child who has been born king of the Jews? For we observed his star at its rising, and have come to pay him homage."*
>
> —Matthew 2:1–2

Finally, recent historians have suggested that a key to the book of Revelation may well be its interest in interpreting constellations and astronomical phenomenon (comets, heavenly bodies, and so on) as symbolic of future events to come!

Where previously these suggestions would not have been taken too seriously, in fact, the Treatise of Shem is a work that clearly establishes the possibility of Jewish and therefore Christian interest in precisely these kinds of issues.

Because both mainline Jewish and orthodox Christian tradition eventually condemned any kind of astrology as contrary to a belief in God's ultimate control of the universe, you can see why a document like the Treatise of Shem would be controversial. Still, like so many of the other writings that we examine in this book, the Treatise shows the wide variety of ideas among Jews and Christians in the days before "correct thinking" tended to weed out unapproved interests.

Pseudo-Phocylides: Wisdom and Rules for Living

Phocylides (pronounced fo-*sill*-i-dees) was an actual ancient Greek poet from the sixth century BCE who was famous for writing wise collections of advice. Ancient writers cite him for the work entitled *Pseudo-Phocylides,* and although very little of his own writing has survived, like the Sibyls (refer to the earlier section "The Sibylline Oracles"), Phocylides is a famous "source" of wise and ethical sayings. Therefore, the attributions to Phocylides are another clear example of a Jewish writer "borrowing" the style of a pagan, Greek writer in order to write a Jewish version of a Greek work. It's generally thought that this writer wrote between 50 BCE and 100 CE, so it is roughly from the same time period as Jesus.

"Pseudo" in front of the title of an ancient writing always means the same thing: Modern historians do *not* accept that it was written by the person it *claims* to be written by! The general name used for almost all this kind of material we're looking at in this chapter is "Pseudopigrapha," which means "writings under a false author's name."

Scholars speculate about why anyone would want to write under the name of a non-Jewish poet or philosopher, of course. Some say that the writings were a way for Jews to give advice to non-Jews (or even preach to them) or for Jews to prove that their wisdom was just as good as pagan wisdom. Others believe it was a way for Jews to prove that wise non-Jews still recognized the power of the Jewish tradition. In any case, Pseudo-Phocylides is yet another fascinating example of Jewish interest in using a decidedly non-Jewish form in order to communicate their own values.

Most of the "wisdom" of Pseudo-Phocylides is pretty much standard biblical stuff. Table 7-1 presents some examples from Pseudo-Phocylides with biblical references so that you can see how closely Pseudo-Phocylides parallels biblical ideas.

Table 7-1	Comparison of Pseudo-Phocylides with the Bible
Example from Pseudo-Phocylides	**Example from the Bible**
Do not tell lies, but always speak the truth. (Pseudo-Phocylides 7)	Deuteronomy 5:20 Neither shall you bear false witness against your neighbor.
Do not case the poor unjustly, do not judge partially. (Pseudo-Phocylides 10)	Leviticus 19:15 You shall not render an unjust judgment; you shall not be partial to the poor or defer to the great: with justice you shall judge your neighbor.
	Proverbs 31:9 Speak out, judge righteously, defend the rights of the poor and needy...
Give the laborer his pay, do not afflict the poor. (Pseudo-Phocylides 19)	Deuteronomy 24:14-15 You shall not withhold the wages of poor and needy laborers, whether other Israelites or aliens who reside in your land in one of your towns. You shall pay them their wages daily before sunset, because they are poor and their livelihood depends on them...

The work also contains decidedly modern sounding bits of wisdom, such as this:

> *Do not afflict your heart with bygone evils;*
> *For what has been done can no more be undone.*

> —Pseudo-Phocylides 55–56

But Pseudo-Phocylides isn't without a few surprises, including this one suggesting possible Christian pacifist influences:

> *Put on a sword, not for bloodshed but for protection*
> *But may you not need it at all, neither outside the law nor justly*
> *For if you kill an enemy, you stain your hand.*

> —Pseudo-Phocylides 32–34

You can even find a few howlers, to be enjoyed with a hearty "ain't *that* the truth" by men and women equally!:

We seek noble horses, and strong necked dogs
Plowers of earth, and the very best of dogs
Yet we fools do not strive to marry a good wife,
Nor does a woman reject a bad man when he is rich . . .

—Pseudo-Phocylides 201–204

Ezekiel the Tragedian

The Greeks wrote many plays, and among the most popular form of Greek play was the *tragedy.* (This form was later adapted by William Shakespeare with rather impressive results, as you know.)

Greek tragedy focuses on the adventures — and also misfortunes — of lead characters who are often historical persons. Sometimes, it explores how "the gods" have intervened into the lives of humans. Tragedies are always matters of serious events, as opposed to comedies. Furthermore, they're usually written in a certain Greek literary style (iambic trimeter, as it happens) that happens to be the style adopted by the writer of *Ezekiel* as well!

Tragedies were written in a set form borrowed by a Jewish writer (presumed to be writing about 200 BCE) to write a play about the Exodus. So, *Ezekiel* isn't about the Prophet Ezekiel but rather is the name of the proposed writer of this play.

One historian, R.G. Robertson, suggests that the Greek play forms used by famous Greek playwrights like Aeschylus, Sophocles, and Euripides may have especially influenced Ezekiel the Tragedian because he lived in Alexandria, and the Greek rulers of Alexandria famously stole the originals of the Greek texts from Athens and sent copies to Alexandria. The fame of this daring action — aimed to supply their famous "library" with famous documents — may have partially inspired a Jewish playwright living in Alexandria.

The various "scenes" in *Ezekiel the Tragedian* include:

- The birth of Moses and saving the baby in the basket from the Nile
- Moses breaking up a fight between Hebrews, who then reveal that they know that Moses has killed someone
- Moses at the burning bush
- The Ten Plagues in Egypt
- The escape of the Hebrews

The Exodus . . . live on stage!?

Was this play supposed to be on stage? Was it ever seen? Scholars debate this point, but Robertson observes that the fact that many aspects of the writing have survived suggests that it was especially adapted for the stage. Robertson's English translation attempts to maintain some of the meter (that is, the rhythm of the verse) to preserve the way it may have sounded as it was performed.

One reason these questions are so interesting is that, if *Ezekiel the Tragedian* was seen, it would be a striking indication of how deeply engaged the ancient Jews may have been with surrounding cultures! Did Jewish citizens of Greek cities actually attend Greek plays? Would they have considered the religious associations with ancient Greek theatre to be "pagan worship" and therefore forbidden to Jewish attendance? Perhaps Ezekiel was written precisely to *allow* Jews to attend a theatre performance that wasn't religiously offensive.

The following speech by God describing the plagues and their visceral unpleasantness gives you an idea of the drama of seeing and listening to this play:

> A host of frogs and lice I'll cast on earth
> Then sprinkle aches from the furnace round,
> And ulcerous sores shall thus burst forth on men.
> And swarms of lies shall come and sore afflict
> The men of Egypt . . .
> Darkness I'll decree for three whole days,
> And locusts send, who shall the residue
> Of food consume and every blade of grass . . .
>
> —Ezekiel the Tragedian, lines 135–146

Consider another surviving scene: Picture an Egyptian character as he describes the Hebrews who have left Egypt after the plagues but are now seeing the coming of Pharaoh's forces:

> The Hebrew, when confronted by our host
> Lay strewn about hard by the sandy shore
> In masses there upon the Red Sea's strand
> Some were engaged in caring for the young
> Together with their wives, worn out with toil,
> With many flocks and herds and household stuff.
> And they, all unprotected, without arms,
> On seeing us sent up a doleful cry,
> 'gainst heaven they inveighed, their father's God . . .
>
> —Ezekiel the Tragedian, lines 204–212

It's tempting to stand up, raise your hands in dramatic gesture, and read this out with great flair, imagining such speeches on a stage. Great stuff! It's too bad that more of this play hasn't survived — it would be fascinating to watch an ancient Greek-style play written by a Jewish writer dealing with biblical history! If it weren't for the early Christian writers who quoted heavily from the many different books they read, we wouldn't even have these few fragments.

A display of unusual religious ideas

Historians are also interested in this play from Ezekiel because of the development of certain unusual religious ideas. One scene reminds readers of apocalyptic visions when Moses has a dream that he sees the throne of God and God gets up and motions for Moses to sit down and view the earth from "God's perspective." Such visions are more common in apocalyptic literature, but the prominence given to Moses as one who will "work with God" in heaven is a striking development. Also, the writer dwells a bit on the Egyptian reaction to God's miracles and the destruction of the armies of Pharaoh. We suppose, however, that one would expect more, well, drama in a drama!

Fragments of Greek-Influenced Jewish Writers

If ever there were a truly frustrating exercise, it's the examination of fragments of books that no longer exist. *Fragments* are either of the following:

- ✔ Actual pieces of books that have survived in archaeological discoveries and have deteriorated so badly that they aren't easily read
- ✔ Writings that are quoted in later works

Quotations are, by far, the greatest source of fragments, but they're more frustrating than actual pieces because they raise one very disturbing question: Can we trust this ancient author not only to be right that such a writing once existed but also to have quoted it accurately and in detail? The answer? We may never know!

Obviously, with such questions, it's only possible to look at some samples of these kinds of writings and offer brief observations about how significant they may be. These debated fragments reveal that

- ✔ Jews were very much in dialogue with their surrounding cultures, and especially with Greek culture; historians have only a smattering of the total amount of material they wrote in this dialogue.

- ✔ Jews frequently felt the need to defend themselves in intellectual arguments about their history and their faith, and they took up Greek literary forms to do so.

Clearly, the ancient Jews had plenty to say and didn't back down! The following sections offer a brief selection of some of these fragments.

As modern readers of ancient history, people are often totally dependent on ancient writers who tried to quote heavily from literature that they knew. Sadly, for many ancient writers, these quotes are the only fragments of their literary work that has been preserved. In other words, the writers' works genuinely are "lost books." The vast majority of this material is "defensive" or represents dialogue and explanation to non-Jews. If it was helpful and interesting at the time, it continued to be read, but it's easy to see how some material that was too topical eventually dropped into disuse, was eventually forgotten, and disappeared. It's another case of survival boiling down to "it was still used over and over again."

Philo the Epic Poet

The main interest in the Philo fragments, mostly quoted in a Christian source (Eusebius, fourth century CE), is the Jewish use of a specifically Greek form of poetry. The poetic aspect isn't easily demonstrated in English because of the translation, of course, but we can note one or two interesting themes that are developed in these fragments. What you can presume is that the entire work must have summarized, in poetic form, aspects of Jewish history. Here's an example passage:

> *From them the Most High, great Lord of all created a most blessed spot, even from of old, yea from the days of Abraham and Isaac and Jacob, rich in children, from whom was Joseph, who was interpreter of dreams for the scepter bearer of Egypt's throne, revolving time's secrets with the flood of fate . . .*

> —Fragment 2 (ed. Charlesworth, 783–784)

Orphica: Writings imitating Orpheus the poet

Orpheus, one of the most famous ancient Greek poets, is widely referred to in classical literature. He's believed to have perfected the playing of the lyre and to have written a number of ancient hymns to accompany his playing.

References to Orphean "hymns" and poetic lines are found as early as the fifth century. These particular fragments, however, are clearly Jewish attempts to write "Orphic" poetry in the pagan form, and they're only known because they're quoted in the writings of the early Christian Church Father, Eusebius, from whom comes many such quotations of works that are now lost.

Some of the common questions about Orphica include:

✔ Were these attempts to write a "Jewish Orpheus" — a kind of religious propaganda?

✔ Were they attempts to convert Greeks by using a famous Greek writer and claiming that he came to understand the truth of the Jewish God?

✔ Were they intended for Jewish consumption only?

The answers to these questions are mysteries, as are the lines of poetry themselves, which are rather cryptic descriptions of God but descriptions, nonetheless, that are vaguely familiar to readers of the Hebrew Bible/Old Testament.

For example, compare the following passage of Orphica to descriptions in Isaiah 66:1, "Thus says the Lord: Heaven is my throne and the earth is my footstool":

> *I will sing for those for whom it is lawful, but you uninitiated, close your doors . . .*
> *My son, I will point it out to you, whenever I notice his footsteps,*
> *And the strong hand of the mighty God.*
> *But I do not see him, because around [him] a cloud is set up . . .*
> *Yes he after this is established in the great heaven*
> *On a golden throne. He stands with his feet on the earth.*
> *He stretches out his right hand to the ends of the ocean.*
> *The foundations of the mountains trembles within [his] anger*
>
> —Orphica (ed. Charlesworth, 799)

Aristobulus: The first Jewish philosopher

There are five fragments attributed to the writer Aristobulus. The main interest in these fragments, which are quoted in early Christian writing, is that Aristobulus tries to mix Jewish religious ideas and Greek philosophy. In fact, he's sometimes called the "First" Jewish Philosopher (something that would have been considered an oxymoron in earlier times — Greeks did philosophy, Jews did religion!) and thus is considered part of a tradition that developed more in the work of the later Jewish philosopher, Philo of Judea, from whom many writings are available.

The Aristobulus fragments claim to be explanations to Greek rulers about the religion of the Jews. As such, Aristobulus attempts to explain aspects of Hebrew descriptions of God in the Hebrew writings that may raise objections. For example, early in the second fragment (quoted from Eusebius) Aristobulus notes that the Hebrews talk about God having hands, legs, arms, and so on. But Aristobulus explains that this should not be understood literally:

> *Now "hands" are clearly thought of even in our own time in a more general way. For when you, being king, send out forces, wishing to accomplish something, we say, "The King has a mighty hand" and the hearers are referred to the power which you have. Now Moses indicates this also in our Law when he speaks thus, "God brought you out of Egypt with a mighty hand" and again he says that God said to him, "I will send forth my hand and I will strike the Egyptians" . . .*

> —Fragment 2:6–8 (ed. Charlesworth, 838)

Even more interesting is the claim (apparently quoted with approval by Eusebius!) that many of the Greek philosophers learned some of their better ideas from the Hebrew writings. After referring to the importance of Moses and his laws, Aristobulus writes:

> *And it seems to me that Pythagoras, Socrates, and Plato with great care follow him in all respects. They copy him when they say that they heard the voice of God, when they contemplate the arrangement of the universe, so carefully made and so unceasingly held together by God . . .*

> —Fragment 4 (tr. Charlesworth, 840)

Interestingly, this passage goes on to quote from the Jewish Orpheus passage that we discuss in the preceding section!

Eupolemus: Third-hand quotations

The work of Eupolemus that's available for study is another series of quoted fragments of a history of the Jews written by a Greek-speaking Jewish author who probably completed his work before 100 BCE.

Once again, scholars are dependent on extensive quotations from the two Christian writers Clement of Alexandria (150–216 CE) and the voluminous Eusebius (260–340 CE) to give them a taste of this Jewish writer's work. Both of these Christian writers, however, quote another work by Alexander Polyhistor, and so the Eupolemus fragments are *third*-hand quotations! This separation from the source has led to some interesting mistakes; in one case, scholars have figured out what may have happened to cause a change in the text. Consider this fragment that discusses King David's decision to build a Temple for God in Jerusalem, described in the Bible in 2 Samuel and repeated in 1 Chronicles:

> *Since David wanted to build a temple for God, he asked God to show him a place for the altar. Then an angel appeared to him standing above the place where the altar is set up in Jerusalem and ordered him not to set up the temple, because he was defiled with human blood and had waged war for many years. His name was Dianathan. He gave him a command that he should entrust the building to his son . . .*

—Fragment 2, 30 (ed. Charlesworth, 866)

The biblical story of David and the Temple doesn't describe an angel in this episode about the Temple, but it does describe the intervention of the Prophet Nathan. Furthermore, although the passage in 1 Samuel states that David was not to build the Temple, it only explains the reason — because David was a man of war — in 1 Chronicles. It seems clear that somewhere along the line the prophet Nathan's involvement turned into the intervention of an "angel" with the name "Dianathan" (dia means "through" or "by means of," so it's possible that the name was intended to mean "by means of Nathan").

The fragment also gives rather extensive details about the actual construction of the Temple — no doubt intended to impress non-Jewish readers already familiar with impressive Greek structures!

This work of Eupolemus also contains some interesting letters written by Solomon to seek assistance in building the Temple — letters to foreign rulers who seem only too pleased to help him out! None of this is in the Bible, of course, but you have to admit that it adds a nice flair to the story!

Cleodemus Malchus and where the word "Africa" came from

In a short paragraph quoted by Josephus (and thus thought to date before 100 BCE), a certain "Cleodemus Malchus" (whoever he was) indicates some rather spurious historical claims about the origins of the word "Africa."

He claims that the continent's name is derived from two of the sons of Abraham:

- ✔ Iafra
- ✔ Afera

Such claims to speak with authority about foreign places and people are very common in ancient writings and are usually to be treated with *great* suspicion.

Artapanus: A story about Moses the inventor!?

A certain ancient writer called Artapanus is quoted in Eusebius, and although thought to have written 300–200 BCE, Artapanus is quoted indirectly by Eusebius from Alexander Polyhistor.

Artapanus is quoted as defending the history of the Jews and Jewish ideas from attacks by Greeks and other pagan writers. So, these fragments contain high praise for Jewish "heroes" like Abraham, Joseph, and especially Moses. In fact, there's a lot of material about Moses from some source entirely unknown to us now.

The bottom line is that the ideas quoted from Artapanus are probably simply made up, such as the notion that Moses was an inventor:

> . . . *he invented boats and devices for stone construction and the Egyptian arms and the implements for drawing water and for warfare and philosophy* . . .

> —Fragment 3

According to the fragment, Moses was loved by the masses, who then called him Hermes (the name of a Greek god). This is a clear attempt to mix Jewish characters with Greek religious ideas.

Pseudo-Hecataeus on the Jews

Some fragments are attributed to the real historian, Hecataeus of Abdera (who lived in the fourth century BCE). Scholars have many extensive quotations from the genuine Hecataeus, and many of these deal with the Jews. It appears that he knew something about them, but even the genuine parts (quoted in the work of a later writer) have some very interesting variations on the descriptions of Moses.

However, modern historians are highly doubtful of other fragments *attributed* to Hecataeus, no doubt because of his significance as a writer; as a result, they refer to the writings as *Pseudo-Hecataeus*. It seems that many early Jewish and Christian writers made overly enthusiastic claims by using sources that they couldn't possibly hope to confirm (sometimes on hearsay, other times from written sources), but they went ahead and used this material if it served their purpose!

The most interesting of these Pseudo-Hecataeus quotations claims to illustrate the argument that the Jews were a steadfast people who wouldn't give up their faith:

> *Therefore, even though spoken ill of by their neighbors and by foreign visitors, and even though frequently treated with disrespect by the Persian kings and satraps, their determination could not be shaken. Without defense, they meet tortures, and the worst kinds of death on behalf of these laws, and they do not disown their hereditary way of life.*

> —Pseudo-Hecataeus 191 (ed Charlesworth 918)

Chapter 8

Apocalyptic Literature (a.k.a. *Really* Strange Books)

● ●

In This Chapter

▶ Hearing from Zephaniah, Ezra, and Sedrach

▶ Digging into the books of Baruch

▶ Reading non-biblical accounts about Abraham, Adam, and Elijah

▶ Following Isaiah's path of martyrdom and ascension

▶ Elaborating on the story of Jacob's ladder

▶ Charting the course of a geographical apocalypse

● ●

*A*s we explain in Chapter 3, an entire category of ancient religious writing is known as "apocalyptic" literature (from the Greek word meaning "revelation"). Typically, these writings involve long, detailed descriptions of visions experienced by the writer. They often use bizarre imagery (multi-headed animals, combinations of animals, seas of glass, many days of travel into the heavens, and so on) and just as often involve gruesome descriptions of "final judgment" that punishes evildoers and rewards good people.

Part of the point of these writings appears to be conveying the message, "Be good . . . or else you'll experience *this* stuff!" Also, these writings typically involve a conversation between the person seeing the vision and an angel or heavenly being who explains some of the meaning of the vision. Most of these visions symbolically describe events in the writers' own time, but they also shed light on things that were expected to happen soon. In short, the message is that change is coming.

So much apocalyptic literature has survived that scholars can easily conclude that *lots* of it was written and that it must have been very popular reading indeed! Suffice it to say that these strange visions allowed the writers to explore all kinds of ideas and emotions that readers were eager to absorb.

Although there were lots of apocalyptic writings, only a couple of them made it into the Bible: Daniel in the Hebrew Bible/Old Testament and the Revelation to John in the New Testament. In general, apocalyptic imagery was controversial and had little enduring moral or spiritual value beyond its bizarre imagery. The *strongest* reason cited by many historians for why there isn't more of this type of literature in the Bible is that there was a great deal of apocalyptic enthusiasm behind the Bar Kochba Revolt of 132–135 CE, and when that ended badly (there was heavy loss of life when Rome put down the revolt), Jewish communities lost interest in apocalyptic speculation. When the angels didn't show up to help with the revolt, people may have thought that it was time to read the religious stuff about "settling in for the long haul" rather than preparing for coming judgment.

In this chapter, we explore some of these strange writings that never made it into the Bible (and in most cases, you can be thankful for that!), giving you brief samples so that you can decide for yourself whether they're something you'd like to read fully in an English translation. *Note:* For this chapter, most of the English translations are found in the two-volume work edited by Charlesworth, *Old Testament Apocrypha and Pseudopigrapha* (see the appendix for all references used).

The Apocalypse of Zephaniah

The first century BCE to first century CE work the *Apocalypse of Zephaniah* is named for the Prophet Zephaniah of the Bible only because the visionary says in the writing, "I, Zephaniah, saw these things in my vision. . . ." Of course, this work was written many centuries after the traditional time of the Prophet Zephaniah and thus was written under a pseudonym borrowed from the earlier history of ancient Israel. Zephaniah was actually a Prophet from the sixth century BCE.

This apocalyptic work is notable for themes that are familiar to readers of the book of Revelation in the New Testament: For example, angels blow on trumpets, and there are descriptive passages in which the visionary talks about seeing people being punished in judgment. What's really interesting about the Apocalypse of Zephaniah, however, is that the vision has a very personal impact on the visionary; when he sees people being punished in Hades by horrible-looking creatures, he wonders what they are:

> When I saw them, I was afraid. I said to that angel who walked with me, "Of what sort of are these?" He said to me, "These are the servants of all creation who come to the souls of ungodly men and bring them and leave them in this place. They spend three days going around with them in the air before they bring them and cast them into their eternal punishment."
>
> I said, "I beseech you, O Lord, don't give them authority to come to me!" . . .
>
> —Apocalypse of Zephaniah 4 (ed. Charlesworth, 511)

The Apocalypse of Zephaniah also expresses the idea of a heavenly book in which one's sins are recorded! Zephaniah, to his horror, is allowed to read the book on his own sins, and describes the experience as follows:

> *I found that all my sins which I had done were written in it, those which I had done from my youth until this day. They were all written upon that manuscript of mine without there being a false word in them. If I did not go to visit a sick man or a widow, I found it written down as a shortcoming upon my manuscript. If I did not visit an orphan . . . A day on which I did not fast or pray . . .*

> —Apocalypse of Zephaniah 7 (ed. Charlesworth, 513)

In this passage, you can see early reference to ideas, such as the Book of Life and places of judgment, that are taken up in other Jewish and Christian writings. Of particular importance is the following prayer addressed to God by Zephaniah, who begs God for help by reminding God how God saved others in the past:

> *You are the one who saved Israel from the hand of Pharaoh, the king of Egypt. You saved Susanna from the hand of the elders of injustice. You save the three holy men, Shadrach, Meschach, Abednego, from the furnace of burning fire. I beg you to save me from this distress . . .*

> —Apocalypse of Zephaniah 6:10 (ed. Charlesworth, 513)

The reason that these references to the book of Daniel are important is because Susanna was only added to Daniel in the Greek versions, after 200 BCE, so the reference helps scholars date this writing! By Chapter 9, Zephaniah gets good news: "Be courageous! . . . Your name is written in the Book of the Living!" So, in the end, the book encourages the reader to work so that his life is listed in the right book!

The Ezra Books

Ezra the Scribe was one of the most famous characters late in Hebrew Bible history (around 450 BCE). Because the Bible famously celebrates Ezra as "bringing the scrolls of the law" on his visit to Palestine and teaching people from these scrolls in what looks like a formal gathering (Nehemiah 8:1–2), he's often spoken of in early Jewish tradition as the one responsible for gathering the old writings into what would become the Bible.

Virtually all the Ezra writings discussed in this section are considered rather late (perhaps even up to the ninth century CE!) in comparison to the other writings that we examine in this book. But they're often included in discussions about lost books because there's great suspicion that they may be based on older material. Although they may be based on older Jewish writings or tradition, these writings also show signs of Christian influence, probably because they were kept among Christian churches longer than they were in the Jewish communities.

Given that many early Christians were also Jewish, it seems hardly surprising that ancient Christian writing would also honor Ezra and his legacy and that such a central character would feature in later books as well. Quite a few later apocalyptic visionary works also were attributed to Ezra; the following sections guide you through them.

The Greek Apocalypse of Ezra

In the *Greek Apocalypse of Ezra,* Ezra is taken up into heaven and shown the various punishments reserved for evil persons. The following elements from the Greek Apocalypse of Ezra are typical of all the Ezra writings (non-canonical writings that prominently feature Ezra):

✔ Detailed descriptions of the various places of heaven and hell (usually featuring numbers 7 and 12, as in seven gates, seven steps up, twelve mountains, twelve beings or seven beings, and so on)

✔ Details of gruesome punishments

✔ Detailed descriptions of the glorious throne of God, surrounded by strange animals and angelic beings

Many of these descriptions are clearly influenced by and further developments of the famous description of the Throne of God in the biblical book of Isaiah, chapter 6.

A very important feature of these Ezra writings, however, are the questions being asked by Ezra himself. Not only does Ezra ask about what he is seeing (such as, "Why are these people suffering?"), but he also asks rather heavy questions of the angels, like "Why don't you help them?" to which the invariable reply is some form of "They had their chance!" In a sense, these books frequently anticipate the obvious questions from readers — questions still asked by modern readers!

Among the intentionally frightful scenes in the Greek Apocalypse is when Ezra is shown the Antichrist — a decidedly Christian concept. The idea that a future religious leader will claim to be the returned Jesus is a notion frequently taken up in Christian discussions (see Epistle of 1 John in the New Testament) and one that seemed to intrigue people. The idea of warning people against this seems to be motivated by warning people about false religious teachers in general, no matter *who* they claim to be!

The Vision of Ezra

In the *Vision of Ezra,* Ezra is carried into "the infernal regions" (the gates of hell) and shown a variety of different kinds of sins. Among the expected sins (lust and adultery) are a few somewhat surprising sins, such as the people shown to Ezra who "did not receive strangers and they did not give alms, they took unjustly the things of others for themselves" (*Vision of Ezra* 30–33).

But as in the Greek Apocalypse, the Vision touches on a clear worry about false teachings, and some of the sins shown to Ezra include people who were ". . . Doctors of the Law who confused baptism and the law of the Lord, because they were teaching with words, but they did not spur on to works . . ." (*Vision of Ezra* 46–47).

Many Roman era works like the Vision mention exposure of infants as a dreadful sin. Apparently, one way to deal with unwanted children was simply to abandon them in the wilderness to die after birth; this practice also is frequently condemned in early Christian literature.

The Questions of Ezra

The *Questions of Ezra* is precisely that: Ezra asks questions of God with regard to the future and especially to the rewards and punishments of the future era.

All the Ezra-focused materials refer to the soul's fate after death (suggesting Greek philosophical influence), and the Questions of Ezra is no exception. But in this writing, readers also encounter a rather charming little proverb on prayer:

> *For your prayers are thus: just as a farmer goes forth, comes to sow, and the Shoot comes forth joyous and graceful and desires to produce numerous fruit, and thorn and weeds also come forth and choke it and do not let numerous fruit be assembled. Similarly, also you, when you go inside the church and desire to offer prayers before the Divinity, the cares of this world and the deceit of greatness (wealth) come forth and choke you and do not let numerous fruit be sown . . .*
>
> —Questions of Ezra 7–38 (ed. Charlesworth, 599)

The Revelation of Ezra

The *Revelation of Ezra* is a short fragment that seems almost like a horoscope. It consists of a prediction of the kinds of good and bad things that will happen during a year if that year begins with a particular day of the week.

What's with all this judgment stuff?

Modern readers of religious writings — especially apocalyptic writings — often express shock and even revulsion at the subject of judgment. Typically, modern readers think that judgment was a crude way to scare people into being good and that some modern people talk too much about judgment and not nearly enough about love. Sometimes talk about punishment and judgment comes off as so, well . . . judgmental! That's what *we* think, but what did *they* think — the writers and readers of apocalyptic literature? Were these people just angry or something?

Consider this: Judgment is usually only bad if you feel that *you* are the one being judged — especially if you consider the judgment to be unfair! There are other situations in which you actually *expect* people to be judgmental. For example, you expect judges in court to say to guilty people, "Shame on you!" People applaud that kind of judgment when they feel that justice is served.

So, the next time you read ancient writings that talk about judgment, ask yourself, "Who wrote this? Why are they talking about judgment so much?" For an ancient people like the Jews, who were often harassed, often conquered, sometimes horribly treated, life didn't feel very fair at all. The early Christians, too, often faced persecution and suffering, especially in the first 300 years of Christianity. It's clear that they sometimes wondered, "Where is our God?" And that is where judgment comes in.

For these ancient people feeling oppressed and abused, judgment was something that sounded good! It gave them the sense that the abuse was going to stop soon and that right would be right and wrong would be wrong. The next time you think about how judgmental these ancient writings are, ask yourself why *you* watch *Law and Order, Boston Legal,* or *Judge Judy. . . .* Truth be told, we have our own judgment literature, too!

Here is a sample, based on Monday:

> *The day of the Moon (Monday) makes both winter and summer moderate. There will be great floods and sickness, infantry warfare, changes of rulers, and many wives will sit in lamentation, there will be much ice, kings will die, there will be a good vintage, bees will die . . .*

—Revelation of Ezra 4

The Apocalypse of Sedrach

The first- to fifth-century CE text the *Apocalypse of Sedrach* is a good example of a book from a very late source (15th century CE Greek manuscript) that's generally held to be based on older materials (from perhaps as early as the first centuries of Christianity).

The nice thing about the Apocalypse of Sedrach, and the reason that it's notable, is that, compared to other apocalyptic literature, it has a much more hopeful tone and a stronger emphasis on love. The work starts off with a sermon, beginning with this positive note: "Beloved, we must prefer nothing more than unfeigned love . . .", and continues along these lines. Along the way, the writer quotes from 1 John:

> *Do not be advised to do anything without love. If you say, "I hate my brother but I love Christ" you are a liar, and John the Theologian rebukes you, for how can one who does not love his brother whom he has seen, love God whom he has not seen . . . Oh how extraordinary and paradoxical is the miracle that he who has love fulfills all the law!*
>
> —Apocalypse of Sedrach 9–10 (tr. Charlesworth, 609)

Like the Ezra materials covered earlier, the Apocalypse of Sedrach features conversations between Sedrach the seer and God. In one line of questioning, Sedrach asks if a person who lives a sinful life for over a hundred years but repents at the very end will be forgiven. God says that the person will be forgiven if he repents in his last three years.

Like Abraham bargaining with God in the book of Genesis, Sedrach doesn't let the question drop, asking, "What about if a person repents within one year of their death, God? What about only 40 days, God?" Each time, God offers to forgive. In fact, the entire conversation is an emphasis on the forgiving love of God, and in some ways, the Apocalypse of Sedrach is a nice antidote to the rather harsh tone of other works! However, it does get in some licks: Those who refuse to repent of their sins aren't spared!

Further Books of Baruch

Baruch was the scribe who wrote the book of Jeremiah in the Bible (Jeremiah 36:4) and may have been responsible for major sections of 1–2 Samuel and 1–2 Kings as well. His famous association with Jeremiah led to Baruch becoming a rather important biblical character in later tradition — especially because Baruch apparently was a scribe who knew how to write, and that skill was very rare in the ancient world!

Few biblical characters could make that claim, so Baruch is an obvious candidate for later writers to pick up on and develop further! Similar to the Ezra traditions of a later era, more Baruch writings were composed also portraying the great scribe as taking journeys to heaven and writing what he saw. The context of these visions, however, is the times of the actual historic Baruch. Following are those "further" books of Baruch:

✔ 2 Baruch (early second century CE)

✔ 3 Baruch (first to third centuries CE)

✔ 4 Baruch (first to second centuries CE)

The historic Baruch, with Jeremiah, lived in the tumultuous times surrounding 587 BCE when Nebuchadnezzar the Babylonian Emperor conquered Jerusalem and carried away many prisoners of war. These events, known as the *Babylonian Exile,* are symbolically used in 2 and 3 Baruch to speak of a later time. 4 Baruch goes in a somewhat different direction, as we explain in a later section.

2 Baruch

It seems a short step to go from inviting readers from later times to *compare* their situations with that of Baruch in an earlier time to suggesting that Baruch could actually *anticipate and speak about* those later developments! 2 Baruch is set in the context of the destruction of the Temple of Jerusalem in 587. The Temple was destroyed this first time by Nebuchadnezzar and a second and final time in 70 CE by the Romans. The two events seem to scream out for comparison, and that's precisely the idea behind 2 and 3 Baruch.

The central questions on the lips of Baruch in 2 Baruch are likely the same questions asked by Jewish faithful when the Romans destroyed Jerusalem in 70 CE:

✔ How could God have allowed this?

✔ Has God abandoned us?

A major section of 2 Baruch consists of a conversation between Baruch and God on precisely these questions. For example, 2 Baruch portrays God's angels actually assisting in the destruction of the city walls of Jerusalem back in 587 BCE, so that the people know that God's doing this, not the forces of Babylon. In other words, the first fall of Jerusalem was the result of judgment, not merely military defeat. When Baruch protests, God clarifies that evil will be punished and God will not spare his own from punishment if they have sinned. However, those who are righteous will also have their rewards. And after all, says God, if a person has a bad youth but a happy older life, he forgets the youth! The implication seems to be that punishments are temporary and better times ahead will prove more memorable.

There follows a series of mystical numbers and symbolic language that communicates basically one thought: Things will appear to get bad, and just when people begin to loose all hope, "the time will awake." People in bad circumstances were comforted by the idea that they weren't abandoned no matter how bad things looked.

A promise in 2 Baruch includes the future fruitfulness of the land — the peace enjoyed by people who know only violence now — and the fact that all will be fed. Much of the symbolism and themes of judgment followed by paradise parallels the language of the New Testament book of Revelation, especially when 2 Baruch speaks of the coming of the "Anointed One" who will officiate over the resurrection of the dead.

The final chapters are these words of encouragement from Baruch to Jewish believers everywhere: Stand firm! Study the signs of the times! Be encouraged about the future!

3 Baruch

3 Baruch has a similar theme to 2 Baruch: It uses the historical tragedy of 587 BCE to muse about later tragedies such as the Temple destruction in 70 CE, or perhaps later events like the suppression of the ill-fated Bar Kochba Revolt in Palestine (132–135 CE).

Particularly intriguing about 3 Baruch, however, is a series of visits into different layers of heaven (which is why 3 Baruch is reminiscent of similar travels in heaven and hell in the famous Book of 1 Enoch, which you can read about in Chapter 6).

Visiting First Heaven

As Baruch is weeping over the fate of Jerusalem, an angel of God whisks him off to the heavens, where they enter a gate at the First Heaven. Here, Baruch is curious about the size of the plains of heaven and also asks about the strange beings he sees there. The angel tells him that these beings (who seem to be mixtures of people and animals) were the ones who tried to build the Tower of Babel (in Genesis 11) and were punished.

Visiting Second Heaven

Baruch then proceeds to the Second Heaven where he encounters more strange people, specifically the ones who tried to build the bricks for the Tower of Babel. As Baruch continues with the angel, he's shown the vine that grew the fruit that tempted Adam and Eve but was destroyed by the Great Flood (3 Baruch Chapter 4). It's said that Noah replanted the vine because God had positive plans for the continued life of the plant. A Christian editor then inserts a sentence about Jesus being the result of that vine (John 15:1), but the original work carries on without strong Christian references.

More layers of heaven

3 Baruch continues with many unusual references as Baruch ascends into various layers of heaven. In one layer, he's shown a version of the phoenix bird that protects the earth from too much of the sun's light (kind of like an

ancient ozone layer!). This section also has a mythical interpretation of the moon as an angelic being that helped to tempt Adam and Eve and was there-fore reduced in light, compared to the sun, as punishment.

Visiting Fifth Heaven

At the Fifth Heaven, Baruch and the angel meet Michael, the "commander in chief" of the angels. Michael is, of course, famously an important angelic per-sonality already in Scripture (Daniel 10:13 and 12:1, and Revelation 12:7) and assumes even greater significance in 3 Baruch. Here, Michael is portrayed as carrying a large bowl of the good works of people upwards to God, and then he explains the inevitability of judgment on evil to Baruch.

4 Baruch

Finally, we come to 4 Baruch. This one isn't really an apocalyptic book but rather an expansion of biblical tradition. However, it does have apocalyptic elements, such as the prominent role of angels. 4 Baruch elaborates on the tragic events of 587 BCE when Jerusalem was conquered and destroyed by Babylon. However, contrary to biblical history, in 4 Baruch the prophet Jeremiah is taken among the captives!

An interesting part of the story has to do with Jeremiah's trusted friend, Abimelech the Ethiopian. In the story, when Jeremiah learns of Jerusalem's fate (before it happens), he pleads with God to spare his friend Abimelech. God grants this in a course of events that may remind you of Rip Van Winkle — Jeremiah sends Abimelech out of Jerusalem to gather figs, and when Abimelech sits down to rest by a tree, he sleeps for 66 years! When he awakes, he discovers the awful truth about Jerusalem's fate and the fact that Jeremiah is gone. But Baruch sends a letter to Jeremiah saying that Abimelech is alive.

In the final chapter of 4 Baruch, which obviously was edited by later Christian writers, Jeremiah dies and then rises to life three days later to announce the coming of Jesus centuries later! There follows a brief series of apocalyptic-style predictions focused on events surrounding the future coming of Jesus. Then you come to a strange ending in which Jeremiah dies for good, but not before a stone image of him distracts his opponents long enough for him to explain everything that he saw to Baruch. (It seems that there may be missing parts of this work because Jeremiah claims that he has explained many mysteries to Baruch, but all that scholars have is this brief Christian section.)

When the mob discovers that they're stoning a mere stone image of Jeremiah, they find the real guy and kill him. This element certainly reflects the opposition that Jeremiah faced among his own people during his lifetime, according to the biblical book of Jeremiah.

The Apocalypse of Abraham

The *Apocalypse of Abraham* begins with the biblical tradition that Abraham grew up in Mesopotamia with his father Terah. Terah was a maker of idols, and Abraham is said to have taken some on the road to sell. Some were destroyed by accident, leading Abraham to contemplate their reality and wonder if they really are gods. After all, his father had to *make* them, and they couldn't even save themselves from falling off Abraham's donkey! Later, a god even burns in the fire as Abraham prepares food for his father.

Somewhat humorously, Terah doesn't see the obvious and instead decides that the god "prepared my food" when the idol burned in the fire. Abraham laughs at this thinking, and you see his emerging disbelief in the various idols.

A real gem in this book, however, is Abraham's speech to his father. Abraham says that Terah's "gods" aren't even as venerable as gold gods, which are made of something valuable like silver or gold. But none of them are gods; fire is more powerful than all of them because it destroys even silver and gold, but fire isn't a god. Water is more powerful than fire, but it isn't a god. By extension, the sun is more powerful than all this, but it disappears at night, so it's hardly a god either.

You can see an interesting philosophical idea emerging in Abraham's speech as he arrives at the notion that there must be something even higher and greater that is creator of all. God finally appears to Abraham and says, "You are searching for the God of gods, the creator . . . I am he!" (*Apocalypse of Abraham* 8:3–4).

After Abraham's speech, the Apocalypse of Abraham borrows from the biblical accounts of Genesis and portrays the famous animal splitting sacrifice (Genesis 15) as a rite instructed by an angel of God to prepare Abraham for a series of revelations. While Abraham waits, he's briefly tempted by Azazel, the evil angel, but another good angel drives Azazel away and prepares Abraham for his visions.

The visions begin with a spectacular description of the throne of God in flames, surrounded by strange beings that combine aspects of different animals (this vision is very similar to that given in the book of the biblical Prophet Ezekiel, chapters 1–3). In subsequent chapters, Abraham is called upon by God to view different scenes on earth: masses of people divided into good and bad; specific sins committed by people, including Abraham's own people; and then finally an explanation of the coming judgment.

Like many of the apocalyptic books that we consider in this chapter, the Apocalypse of Abraham ends with a series of generalized predictions of disasters coming upon the earth just before the final judgment occurs, exemplifying the modern saying, "It is always darkest just before the dawn."

This first to second century CE work, probably originally written in Hebrew in Palestine, has been passed through Slavonic languages into Russian, and thus scholars are dependent on Russian versions to help reconstruct the original as best as they can.

The Apocalypse of Adam

The *Apocalypse of Adam* is a first- to fourth-century CE Gnostic writing that was found among the Nag Hammadi manuscripts discovered in Egypt in the early 20th century. Seth, the son of Adam, became very important in Gnostic belief because he was supposed to be the one to whom Adam revealed many secrets, which Seth passed on to the people who called themselves *Gnostics* (see Chapter 12 for more on Gnostic beliefs). "Gnosis" is the Greek word for "knowledge."

The Gnostic philosophy, which appears to have arisen in the second century CE, influenced many other religious traditions, including Judaism and especially Christianity. There were many Christian Gnostic writings, but the Apocalypse of Adam appears to be a Gnostic Jewish writing — that is, a work that draws on the Jewish instead of the Christian tradition in order to argue Gnostic beliefs.

In short, the Gnostics believed that the material world isn't real in any profound sense and that the only reality is spiritual. The God of the Hebrews, the creator of this world, is an evil god who tries to cover up the truth about the Higher God, the God of Light and Truth.

Thus, in Gnostic writings, the Hebrew biblical narrative is typically told as a narrative of enslavement to an evil god who doesn't want humans to know the truth. But according to the Apocalypse of Adam, an Illuminator will come with the truth.

This work has a long poetic sequence that describes this Illuminator as one who was carefully chosen and cared for by the angels of the Higher God. There are 13 sections in the sequence, and each section ends with the phrase, "thus, he came to the water." Given that water and "coming to the water" are themes throughout the entire writing, it's possible that this writing had something to do with a kind of water ritual (perhaps a sort of baptism) conducted as part of entry into a Gnostic sect.

According to the Apocalypse of Adam, the Illuminator eventually reveals the truth to humanity, and the truth is the knowledge that's passed on to Seth for safekeeping.

Note: Although most of the surviving Gnostic writings are Christian Gnostic writings, the Apocalypse of Adam stands out as one that appears to have no specifically Christian elements at all, suggesting the wide range of religious themes and sources that Gnostic religious writers could use in the ancient world.

The Apocalypse of Elijah

A first- to fourth-century CE work, the *Apocalypse of Elijah* is considered an older Jewish work with later Christian editing in various locations. It begins with a praise of fasting as a form of spiritual battle against temptation and sin. The writer is reacting, apparently, to those who have questioned the importance of fasting, but this writer is strongly set in favor of fasting as a spiritual practice that prepares one for facing evil in the same way that a craftsman must use tools and a warrior must use weapons.

There follows a section that appears to be a visionary prediction of the rise of evil rulers in the countries surrounding the writer (some suggest that the writer must be in Egypt). These predictions are typically vague, as in "A king will rise in the West," but there's a strong warning that this ruler will be seductive in using the language of peace and joy. The writing even tells how to recognize him: He will have two sons, and from the one with a demonic face, evil kings will arise, and people will cry out because of the oppression he will bring. Even 12-year-old children will be drafted into this evil king's armies.

A later Christian editor read these references to be the Antichrist, and so develops this theme further. The writer warns that the Antichrist will accomplish many impressive things and then helps readers out by giving a strange physical description to aid in recognizing him: "skinny-legged young lad . . . tuft of gray hair . . . his eyebrows will reach to his ears . . ." (*Apocalypse of Elijah* 3:15).

The sequence of events in the Apocalypse of Elijah becomes even odder: You're introduced to a virgin named Tabitha who chases the Antichrist. The Antichrist kills her and casts her body on the Temple, but it's revealed that her blood will produce healing. Then you read about the martyrdom of Elijah and Enoch as they also take up the fight against the Antichrist. They rise from the dead and keep up the battle.

This theme of conflict is maintained through the persecution of Christians. Jesus appears, takes up the faithful (similar to the Rapture idea in Revelation in the New Testament). Afterward, however, the writing foresees earth experiencing frightening evils:

And on that day the earth will be disturbed, and the sun will darken, and peace will be removed from the earth. The birds will fall on the earth, dead. The earth will be dry. The waters of the sea will dry up. The sinners will groan upon the earth saying, "What have you done to us, O son of lawlessness, saying I am the Christ, when you were the devil!?"

—Apocalypse of Elijah 5:7–11

In the end, Christ returns with the faithful and reigns for a thousand years. The evil ones cry out, "We thought we had time, but we did not!" Like many apocalyptic writings, the entire Apocalypse of Elijah revolves around the theme and goal of the last judgment.

Clearly, this work shares similar themes with the famous book of Revelation in the New Testament, but it's likely that these themes come from general apocalyptic lore and not directly from the New Testament work.

The Martyrdom and Ascension of Isaiah

The *Martyrdom and Ascension of Isaiah* is clearly a book composed of two major sections that describe the martyrdom and ascension of the prophet Isaiah, a historic figure who began preaching in ancient Israel around 740 BCE. From his influence came the enormously important writing known as the book of Isaiah in the Hebrew Bible. The Martyrdom and Ascension is believed to be dated to the second century BCE for parts of the book and up to the fourth century CE for other portions.

Isaiah's martyrdom

The first section of the book, considered the older portion, is a legend about the martyrdom of Isaiah that's similar in many respects to other second century BCE martyr stories, especially those contained in 2 Maccabees and the "near martyr" stories of Daniel 1–6. It's often thought that the dramatic increase in martyr stories as religious literature among the Jews probably increased with the persecution of Jews under the Greek rulers over Palestine between 200–150 BCE, which gave rise to the Maccabean revolts near 164 BCE. Typical of all these stories is a conversation between the evil ruler and the faithful person in which the faithful person is offered clemency to renounce his faith. This element appears in this work.

The legend speaks of the evil king Manasseh murdering Isaiah at the instigation of Satan (under the name "Beliar," used frequently in other apocalyptic literature). According to this legend, Isaiah is literally sawed in half after refusing to abandon his faith in God.

Isaiah's ascension

The second portion of the book, often called the *Ascension of Isaiah,* seems to be a Christian work (although the Christian elements may have been edited into an older Jewish work). Isaiah is visited by angels who raise him upward through seven heavens. Briefly stopping at each of the seven heavens, Isaiah sees angels singing and praising God, and he's told to go higher to see whom they're praising. Finally, Isaiah reaches the seventh and final heaven only to meet Jesus before he's born as a human child. There follows a summary of the life of Jesus, all viewed in short order by Isaiah before the risen Jesus rises once again to the seventh heaven.

The fact that the biblical Isaiah didn't tell this story is addressed at the end of the Ascension, where it says that Isaiah was sworn to secrecy until all these predicted events took place.

Sorting out the different sections of this work, however, isn't easy. It's widely held that the actual visits of Isaiah in heaven form an older part of the work and the martyrdom section may be a Christian addition. However, if you remove the really obvious Christian references, it's possible to argue that the entire work is pre-Christian and thus entirely Jewish in character.

The Ladder of Jacob

Jacob's famous dream described in Genesis 28 is obvious inspiration for an apocalyptic text — it seems ready-made for such an interpretation! In the *Ladder of Jacob,* Jacob's dream is elaborated. In the biblical passage, Jacob sees a ladder with angels going down and up from heaven to earth (already pretty striking imagery); but in this writing, God tells an angel named Sariel to explain to Jacob the symbolic meaning of the dream. Here's part of Sariel's explanation:

> *You have seen a ladder with twelve steps, each step having two human faces which kept changing their appearance. The ladder is this age, and the twelve steps are the periods of this age. But the twenty-four faces are the kinds of the ungodly nations of this age . . .*

—Ladder of Jacob 5:1–2

There follows the typical series of vaguely general predictions that give historians headaches and raise more questions, such as, "Is this symbol a reference to a real ruler? If so, which one?" and so on. Among the specific predictions is the following reference most likely to the enslavement in Egypt before Moses and less likely to the Babylonian conquest of Jerusalem in 587 BCE:

> *Know, Jacob, that your descendants shall be exiles in a strange land, and they will afflict them with slavery and inflict wounds on them every day . . .*
>
> —Ladder of Jacob 5:16

It's precisely the vagueness of this kind of prediction that allows people to read the Ladder of Jacob and say, "Wow! That's just like us today!" This has been the case particularly when the work has been read by Jews who face persecution and mass movements after

✔ The Assyrian conquests of 722 BCE

✔ The Babylonian conquests of 587 BCE

✔ The Greek conquests of 333 BCE and 200 BCE

✔ The Roman conquests of 64 BCE

✔ The Roman destruction of Jerusalem in 70 CE

✔ The Roman suppression of the Bar Kochba Revolt in 132–135 CE

Hopefully you get the idea that, when experiencing these kinds of bad times, people get some kind of comfort from believing that it's all part of some plan . . . and especially when that plan includes changes coming!

This short little first century CE writing is only available to modern readers from Slavonic and Russian sources (for example, from Eastern Christian traditions in the vicinity of modern Bulgaria), but it was most likely originally composed in Greek.

The History of the Rechabites

Consider one last odd first- to fourth-century CE work with somewhat unusual apocalyptic elements. The *History of the Rechabites* sets itself in the time of the Babylonian conquest of Jerusalem, similar to many of the texts reviewed in this chapter. This context is probably because of the parallels that readers sensed between that time and their own time of persecution — especially around the time of the Roman destruction of Jerusalem in 70 CE.

In the History, Zosimus is fasting in the wilderness in hopes that God will show him where the "Blessed Ones" dwell. There's no explanation of who these Blessed Ones are until later in the writing. An angel, who appears to transform into a strange animal, brings Zosimus to a beautiful island. Typically, Jewish apocalyptic writings emphasize that the visionary visits heavenly locations (or occasionally, the "other place"). But in this writing, Zosimus appears to go on a literal journey to another location on earth! The island is occupied by strange and unusual people, and one of these Blessed Ones actually appears to

Zosimus to be like an angel. Like the proverbial "take me to your leader" encounter, Zosimus is taken to the Blessed Ones' gathering, where he must answer a series of questions, particularly questions dealing with the final events of history (ah . . . we knew we'd get to *that* subject, right?).

Zosimus is so bothered by the Blessed Ones' constant questions that he tells a messenger to lie to them and say that he's not available. When the lie is discovered, Zosimus is nearly kicked out of paradise! He apologizes, and the Blessed Ones explain to him who they are, which is what today might be called an "order" in the Catholic sense of people who make a vow to form a special and unique religious community. They live a nomadic existence in tents apart from regular society, and they don't drink wine. (In fact, there's a historical basis for this explanation in Jeremiah 35, where Jeremiah affirms the Blessed Ones' faith and tells them that they will survive even when Jerusalem is conquered.)

The History then elaborates that the entire order was magically transported to this island where they live an idyllic existence without war, money, sin, or impurities. Even the weather is perfect, so they live off the produce of the land. They sleep with their wives only once in their lives and produce two children, one for marriage and one for virginity. From the perspective of the writer, obviously, these are characteristics of some kind of perfect society, and the History is intriguing from that perspective if for nothing else. A Christian editor has inserted some comments about the significance of Jesus, but it seems an obvious intrusion in what is generally thought to have been a Jewish writing.

The History is like a geographical apocalypse rather than a future apocalypse and is clearly among the more unusual of the writings we survey in this chapter.

Other "Travels with God" Literature: 2 Enoch, 3 Enoch, and 3 Baruch

Although 1 Enoch (which is discussed in detail in Chapter 6) is the most famous, there were two other ancient books that use the Enoch character, both of which were written much later than 1 Enoch. They're known as 2 Enoch and 3 Enoch.

These two related books cover very similar territory:

- ✔ Descriptions of travels upwards through the levels of heaven
- ✔ Descriptions of what is learned from the travels

One of the interesting things about all Enoch literature is that it all describes travels from Earth to other, spiritual places where information is gathered and then passed back to humans.

Like the Greek Prometheus who stole fire from heaven and brought it to earth, so these writings take information about and from heaven and bring it back to earth. But 2 and 3 Enoch books aren't the only books about travels in heaven; another example worth mentioning is 3 Baruch.

2 Enoch

In 2 Enoch, Enoch gives a short speech to his sons that contains ethical instructions for things like taking care of the poor and avoiding injustice, and then Enoch is taken up into heaven.

Levels of heaven

2 Enoch describes each level of heaven with the authority of someone who's been there. Here's a rundown of the ten levels:

- ✔ **Level 1** is where the "storehouses" of weather are kept, including rain, snow, ice, and fire (which perhaps refers to lightning).

- ✔ **Level 2** is the place of punishment for the wicked.

- ✔ **Level 3** is the pleasant place for the righteous and for those who have done justice in their lives.

- ✔ **Level 4** contains the physical bodies of the universe. It's where Enoch is able to measure the flights and path of stars and the sun as well as the movements of the angels that accompany these heavenly bodies. The description of this level contains complex calculations of the length of days and the movement of stars.

  An interest in astronomical numerical detail is also a part of 1 Enoch.

- ✔ **Level 5** is where Enoch meets the famous fallen angels, led by Satan.

- ✔ **Level 6** is where Enoch sees the archangels in charge of all the heavenly beings.

- ✔ **Level 7** (Seventh Heaven!) is the place where Enoch sees heavenly armies and catches a glimpse of God on God's Throne in Heaven. Enoch is so overcome by his visions that the angels encourage him to "be strong."

- ✔ **Levels 8 and 9,** which Enoch passes through rather quickly, are where Enoch sees zodiac signs.

- ✔ **Level 10** is where Enoch finally sees of the face of God.

Note: If this sounds a bit like 2 Corinthians 12:2, then you're paying attention! The notion of levels of heaven *may* have been an influence on Paul from none other than Enoch, although other ancient Jewish writing also uses this theme.

Dating dilemmas for 2 and 3 Enoch

The dating of 2 Enoch is controversial, with some historians suggesting the first century BCE but other estimates as late as 900 CE.

The fact that some details (such as specific terms and even wordplay that only make sense in Greek but not in the later Slavonic translations) suggest a Greek origin for this book, however, has suggested to many historians that original parts of this work must go back to early centuries of Rabbinic Judaism and Christianity.

3 Enoch, on the other hand, is normally dated after 70 CE, after the destruction of the Temple in Jerusalem by the Romans in that year. 3 Enoch has references to Rabbi Ishmael, an early Jewish leader who was born in the first century, just before 70 CE, so the writing can't be any older than that. The book as it exists today, however, contains material that was clearly added for a long time after that 70 CE.

A sitdown with God on Level 10

Upon reaching Level 10, God explains the creation of the world to Enoch in much more detail than provided in the creation stories of Genesis. It's made clear to Enoch that he's intended to learn from this explanation and carry it back to earth.

This description has some genuinely charming details, such as the suggestion that God made man from seven components:

- His flesh from earth
- His blood from dew and the sun
- His eyes from the bottomless sea
- His bones from stone
- His reason from the mobility and speed of angels and clouds
- His veins and hair from the grass of the earth
- His spirit "from my spirit" and from wind

Enoch is an eager student and takes good notes, which he needs because he's granted 30 days back on earth to explain to his sons and anyone else who will listen what he has learned before he returns to heaven forever.

3 Enoch

3 Enoch contains even stranger descriptions of the levels of heaven but is generally similar in content to 2 Enoch. One difference is that in 3 Enoch, readers are introduced to Rabbi Ishmael, who encounters the angel named Metatron. Metatron clarifies to Rabbi Ishmael that he is, in fact, Enoch.

3 Enoch draws from descriptions of the levels of heaven in 2 Enoch (refer to the earlier section, "Levels of heaven," for the list) but is especially fascinated with the gathering and listing of names, including providing 70 names of God, more than 70 names for Metatron/Enoch, and a slew of names of various archangels. All this suggests an interest in the details of the heavens, and some historians believe that these names may have been believed to have magical properties.

3 Baruch

We should start by pointing out that there is both a Book of Baruch (1 Baruch) and a 2 Baruch, both of which are well known and accepted by Catholics as part of the Apocrypha (see Chapter 4). All this Baruch literature, like the Enoch literature, is based on a famous biblical persona, Baruch, a real historical figure responsible for writing down the sayings of the Prophet Jeremiah. But fascination with Baruch led to a series of works attributed to him, including two apocalyptic writings.

1 Baruch and 2 Baruch are quite different from Enoch-like writings about journeys in heaven, but 3 Baruch is very similar to Enoch. It includes descriptions of journeys into at least five levels of heaven. In 3 Baruch, Baruch is shown good places for good people and places of punishment for bad people as well as the workings of heaven and the various heavenly beings.

The interesting part of 3 Baruch is the fact that God allows Baruch to plead for the fate of evil persons, that they may be spared punishment. This is a somewhat unique feature of ancient literature that's almost always rather graphic in its description of the punishment of evil people.

Chapter 9

Popular Legends and Expansions of Older Hebrew Traditions

*T*his chapter covers some of the interesting writings from the Greek and Roman periods of Jewish history that are loosely based on older Jewish writings — most of which ended up in the Bible. Typically, historians and Bible scholars are interested in these kinds of writings because they represent an interesting form of "interpretation" of the older biblical stories in which the authors literally add details and sometimes retell the older material in a new fashion.

The most intriguing question to ask when studying these materials is whether any of these writings supply "missing elements" from the older biblical materials. In other words, were some of the episodes, short pieces, or elements of these stories based on older oral traditions? Or are they simply later "elaborations" of the older tradition?

It's clear that all the writings discussed in this chapter are later elaborations on biblical traditions — a kind of Jewish (and often also Christian) entertaining folklore with some ethical instructions. Furthermore, some of these writings contributed to magical beliefs that eventually raised suspicions among Church and Rabbinic leadership, who often looked askance at such practices that were often popular rituals among (frightened!) common people — if not the scholars as well!

The Odes of Solomon

We consider this late-first to early-second century CE collection of poetry to be the star of the show in this chapter. We confess that much of this judgment is based on the sheer beauty of the language. Whoever wrote these lines poetically describes what seems to be a profound experience of faith. It's likely that the work is ascribed to "Solomon" only because other Old Testament poetry is assigned to him even if it was written centuries later (like Proverbs and especially Ecclesiastes).

The Odes of Solomon contain some genuinely moving lines, and the general consensus, although occasionally disputed, is that these are *Christian* works so deeply influenced by Jewish ideas that they represent spiritual poetry of early Jewish Christians.

Jewish-Christianity was a part of early Christianity that eventually died out as Christianity became an increasingly non-Jewish religious movement. Of course, the New Testament was largely written by Jewish-Christians. When scholars speak of Jewish-Christianity, they usually mean those Jewish-Christians who were not entirely in agreement with St. Paul's open attitude toward non-Jews and who didn't accept Jewish practices when they became Christians. St. Paul's "missionary" movements, however, led to increasing numbers of non-Jews being accepted into the Christian movement without first becoming Jews, and later, even without much familiarity with Jewish tradition.

In the poems that comprise the Odes of Solomon, you hear something of the spirituality of these early Jewish-Christians. The poems also have the occasional odd turn of phrase and even some images that are a bit unorthodox. For example, the notion that Jesus didn't really die raises some theological problems; however, it may just be a poetic way of speaking of the Resurrection, or it may be a quite *un*orthodox statement that Jesus wasn't actually fully human and therefore only *appeared* to die — an idea that Christians argued about rather vehemently in the early centuries.

Despite these occasional doctrinal "hiccups" (which were sufficient enough to keep the collection out of the New Testament, we dare say), much of the poetic imagery of the Odes is undeniably quite expressive. For example:

> *As the wind moves through the harp and the strings speak,*
> *So the Spirit of the Lord speaks through my members,*
> *And I speak through his love*
>
> —Ode 6

> *My joy is the Lord and my course is toward him,*
> *This way of mine is beautiful.*
> *For there is a Helper for me, the Lord*
> *He has generously shown himself to me in his simplicity*

Because his kindness has diminished his grandeur
He became like me, that I might receive Him . . ."

—Ode 7

You also can see a level of social comment about Jesus and the poor in the midst of these rapturous lines of worship:

Stand and be established,
You who once were brought low.
You who were in silence, speak,
For your mouth has been opened.
You who were despised, from henceforth be raised
For your Righteousness has been raised
For the right hand of the Lord is with you
And he will be your helper . . .

—Ode 7

Joseph and Asenath

Joseph and Asenath is a charming story written sometime between the first century BCE and the second century CE. It's a romantic tale that may remind you of *Kiss Me, Kate* and *My Fair Lady* set in the biblical world. It's a tale with all the trimmings: drama, charm, and even animal characters!

Here's a breakdown of the story: Asenath, the daughter of an official of Pharaoh, hates all men, but somewhat inconveniently for her, she's also very beautiful and thus is a magnet for the males with whom she comes into contact. She hates all of them, that is, until she sets eyes on the handsome Joseph, portrayed as a young official in the Egyptian administration (based *very* loosely on the book of Genesis stories of Joseph).

But Joseph won't even consider a relationship with a non-Jew! Asenath is terribly sad, but Joseph says a prayer for her, and while he's away, Asenath goes through a significant conversion experience, abandoning the many gods of the ancient Egyptians for the Jewish God. In a notable prayer, she acknowledges that she has been wrong worshipping false gods but is hopeful for grace:

But I have heard many saying
That the God of the Hebrews is a true God
And a living God, a merciful God
And compassionate and long-suffering and full of pity and gentle
And does not count the sin of a humble person . . .

—Joseph and Asenath 11:10

The mighty angel Michael comes to announce that Asenath's prayers have been heard, and she is transformed. In a slightly strange scene, a hive of bees surrounds her in the moment of spiritual transformation. Joseph returns sometime later to find that she's transformed, and they are married in the household of the Pharaoh.

The work, charming as it is, has some interesting aspects that scholars focus on:

- ✔ **Joseph maintains his clear Jewish identity despite working in foreign service.** This is reminiscent of the older tales of Daniel, Tobit, Esther, and others. But this story contains little hint of the danger of being with foreigners that you see in the older tales.

- ✔ **The "conversion" of Asenath may say a lot about mixing with foreigners.** There's a considerable debate among historians as to whether the conversion means that this tale actually attempts to argue for the acceptance of foreigners as legitimate wives (under certain spiritual conditions). If so, then it's literature that very much goes against the grain of a general antipathy about mixing with foreigners that is evidenced in *most* of the literature from the Greco-Roman period of Jewish society (circa 333 BCE–300 CE).

Moreover, scholars debate whether the initial prayer of Joseph over Asenath, praying for her to be among the chosen ones, was from an actual prayer tradition over non-Jews. There's no proof of this practice, but it seems like something that could apply in situations other than just this story.

Life of Adam and Eve

This first-century CE "expansion" of the biblical story of Adam and Eve from Genesis has survived in two rather different versions. One has more apocalyptic-like elements than the other, but they both follow the same general lines. In this section, we summarize the general story line of both surviving versions.

As the story opens, Adam and Eve are hungry, having been expelled from the famous Garden where they never had to worry about food. In their desperation, Adam tells Eve that they must beg God to either let them back in or at least let them have some food. They decide to go about begging God in a very strange manner: Adam will go to the River Jordan and Eve will go to the River Tigris (in modern Iraq), and they'll stand up to their necks in the water and fast and pray. Soon, fish and marine animals gather with them, and they actually stop up the rivers' flow!

Satan, however, tricks Eve into breaking her fast by pretending to be an angel of God who has heard her prayers. When Satan is confronted by Adam for tricking Eve "once again" (the tradition that the snake in the Garden was actually Satan is a late tradition that does *not* appear in the original biblical story of Genesis but appears in the late Jewish work, the *Wisdom of Solomon*), Satan explains why he's so angry with them: Satan's original refusal to honor God's creation of humans led to his expulsion from heaven. ***Note:*** A somewhat different version of Satan's expulsion is provided in the older and more famous 1 Enoch (see Chapter 6).

After Adam and Eve recover from this initial deception, the rest of the narrative describes how they come to accept the reality of pain and death. In a poignant scene, the sons of Adam gather around their dying father demanding to know what pain and death are — after all, nobody has died yet! Before he dies, Adam is taken into heaven and given a number of revelations, which he's allowed to tell to his son Seth (who was born to replace the murdered Abel).

Because this writing doesn't contain an extended discussion of what Adam was told in heaven, the book isn't really a full apocalyptic-like writing — and readers are left wondering if something is missing. What is certainly the case, however, is that later Jewish and Christian mystical movements centered their traditions on Seth, who became famous for insights and knowledge, and this tale may be among the ancient stories that tried to explain the importance and significance of Seth. After all, this writing does suggest that Adam left important writings in Seth's care.

Additional Psalms from the Dead Sea Scrolls

Among the materials found in the Dead Sea Scrolls (see Chapter 5) were scrolls that included some additional Psalms.

The Bible has 150 Psalms, but the Scrolls provided the famous "151–155" Psalms. For the most part these Psalms, dated to between the third century BCE and the first century CE, are explicitly based on stories of David and deal more directly with David than most of the biblical Psalms do. This fact suggests that they were written much later than the more familiar Psalms in the Bible, carefully drawing on the established traditions about David. Many of the biblical Psalms aren't nearly as specific as those found with the Scrolls, such as Psalm 152, which alludes to enemies as lions:

> *It is not sufficient for them to ambush my father's flocks;*
> *and to tear a sheep from his sheepfold?*
> *They are even wishing to slay me.*
> *Spare, O Lord, your elect one;*
> *and deliver your holy one from destruction . . .*

—Psalm 152:3–4

Psalm 154, however, has an interesting association with Wisdom Mystical teachings, such as the continued tradition of personifying wisdom as a woman (discussed in Chapter 3):

> *For to announce the glory of the Lord*
> *Wisdom has been given*
> *And to recount his many deeds,*
> *She was made known to humanity*
> *. . . From the utterances of the righteous ones is heard her voice;*
> *And from the congregation of the pious ones her song.*
>
> —Psalm 154:5–6, 154:12

It remains an open question why these Psalms weren't included in the Bible, although the best guess seems to be their late date. In other words, it's possible that they were written too late to make it in.

Psalms of Solomon

Another body of Psalms not included in the Bible is traditionally assigned to the famous son of David who became King after him, namely "Wise" King Solomon. Historians point out that these Psalms from the first century BCE seem to focus on the Jewish confrontation with the Romans in Palestine in the first century BCE. Pompey took over Palestine in about 64 BCE. Here's an excerpt from one of the so-called Solomonic Psalms:

> *The lawless one laid waste our land, so that no one inhabited it;*
> *They massacred young and old and children at the same time.*
> *In his blameless wrath he expelled them to the west*
> *And he did not spare even the officials of the country from ridicule*
> *As the enemy was a stranger*
> *And his heart alien to our God, he acted arrogantly*
>
> —Solomonic Psalm 17:11–13

There are 18 of these Solomonic Psalms, and thankfully historians have lots of manuscripts that have preserved them. The manuscripts date from the tenth to sixteenth centuries CE, but the Psalms are presumed to date much earlier, of course, and were written originally in either Hebrew or Greek.

Many of these Psalms of Solomon include themes of judgment and expulsion of foreigners or judgment of the foreigners. If you overlook this vindictive streak (especially given the historical circumstances involved), you can enjoy some genuinely beautiful lines that are very reminiscent of the more lyrical and evocative lines of the biblical Psalms. To be fair, the biblical Psalms also occasionally give in to some judgmental attitudes.

Prayer of Manasseh

According to the biblical history books 1–2 Kings, Manasseh, the son of Hezekiah, was one of the most evil and corrupt kings in all Jewish history. Many evil Kings are compared to him in the Bible, and he seems to have set the standard for despotic, pagan rule. Still, a tradition arose that Manasseh eventually repented of his evil deeds — and the *Prayer of Manasseh* is the prayer of that confession.

This prayer from the second century BCE to first century CE is found in many older Greek manuscripts but isn't considered a legitimate part of the older biblical traditions. It's widely noted that the Prayer borrows many lines from Psalm 51 and thus is pretty clearly a derived tradition. However, one could possibly argue that this prayer form is found in somewhat older biblical books; such "prayers of confession" became more widely used in the centuries after the destruction of Babylon in 587 BCE (see, for example, Daniel 9, Ezra 9, and Nehemiah 9), and this prayer shows some resemblance to that tradition.

It seems clear that the prayer arose because of concern on the part of latter readers that the Bible never "resolved" the issue of evil kings of ancient Israel. Thus, prayers of confession like the Prayer of Manasseh attempt to "clean up" some religious loose ends that are perceived in the biblical traditions.

I (coauthor Daniel) would suggest that such literary editing and additions made to the older tradition are entirely harmless, even if they come rather late in the game. The sentiment behind the prayers — that people come to see the error of their ways — obviously is rather nice and reassuring!

Testament Literature: Famous Last Words

The works covered in the following sections are all classified as *Testaments* because they all revolve around final speeches made to a man's family before he dies. The Bible seems to feature such monumental last words as a literary style of focusing on enduring messages left by famous people.

Although the Testaments contain a mix of material — including apocalyptic visits to heaven and hell — the major content is famous biblical characters' final statements made before they die. Think of them as a last will and testament.

The main precedent for this kind of writing, of course, is the book of Genesis; in chapters 49–50, Jacob gathers his 12 sons and offers a kind of prophetic word about each of them as he blesses them. You can also find a biblical precedent for this kind of practice in 1 Kings 2, when David talks to Solomon and begins by informing his son that he, David, is about to "go the way of all the earth . . ." and then offers important advice.

The following Testaments are therefore expansions of biblical material that in many cases carry the discussions and historical references down to the Greco-Roman period, which helps historians identify the approximate dates of the actual writing.

The Testaments of the Twelve Patriarchs

Unlike the book of Genesis, in the second-century BCE writing *Testaments of the Twelve Patriarchs,* each of the 12 sons of Jacob does the talking. Many of them begin with a confession of their particular sins and then provide advice to "my children" — the presumed readers of the Testaments.

One of the reasons that this particular writing was popular — and continues to be read with great appreciation — is the profound ethical advice that many of the brothers give to their children. The writing has a striking peacefulness at a time when violent events were rocking the Jewish communities (in the second century BCE through to the first century CE).

Starting with Reuben, the first of the twelve

The first of the confessors in *Testaments of the Twelve Patriarchs* is Reuben. Reuben confesses to sexual sin, and in the process of repenting of this sin, he comes to understand the "seven spirits of deceit." These are spirits aligned against humanity that are also given seven spirits of life. The idea seems to be that each positive spirit has a negative counterpart. The positive spirits are as follows:

- **The spirit of Life:** Humanity created as a composite being

- **The spirit of Seeing:** Which brings desire

- **The spirit of Hearing:** For instruction

- **The spirit of Smell:** From which comes taste and drawing breath

- **The spirit of Speech:** From which comes knowledge

- **The spirit of Taste:** From which comes consuming food and drink

- **The spirit of Procreation and intercourse:** From which could come sin from an overly strong fondness for pleasure

After noting an eighth spirit of Sleep, which appears somewhat neutral, Reuben lists these spirits of error:

- ✔ **The spirit of Promiscuity**
- ✔ **The spirit of Insatiability**
- ✔ **The spirit of Strife**
- ✔ **The spirit of Flattery and trickery**
- ✔ **The spirit of Arrogance**
- ✔ **The spirit of Lying**
- ✔ **The spirit of Injustice**

Hopefully you can clearly spot the beginnings of what will evolve into the seven deadly sins paradigm in later medieval thought, although there's also a tradition of "sin lists" that, at the time of the Testaments, had already begun in the New Wisdom Literature of the Bible. Consider this example:

> *There are six things that the Lord hates, seven that are an abomination to him: haughty eyes, a lying tongue, and hands that shed innocent blood, a heart that devises wicked plans, feet that hurry to run to evil, a lying witness who testifies falsely, and one who sows discord in a family. My child, keep your father's commandment, and do not forsake your mother's teaching."*

—Proverbs 6:16–20

More confessions from the remaining sons

Following Reuben, each son of Jacob discusses a particular sin or sins. Simeon, for example, confesses to deceit and envy of his younger brother, Joseph.

However, not all the sons discuss sins and results. Levi, for example, reveals aspects of the heavenly realms, including a description of what occurs in the three "layers" of heaven. There follows an extended discussion of Levi's descendants, who become the Priests of the Temple service in ancient Israel.

Of particular interest in this section on Levi is a "Priestly Messiah," a poetic description of a future Priest-King that may refer favorably to the Maccabean rulers (who also proclaimed themselves High Priests — much to the disgust of some aspects of the Israelite population in the second and first centuries BCE) or that may simply indicate yet another variety of "expectation" among pre-Christian Jewish movements.

The confessions of Zebulon include a recounting of his attempts to live a good life, offering food to the poor and care for the sick; he gives this advice based on his observations of life:

> *To the extent that a man has compassion on his neighbor, so that extent the Lord has mercy on him. For when we went down into Egypt, Joseph did not hold a grudge against us. When he saw me, he was moved with compassion. Whomever you see, do not harbor resentment, my children, love one another, and do not calculate the wrong done by each to his brothers. This shatters unity, and scatters all kinship, and stirs up the soul. He who recalls evil receives neither compassion nor mercy.*
>
> —Zebulon 8:3–6

Much of the sons' teaching seems to build toward a picture of Joseph, whose compassion on his brothers in Egypt (as recorded in Genesis) is seen as a model of patience and long-suffering nature. In fact, when you get to the Testament of Joseph, there's a section that suggests rather dramatically that Joseph's attempts to live a good life are parallel to the teachings of Jesus. Either this is a Christian insertion into the work or a rather dramatic anticipation of Jesus's teachings in Matthew 25:31–46. Consider Joseph's words:

> *I was taken into captivity: the strength of the Lord came to my aid*
> *I was overtaken by hunger — the Lord himself fed me generously*
> *I was alone — and God came to help me*
> *I was in weakness — and the Lord showed his concern for me*
> *I was in prison — and the Savior acted graciously on my behalf*
> *I was in bonds — and he loosed me . . .*
>
> —Joseph 1:5–7

Like that of the 11th son, Joseph, the final confession of Benjamin contains profound calls to peacefulness:

> *If your mind is set toward good, even evil men will be at peace with you; the dissolute will respect you and turn back to the good. The greedy will not only abstain from their passion but will give the oppressed the things which they covetously hold . . . for if anyone wantonly attacks a pious man, he repents, since the pious man shows mercy to the one who abused him, and maintains silence . . .*
>
> —Benjamin 5

The Testament of Job

Job is one of the most perplexing books of the Old Testament. The *Testament of Job*, a work from the first century BCE to first century CE, purports to be about a non-Jew named Job. In the Testament, God and Satan make a wager to see how loyal Job will remain if his life is made miserable. Satan doesn't believe that Job will continue to praise God if Job has nothing to be thankful for.

The entire biblical book of Job consists mostly of conversations between the suffering Job and his "friends" who come to discuss his situation with him; each one advises Job in a different way, and none of them believe that Job is really innocent of sin. The book appears to be a frank reflection on suffering in this life and is also famous for featuring some of the most striking poetry in the Bible.

The Testament of Job, however, is an expansion on the biblical material. Even though the discussion of Job's losses is very brief in the Bible, in the Testament, it's the subject of considerable attention. Job's piety and his widely known generosity to the poor are expressed in great detail, and this is followed by a detailed ledger sheet of his losses (for example, Satan destroyed "7,000 sheep . . . 3,000 camels . . . 500 donkeys . . . 500 oxen") as well as more details on the death of his family.

The Testament elaborates on the biblical story and occasionally stops to tell a "back story" explaining why the biblical text reads the way it does. Among these unusual stories is the story of three "sashes," or pieces of cloth, that God gives Job, who then gives them to his daughters to perform miraculous feats such as speaking in heavenly languages. Finally, the Testament describes Job's own death.

Other than glorifying Job's deeds for the poor and his generosity before Satan's intervention, there seems little in this writing that is particularly memorable or rewarding other than a few entertaining tales only awkwardly related to the older tradition surrounding the biblical book of Job.

The Testaments of the Three Patriarchs

Clearly, Testament literature is a popular literary form used to sum up the important wisdom of life in order to pass it on to the next generation. It's natural, then, that writers would assign "last testaments" to other famous people in the Bible as well — as the *Testament of the Three Patriarchs* does with famous characters from Genesis. However, the odd thing about these three sections is that the famous people are rather apprehensive about their deaths and even try to postpone their final hour!

In each of the three testaments, Michael the archangel is sent to the famous earthly person to explain that he's about to die and that Michael is there to take away his spirit and bring him to heaven.

The Testament of Abraham

As the *Testament of Abraham* begins, God sends Michael to fetch the spirit of Abraham because it's time for Abraham to die. As in the famous scene in Genesis 18 when heavenly visitors come to see Abraham, here Abraham doesn't seem to understand at first why Michael has come to visit. Michael returns to heaven to protest to God that he just can't take Abraham's spirit because old Abraham is such a righteous man!

God and Michael hatch a plot to plant a dream in Abraham's son Isaac's sleep about his father's death so that when Isaac describes his dream to his father, Abraham will come to understand that it's finally his time.

The rest of the Testament of Abraham essentially consists of Abraham asking questions of Michael, attempting to stall his death until he gets a number of questions answered. Abraham wants to see the heavens and to understand more about the judgments against humanity. Michael (and God) agrees to these requests, and Abraham is taken up into the heavens to be shown the glories of heaven and the judgments prepared for human beings.

Along the way, Abraham sees human beings in the very acts of sinning, including fighting with swords, engaging in sexual immorality, and thieves breaking into a house to steal from it. In each case, Abraham demands that the sinners be punished, and Michael agrees. But God becomes concerned with Abraham's overzealous attitude toward the punishment of sinners:

> . . . *Abraham has not sinned and he has no mercy on sinners. But I made the world, and I do not want to destroy any one of them, but I delay the death of the sinner until he should convert and live . . .*

> —Testament of Abraham 75

Abraham is shown how the judgment of God attempts to draw people away from their sins. This writing seems to include a criticism of other Jewish writings that are too zealous about punishment, and it calls for more compassion than even Abraham managed to exhibit.

Abraham also asks Michael about the understanding of evil. So death himself comes to visit Abraham, but what Abraham sees is a handsome man dressed in colorful robes! Eventually, Abraham figures out who this is and demands that he show himself as he truly is. There follows a frightening description that includes:

- Seven fiery heads
- A lion
- A cobra
- A serpent
- The face of swords
- Storm-tossed seas
- Poisons
- Every disease known to humans

After a discussion about the nature of death and the fact that people are destined to die in different ways, death promises life and strength to Abraham if Abraham kisses his hand. Thus Abraham is deceived by death, and immediately Abraham's spirit is taken from his body. The book ends with the mourning of his family.

The Testament of Isaac

This second-century CE work, which is the second installment of the *Testaments of Three Patriarchs,* begins like the *Testament of Abraham* (see the previous section) except that there's no "bargaining" with Michael that leads to extended discussions about death, the nature of judgment, and the heavens. The *Testament of Isaac* is more ethical in its teachings, including an extended passage about Isaac's advice to his children. Among the ethical injunctions advised to his child Jacob, Isaac advises:

> *. . . continue to supplicate God with repentance for your past sins, and do not commit more sin. Accordingly, do not kill with the sword, do not kill with the tongue, do not fornicate with your body, and do not remain angry until sunset. Do not let yourself receive unjustified praise, and do not rejoice at the fall of your enemies or of your brothers. Do not blaspheme; beware of slander. Do not look at a woman with a lustful eye . . .*

> —Testament of Isaac 4:49–54

After a lengthy ethical speech, Isaac (like Abraham) is taken up into heaven and allowed to see the judgments against sinners. Some of these visions are very strange, such as the person being eaten by lions over and over again. When Isaac asks why this person is suffering in this way, he's told that the man was angry with his brother for hours and died before he could be reconciled to him.

Eventually, Isaac meets Abraham, who gives him further spiritual advice, and then Isaac briefly returns to earth to say a final goodbye to his son Jacob, after which Isaac dies. At the end of this work is a recognition that these stories are to be read on a special day of the year. This detail probably applies to the entire work of the Testaments of the Three Patriarchs, not only the material dealing with Isaac.

The Testament of Jacob

This roughly second- to third-century CE work seems to complete the three works, identified in some modern collections of non-biblical writings as *Testaments of Three Patriarchs.*

The *Testament of Jacob* features Jacob commenting on the future of the Israelite peoples. It also includes ethical advice for his descendants. Scholars generally think that this writing doesn't add a significant amount to the material covered in the testaments of Abraham and Isaac.

In the Testament of Jacob, an angel appears to Jacob and explains that it's the same angel who has been protecting Jacob throughout his life (referring to episodes noted in the biblical story of Jacob in Genesis). An interesting difference between this work and the testaments of Abraham and Isaac is that this work frequently advises its readers to consult the books of the Bible for more information. But, like the others, it features a list of sins to avoid and ethical practices and spiritual practices to maintain.

The Testament of Moses

The *Testament of Moses* is a first-century CE work that purports to be a word of advice and prophecy given to Joshua, the successor of Moses in the Israelite story of the Exodus and conquest of the land of Canaan.

But in this Testament, Moses informs Joshua of the unfortunate events in the future of Israel, including the sins of the people leading to the destruction of the Temple and the events of the Maccabees and their taking over the Temple in Jerusalem. This writing appears to contain serious hostility toward the Maccabean family, a point which has led many scholars to wonder if this work is to be associated with the Dead Sea community, which also held deep animosity toward the Temple officials who descended from the Maccabean conquerors of Jerusalem.

Chapter 6 of the Testament of Moses contains a description that many historians presume to be a description of Herod the Great and his overcoming of the Hasmonean (Maccabean) dynasties between 37 BCE and 4 CE:

> *Then powerful kings will rise over them, and they will be called priests of the Most High God. They will perform great impiety in the Holy of Holies. And a wanton king, who will not be of a priestly family, will follow them. He will be a man rash and perverse, and he will judge them as they deserve. He will shatter their leaders with the sword . . .*

> —Testament of Moses 6

Joshua is overcome with grief at knowing that Moses is soon to die, but Moses continues to encourage him despite the warnings of unfortunate developments in the future. This work is a word of hope for the righteous: Despite the coming problems, they will flourish!

The Testament of Solomon

The first- to third-century CE *Testament of Solomon* is one of the most enter-taining and strange writings that we survey in this chapter. This work is at once shocking and entertaining: It reveals that there was a large Jewish population (and a Christian population) who maintained a very detailed and deeply held belief about magical amulets and warding off demons. It also reveals that this population felt that it was very important to have highly technical and detailed information about the precise names of the demons and the precise names of the angels used to ward off the power of the demons.

The setting and context of this book is the great building of the Temple in Jerusalem. As you know from the biblical history, although David has the notion to build a Temple in Jerusalem for the God of Israel, David isn't able to carry out his plan. Solomon, his son, is the one chosen for the task. This writing, however, elaborates an entire series of legends about the construction of the Temple.

As the story begins, you're introduced to a Temple construction worker whose son (also working on the Temple, it seems) is plagued by a demon who is not only stealing the wages of his work but is also literally sucking the life out of the boy (out of his thumb!) every night. When this situation comes to the attention of King Solomon, the King gives the boy a magic ring with powers over demons. When the demon shows up, the boy throws the ring at the demon and demands that he go to King Solomon himself! The demon is com-pelled to go, and this is where the story gets interesting.

King Solomon demands to know the name of the demon, who is "Ornias." Ornias explains not only his name but also the zodiac sign he resides in (this is another indication of Jewish interest in astrology at this early date). As King Solomon is about to punish Ornias with forced labor, Ornias begs for mercy, whereupon Solomon demands to meet the King of Demons himself! Using the magic ring, "Beelzeboul" (similar to the name in Matthew 10:25) is brought to Solomon.

For the next few chapters, Solomon forces the King of Demons to call up indi-vidual demons one by one. The demons are forced to explain who they are and which heavenly angels have power over them. In each case, a heavenly angel is named, suggesting that this writing may have been partially intended to provide a guide for the making of magical amulets against particular evils. What's truly fascinating, however, is that each time a demon is controlled by Solomon, he then puts the demon to work on some portion of the Temple — cutting stones, making ropes, cutting wood, and so on. Here's a brief example of this enslavement of a demon using a kind of magical action:

Finally, I asked him, "By what name are you thwarted?" He responded, "The name of the archangel Azael." Then I placed my seal on the demon and commanded him to pick up stones and hurl them up to the heights of the Temple for the workmen . . .

—Testament of Solomon 7:7–8

One "giveaway" explanation for all the technical names in this work comes in Chapter 13, when one of the demons named Obyzouth, who causes babies to die in birth, admits that he's resisted by people writing the name of the Archangel Raphael on ". . . a piece of papyrus and I shall flee from them to the other world!" In fact, in Chapter 15, Solomon explains that he's writing this work so that, after his death, his descendants will know how to exert power over demons.

Sadly, at the end of the Testament of Solomon, Solomon succumbs to his passion for a woman who insists that he offer sacrifices to her gods or she won't marry him. Because of this sin, Solomon confesses that God's spirit departed from him, and he warns his readers that he's leaving this information for those who would "find grace forever."

Part III

Lost Books about Jesus

The 5th Wave

By Rich Tennant

"Deciphering the lost books of the Bible must have been difficult, but the late fee must have been astronomical."

In this part . . .

This part proves that Jews definitely didn't have all the fun in the ancient world. When it came to writings about Jesus, the earliest Christians had their books that they trusted and revered (the four canonical Gospels), but they also knew about a number of writings that were probably intended to be pious entertainment and a few that were downright unsettling. In this part, you discover that some early Christian writings about Jesus seemed to be inspired by sheer curiosity, approaching questions like "What happened to Jesus as a young man?" and "Did Jesus say much outside of the four Gospels?" Ask a question often enough, and somebody comes up with some creative answers . . . and you find that some of the early Christian writings about Jesus are nothing if not creative!

Chapter 10

Ancient Writings on the Youth and Infancy of Jesus

. . . .

. . . .

Most modern Christians don't realize that the birth of Jesus held little importance in earliest Christianity compared to the Resurrection — as evident from the fact that the infancy of Jesus is dealt with so briefly in the New Testament. Most of the charming tales and traditions about Christ's birth and infancy arose much later — beginning in the second century but expanding exponentially as people became more interested in the subject.

For the study of the Infancy Gospels of Jesus, we turn to a marvelous resource produced by the noted New Testament and Apocrypha scholar, J. K. Elliott. He has actually categorized all the major Infancy Gospels into "synopsis form" so that you can follow the general outline of each work, comparing each section as he moves along. This is a tremendous resource for study, and it indicates the major episodes of most of these writings. In other words, most of these works have some version of the traditions listed in the next section.

What's Covered in the Infancy Gospels and Why

What follows is the list of Infancy Gospel categories created by J. K. Elliott. This organizational structure has become the standard arrangement in biblical scholarship regarding the Infancy Gospels:

✔ Mary's birth and upbringing

✔ The Annunciation

✔ Mary visits Elizabeth

- ✔ Mary's pregnancy and its explanation
- ✔ The birth of Jesus
- ✔ The Adoration of Jesus
- ✔ The presentation at the Temple
- ✔ The Magi (whom you may know as the "Wise Men")
- ✔ The slaying of the infants and the flight to Egypt
- ✔ Jesus as a child

There are no real surprises here. In fact, this list is pretty close to what one might formulate by using the Infancy stories in the two Gospels that feature birth narratives: Luke and Matthew.

Most historians believe that these additional writings, the Infancy Gospels, arose from the sheer curiosity of the early Christians and their persistent question, "What was Jesus like as a youth?" This interest seems hardly surprising given that people tend to be curious about the backgrounds of major personalities from more *recent* history. So, could you suppose that perusing the Infancy Gospels is like reading a second-century *People* magazine? Perhaps, but with a considerable amount of religious piety added in, to be sure! These writings were intended to encourage faith, not make fraudulent claims.

Take care not to think like a modern when evaluating what amounts to religious folklore. Some folklore is intended to be *very* pious and devotional and is expressed with exaggerated claims that often aren't historical, although intended with positive motives!

Primary Sources about the Infant Jesus

There are two basic sources for info about the infant Jesus. The *Proto-Evangelium of James* and the *Infancy Gospel of Thomas* (not to be confused with the *Gospel of Thomas,* a different work that we cover in Chapter 11) are the two oldest of the Infancy Gospels. Others were written that add new episodes or ideas, but they largely draw on the two older writings as sources.

Over 150 Greek texts of the Proto-Evangelium of James are on record, showing that it was widely read and appreciated. It's dated sometime in the second century CE. Similarly, the Infancy Gospel of Thomas is also dated to roughly the second century CE.

Some very important ideas, especially in Roman Catholic and Orthodox piety surrounding Mary, can be traced to the influence of these writings. A key example is the Immaculate Conception of Mary, which refers to the belief in these later traditions that Mary was born without original sin and had an extraordinarily "pure" life (pure meaning "no sex").

The Proto-Evangelium of James

The notion of a "Proto-Evangel" literally means "*before* the Good News." These are events that are purported to take place before the events covered by the biblical Gospels. As such, the *Proto-Evangelium of James* sets up the Gospel stories with additional information about the characters in the early years of Jesus but also introduces characters that will turn up later. This is a classic example of early Christians being *so* curious about some of the familiar characters of the Gospel story that they wanted what we *now* call in the movie biz a "prequel" to the story as well as the many "sequels" that were written about events *after* the Gospel stories.

Note that all the information supplied in the Proto-Evangelium takes place *before* you actually find out about Jesus himself, and most of the writing is about the supporting characters in the story.

Episode one: Mary is born

The Proto-Evangelium of James begins with a sad scene as Joachim, the father of Mary, appears to offer gifts at the Temple in Jerusalem. An official stops Joachim and says that it isn't proper for a man who hasn't contributed a child to Israel to offer gifts ahead of those who have. This insult saddens Joachim, and after checking to be sure that indeed most of the major figures of Israelite history have had children, he retires to the wilderness to fast for 40 days and nights.

Meanwhile, his wife Anna is also lamenting her childless state. Outside under a laurel tree, Anna sings a song of lament to God, praying that she, like Sarah in the Old Testament, might still be given a child. Immediately an angel appears to announce that Anna will have a child and that two other angels have also told Joachim, who is already preparing to make a huge sacrifice from his flocks for a celebration. When he returns from his fast, Anna meets him in great joy, and they rest that night.

Joachim's gift at the Temple is accepted, and soon Anna gives birth to a female child and names her Mary. As soon as Mary can walk, Anna makes a pact with God that Mary will be dedicated to God at the Temple and be cared for by Hebrew virgins. Mary's first birthday is celebrated with great joy, and the Priests bless Mary:

> *O God of the heavenly heights, look upon this child and bless her with a supreme blessing which cannot be superseded.*
>
> —Proto-Evangelium of James 6:2 (tr. Elliott)

Upon Mary's third birthday, Joachim and Anna fulfill their promise to God that Mary will serve in the Temple, and she's taken there. The people at the Temple are amazed that a 3-year-old is so willing to stay at the Temple:

And her parents returned marveling, praising the Lord God because the child did not turn back. And Mary was in the Temple of the Lord nurtured like a dove and received food from the hand of an angel.

—Proto-Evangelium of James 8:1–2 (tr. Elliott)

Episode two: Joseph is chosen as Mary's husband

This episode is quite interesting. The Priests at the Temple decide that Mary must leave the Temple as she approaches age 12 because if she were to begin menstruating while at the Temple, the Temple would become unclean. So, they search throughout Judea to find an appropriate husband for her. A miraculous sign chooses Joseph, who in this writing already has sons and is an older man. At first, he protests that he will be a laughingstock for marrying a young girl! But the Priests advise him to obey God's selection, so Mary is taken into Joseph's house as a ward. Meanwhile, Joseph goes on a building campaign (he is, you recall, a carpenter).

Episode three: Mary weaves the veil that will be torn

A clever episode is inserted here. The Priests of the Temple determine to have a veil made for the Holy of Holies in the Temple, and they find seven virgins to weave and make this sacred cloth. They remember Mary and choose her to do part of the work. This is the same veil, of course, that's miraculously torn at the crucifixion of Jesus, so this episode has some clever foreshadowing.

Episodes four and five: Behold, a virgin shall conceive . . .

Episode four is the announcement by an angel to Mary that she is to give birth to Jesus. This episode doesn't seriously diverge from the New Testament accounts in Luke, and episode five, in which Mary's cousin Elizabeth (mother of John the Baptist) visits with Mary, is even shorter than the account in Luke.

As Mary starts to show her pregnancy, the Proto-Evangelium elaborates on something that readers of the New Testament have wondered about for centuries: Surely there was a serious reaction from Joseph! This writing deals with the issue in a big way:

And he struck his face, threw himself down on the ground on sackcloth and wept bitterly saying, "With what countenance shall I look towards the Lord my God? What prayer shall I offer for this maiden? For I received her as a virgin out of the Temple of the Lord my God and have not protected her. Who has deceived me? Who has done this evil in my house and defiled the virgin? Had the story of Adam been repeated in me? For as Adam was absent in the hour of his prayer, and the serpent came and found Eve alone and deceived her, so also has it happened to me!"

—Proto-Evangelium of James 13 (tr. Elliott)

Joseph asks Mary why she has done this. Joseph is perplexed: If he doesn't reveal the truth to the religious authorities, he fears that he's sinning, but if he turns Mary over to the authorities (Priests, or local elders), she will die. He decides to try to spirit her away quietly. However, in time, she's discovered, and the Priests demand to know why Joseph has violated Mary and consummated a marriage with her — a marriage that hasn't taken place as yet! They both plead innocence, but of course no one believes them. The Priest puts them through an ordeal of drinking a special potion that reveals guilt, and they both survive, indicating innocence (this scene is similar to the ritual in Numbers 5). The Priest honors the results of the test and sends Joseph and Mary home.

The time for the birth approaches, and like in the New Testament story (Luke 2:1), Joseph must go and register his family. Along the way, Joseph sees Mary first sad and then laughing because she has had a vision of one group of people weeping and another group rejoicing. Soon, Joseph finds a cave where Mary can give birth.

In one version of the tradition, Joseph sees a vision of everything in heaven coming to a stop — heavenly rivers stopped, heavenly animals stopped, workmen stopped — all apparently in awe of the approaching birth. A midwife happens to walk by, and Joseph sends her to Mary in the cave. After a bright light, Jesus is born and begins to feed at Mary's breast. The midwife, however, doesn't believe that a virginal birth is possible, and she tells Mary to prepare for her to test with her finger. When the midwife does this, she cries out: "Woe for my wickedness and unbelief; for I have tempted the living God!" *(Proto-Evangelium of James 20)*. Her hands are immediately stricken, and an angel tells her to touch the child and be healed.

The appearance of the Wise Men follows rather closely to the account in the Gospel of Matthew.

Episode six: Zacharias, John the Baptist's father, is martyred

The Proto-Evangelium adds an entirely new and final episode with regard to King Herod seeking the child John (Jesus's cousin, the future "Baptizer"). Elizabeth and the child are miraculously hidden in a mountain with an angel, but John's father Zacharias, who is a Priest in the Temple, faces Herod's anger. Herod has him slain, and Zacharias's blood stains the Temple. Eventually, the Priests choose another Priest, Simeon, to replace Zacharias. Simeon eventually appears in the New Testament in Luke's account of Jesus's birth.

The Proto-Evangelium concludes with a brief note claiming that James has written the account.

The Infancy Gospel of Thomas: A mischievous young Jesus

The *Infancy Gospel of Thomas* has gained some notoriety precisely because of the unexpected way in which the young boy Jesus is portrayed as a rather mischievous prankster whose pranks are more dangerous because of his miraculous powers! Many people have heard of one or two of the stories featured here, but it's important to get the whole story, because the point of the writing seems to be the maturing of Jesus, which you can only grasp from reading the entire work. It was hardly intended to be a blasphemous work, but those who only know an episode or two may think differently!

Episode one: Bringing clay sparrows to life

The Infancy Gospel of Thomas begins when Jesus is 5 years old. The first episode involves Jesus playing in mud (sounds right for a 5-year-old) and making clay sparrows. But it's Sabbath, and someone tells Joseph that his son is profaning the Sabbath by making things. When Jesus is confronted, he claps his hands and the clay sparrows turn to real birds and fly away.

Episode two: The young Jesus kills a playmate

In the second episode, Jesus gathers pools of water, and the son of Annas the Scribe disperses the pools with a stick. The young Jesus is angry:

> *You insolent, godless ignoramus! What harm did the pools and the water do to you? Behold, now you also shall wither like a tree and shall bear neither leaves nor root nor fruit!*

> —Infancy Gospel of Thomas 3:2 (tr. Elliott, 76)

The boy dies immediately, and his parents yell at Joseph: "What kind of child do you have, who does such things?" What kind indeed! Another child bumps Jesus, and he too is struck dead by the child Jesus. Parents begin to complain to Joseph to control his kid. When Joseph confronts Jesus, Jesus strikes the other children's parents blind! Fed up, Joseph takes Jesus by the ear to scold him — whereupon Jesus protests at being treated this way.

However, a man called Zacchaeus overhears the exchange between Jesus and Joseph and is impressed with how Jesus can speak; he asks Joseph if he can tutor the clever boy. Zacchaeus starts with the Greek alphabet, but after a time, Jesus asks the teacher about the first two letters, Alpha and Beta:

> *How do you, who do not know the Alpha according to its nature, teach others the Beta? Hypocrite, first if you know it, teach the Alpha, and then we shall believe you concerning the Beta.*

> —Infancy Gospel of Thomas 6:3-4 (tr. Elliott, 77)

This excerpt suggests a Gnostic quality to this writing, especially in the sneering attitude toward those who are considered ill-informed. Further, it's a strange saying, suggesting that most people don't understand truth beyond simple basics, and an all-knowing young Jesus almost ridicules people for not knowing these deeper truths. Zacchaeus begs Joseph to take Jesus back because the tutor can't handle Jesus or understand what Jesus has been saying: ". . . Whatever great thing he is, a god or an angel I do not know what I should say . . ." *(Infancy Gospel of Thomas 7:4)*. Then Jesus laughs and talks about his calling:

> *Now let those who are yours bear fruit, and let the blind in heart see. I have come from above to curse them and to call them to things above, as he who sent me ordained for your sakes. . .*

—Infancy Gospel of Thomas 8:1

Note the clear Gnostic hints: the nasty laughter, the idea of "being sent" from the higher God of light, and the notion of coming to teach rather than act.

Episode three: The young Jesus resurrects a playmate

This episode has Jesus playing on an upper story of a house. The boy playing with Jesus falls and dies, and Jesus is accused of killing yet another child. But Jesus asks the dead child, "Arise — and tell me, did I throw you down?" *(The Infancy Gospel of Thomas 9)*. The child rises to life and tells everyone that he wasn't pushed. From this time on, the miracles that Jesus performs are somewhat more positive than in earlier episodes, but not entirely. For example, Jesus heals a man who accidentally chops into his foot while chopping wood, he makes corn grow so abundantly that everyone in the village shares the extra food, and he also stretches a piece of wood that Joseph has cut too short for a project.

At age 8, Joseph tries another teacher. But when Jesus answers this teacher, the teacher slaps Jesus, and Jesus strikes him dead. When a third teacher tries to teach Jesus, he immediately recognizes Jesus's wisdom and allows Jesus to teach instead. When Joseph comes to check on his son, the third teacher tells Joseph to take Jesus because he already knows what he needs to know. Jesus is pleased with the third teacher and to honor him raises to life the second teacher who was stricken.

Jesus performs a series of miracles — raising a dead child and a dead worker to life to the amazement of all. Finally, one of the traditions of this writing ends with Jesus, at age 12, teaching the elders in the Temple (following the biblical tradition you see in Luke and from artist Heinrich Hofmann's rendering in Figure 10-1). It's likely that this episode in the actual Gospel of Luke inspired some of the ideas further developed in somewhat controversial ways in the Infancy Gospel of Thomas. It's worth remembering this interesting tradition in Luke in order to see how a line or two may have led to further development of the "youth of Jesus" folklore explored in writings like the Infancy Gospel of Thomas. Here's the passage from Luke:

And when he was twelve years old, they went up as usual for the festival. When the festival was ended and they started to return, the boy Jesus stayed behind in Jerusalem, but his parents did not know it. Assuming that he was in the group of travelers, they went a day's journey. Then they started to look for him among their relatives and friends. When they did not find him, they returned to Jerusalem to search for him. After three days they found him in the Temple, sitting among the teachers, listening to them and asking them questions. And all who heard him were amazed at his understanding and his answers. When his parents saw him they were astonished; and his mother said to him, "Child, why have you treated us like this? Look, your father and I have been searching for you in great anxiety." He said to them, "Why were you searching for me? Did you not know that I must be in my Father's house?" But they did not understand what he said to them. Then he went down with them and came to Nazareth, and was obedient to them. His mother treasured all these things in her heart. And Jesus increased in wisdom and in years, and in divine and human favor.

—Luke 2:42–52

Figure 10-1:
Jesus as a child teaching the elders in the temple.

Bildarchiv Preussischer Kulturbesitz / Art Resource, NY

The idea of Jesus not behaving entirely as expected toward his parents may have inspired the authors to push this idea farther in the Infancy Gospel of Thomas. But what you should notice is that Jesus moves from youthful prankster to more mature healer and miracle worker at age 12. The goal of this Infancy Gospel is to magnify the maturing of Jesus into a full realization of his relationships to human beings — less judge and more loving.

Professor J. K. Elliott, one of the modern experts on non-canonical Christian literature, points out that the Infancy Gospel of Thomas is really misnamed because it doesn't deal with the birth of Jesus at all, but his early boyhood! Furthermore, no part of the text actually claims to be written by a "Thomas"!

Secondary Infancy Gospels

Well, one good idea deserves another, right? It seems clear that the Infancy Gospel of Thomas, although interesting in many ways, was also offensive to many early Christian readers and thus spun off into "sequels" or even different versions! The next few writings appear to be elaborations of the Thomas-type stories.

The Gospel of Pseudo-Matthew: Taking the older works a step farther

The Gospel of Pseudo-Matthew, which Professor Elliott and others date to the sixth century CE, is considerably later than the two major writings covered earlier in this chapter, but this document made many of the traditions in the older works known throughout medieval Europe.

In other words, Pseudo-Matthew ("pseudo" means there's no concrete evidence as to who the actual author was) was more widely known than the older writings the Proto-Evangelium of James and the Infancy Gospel of Thomas. Pseudo-Matthew passes on many of the traditions from those writings, but it also adds considerably to the traditions about Mary. Some suggest that it was written to promote the piety about and the traditions of veneration of Mary in the early and middle medieval Christian traditions.

Emphasis on Mary's piety

The earliest divergence from the older traditions is the lengthy descriptions of Mary's youth in the Temple. At length, Pseudo-Matthew describes Mary's piety, her time spent in prayer, and the fact that she greeted everyone with "Thanks be to God" (and the writing notes that she started the tradition of using this greeting among Christians). When the Priests tell Mary that it's time for her to marry and bear children and that this is acceptable in the Israelite tradition, Mary answers in terms that suggest her continued devotion to sexual purity — which will not be violated, of course, by a "virgin birth":

> It cannot be that I should know a man, or that a man should know me. . . . God is first of all worshipped in chastity. For before Abel there was none righteous among men, and he by his offerings pleased God, and was without mercy slain by him who displeased him. Two crowns, therefore, he received — of oblation and of virginity, because in his flesh there was no pollution . . .

> —Gospel of Pseudo-Matthew 6–7 (tr. Elliott, Synopsis, 16)

Pseudo-Matthew then follows the Proto-Evangelium of James closely up to the point when Mary is given to Joseph, but Pseudo-Matthew also adds the detail that Joseph was away for over nine months working before he returned to his home to find Mary pregnant. The detail, obviously, serves to further protect the reputations of Mary *and* Joseph!

The ritual of the test in the Temple

Pseudo-Matthew elaborates on the Temple ritual of drinking the mixture ordered by the Priest to reveal guilt. After drinking the potion, the ritual includes circling the altar seven times. Joseph survives the test, indicating innocence, and then attention is on Mary; the Priests presume that she must be guilty if Joseph is innocent. Everyone is astonished when she also circles the altar seven times and survives, insisting on her innocence.

The addition of these ritual actions to the story suggests ritual performances, and it's possible to see in these later writings the beginnings of *liturgical drama,* which led to many forms of Passion plays and biblical-based medieval dramas in Southern European churches.

The examination of Mary after Jesus's birth

The next major scene in Pseudo-Matthew elaborates on the examination of Mary immediately after the birth of Jesus. In the older tradition, only one woman examines Mary, and her hands are crippled as a result. In Pseudo-Matthew, however, more midwives are involved in the birth, and the first one who examines Mary is amazed and praises God. But the second midwife doesn't believe her and also requests to examine Mary. She's stricken, apparently as a result of her doubts. But like the older tradition, the stricken midwife is healed by worshipping the child.

The Holy Family's journey to Egypt

The major sections in which Pseudo-Matthew adds a great amount of material are in the journey of the Holy Family to Egypt to escape the persecutions of Herod. Even on the road in the opening paragraphs of these additional stories, you get an idea of the folkloric (or better, "piously legendary") nature of this material. When they pass some caves, the traveling party (which has picked up some companions along the way) is terrorized by dragons:

> *Then Mary put Jesus down and even though he was not yet two years old he stood on his feet before the dragons, which worshipped Jesus before departing. This fulfilled the prophecy of the Psalmist, which says, "Praise the Lord from the earth, ye dragons; ye dragons, and all ye deeps." Jesus walked before the dragons, commanding them to hurt no one. However, Mary and Joseph were very much afraid that the dragons should hurt the child. Jesus said to them, "Do not be afraid, and do not consider me to be a little child; for I am and always have been perfect; and all the beasts of the forest are tame before me."*

> —Gospel of Pseudo-Matthew 18-24 (tr. Elliott, Synopsis, 113)

This interesting passage clearly draws from Psalm 148:7: "Praise the Lord from the earth, you sea monsters and all deeps. . . ." The passage probably refers to legendary sea monsters believed to exist by many of the peoples surrounding the ancient Israelites. This may be a kind of taunt from the ancient Israelites against those beliefs. However, the tradition merges with medieval belief in dragons of a different sort!

According to Pseudo-Matthew many animals accompanied the travelers, to the delight of the young Jesus. Also, when they stop at an oasis, Jesus makes the palm trees bend over to make it easy to pick fruit and uproot from their roots a source of water. Finally, Jesus makes the long journey much shorter.

When they arrive in Egypt, the party comes to a pagan Temple with many idols of gods. When Mary and the child enter the Temple, all the idols bow in submission to Jesus and then shatter. When a local official approaches with his army, the priests of the Temple fear that the family will be killed. But the officer says that the idols would not have bowed if Jesus weren't God of Gods and King of Kings, and he honors the child Jesus.

Jesus as a youth

Pseudo-Matthew picks up with significant additional material in the story again after the return from Egypt and begins to follow the traditions of the Infancy Gospel of Thomas (refer to that section earlier in this chapter to find out more about these traditions). In Pseudo-Matthew, however, the first boy who's struck dead for messing with Jesus's pools of water is eventually brought back to life after Mary pleads with Jesus. Furthermore, the boy who nudges Jesus (presented as intentional bullying in Pseudo-Matthew) is also healed after Mary and Joseph plead with Jesus. However, Pseudo-Matthew also makes a stronger appeal about the nastiness of those who interfered with Jesus even as a boy — suggesting that they were no angels! The Infancy Gospel of Thomas doesn't mention this, and it's clear that the later writer of Pseudo-Matthew wants to present Jesus in a somewhat more flattering light in these stories.

Pseudo-Matthew also elaborates heavily on the exchanges between Jesus and his proposed teachers. In this version, the teachers are more malevolent, there's a bit less esoteric mystery, and there's still a discussion of Alpha and Beta. In the end, Jesus is presented in a more positive (and less mysterious) light than he is in the Infancy Gospel of Thomas; for example, his laughter is joyful instead of the laughter of one reviling stupid people:

> *Jesus, smiling . . . with a joyful countenance, said in a commanding voice to all the sons of Israel standing by and hearing, "Let the unfruitful bring forth fruit, and the blind see, and the lame walk right, and poor enjoy the good things of this life, and the dead live, and each may return to his original state, and abide in him who is the root of life and perpetual sweetness." And when the child Jesus had said this, forthwith all who had fallen under malignant diseases were restored. And they did not dare to say anything more to him . . .*

—Gospel of Pseudo-Matthew 30–31 (tr. Elliott, Synopsis, 148)

Pseudo-Matthew finishes with two charming stories: one episode in which the young Jesus plays with a lioness and her cubs to the astonishment of everyone who watches (". . . they recognize who I am, why don't you?"), and another episode in which Jesus assists Joseph in healing an older man who was sick and died. At this point, Pseudo-Matthew seems to lead into a discussion of the ministry of Jesus, probably intending to be followed by readings from the New Testament Gospels.

The Arabic Infancy Gospel

The *Arabic Infancy Gospel* is another collection of early Jesus legends, based heavily on the Proto-Evangelium of James and the Infancy Gospel of Thomas (both of which we cover earlier in this chapter). This work is likely to be fifth century at the earliest and is often thought to be based on an origin work written in Syriac (an early Semitic language related to Hebrew and Aramaic) and coming from Christian traditions of the East. Eastern Christians (in Syria and farther east) used Syriac heavily from the second century CE onwards, and Christian historians and theologians to this day study the rich tradition in Syriac.

A considerable amount of the material that's unique to the Arabic Infancy Gospel focuses on the Holy Family in Egypt. Also, the work adds more miracles to the journey through Egypt, with a series of visits to different towns and a new miracle in each town. The miracles include:

- ✔ Healing a bride who couldn't speak
- ✔ Driving demons from a young women
- ✔ Scaring away robbers with miraculous sounds of many people
- ✔ Driving away a serpent who had tormented an important woman in another village

In one of these longer, more elaborate stories, a princess cries privately until companions of the Holy Family find her and ask what's wrong. She explains that after a long time, she finally provided a son to the Prince, but the child was stricken with leprosy and the father wanted nothing to do with him. The companions of the Holy Family arrange to take water used to wash the child Jesus and pour it over the princess's son, who's instantly healed to great joy and celebration.

Finally, when Mary and Jesus are traveling, two robbers in hiding discuss whether to attack them. One of the robbers begs to leave them alone, but the other refuses. Mary overhears the conversation and blesses the good robber, named Titus, for trying to do a good work. Although they're prevented from doing Mary and Jesus any harm, the young Jesus identifies the men as the two robbers who will eventually be crucified on either side of Jesus, and Jesus will forgive Titus for having tried to do the right thing years earlier.

We can't conclude our survey of the Arabic Infancy Gospel without mentioning one more charming miracle story from the youth of Jesus. In the story, Jesus is playing with some children near the dye works of a man named Salem. When cloth accidentally spills into a vat of dye and everything is colored indigo, Salem is angry that his work is ruined. The young Jesus, however, offers to change the colors of the cloth, and as Salem calls out a color, Jesus draws out cloth from the indigo vat that's miraculously colored the very color that Salem asks for!

Other infancy traditions of later vintage

Christian history beyond the fourth century CE knows many more infancy traditions that contain even more elaborations on the earlier traditions. Surveys include such writings as

- ✔ The Arundel Manuscript: A Latin text that may go back to the fourth to fifth centuries CE and contains a few additional traditions but mostly testifies to the Latin traditions that became more widely known in the West

- ✔ The History of Joseph the Carpenter: A text that's narrated by Jesus in the first person and adds a tradition about the death of Joseph

- ✔ Later materials that show that these traditions arrived in Ireland very early (perhaps in the seventh century CE) and were subject to copying and additional development there (for example, the three Wise Men are called "Druids" in one version)

Most of these tales of the birth of Jesus and the boyhood of Jesus are rather innocent, at times quite entertaining, and even occasionally quite moving.

In some places, however, these traditional stories are taken quite seriously as stories of faith. Among the Coptic Orthodox churches of Egypt, for example, Egyptian Christians have journeyed an entire "itinerary" of the travels of the Holy Family as a kind of spiritual pilgrimage for centuries, with travelers celebrating the specific miracles at each stop along the way. An American writer recently wrote about his experiences following this old traditional path in modern Egypt, and it's a wonderful read; we recommend that you check out *Jesus in Egypt: Discovering the Secrets of Christ's Childhood Years,* by Paul Perry (Ballantine Books).

Chapter 11

Lost Gospels and Sayings of Jesus

● ●

In This Chapter

▶ Finding the lost sayings of Jesus

▶ Identifying Jesus's sayings in early Christian literature

▶ Reviewing the major "other" gospels

● ●

*J*esus spoke. And according to some ancient "lost books," he spoke words that didn't end up in the Bible as you know it. Sometimes, these sayings are found in quotations from early Christian writers. In other cases, they're ancient fragments of texts that mention a saying or two of Jesus. Finally, however, there's an entire collection called the *Gospel of Thomas* that has dozens of sayings claimed to be from Jesus.

In this chapter, we examine some of these traditions about Jesus that circulated from the first to third centuries CE — the first "Christian" centuries. In some cases, you see that these writings represent a kind of sequel to known sayings of Jesus from the Gospels, but in other cases, intriguing sayings are quoted that seem reasonably similar to the Jesus known from the Gospels. And, if it *looks* like his words and *sounds* like his words . . . well, then maybe it *is* his words! You come to find out, however, that this discussion can get understandably controversial when dealing with Jesus, the central figure in the largest religion in the world.

With the intriguing exception of the *Gospel of Thomas,* virtually all the writings discussed in this chapter are *derivative* — that is, they're clearly based on knowledge of the older, canonical gospels. They don't add significant information on the historical Jesus. Thomas, however, is treated as a special case because it may contain a few genuine sayings; but without any narrative description of Jesus, and because Thomas includes some obviously Gnostic forgeries as well, it's easy to see why the work was also excluded from the Bible.

Sources for Lost Sayings of Jesus

Many "sayings" of Jesus don't appear in the canonical Gospels you know (Matthew, Mark, Luke, and John). In fact, some of the most famous sayings of Jesus *are* in the New Testament but *aren't* in the Gospels! Consider the following well-known quotation of Jesus cited in the *Book of Acts* but unknown in the four Gospels:

> *In everything I did, I showed you that by this kind of hard work we must help the weak, remembering the words the Lord Jesus himself said: "It is more blessed to give than to receive."*
>
> —Acts 20:35

Fair enough — but what about sayings that are completely outside the New Testament? Plenty of those exist, too, and we have three main "sources" for these kinds of sayings. This section walks you through each one.

First source: Works by later Christian writers

Many such sayings of Jesus are quoted by later Christian writers, including

- Origen
- Tertullian
- Jerome
- Clement of Alexandria

Many other writers from the second to fifth centuries CE and beyond also quote sayings of Jesus. Sometimes it's difficult to know what they're quoting — a book, an oral saying, or someone they heard — but historians have tried (and keep trying) to sort this out. You can understand the difficulty if someone just says, "It is said. . . ." Does that mean the source is oral or written? You get the idea.

Second source: Small fragments of papyrus

Other sayings of Jesus are noted in small fragments of papyrus (the main writing material in ancient Egypt and elsewhere) located mainly in Egypt (because papyrus lasts longer in the dry heat there, especially if it's buried).

Sometimes these fragments of texts are large enough to read many lines; other times, unfortunately, scholars can hardly read anything at all on the fragments.

Third source: Complete writings that have survived

Some of the lost sayings of Jesus have survived as complete (or very nearly complete) writings, such as the Gospel of Thomas (as opposed to the *Infancy Gospel of Thomas,* a quite different writing that we examine in Chapter 10) or the shorter *Gospel of Judas.* Although historians often refer to these as "books," they're usually collections of papyrus pages or parchment (animal skins made into pages).

Did Jesus Really Say That? Separating False from Genuine

Different Gospels (writings about Jesus) were written for different reasons, and each Gospel writer decided to include things that the writer thought was important. Matthew, for example, includes episodes that remind his reader of the history of Israel and the life of Moses. Only Matthew has the family of Jesus fleeing to Egypt, thus reproducing aspects of the history of Israel. Only Matthew has Jesus deliver his famous "sermon on a mount" — thus reminding his readers of Moses on Sinai. On the other hand, only John shares the famous "farewell speeches" of Jesus, such as John 17, where Jesus expresses serious concern about the safety and well-being of the disciples after Jesus leaves them.

The point of this is to say that *all* the Gospels have a perspective on Jesus. The problem, however, is that some of the perspectives taken by some early Christians were considered to be in error — or outright heresies — in the judgment of the "orthodox" Christian movement (that is, the movement that eventually became the main interpretation of the Christian faith). These writings were accused of misrepresenting Jesus and, even worse, were sometimes accused of literally making up sayings of Jesus to back up their own religious ideas. Thus scholars are faced with the problem of misrepresenting, or even making up, Jesus quotations.

Understand that misrepresentation and fabrication are two different things. In some cases, a saying of Jesus may be more or less accurate but is quoted in a misleading way. In other cases, the saying is an outright fabrication.

Sometimes it's easy to tell the difference between misquotings and fabrications, but not always. If you know the general ideas of a religious challenge to early Christianity (like Gnosticism), it's easier to identify a misrepresentation or even a fabrication. For example, even though the present form of the Gospel of Thomas (discussed later in this chapter) is clearly a product of Gnostic Christians who were pressing their own Gnostic agenda, *some* of the quoted sayings may be genuine sayings from early traditions about Jesus.

Sayings of Jesus Quoted in Early Christian Literature

As we discuss earlier in this chapter, many sayings of Jesus were cited by early Christian writers. Sometimes, these writers were quoting these sayings with approval — they liked them and used them to support an argument. Because we aren't terribly concerned here with those arguments, we simply cite some of the supposed quotations from Jesus that they use.

But in many other cases, these early Christian writers were attacking writings that they thought were false, and they quoted passages to show how they should be dismissed or avoided! In many cases, these early Christian writers cite writings that are no longer available. Yes, many of them are truly "lost." Maybe someday someone will find a copy of the *Gospel of the Ebionites* or the *Gospel of the Hebrews,* works that are quoted from by early Christian writers. That will be an exciting day, and then we can decide for ourselves if the quotes are fair representations of these "lost Gospels."

Quotations from the Jewish-Christian gospels

Jewish-Christians were a group of early Christians who were Jews and who taught that Christians should still maintain a strong tie to Jewish tradition and practice. A number of gospels discussed in early Christian writings are assumed to have been written by these Jewish-Christians, although, sadly, none of the writings themselves are in possession today. However, they're cited by early Christian writers who occasionally include actual quotes.

It's assumed that the gospels were written by Jewish-Christians because of these strong suggestions of maintaining Jewish traditions and the positive statements made about Jewish traditions. For example, strong statements honoring the Mosaic Law and a strong sense of social responsibility to fellow believers have a very positive and very Jewish emphasis as opposed to strictly spiritual discussions.

A further problem is whether all the different titles mentioned in early Christian writings are actually different books — or different titles for some of the same writings. Gospel of Nazarenes? Gospel of Hebrews? Gospel of Ebionites? Are they *all* different?

The following titles are mentioned in early Christian writings and are believed to come from the Jewish-Christians.

The Gospel According to the Hebrews

The lost *Gospel According to the Hebrews* is specifically cited by early Christian writers such as:

- Clement (150–circa 216), an early Christian philosopher in Alexandria

- Origen (185–254), one of the most famous early Christian philosophers in Alexandria

- Jerome (331–420), a translator of Scripture into Latin who was therefore familiar with many early texts, including many that historians don't have now

- Eusebius (263–339), an early Christian historian who has provided a great deal of information about events and texts circulating among early Christians

Jerome cites the following saying of Jesus quoted in this gospel: "Never be glad unless you are in charity with your brother." What's notable about this is it mandates a social concern for taking care of each other — a principle that seems typical of Jewish ethical concern that goes right back to the Mosaic law (Deuteronomy 15:4, 15:8, 15:11, and so on)! In fact, it sounds like it comes from Jesus precisely because Jesus often speaks of this kind of compassion for your "brothers and sisters." Not surprising for a Jewish teacher, of course.

A second, longer quotation from the Gospel According to the Hebrews is even more interesting because it highlights the importance of James in the Jewish-Christian tradition. James was revered as a pious Jew as well as a Christian leader of the Church in Jerusalem, so it's hardly surprising that a reputed Jewish-Christian gospel features a resurrection appearance to James that doesn't receive attention in the four canonical Gospels:

> *Now the Lord, when he had given the cloth to the servant of the priest, went to James and appeared to him. For James had taken an oath that we would not eat bread from that hour on which he had drunk the cup of the Lord till he saw him risen from the dead. Again a little later the Lord said, "Bring a table and bread," and forthwith it is added: "He took bread and blessed and broke it and gave to James the Just and said to him, 'My brother, eat your bread, for the Son of Man is risen from those who sleep . . .'"*

> —Jerome, de Viris Illustribus, 2

Jerome quotes this same Gospel of the Hebrews with another very Jewish-sounding ethical teaching of Jesus:

> In the Gospel of the Hebrews which the Nazarenes are in the habit of reading it belongs to the greatest sins when "one afflicts the spirit of his brother."

—Jerome, On Ephesians

The Gospel of the Nazareans

Origen also cites from what he calls a *Gospel according to the Hebrews,* which exhibits characteristics similar to the social and ethical emphasis of Jewish Mosaic Law as well as positive statements about Jewish faith and tradition. It's often suggested that this is the same work that in other early citations is referred to as the *Gospel of the Nazareans.*

Origen cites this Gospel of the Nazareans, which he says contains the following fascinating expansion of a Gospel saying, most of which is familiar from the known Gospels, except for the final sentence:

> Another rich man said to him, "Master, what good things shall I do to live?" He said to him, "O man, fulfill the law and the prophets." He replied, "I have done that." He said to him, "Go, sell all that you possess and distribute it to the poor, and come, follow me." But the rich man began to scratch his head and it did not please him. And the Lord said to him, "How can you say, 'I have fulfilled the law and the prophets' since it is written in the law: You shall love your neighbor as yourself, and lo! Many of your brethren, sons of Abraham, are clothed in filth, dying of hunger, and your house is full of many goods, and nothing at all goes out of it to them." And returning to Simon, his disciple, who was sitting by him, he said, "Simon, son of Jonas, it is easier for a camel to enter the eye of a needle than for a rich man (to enter) the kingdom of heaven."

—Origen, On Matthew

According to Matthew 19, Jesus did say something very much like this, but when you compare the two verses, you see that in the saying from the Gospel of the Nazareans, Jesus goes into much greater detail about the social expectations of what it means for people to share with each other and take responsibility for each other. Furthermore, there's also the unique and interesting reference to your brothers, "sons of Abraham," a phrase that Jesus never uses in the known Gospels. In short, the saying from the Gospel of the Nazareans presumes a unique emphasis on concern for fellow Jews that's to be expected in a Jewish-Christian gospel.

The Gospel of the Ebionites

The word "ebionites" comes from the Hebrew word for "poor or needy" (Deuteronomy 15:4, 15:7, 15:9, and 15:11) and may have been adopted as a name from the saying of Jesus, "Blessed are the poor," or Jesus's otherwise generally favorable comments toward the poor.

The term is typically associated with a group of Jewish-Christians known as *Ebionites.* Many of the quotations from the *Gospel of the Ebionites* are simply rearrangements of known canonical material, but there also are some striking and unknown sayings, such as the following that's quoted by the early Christian writer Epiphanius (320–403 CE):

> *I have come to abolish the sacrifices: if you do not cease from sacrificing, the wrath of God will not cease from weighing upon you . . .*

> —Epiphanius, Against Heresies

This saying is a striking attack on the ritual of sacrifice but may not be entirely foreign to a group of Jews for whom the sacrificial system has been corrupted, or even stopped, by the "sacrifice" of Jesus. It furthermore appears that the Ebionites were vegetarian, having rejected not only the sacrifice but also consumption of meat entirely.

Quotations from other gospel traditions

Some of the unusual early gospels reflect the ideas or odd notions of a particular sect or group quite different from the mainstream Christian movement. They wrote their own versions of the teachings of Jesus in order to justify those beliefs. Although the gospels show great diversity in early Christianity, sometimes they're downright surprising in their strange versions of Jesus! When you come across quotes that sound strange, they were sometimes quoted by early Christian writers to prove that they're *not* genuine sayings!

The Gospel of the Egyptians

The *Gospel of the Egyptians* is a writing that seems to have been used to promote the views of a small group of Christians who completely ceased to believe in marriage and sexuality. (They must have been a fun bunch, eh?) Clement of Alexandria, who had little sympathy for this group, quoted their writings where they claim that Jesus was opposed to marriage and giving birth:

> *For they say: the Saviour himself said, "I have come to undo the works of the female," by the female meaning lust, and by the works — birth and decay.*

> —Clement, Stromateis ("Miscellanies")

Such a saying has so little in common with what's known of Jesus and of Jewish tradition and its praise of marriage that it seems a clear example of a fabricated word to defend a particular religious idea — specifically, celibacy.

The Gospel of Matthias

It was Clement who identified the late-second-century CE writing the *Gospel of Matthias* as a Gnostic writing, although some modern historians aren't so sure if Clement was right. However, if the following is an authentic quotation from this source, it certainly sounds like the typically anti-physical, "against the body" bias of the Gnostics:

> . . . *Matthias also taught thus: that we should fight with the flesh and abuse it, not yielding to it at all for licentious pleasure, but should make the soul grow by faith and knowledge . . .*
>
> —Clement, Stromateis

On the other hand, Clement cites another saying from this same source that sounds somewhat different in orientation, although it could be interpreted to mean some kind of sexual sin or activity, in which case it would be very much in the spirit of the previous quote:

> *They say that in the Traditions, Matthias the apostle always states, "If the neighbor of a chosen one sin, the chosen one has sinned: for had he behaved himself as the world enjoins, the neighbor also would have been ashamed of his way of life, so as not to sin."*
>
> —Clement, Stromateis

Fragments of Jesus Sayings: Pieces of Unknown Gospels?

In his recent translation of a series of fragments of Jesus sayings, Professor J. K. Elliott, one of the most important scholars of non-canonical Christian literature, includes the *Oxyrhynchus* fragments found in 1905 (they're named for an ancient Egyptian town about 100 miles south and west of modern Cairo) and other fragments named for places or persons who first identified them or even the wealthy benefactors who donated to museums (like the *Egerton Papyri*, which we cover in a later section). These fragments are normally dated late second century CE and as late as the fifth century.

In the following section, we discuss some of these fragments.

Such fragments are usually identified by the place they were found and by a number to identify the particular fragment (because there are sometimes *hundreds* of little fragments!).

Oxyrhynchus 840

Oxyrhynchus 840 is the name given to a tiny fragment containing an interesting piece written in very small letters, apparently so that it could be rolled up and worn as an amulet inside some kind of casing.

In this long quotation, Jesus and his disciples are confronted by a Pharisee and Priest who challenge Jesus as he walks in the Temple. He's apparently not supposed to be walking in a place of purity in an unclean state. Jesus responds and engages in a polemical conversation:

> . . . *Thereupon the Saviour stood with his disciples and answered him: "Are you then clean, here in the temple as you are?" He said, "I am clean, for I have bathed in the pool of David and have gone down by one staircase and come up by the other, and I have put on clean white clothes. Then I came and viewed the holy vessels." "Alas," said the Saviour, "you blind men who cannot see! You have washed in this running water, in which dogs and pigs have wallowed night and day, and you have washed and scrubbed your outer skin which harlots and flute-girls also anoint and wash and scrub, beautifying themselves for the lusts of men while inwardly they are filled with scorpions and unrighteousness of every kind. But my disciples and I, whom you charge with not having bathed, have bathed ourselves in the living water which comes down from heaven . . ."*
>
> —Oxyrhynchus 840

When you compare this excerpt to Matthew 23:25–27, the saying from Oxyrhynchus 840 seems rather close to many of Jesus's own teachings about purity regulations (which Jesus often took issue with):

> *Woe to you, scribes and Pharisees, hypocrites! For you clean the outside of the cup and of the plate, but inside they are full of greed and self-indulgence. You blind Pharisee! First clean the inside of the cup, so that the outside also may become clean. Woe to you, scribes and Pharisees, hypocrites! For you are like whitewashed tombs, which on the outside look beautiful, but inside they are full of the bones of the dead and of all kinds of filth.*
>
> —Matthew 23:25–27

Oxyrhynchus 1224

Other fragments, such as *Oxyrhynchus 1224,* seem to be variations on known Gospel traditions. In the following excerpt, the brackets indicate presumed words filled in by Professor Elliott in his translation:

And the scribes and [Pharisees]
And priests, when they saw him
Were angry [that with]
Sinners in the midst he [reclined]
At table. But Jesus heard [it and said:]
The healthy do not need [the physician] . . .

—Oxyrhynchus 1224

Compare this excerpt to a passage from the Gospel of Matthew:

And as he sat at dinner in the house, many tax collectors and sinners came and were sitting with him and his disciples. When the Pharisees saw this, they said to his disciples, "Why does your teacher eat with tax collectors and sinners?" But when he heard this, he said, "Those who are well have no need of a physician, but those who are sick. Go and learn what this means, 'I desire mercy, not sacrifice.' For I have come to call not the righteous but sinners."

—Matthew 9:10–13

As you can see, the Oxyrhynchus 1224 selection is quite close to the known Gospel tradition, suggesting that different *versions* of sayings of Jesus were also circulating among early Christians.

The Egerton Papyri

In 1934, an Egyptian antiquities dealer sold a series of second-century CE papyrus fragments to the British Museum. The source of these celebrated documents, called the *Egerton Papyri,* is unknown.

The collection is generally dated between 100 and 150 CE and thus is one of the oldest fragments of Jesus writings in possession. It doesn't appear to have any Gnostic tendencies, although historians continue to debate that point. The Egerton Papyri contains a number of fascinating portions, including the following debate between Jesus and other Jewish scholars:

. . . And Jesus said to the lawyers: "Punish every wrongdoer and transgressor, and not me . . ."

Then, turning to the rulers of the people he said this word: "Search the scriptures, in which you think you have life. It is they which bear witness to me. Do not suppose that I have come to accuse you to my father. There is one who accuses you: Moses, in whom you have hoped."

And they said: "We know that God spoke to Moses, but as for you, we do not know, where you are from."

Jesus answered and said to them: "Now your unbelief is exposed to the one who was witnessed to by him. If you had believed [in Moses] you would have believed me, because he wrote to your fathers about me . . ."

—Egerton Papyri

The Egerton Papyri also records an unknown miracle:

"Why is the seed enclosed in the ground, the abundance buried? Hidden for a short time, it will be immeasurable." And when they were perplexed at the strange question, Jesus, as he walked, stood on the banks of the River Jordan, and stretching out his right hand, he filled it with seed and sowed it upon the ground. And thereupon he poured sufficient water over it. And looking at the ground before them, the fruit appeared . . .

—Egerton Papyri

Whole Writings That Contain Sayings of Jesus

When it comes to sayings of Jesus, fragments are just the beginning. Longer works also exist, and it's presumed that most if not all of these writings are in possession. Of course, these are among the most spectacular writings about Jesus from early Christianity precisely because of their size and the amount of material. Don't forget, however, that the fragments we consider in this chapter (especially Egerton) are important because they're *old.* The complete writings — namely the *Gospel of Thomas* and the *Gospel of Judas* — are available in versions that aren't nearly as old as the fragments. Both of these writings, however, are clearly Gnostic in spirit. Note that the Gospel of Judas is much more deeply Gnostic than the more famous Gospel of Thomas.

The Gospel of Thomas

Although in Chapter 12 we talk about the Gnostic writings found in 1945 in Egypt at Nag Hammadi, we cover the second-century CE *Gospel of Thomas* in this chapter because it's perhaps the most important fuller writing about Jesus that's in possession outside of the biblical Gospels and because references to Thomas are made even outside the Nag Hammadi Library.

The Gospel of Thomas gets scholars' and historians' juices flowing for a number of reasons:

- It's a lengthy work and therefore lends itself to serious study.

- It consists mostly of 114 sayings of Jesus with very little narrative description of the life of Jesus (as is found in the canonical Gospels).

For decades, scholars have proposed that Matthew and Luke must have used a collection of sayings of Jesus when they wrote their Gospels because so many sayings of Jesus are the same word for word in both Gospels. Many historians doubted that such a document (called "Q" for the German word "quelle," or in English, "source") could have existed . . . until the Gospel of Thomas was found! *Note:* We aren't saying that Thomas *is* "Q." In fact, *nobody* is saying that. However, the very existence of an early collection of sayings of Jesus like Thomas suggests that writings like this did exist, and thus the possibility of "Q" is more likely.

- Many New Testament scholars believe that *some* of these sayings of Jesus may well be genuine because of the work's age. Origen was already talking about a Gospel of Thomas in the second century CE! Just because they ended up in a collection with other sayings that probably *aren't* genuine doesn't mean the whole collection is worthless.

So, how do you tell the difference between the genuine sayings and the fabricated ones? Now there's a question for the scholars to argue about for years and years . . . and years. Determining which sayings are authentic is tricky business, of course, so two common criteria are applied to sayings-in-question:

- Does it *sound* like Jesus based on things Jesus taught?

- Does it *sound* like other things Jesus actually said?

The following sections discuss passages that obviously don't meet these criteria, passages that do, and passages that meet one but not the other.

Passages that are strange enough to obviously not be from Jesus

In some cases, it's easy to tell that a saying is just made up. Consider the following examples from the Gospel of Thomas:

> Jesus said, "Blessed is the lion which the man shall eat, so that the lion will become man; and cursed is the man whom the lion shall eat, and the lion will become man."
>
> —Gospel of Thomas, Saying 7

> The disciples said to Jesus, "Tell us which way our end will occur?" Jesus said, "Have you indeed discovered the beginning, that you search for the end? In the place where the beginning is, there the end will be. Blessed is he who will stand at the beginning: he will know the end and he will not taste death."
>
> —Gospel of Thomas, Saying 18

> *Jesus saw some infants being suckled. He said to his disciples, "These children who are being suckled are like those who enter the kingdom." They said to him, "If we are children shall we enter the kingdom?" Jesus said to them, "When you make the two one, and when you make the inner as the outer and the outer as the inner and the upper as the lower, and when you make the male and female into a single one, so that the male is not male and the female is not female, when you make eyes in place of an eye, and a hand in place of a hand, and a foot in place of a foot, an image in place of an image, then you shall enter the kingdom . . ."*
>
> —Gospel of Thomas, Saying 22

Um, what was that again? Does the lion thing have something to do with the persecution of Christians — with them being fed to lions in the Roman Circus? And what the heck does "discovering the beginning" mean? And that last one, Saying 22, is a real conundrum . . . and quite frankly, we don't buy for a minute that Jesus said *any* of these things!

Saying 7, about the lion and man, seems to make very little sense, and that's not typical of Jesus, who always explained his images rather well. The other sayings are also just plain too cryptic — but they *are* typical of the Gnostic movement's love of strange and puzzling images. Because he taught simple folk most of the time, Jesus was rarely this cryptic and unclear.

Sayings that sound like canonical Gospels and are probably genuine

Some of the sayings in Thomas, however, are very much like what is found in the canonical Gospels. For example, this saying from Thomas expresses much the same idea as the verse from Luke:

> *Jesus said, "Those who seek should not stop seeking until they find . . ."*
>
> —Gospel of Thomas, Saying 2

> *So I say to you, Ask, and it will be given you; search, and you will find; knock, and the door will be opened for you.*
>
> —Luke 11:9

Other sayings from the Gospel of Thomas are slightly different versions of well-known parables in the canonical Gospels. In the case of the story of the Sower, some New Testament scholars wonder if Thomas preserves a more original form of the story that traces to Jesus himself:

> *Look, the Sower went out, took a handful [of seeds], and scattered [them]. Some fell on the road, and the birds came and gathered them. Others fell on rock, and they did not take root in the soil and did not produce heads of grain. Others fell on thorns and they choked the seeds and worms ate them. And others fell on good soil, and it produced a good crop: it yielded sixty per measure and one hundred twenty per measure . . .*
>
> —Gospel of Thomas, Saying 9

If we were to ask what a Gnostic gospel's interest would be in a genuine saying of this kind, the answer is fairly straightforward: The Gnostics wanted to differentiate between the people who truly understood Jesus's message (namely, the Gnostics!) and those who did not. So, even if it were genuine, any saying that could be bent or interpreted toward the Gnostic frame of reference could still serve a purpose!

Passages that sound like Jesus but have no parallel in the canonical Gospels

Some passages in the Gospel of Thomas have *no* parallel in the canonical Gospels but sound very much like something Jesus would say.

Here's a fascinating example: a parable about the Kingdom of God being unintended goodness. In the canonical Gospels, Jesus speaks about doing righteousness even if nobody is watching; this seems to be the idea behind the following story from Thomas:

> *Jesus said, "The Father's imperial rule is like a woman who was carrying a [jar] full of meal. While she was walking along a distant road, the handle of the jar broke and the meal spilled behind her [along] the road. She didn't know it; she hadn't noticed a problem. When she reached her house, she put the jar down and discovered that it was empty."*

> —Gospel of Thomas, Saying 97

Now, the fact that the meaning of this parable is a bit hard to work out doesn't necessarily mean that Jesus didn't say it. It may well simply refer to the idea that people should live their lives so that they're surprised by unusual things happening as opposed to expecting unusual things or even living a good life just for the rewards!

Consider a very unusual parable-like saying attributed to Jesus in the Gospel of Thomas:

> *The Father's Imperial rule is like a person who wanted to kill someone powerful. While still at home he drew his sword and thrust it into the wall to find out whether his hand would go in. Then he killed the powerful one.*

> —Gospel of Thomas, Saying 98

Frankly, the violence of this image is shocking and isn't at all consistent with the nonviolent teachings of Jesus. But it's a parable — not an ethical example. Jesus isn't advocating violence but rather is advocating taking preparations and being ready for a task.

So, at first, you may be tempted to reject this saying. But think again: this particular story uses a startling example, which, of course, is *very much* in character with Jesus. After all, Jesus uses serpents as a positive example, contrary to Hebrew tradition (see Matthew 10:16, ". . . be wise as serpents . . ."), and he speaks of servants being killed and cities destroyed as part of a parable (see Matthew 22:1–7). Along these lines, then, many New Testament scholars wonder if Saying 98 — without parallel in the canonical New Testament — is nonetheless genuine.

The Gospel of Judas

The announcement of the discovery of the *Gospel of Judas* has generated a flurry of interest over the past ten years. *National Geographic* sponsored a major media event about this writing, complete with extensive publicity, a television special, and books. However, the initial thrill has calmed down rather significantly.

A number of people suggested that this was a "genuine" work, a genuine gospel, and lots of people believed that *the* Judas is the one who wrote it. Same name and all, right? Has to be him, right? Wrong.

The historical Judas did *not* write the Gospel of Judas. This document is actually a Gnostic writing from (probably) no earlier than the late second century CE, and perhaps even later. As a Gnostic work, therefore, it has a great deal in common with the Nag Hammadi manuscripts that are the subject of Chapter 12, but because it was found apart from the Nag Hammadi collection and released only recently to public attention, we choose to briefly talk about it in this chapter on early non-canonical traditions about Jesus.

This short work, the publication of which had all the intrigue of a modern mystery novel, finally came to light in 2005 after a long series of secretive negotiations and meetings. The actual contents of the book hardly justify such excitement — the Gospel of Judas is a rather typical example of Gnostic spirituality.

A typical Gnostic tract

The Gospel of Judas features many of the common traits of Gnostic Christianity, including

- The notion that the Jewish God is a lower and somewhat malevolent god compared to the "higher god" of Light who originally sent Jesus
- The rejection of the material world, including the significance of human bodies

In keeping with these themes, the Gospel of Judas portrays Jesus as laughing at the notion of the Eucharist! The meal, as an expression of the material presence of God in the world, is depicted as honoring the wrong God — the material God rather than the spiritual God of Light. This further suggests some material connection in the Gnostics' minds between the Eucharist, the world, and God.

Furthermore, the Gospel of Judas highlights the Gnostic sense of elite knowledge. Jesus rather crudely taunts the disciples: "Do you think you know me?" Note the emphasis on knowledge; they *think* they know, but they do not. Not surprisingly, the disciples react with some indignation at this abuse from Jesus; note that their anger is seen in the Gospel of Judas as itself an indication of "lower understanding."

Judas, the Jesus "insider"

In the Gospel of Judas, Jesus shows special treatment to Judas and privately reveals information to him. Again, the theme of secrecy and privileged information is typically Gnostic. In this gospel, the information given to Judas is a series of meditations on the nature of the heavens and somewhat obscure notions that are quite typical of the kind of esoteric, symbolic, and opaque "spirituality" found in the Nag Hammadi texts (see Chapter 12).

Of particular interest is a series of "teachings" about the nature of God as the first, ungenerated ground of all existence and how everything that exists is in some form derived from God's existence, either negatively by ignoring or disobeying this god or positively as an emanation from this god. However, this information seems a somewhat awkward addition to the story of Jesus, the disciples, and Judas — an opportunity, if you will, to splice in Gnostic ideas.

In the end, astonishingly, Jesus praises Judas for betraying Jesus because Judas's act finally allows Jesus to be rid of his earthly prison — his earthly body:

> But you [Judas] will excel all of them. For you will sacrifice the man that clothes me . . .
>
> —Gospel of Judas

Physical death leads to spiritual life, so Judas is a hero!

A serious reading of the Gospel of Judas is difficult because it seems altogether taunting and abusive of Christian orthodoxy in its attempt to take the ultimate "villain" in Christian tradition, Judas, and make of him a laudable, heroic figure. The writing seems almost calculated to enrage non-Gnostic Christians. While many historians argue that the Gospel of Judas is a pious work by a Gnostic writer that reveals a very positive attitude toward Jesus, the depiction of Jesus, much less Judas, is also rather disturbing.

Consider this example: In ancient manuscripts, laughter is rarely the reaction to harmless amusement or enjoyment; rather, it's typically a sign of ridicule (consider Daniel laughing at Nebuchadnezzar in the story of Bel in the Deutero-Canonical version of Daniel). To have Jesus ridiculing the twelve disciples with malicious laughter is difficult to reconcile with a respectful attitude!

The Gospel of Peter

The *Gospel of Peter* is an elaborate resurrection account referred to by Origen in the second century and Eusebius in the fourth century. The actual document, however, wasn't discovered until 1886 in Egypt.

This second- or third-century CE work is virulently anti-Jewish and similar to attitudes seen in early Christian writings like the *Epistle of Barnabas* (see Chapter 14 for more on this work). This gospel transfers the blame for the death of Jesus from the Romans (who were, after all, the ones really responsible) to Jewish opposition to Jesus.

The Gospel of Peter portrays the Resurrection of Jesus in grand fashion. This text actually provides a description of how two angels sent down from God opened the tomb of Jesus and how the soldiers guarding the tomb saw it all. At that point, things start to get a bit strange:

> . . . *[the soldiers] saw three men come out from the sepulcher, two of them supporting the other and a cross following them and the heads of the two reaching to heaven, but that of him who was being led reached beyond the heavens. And they heard a voice out of the heavens crying, "Have you preached to those who sleep?" and from the cross there was heard the answer, "Yes."*

> —Gospel of Peter 10 (tr. Elliott, 156–157)

To recap, the angels brought Jesus out of his tomb, but their heads extended up into the sky (not sure how that works, but anyway) . . . and a walking wooden cross followed behind them and spoke. Right. We think it's fair to say that the Christians who are aware of this text are thrilled that this "gospel" wasn't taken seriously . . . but it does raise interesting questions as to why an early Christian writer thought that this was important information.

The idea of the talking cross has especially fascinated modern scholars, who wonder what this image is intended to communicate. Is a talking cross symbolic of the death of Jesus as part of a cosmic plan, so that even the wooden cross "knows" what's happening? Does it suggest later traditions of a cross being a site of an early Christian Oracle like the ancient Delphi Oracle? Symbolic scenes, however, figure prominently in some Gnostic circles and certainly in apocalyptic visions, so either tradition could have influenced this presentation.

In the mid-19th century, in the Mayan-populated area of the Yucatan Peninsula, a group of Mayan peasants who rebelled against their European overlords believed that they were led by God through a "talking cross" who spurred on the revolutionaries. There's no evidence that the ancient Christian Gospel of Peter could have possibly influenced the Mayan phenomenon, but more than one reference to a talking cross certainly is an interesting coincidence, isn't it?

It's highly unlikely that the Gospel of Peter adds anything to modern historical knowledge, but it certainly does add to the view of the variety of ideas circulating among early Christians. Thankfully, the nasty attitude toward the Jews that's represented in this writing wasn't made part of the New Testament.

The Gospel of Bartholomew (Or "You sure do ask a lot of questions, Bart!")

The fourth-century CE early Christian theologian and translator of the Bible, Jerome, mentions yet another gospel written under the name of another of the disciples of Jesus, a *Gospel of Bartholomew*.

In their study of early non-canonical gospels, scholars point out that no document under this name has survived, but the following available texts do feature the name "Bartholomew":

 ✔ Questions of Bartholomew
 ✔ Book of the Resurrection of Jesus Christ by Bartholomew the Apostle

There's no way of knowing if these other two writings have any connection with what Jerome calls the Gospel of Bartholomew.

Questions of Bartholomew

The *Questions of Bartholomew* writing is precisely that: The disciple Bartholomew asks Jesus a series of questions when the resurrected Jesus reappears to the disciples after his crucifixion.

It's easy to see why such Questions literature would arise: People had legitimate questions about specific interpretations of some of the sayings of Jesus.

Following are a few of the more interesting selections from this work.

Bartholomew asks Jesus about his disappearing on the cross

Questions of Bartholomew contains some wondrous accounts. In the first question, for example, Bartholomew tells Jesus that he watched the crucifixion from a distance and saw that Jesus actually disappeared from the cross for a while. Bartholomew wonders where he went! Jesus answers,

> *Blessed are you, Bartholomew, my beloved, because you saw this mystery, and now I will tell you all things whatsoever you ask me . . .*

—Questions of Bartholomew 1:8 (tr. Elliott, 655)

Jesus describes how he went into Hades to free Adam and other entrapped souls. (In other words, you may read this as a "reversal" of the curse of Adam's sin on humanity, a notion taken up by Paul in Romans 5:12.) Clearly, this task is an expansion of the famous tradition that Jesus "descended into hell" upon his physical death and did battle with Satan, and thus the Resurrection was not only his defeat of his own death but the defeat of Satan and death *in general*. These are themes already encountered in brief form in Paul's New Testament writings, but they're considerably expanded in the Questions of Bartholomew.

Particularly provocative is Jesus's comment that 30,000 people die every day. When Bartholomew asks how many of this number are righteous, Jesus sadly answers, "Hardly fifty-three!" Jesus also informs his disciple that 30,001 souls are born every day — that is, one more than die every day.

Mary risks global Armageddon

Jesus wasn't the only one bombarded with questions in this work. In the next very strange section, the disciples ask Mary what it was like to have the child Jesus formed within her. Surprisingly, she pleads with them that she not be asked to describe this, but when the disciples insist, she asks them to surround her and literally brace her on all sides to "hold her together," lest the holiness of what she is about to describe blow her apart! Just as she finishes the story, Jesus suddenly appears and warns Mary not to finish the story or the world will end! You can presume that there are some questions you won't get answers to . . . unless, of course, you don't mind triggering the apocalypse.

Asking about sin, humanity, and judgment

After Jesus is back in the picture, the disciples want to ask him further questions. What's rather funny, however, is that everyone is so afraid to ask that they argue with each other about who should do the asking! Peter, for example, tells Mary that because she bore the child who reversed the curse of Adam and Eve, she should ask. Mary fires back that Peter's the one who Jesus put at the head of the group, so *he* should ask. Meanwhile, Bartholomew steps up and asks the questions.

Bartholomew's questions concern

- ✔ The nature of hell and judgment
- ✔ The nature of the creation of humanity
- ✔ The nature of specific sins

Asking about the unforgivable sin

In a final series of questions, Bartholomew asks Jesus about the famous "unforgivable sin." This draws on the Gospel tradition of Mark in which Jesus states, ". . . but whoever blasphemes against the Holy Spirit can never have forgiveness, but is guilty of an eternal sin" (Mark 3:29). Jesus's clarification to Bartholomew is quite startling:

Whosoever shall decree against any man who has served my holy Father has blasphemed against the Holy Ghost. Every man who serves God with reverence is worthy of the Holy Ghost, and he who speaks anything evil against him shall not be forgiven!

—Questions of Bartholomew 5:4 (tr. Elliott, 667)

It seems that persecution of Christians is what's intended here: Because every Christian is worthy of the Holy Spirit, attacking Christians is also attacking the Spirit within them. This is a very interesting interpretation, to say the least.

Book of the Resurrection of Jesus Christ

The related Bartholomew work known as the *Book of the Resurrection of Jesus Christ* is actually a combination of a series of episodes, all dealing with appearances of Jesus after his resurrection. Here's a recap of four episodes:

- In an opening sequence that flashes back to before the crucifixion, one of the disciples brings a chicken to the table and relates how some Jews told him that when the chicken was killed, Jesus would bleed and die just like the chicken! And what's Jesus's response to this? He says, "It is true," and proceeds to bring the chicken back to life, after which it flies away. Many historians consider this episode a prediction of the death and resurrection of Jesus.

- Jesus is visited in his tomb by demonic figures who are shocked to find him alive, and thereafter, Jesus goes to hell and releases all the souls but three:
  - Herod
  - Cain
  - Judas (and Jesus apparently scolds Judas)

- A gardener describes Jesus's resurrection to nine women who have come to visit the Tomb of Jesus, and then Jesus appears to them on a fiery chariot.

- Thomas raises his own son to life after seven days of death, and the boy describes the scenes that he saw in heaven, including 12 seats in heaven reserved for the Apostles. This episode elaborates on the tradition of "doubting Thomas," the story of the Apostle Thomas, who refused to accept that Jesus had risen from the dead and demanded to feel his wounds as proof (see John 20).

These writings attributed to Bartholomew have clear parallels with apocalyptic visionary material seen in both Jewish and other early Christian writings, and they're particularly similar to the much more popular writing the *Shepherd of Hermas* (see Chapter 13 for details on Hermas).

Writings on the Death of Jesus

Other writings purport to add to the knowledge of the events leading up to, and after, the death of Jesus. Among these are documents in which Pilate plays a significant part. One of these documents has actually been called the *Acts of Pilate;* it's the first part of the *Gospel of Nicodemus.* The Acts of Pilate is collected with other writings including *Christ's Descent into Hell* (which is the second part of the Gospel of Nicodemus), a series of letters from an alleged correspondence between Pilate and Herod, and other letters from Pilate to other Roman officials.

The Acts of Pilate, or the Gospel of Nicodemus

In the writing known as the *Acts of Pilate,* Nicodemus is a pious Jew who attempts to defend Jesus and then investigates the events of the resurrection after Jesus's death.

The resurrected Jesus also appears to Nicodemus. The work begins with the known canonical Gospel accounts of the trial, death, and resurrection of Jesus, but then it expands far beyond the basic information in the Gospels and provides some fascinating details.

When Jesus first walks into the presence of Pilate, the Roman Standards (the eaglelike symbols held on poles) bow before Jesus, angering Pilate because he thinks that some of his soldiers either are playing games or are secret admirers of Jesus. When Pilate orders stronger soldiers to hold the standards, the images atop the standards bow once again when Jesus enters. This is a charming detail — with perhaps some political implications.

The book features some rather nasty debates between Jesus, Pilate, and the Jewish Elders that surely summarize some of the real debates between Christians and Jews throughout the first centuries of Christianity. The debates include what were probably common accusations faced by early Christians, including claims that

- Jesus was an illegitimate child.
- Jesus was a sorcerer.
- Jesus's family fled to Egypt because they were driven out by their neighbors rather than because of God's protection.

Pilate hears a number of testimonials by those who were healed or exorcised of demons, but Jewish crowds overrule them and insist on the crucifixion of Jesus. Throughout the actual trial, Pilate protests Jesus's innocence and tells the Jewish speakers to deal with Jesus in their own way. The crucifixion, however, carries on as stated in the Gospels, with some expansions of the story, including an extended discussion of Joseph of Arimathea, who donated a tomb for the body of Jesus.

The main expansion of the traditional story, however, takes place *after* the crucifixion. The Acts of Pilate features an extended investigation by priestly Jewish leaders, who attempt to learn the fate of Jesus because of the empty tomb. The risen Jesus, however, appears to many, including Joseph of Arimathea, and eventually many of the Jewish leaders come to recognize the true identity of Jesus.

Christ's Descent into Hell

Christ's Descent into Hell is a dramatic presentation of Jesus storming the gates of Hades, defeating the attempts of Satan and Hades (here presented as two different characters) to keep Jesus out.

Jesus comes to hell and releases all the people who were trapped there because of Adam's original sin (including many historic figures of the Old Testament and Adam himself, who has a prominent part in the story). In one version of Christ's Descent, a cross is planted in hell to serve as a powerful symbol of Christ's defeat of death and sin.

The general description of Christ's entry into hell is very similar to elements of the Questions of Bartholomew (see the earlier section), suggesting that both draw from popular early Christian folklore surrounding the canonical descriptions of the death and resurrection of Jesus.

Brief letters and correspondence of Pilate

A number of short works purporting to be letters sent by Pilate to other officials suggest that Pilate wasn't a willing participant in the crucifixion of Jesus and generally exonerate the entire Roman Empire. Indeed, in one of these letters, Caesar is angry at "the Jews" for the crucifixion of Jesus and commands serious retribution.

In general, the tone of the Pilate materials is polemic, accusatory, and clearly anti-Semitic. Furthermore, the positive depiction of the Roman Empire is quite likely to reflect the period after 313 CE when Constantine started the process that led to the Roman Empire itself becoming Christian. That is to say, anti-Semitism during the period when Christians held the power of government — the Roman Empire — was seriously deadly for Jewish communities who chose not to be converts. For many Jews after the seventh to eighth centuries, the Islamic world afforded at least some level of security and protection when persecution was a serious danger in the Christian world. Writings like the Pilate materials show how religious propaganda can be used to stir up hatred and animosity.

Part IV

Lost Early Christian Books

The 5th Wave By Rich Tennant

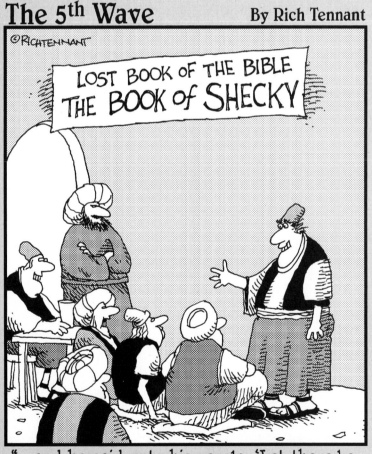

"...and he said unto his people, 'Let there be stand up.' By the way, have you seen some of these camel drivers...?"

In this part . . .

The New Testament isn't just about Jesus. One of the most important books for Christianity is a "history book" called the *Acts of the Apostles* that tells some of the stories of early followers of Jesus like Stephen, Peter, and Paul (and Mary, for that matter). St. Paul, of course, became one of the most influential early Christians, and many of his letters became so popular that they were in the New Testament. But other stories were written about Paul, Peter, Mary, and even some of the other disciples that no one hears much about at all — Andrew and Thomas, for example.

In this part, we explore many of these early Christian writings that talk about early Christian leaders. Again, there are lots of entertaining legends and a few disturbing ideas, but altogether it's fascinating reading. We also introduce you to Christian legends, early visions, and adventures that aren't for the faint of heart. We summarize all these works for you so that you know which ones to track down at the local library or bookstore and read for yourself!

Chapter 12

The Gnostic Christian Writings

*W*e use the word "esoteric" a lot in this chapter. From the Greek meaning "inner," it refers to ideas that are difficult or impossible to understand for "outsiders" because these ideas are described in images or language that's meaningful only for those initiated into the mysteries or secrets. There can be esoteric symbols and drawings (like Masonic symbols or those of other secret clubs) or esoteric writings (like the stuff we look at in this chapter).

Many Gnostic writings are almost completely esoteric, and some of these writings use language, terms, names, and ideas so totally strange as to defy modern understanding. Happily, however, some of the writings can be worked out enough to reveal at least some of what the writers were thinking, and that's what we tackle in this chapter. In doing so, we draw on the English translations edited by James Robinson *(The Nag Hammadi Library)* and also Bentley Layton *(The Gnostic Scriptures)*. See the appendix for both sources.

In this chapter, we conduct a survey of Gnostic Christian writings. Gnosticism was an early Christian "heresy" that was attacked and debated by the early Christians, whose views emerged as "orthodox Christianity." Therefore, none of these writings were ever considered for inclusion in the New Testament, even though the Gnostic Christians obviously treasured them!

Some of these writings have been known for some time, whereas others were more recently discovered in the spectacular find in Egypt at the place known as "Nag Hammadi," and so they're referred to as the *Nag Hammadi Library*. Because of this discovery, much more is known about early Gnostic Christian thought — but not as much as scholars and historians would like to know! (You'll see what we mean as you read on.)

Understanding Gnostic Christianity

"Gnosis" is a Greek term that means "knowledge." So, a Gnostic would be someone with knowledge. Simple, right? Not so fast. Historically, the term "Gnostic" is most often used specifically to refer to an ancient religious movement that began probably early in the second century CE, if not earlier. Modern historians refer to this movement as *Gnosticism* (although it isn't the term the ancient Gnostics used for themselves).

Some ancient Gnostics were interested in Christianity, and it's also probably the case that some early Christians were impressed with a Gnostic way of understanding Christianity.

Gnostic Christianity can be described as a form of Christianity concerned with typically Gnostic themes, particularly

- ✔ The nature of spiritual reality
- ✔ The origin of the spiritual beings
- ✔ The origins and fate of the human soul
- ✔ The meaning of Jesus
- ✔ The nature of salvation

However, it seems quite clear that Gnostic Christianity dwelt on ideas that were either very minor in other forms of Christianity (like the true nature of the creation of the world — not a huge theme in the New Testament) or even openly hostile to ideas in other forms of Christianity (for example, Gnosticism did *not* like the New Testament emphasis on the physical suffering and bodily resurrection of Jesus).

What Gnostic Christians believed, in a nutshell

All Gnostics, whether Christian or not, were interested in the origins of the world and also in understanding the origins of good and evil. In the Christian Gnostic *cosmology* (a system of beliefs about what exists), we can identify some basic ideas common to all Christian Gnostic literature.

Being of light

Christian Gnostics believed in an all-knowing, entirely independent being of light, the origin of everything, who wasn't created but always was. This "being" existed before anything or anyone else. Everything that now exists is, in some way, derived from this first perfect being that the Gnostics call by many different names: divine source, omnipotent one, the "ineffable" . . . you get the idea. This being is purely good.

A created second being

The original being gave rise to a second being, although Gnostic writings never quite explain why. Think of this concept in terms of amending the famous line from the philosopher Descartes, "I think, therefore I am"; for Gnostics, it's "*He* thought, therefore *others* came about."

Gnostics sometimes call this second being after pure perfection "Barbelo," a name that some speculate is formed by Coptic terms for "projectile" (thus one "emitted" from the oneness) or, some suggest, the Hebrew terms for "god in four" ("b" = "in" + "arba" = 4 + "El" = god).

Although Gnostics usually refer to this second being as male, they occasionally use feminine terms. This second being then expanded into additional beings, most importantly the personified Wisdom, usually called by the Greek term for "wisdom," Sophia. She's often described as a feminine being growing out of the thought of the unknown and unknowable god of light. Different Gnostic texts go into intricate detail on the number of "beings" that were generated at this stage after Barbelo, speculating that it was 365 for every day of the year, or perhaps 70. Sometimes these beings appear to embody certain traits — good ones like wisdom, happiness, and courage; or bad ones like jealousy and hatred.

Making of matter

For Gnostics, following the creation of the second being and subsequent beings is the stage involving the creation of the material universe — that is, the one we experience every day. This involves the creation of a being almost always called by the name "Yaldaboath."

This being is considered a lesser being, and in many Gnostic myths, this lesser being creates the known world with flaws. Why? Because the being is flawed. Where do these flaws come from? Why is there evil in the world? There are various, strange explanations for how evil could come from an originally pure good, but philosophers have been beating their heads on that one for centuries. In their writings, the Gnostics seem to answer that evil was made by Sophia, a lesser power, as a rebellious act apart from the higher god's permission. This Yaldaboath is usually pictured as trying to convince humans that he's the true god because he initiated the physical creation (but not the spiritual, inward part of humanity).

Making of man

In Gnostic writings, the creation of humanity is a special case. Although they are material beings, Sophia (or other beings in some versions) attempts to take away (or perhaps balance) the powers of Yaldaboath, so she gives humans a "piece" of pureness even though they're tainted by being creatures in this lesser, material universe. But Yaldaboath strikes back by convincing these humans that he, in fact, is their god, not the original God of light and goodness.

You can see the lines drawn from a kind of spiritual battle in history as the forces of good struggle over humanity against the forces of evil.

How Gnostic beliefs clashed with traditional Jewish and Christian beliefs

Okay, we admit it: The Christian Gnostic cosmology all sounds totally bizarre. But there are some rather startling implications to it all; here are the highlights:

✔ **Many Gnostic Christians believed that the "Jewish God" was precisely Yaldaboath: the lesser, even evil, being that sought to fool humans into believing that he was, in fact, their god.** Thus, Gnostic Christians tended to deny the significance of the entire Jewish tradition for their own faith and practice, or at least interpret it according to their own ideas!

✔ **Because the Gnostics believed that the material world was the result of a lesser god, material things weren't important — even material bodies weren't important.** They believed that they would be free upon death to regain their true spiritual nature and rejoin the spiritual world of good.

✔ **In general, ethical practices that tended to value material issues of care and concern for bodies were a very minor concern.** There is, quite frankly, very little ethical instruction in Gnostic literature, although to be fair, it isn't entirely absent.

✔ **Because the physical body was part of the unimportant world, sexual pleasure and sexual procreation were usually seen as corrupting, although not always flatly condemned.** In short, the material world was rejected in favor of spending time speculating on a heavenly world and awaiting one's freedom to reunify with the God of light and goodness.

In Gnostic Christianity, Jesus is the great informer or messenger. He's the one sent from the higher light to inform humans of their true inward nature and their intended destiny to escape the material universe and rejoin the forces of light and good. In all Gnostic literature, Jesus begins as a pre-existent being who "takes on" the form of material humans. But most Gnostic scriptures deny that Jesus was truly physical or really suffered. Gnostic Christians believed that people could be saved by knowledge of the truth and by know-ing who they were. Thus, you're no longer "asleep" in the material world. This is why most of these writings consist of attempts to teach or inform the reader about "the truth."

Gnostic Writings Galore: The Nag Hammadi Library

After the Dead Sea Scrolls of 1948–1952, one of the most dramatic discoveries of the 20th century is easily the discovery of the Christian Gnostic writings at Nag Hammadi in Egypt in 1945. Included in this discovery were 13 bundles of texts in varying condition from excellent to very fragmentary. There are some 45 different documents in the Nag Hammadi collection, virtually all of them Gnostic in the sense that they're either overtly Gnostic or lend themselves to Gnostic interpretation.

The language of the Nag Hammadi manuscripts is Coptic, the ancient written language of the Egyptians. It's clear that virtually all these writings, however, are translations from Greek. Historians debate where they came from: Were they buried by an ancient monk because the writings would otherwise have been burned? They were found near the location of ancient monasteries, so most historians think that early Christian monks must have had something to do with these writings.

In this chapter, we don't take time with the Gnostic writings from Nag Hammadi that aren't clearly Christian; instead, we focus on the most notable Christian writings. Some of the writings (including a fragment from Plato) have no Christian connection whatsoever, while others are only mildly Christian (perhaps featuring a brief insertion here and there into what's otherwise clearly a non-Christian work).

Most of these writings clearly have Gnostic philosophy at the heart of their argument. As we indicate, Gnosticism was rejected as denying orthodox beliefs about the Old Testament and the physical nature of Jesus and his existence and suffering. Gnosticism appears to have promoted some rather strict ascetic tendencies that supported a denial of the importance of the physical, either in physical care for other persons' needs for food and shelter or in positive views of sexuality and family life. There are exceptions to these generalizations, of course, but they *are* exceptions.

These writings are typically so difficult to understand and are written with such strange imagery using such bizarre language that it's often impossible to be certain that you really do understand what they're talking about!

Although historians and scholars find these writings interesting, sometimes inspiring (like *The Sentences of Sextus*), and occasionally entertaining (coauthor Daniel is quite fond of *The Acts of Peter and the Twelve Apostles*), their value is in revealing the diversity of early Christian ideas — even the weird ones!

Although it may be dangerous to propose an "organization" for books that are inherently difficult to understand, in this chapter we propose to examine the Gnostic writings by the general subjects they address. If they speak mostly of the Gnostic ideas of Creation, or about Jesus, then we group them accordingly. We hope this makes this survey a bit easier to work through.

Many of these writings present different versions of the same kind of material, namely a recitation of the Gnostic ideas about the creation of all things from the one, uncreated God, the present state of many beings, the material universe, and the spiritual conflicts within the cosmos.

Questions for Jesus

One interesting form of Gnostic Christian writing is what we might call "Questions for Jesus." Although the specific ways that Jesus shows up to talk with disciples may vary, the point seems to be the same in each case: an opportunity to quiz Jesus on matters of concern to Gnostic spirituality. Of course, this scenario is also a rather effective tool for promoting Gnostic ideas by assigning them to Jesus, now isn't it?

The Apocryphon of James

The *Apocryphon of James,* from around 150–200 CE, exemplifies the "question time" genre of Gnostic writing.

According to the writing, 50 days after the Resurrection, James and Peter ask the risen Jesus a number of questions about the nature of the universe and especially about what happens after death. Jesus tells them not to fear death: "Scorn death, therefore, and take thought for life! Remember my cross and my death, and you will live!" *(Apocryphon of James 5:30-35, ed. Robinson, 32).*

This work, which features an unusually large amount of understandable language, even contains variations on parable forms, though the message of the parable isn't immediately obvious:

> . . . *the kingdom of heaven is like an ear of grain after it had sprouted in a field. And when it has ripened, it scattered its fruit and again filled the field with ears for another year. You also, hasten to reap an ear of life for yourselves that you may be filled with the kingdom* . . .

> —Apocryphon of James 12:20-25 (ed. Robinson, 35)

Probably because so much of it is rather clear in its meaning, the Apocryphon is often considered "mildly" Gnostic, but it still features typical aspects of Gnostic portrayals of Jesus — such as Jesus getting irritated with so many questions and apparently getting impatient with his disciples!

The Apocryphon of John

The *Apocryphon of John* is a pre-185 CE work that's another of the "Questions" writings, this time dealing with the origins of evil and how humans are to escape evil.

After John prays for information, a multiple being appears as young, old, and a servant, apparently all at once. This being, intended to be Jesus in various forms, proceeds to explain Gnostic cosmology: God as the *monad* (unitary one) and the creation of the secondary beings Barbelo and a feminine being.

This feminine being's desire to conceive of a thought from herself results in the creation of Yaldaboath, the first *archon* (creator), who then starts to create other beings. In a fascinating extended discussion of the creation of humanity, this writing lists many different beings — each given strange names — who contribute parts of the body of Adam. Here are a few examples:

- ✔ Bano created the lungs.
- ✔ Sostrapal created the liver.
- ✔ Anesimalar created the spleen.

But it's the feminine mother being who gives Adam the power of life and thus the part of good that's in humanity. Referring to elements of the Genesis stories, the Apocryphon describes Adam's son Seth as the one chosen to receive Adam's information about all this creation, but Seth's wisdom is forgotten until Jesus comes to restore the truth.

The prominence of Seth in some of these writings has led many to believe that there was a separate Gnostic group, called *Sethites,* who valued the spiritual being called Seth very highly and sometimes, it seems, identified him with Jesus.

The Book of Thomas the Contender

In the *Book of Thomas the Contender,* which is estimated to be from around 200–250 CE but certainly before 350 CE, numerous sayings of Jesus are clearly modeled on the canonical Gospels but are deeply Gnostic in tone. For example, Jesus is portrayed as very much against any sensuality or sexuality, a common ascetic, anti-material, "anti-physical bodies" theme in Gnostic writing:

Woe to you who love intimacy with womankind and polluted intercourse with them!

Woe to you in the grip of the powers of your body for they will afflict you

Woe to you in the grip of the forces of evil demons . . .

. . . For when you come forth from the sufferings and passions of the body, you will receive rest from the good one, and you will reign with the kind, you joined with him and he with you, from now on, for ever and ever Amen.

—Book of Thomas the Contender 143 (tr. Turner, ed. Robinson, 205)

This work *models* itself on the style of much of Jesus's actual teaching, especially the typical Wisdom-style of teaching that contrasts the behavior of the wise with that of the foolish and the use of "woes" like Prophetic literature from the Old Testament.

The First Apocalypse of James and the Second Apocalypse of James

There are two roughly 100–150 CE Apocalypse of James writings in the Nag Hammadi collection, and they both appear to be discussions between Jesus and his brother James, who was, in fact, historically the first leader of the Jerusalem Christian church after the death and resurrection of Jesus.

In the *First Apocalypse of James,* however, James questions Jesus about his own fate, and Jesus explains how James will die as a martyr. Along the way, James takes the opportunity to question Jesus on matters of Gnostic interest, such as the number of spiritual beings created at certain times in the cosmic order:

> *James said, "Rabbi, are there then twelve hebdomads and now seven as there are in the scriptures?" The Lord said, "James, he who spoke concerning this scripture had limited understanding. I, however, shall reveal to you what has come forth from him who has no number. I shall give a sign concerning their number."*

—First Apocalypse of James 26 (tr. Schoedel, ed. Robinson, 262)

The *Second Apocalypse of James* shows Jesus trying to comfort James as he faces further details about his suffering and martyrdom. James is finally martyred by being thrown from the Temple and, after he survived the fall, being buried up to his waist and stoned to death. The work ends with James uttering a prayer as he dies, asking to be delivered from his body but judged as a good man.

The Apocalypse of Peter

The *Apocalypse of Peter,* from around 200–300 CE, claims to be an explanation of the true nature of spiritual mysteries that Jesus gave to Peter. Along the way, however, you notice serious signs of conflict between the writers (and readers) of this work and the group of Christians who later come to be Orthodox Christians. One can hear the arguments in the following passage:

> *And there shall be others of those who are outside out number who name themselves bishop and also deacons as if they have received their authority from God. They bend themselves under the judgment of the leaders. Those people are dry canals . . .*

—Apocalypse of Peter, 79-80 (tr. Brashler, ed. Robinson, 376)

And Jesus offers advice about waiting for them to fall:

> *The Saviour said, "For a time determined for them in proportion to their error they will rule over the little ones. And after the completion of their error, the never-aging one of the immortal understanding shall become young, and they (the little ones) shall rule over those who are their rulers. The root of their error he shall pluck out, and he shall put it to shame to that it shall be manifest in all the impudence which it has assumed to itself."*

—Apocalypse of Peter 80 (ed. Robinson, 376)

Finally, among the interesting ideas about Jesus, Peter is given to understand that the true Jesus never really suffered but rather watched and laughed as the "fleshy part" was nailed to the cross:

> *The Saviour said to me, "He whom you saw on the tree, glad and laughing, this is the living Jesus. But this one into whose hands and feet they drive the nails is his fleshly part, which is the substitute being put to shame, the one who came into being in his likeness. But look at him and me."*

—Apocalypse of Peter 81 (ed. Robinson, 377)

The Gospel of Mary

The *Gospel of Mary,* a 200 CE or later work, has generated considerable interest because of the prominence of Mary Magdalene and her portrayal as among the *leaders* of the early Christian movement. She even teaches some of the other disciples based on specific instructions given to her. This fragmentary document is quite interesting in its details.

As the work begins, Jesus is explaining some matters to the disciples, with Peter asking one final question about sin in the world. Jesus gives a rather brief and truncated version of the origin of darkness in the world in mildly Gnostic terms and then proceeds to say his goodbyes. After he leaves, Peter and the other men are afraid, saying that they killed Jesus, so there's nothing to stop people from killing them also! Mary steps up and encourages everyone:

> *Do not weep and do not grieve nor be irresolute, for his grace will be entirely with you and will protect you. But rather let us praise his greatness for he has prepared us and made us into men. When Mary said this, she turned their hearts to the Good . . .*

—Gospel of Mary 9 (tr. Macrae and Wilson, ed. Robinson, 525)

Peter, understanding that Mary has some important ideas to teach, asks her to tell them what Jesus taught her. She agrees, but the text appears to be broken, and when it picks up again, Mary appears to be well into a detailed description of a soul experiencing many levels of heaven as it travels. As the soul passes a kind of test at each level, it travels to the next level and learns something new. At the fourth level, seven different forms are perceived. This excerpt shows the esoteric nature of this teaching:

> *The first form is darkness, the second desire, the third ignorance, the fourth is the excitement of death, the fifth is the kingdom of the flesh, the sixth is the foolish wisdom of flesh, the seventh is the wrathful wisdom . . .*
>
> —Gospel of Mary 16 (ed. Robinson, 526)

When the soul announces that it has conquered these things (perhaps through the power of Jesus), it is released to the rest of time, and apparently reunifies with God, or is "silent."

At the apparent end of Mary's teaching, Andrew doesn't believe her and says that he doesn't think Jesus said these things because they're strange ideas. We have to admit that we're with Andrew on this, but in the writing, Peter also begins to doubt and wonders if Jesus really spoke to a woman without their knowledge. They even appear a bit jealous.

At this confrontation, Mary begins to cry and asks if they think she's lying to them. The disciple Levi steps up to defend her against Peter and complains that Peter is always so hotheaded:

> *. . . But if the Savior made her worthy, who are you indeed to reject her? Surely the Savior knows her very well. That is why he loved her more than us. Rather let us be ashamed and put on the perfect man and acquire him for ourselves as he commanded us, and preach the gospel, not laying down any other rule or other law beyond what the Savior said . . .*
>
> —Gospel of Mary 18 (ed. Robinson, 527)

This rather staunch defense of the leadership of a woman among the early Christians is obviously a sentiment of keen interest to feminist scholars and others interested in the issue of early Christian women in leadership within early Christianity. Even people not particularly interested in Gnostic spirituality see in this document at least some evidence of *debates* about the leadership of women in the early movement, suggesting that in some parts of the early Christian world, women most certainly were in leadership until they were suppressed in later Christian practice.

The Letter of Peter to Philip

In this roughly 190–250 CE work, Peter writes to the Apostle Philip, asking him to come to visit. Philip gladly comes, and when he arrives, Peter takes him and others to the Mount of Olives (just outside Jerusalem), where they pray for protection from persecution. A great light appears, and Jesus manifests, asking why they're praying when Jesus already promised that he would be with them forever.

In true Gnostic fashion, however, the disciples decide to ask Jesus some questions (rather like, "So, now that you're here . . . can we ask a few things we forgot about before?"). They ask, "Lord, we should like to know the deficiency of the aeons and their pleroma" — translation: we want to know how evil began, and how things are going to end!

Jesus repeats many of the expected aspects of Gnostic cosmology in a (mercifully) rather brief response. Peter is thrilled with the reassurances about the cosmos and also the end of time, and he enthusiastically preaches to his fellow disciples that although it appeared Jesus suffered and died, "My brothers, Jesus is a stranger to this suffering, but we are the ones who have suffered through the transgression of the mother." In other words, humans will have to suffer to rid themselves of their material bodies, but now that they know this, they can perform wonders in the world as they await their deaths.

Eugnostos the Blessed and the Sophia of Jesus Christ

Eugnostos the Blessed and the *Sophia of Jesus Christ* are an interesting combination of texts from around 100–150 CE. They're printed together in some English editions for a very good reason: Eugnostos is copied and expanded by the Sophia of Jesus Christ.

This pairing provides the very unusual opportunity to see how an ancient Gnostic Christian writer basically cribbed from one work and made it Christian by inserting Jesus answering questions posed by his disciples. Most of the things that Jesus says, however, are clearly copied directly from the first work! The subject of the discussions appears to be a rehearsal of the same cosmic origin myths of God, the emergence of Sophia, and the creation and significance of humanity.

Gnostic ideas on Jesus

Another form of Gnostic literature is a narrative about the nature, identity, and work of Jesus. This isn't written as if Jesus is speaking but rather is a narrative description. As such, the writings in this category are a kind of sermon, and in fact, some of them may have been Gnostic sermons or teachings shared in some kind of gathering.

The Tripartite Tractate

The *Tripartite Tractate* is a longer Gnostic writing than many that we cover in this chapter. From around 200–250 CE, it's a response to critics on Gnostic ideals and thus tries to explain Gnostic beliefs. Don't start thinking it's an easily read work, though. The Tractate is deeply esoteric in tone and in its use of symbols and language. For example, God is described as unknowable by humans

> . . . *because of his inscrutable greatness and his incomprehensible depth, and his immeasurable light, and his illimitable will. This is the nature of the unbegotten one* . . .

> —Tripartite Tractate 54 (tr. Attridge and Mueller, ed. Robinson, 62)

As in typical Gnostic cosmology, the "Logos" (like "Sophia" in other Gnostic forms; this refers to "a created second being") falls short and creates lesser beings. As a result, in the good creation of Jesus and the Church, Logos turns away from its fallen state and assists in the redemption of creation.

The nature of Jesus is described as a good being who ". . . let himself be conceived and born as an infant, in body and soul." Even the disciples are described here as from God. However, the ultimate desire of humanity is reunification with God:

> *When the redemption was proclaimed the perfect man received knowledge immediately, so as to return in haste to his unitary state, to return there joyfully, to the place from which he came to the place from which he flowed forth.*

> —Tripartite Tractate 123 (ed. Robinson, 96-97)

The Gospel of Philip

Professor Isenberg, one of the translators we consulted for the Nag Hammadi works, suggests that the roughly 250–300 CE *Gospel of Philip* may contain a series of sacramental songs and poems, but otherwise, the book seems somewhat disorganized.

Despite its lack of organization, it's among the more entertaining of the Nag Hammadi writings because most of it seems rather clear and understandable. That doesn't mean, however, that some of its ideas aren't strange! In this writing, readers discover that Christ voluntarily laid down his life from the very day the world came into being:

> *Then he came first in order to take it, since it had been given as a pledge. It fell into the hands of robbers and was taken captive, but he saved it* . . .

> —Gospel of Philip 53:10 (tr. Isenberg, ed. Robinson, 142)

This gospel denies some basic orthodox Christian ideas; following are two examples:

> ✔ The virgin birth of Jesus is denied by engaging in rather questionable reasoning that Jesus, in Matthew 16:17, identifies another father: "Jesus replied, 'Blessed are you, Simon son of Jonah, for this was not revealed to you by man, but by my Father in heaven.'" The writer asks why Jesus would identify another as his "father" unless there was already an earthly one.

> ✔ The work contends that water baptism isn't considered "real" because *spiritual* baptism is the really authentic and meaningful form of baptism.

There are also some rather strange sayings of Jesus rendered in a Gnostic orientation, such as, "Blessed is he who is before he came into being. For he who is, has been, and shall be. . . ." For more unusual sayings attributed to Jesus, turn to Chapter 11.

Finally, the Gospel of Philip suggests that the cross of Jesus was made from a tree that Joseph planted, but oil for christening (perhaps used in a Gnostic Christian ritual) comes from the olive tree, described as a "Tree of Life." This christening ceremony seems to be a rite or ritual that's more highly valued than baptism and is mentioned in a few other Gnostic works.

As in other Gnostic writings, the Gospel of Philip also refers to the "Bridal Chamber." This is a very interesting Gnostic idea: As husband and wife become one in the act of making love in a literal Bridal Chamber, this image is used to refer to humanity regaining their unity with God. Thus the Bridal Chamber becomes a popular Gnostic image for reunified *spiritual* persons. Lest you think something literally sexual is implied here, it's worth pointing out that Gnostic writings contrast this spiritual union to physical sexual intercourse, which is considered evil and lustful.

Finally, this gospel contains some of the sneering judgmentalism that we refer to earlier as characteristic of Gnosticism: There are many kinds of people, the writer says, and some will never understand the truth. Thus, the Gospel of Philip portrays Jesus using the image of different animals and then explaining:

> *There are many animals in the world which are in human form. When he (God) identifies them, to the swine he will throw acorns, to the cattle he will throw barley, and chaff and grass, to the dogs he will throw bones. To the slaves he will give only elementary lessons, to the children he will give the complete instruction.*
>
> —Gospel of Philip 81 (ed. Robinson, 157)

The point here is painfully obvious: Some people are little better than swine, who get only acorns; or cattle, who get only barley; and so forth. The true "children of God" (that is, of course, the Gnostics) are the only ones who will get the truth. It's little wonder that some historians accuse the Gnostics of elitism and arrogance.

Dialogue of the Saviour

In the *Dialogue of the Saviour,* from around 150–200 CE, Jesus purports to give the disciples (and Mary) some important information. Although portions of the text are missing, enough remains to appreciate the general tone of the work. Knowing the truth is compared to knowing the source, the origin, the "root," which ties to the Gnostic emphasis on knowing the origins of the cosmos and spiritual reality, as you see in this excerpt:

> *If [one] does not [understand how] fire came into existence, he will burn in it, because he does not know the root of it. If one does not first understand water, he knows nothing. For what use is there for his to be baptized in it? If one does not understand how blowing wind came into existence, he will blow away with it. If one does not understand how body, which he bears, came into existence, he will perish with it . . .*

—Dialogue of the Saviour 134 (tr. Koester and Pagels, ed. Robinson, 250)

Gnostic ideas on creation

As we said earlier in this chapter, how the world came to be is central to Gnostic ideas. It was the creation of the lesser god and that god's creation of this world that caused the whole mess we're in now, according to the Gnostics. So, they explain the creation — and refer to it — again and again in their own idiosyncratic ways. The basic story is the same: Jesus came to solve problems that started with the very beginning of the cosmos. Put that way, it *does* sound like Paul's ideas about the fallen Creation and Christ as the "new Adam" (Romans 5), so you can see that the Gnostics weren't entirely original. Still, the Gnostics dwell on this subject far more than the New Testament ever did.

The Gospel of Truth

A 140–180 CE writing, the *Gospel of Truth* is particularly intriguing for many historians precisely because it *may* be the actual writing of one of the most important early Christian Gnostic teachers, Valentinius. It's not really a gospel of Jesus, though, but a compendium of Valentinian ideas of Gnostic Christianity.

This work reveals the origins of human existence and the origins of darkness and mistakes in the fall of Sophia as well as the importance of Jesus and his role in informing humans of the truth. The work has a joyful tone as it speaks of the bliss of reuniting with God and celebrates the eventual return of all to unity with God.

The gospel is a good example of Christian Gnosticism, and we think it's a good document for newcomers to the study of Gnosticism to read in order to get an idea why some may find these kinds of ideas quite attractive. The

Gospel of Truth contains less of the nasty, sneering streak that you find in other Gnostic Christian writings (Jesus laughing at disciples, many people called "stupid" or compared to swine or cattle, and so on), and one gets the idea that Valentinius was probably a nice old guy!

For example, the celebration of Jesus is quite poetic, but note how it empha-sizes what people learn from Jesus and that salvation is information:

> *For this reason, Jesus appeared; he put on that book; he was nailed to a tree; he published the edict of the Father on the cross. O such great teaching! He draws himself down to death though life eternal clothes him. Having stripped himself of perishable rags, he put on imperishability.*

> —Gospel of Truth 20 (tr. Attridge and Macrae, ed. Robinson, 42-43)

There's genuine compassion in how God reaches out with important informa-tion about reality to fill the void left by "deficiency" and lack of understanding:

> *For this reason incorruptibility breathed forth; it pursued the one who had sinned in order that he might rest. For forgiveness is what remains for the light in the deficiency, the word of the pleroma [fullness]. For the physician runs to the place where sickness is . . .*

> —Gospel of Truth 35 (ed. Robinson, 48)

The Hypostasis of the Archons

The third century CE work the *Hypostasis of the Archons* appears to be a retelling of Genesis chapters 1 through 6, but it claims to be a fuller explana-tion of these chapters in that it expands the biblical writing with Gnostic cosmology.

The writing claims to be the words given to Norea, a proposed daughter of Eve. The standard Gnostic themes are present, including a final suggestion that Christ will eventually come to grant people the critical information they need for salvation.

On the Origin of the World

This roughly 300–325 CE work is another rehearsal of the spiritual beginnings of the cosmos — first the spiritual world and then the material world. Readers are told of the creation of Sophia, the creation of Yaldaboath and Yaldaboath's belief that he's actually God, and the announcement of the coming of Christ to bring knowledge.

One thing that sets *On the Origin of the World* apart from some of the other writings that cover similar topics is an apocalyptic, "last judgment" type of ending as light and dark, good and evil, are sorted out. The work ends:

. . . For everyone must go to the place from which he has come. Indeed, by his acts and his acquaintance each person will make his nature known.

—On the Origin of the World 127 (tr. Bethge, ed. Robinson, 139)

The Apocalypse of Adam

The *Apocalypse of Adam,* from around 100–200 CE, purports to be a long explanation of the nature of the cosmos by Adam to his son, Seth. Many scholars consider it a non-Christian Gnostic work. It's based roughly on the opening chapters of the book of Genesis, and in fact, it has very few Christian features. The Apocalypse illustrates that the Nag Hammadi Library did indeed contain many non-Christian works, thus pointing to the existence of Gnostics outside of the Christian movement.

The Concept of Our Great Power

The *Concept of Our Great Power* is a difficult work from around 300–400 CE that presents a narration of the origins of the cosmos that's similar to other Gnostic documents we consider in this chapter, but it's written without many of the familiar names. Instead, this work presents spiritual beings (the High God as "The Great Power") involved in a conflict that's represented as a conflict between fire and water. Occasionally, a biblical name is cited (such as Judas and Logos) suggesting that the writer was Christian, but as a whole, the work appears to describe a spiritual battle that leads to the salvation of souls who will be reunited with God.

Sethian Gnosticism

Sethian Christian Gnosticism is marked by the apparent importance of the son of Adam known as Seth (Genesis 4 and 5). Works in this category clearly display some unique features, most especially proposing some serious changes in the Jesus story, so it's often proposed that Sethian Gnosticism was a particular branch (perhaps a denomination) of Gnostic Christianity.

The Gospel of the Egyptians

The *Gospel of the Egyptians* is a deeply esoteric and difficult writing from around 150 CE. It's sometimes described as a book of Sethian Gnosticism because of the apparent importance of the son of Adam known as Seth. He's considered a historical repository of ancient wisdom:

Then the great Seth was sent by the four lights, by the will of the Autogenes [perhaps meaning self-generated] and the whole pleroma [fullness], through the gift and the good pleasure of the invisible Spirit, and the five seals, and the whole pleroma . . .

—Gospel of the Egyptians 62-62 (Boehlig and Wisse, ed. Robinson, 216)

The contents of this work reiterate much of the same cosmology of Gnosticism seen in many of the other writings, although this gospel contains what appear to be sounds written as a series of vowel letters — iiiiiiiiiii and ooooooooooo, for example. It's possible that these sounds were interpreted as coming from the spiritual beings. These sounds also could have been symbolic representations of names of gods or even sounds to be repeated in Sethian rituals (kind of spooky, eh?).

The Second Treatise of the Great Seth

In the *Second Treatise of the Great Seth* (likely pre-third century CE), Jesus explains to selected persons how he came about as a higher being; he explains that he didn't die on the cross but that Simon of Cyrene, who carried Jesus's cross, actually died in his place while the spirit of Jesus watched from the cosmos:

> *I did not succumb to them as they had planned. But I was not afflicted at all. Those who were there punished me. And I did not die in reality but in appearance, lest I be put to shame by them . . . I was rejoicing in the height over all the wealth of the archons and the offspring of their error, of their empty glory, and I was laughing at their ignorance . . .*

> —Second Treatise of the Great Seth

Jesus laughing at the ignorance of others? It's not a pretty picture. In ancient writings, laughter was almost always a sign of ridicule — never merely an indication of enjoyment. In other words, the Gnostics are *not* saying that Jesus is "laughing *with* you . . .", if you get our drift. In fact, this work has a kind of sneering disrespect of the Jewish tradition — Adam, Abraham, Isaac, Jacob, David, Solomon, and even Moses are all laughingstocks, and all give witness to another being who is not truth.

Melchizedek

Melchizedek is a curious 200–300 CE work that purports to be an explanation of the significance of Jesus by comparing him to Melchizedek, the priest briefly mentioned in the Old Testament (see Genesis 14:18 and Psalm 110:4). Melchizedek was a priest who spoke to Abraham in the book of Genesis, and he has been a figure of mystery for centuries. According to some scholars, this work may have originally been a document from a unique group of Christians who preserved a strange tradition of honoring this mysterious Melchizedek as a "previous appearance" of Christ in biblical history. Thus, some early Gnostics may have believed that Christ was a kind of "reappearance" of Melchizedek.

These scholars have suggested that the work originally belonged to a small group of Christians perhaps known as *Melchizedekites,* and that it was edited by a Sethian Gnostic Christian who perhaps wanted to read the significance of Seth in some of the features of this work. The trouble, however, is that the text is badly damaged, and filling in the missing words and ideas requires a lot of guesswork.

The Paraphrase of Shem

A deeply esoteric work, *The Paraphrase of Shem* (second century CE) appears to represent conflicts between three levels of reality, in this order:

- ✔ The god of light
- ✔ The "Spirit"
- ✔ Darkness

"Shem" is entrusted with the knowledge given in this work. Throughout, the power of the spirit (often called "Fire") is contrasted with the negative power of water, and thus even the water of baptism is considered unacceptable. It seems that the writer has picked up on water imagery in the Bible (refer to primordial waters in Genesis 1:1–5, as well as references to the Great Flood and baptism) and rendered it as representative of evil in opposition to light and fire. The Paraphrase is only mildly Christian in nature and may be related to Sethian Gnostic literature.

Gnostic wisdom

Another way of grouping Gnostic writings together is to consider those writings that appear to offer advice for living your life. This was the main idea behind Wisdom books like Proverbs in the Old Testament and James in the New Testament. In Gnostic writings, these works seem to be advice for living a *spiritual* life according to Gnostic values and beliefs.

The Teaching of Silvanus

The *Teaching of Silvanus* (from around 300–400 CE) is often described as "Greek Christian Wisdom," which means that its teachings read rather like the *Book of Proverbs* or the *Epistle of James* in the New Testament, both fine examples of Jewish Wisdom teaching (see Chapter 3 for a more complete explanation of what we mean by Wisdom writings).

Some historians seriously doubt that the *Teaching of Silvanus* is a Gnostic tract; there's too much practical emphasis on living in the material world for this to be a deeply Gnostic work, if Gnostic at all. But like a few other writings in the Nag Hammadi collection, it's possible to interpret the work in a Gnostic manner. As in many Wisdom books, the advice in the Teaching often seems quite timeless and worthy of serious consideration by many Christians. Here are some rather pleasant examples:

Do not tire of knocking on the door of reason, and do not cease walking in the way of Christ. Walk in it so that you may receive rest from your labors. If you walk in another way, there will be no profit in it . . .

—Teaching of Silvanus 103 (tr. Peel, Zandee, ed. Robinson, 389)

Let Christ alone enter your world, and let him bring to naught all powers which have come upon you. Let him enter the temple which is within you so that he may cast out all the merchants. Let him dwell in the temple which is within you, and you may become for him a priest and a Levite, entering in purity. Blessed are you, O soul, if you find this one in your temple.

—Teaching of Silvanus 109 (ed. Robinson, 391)

The Sentences of Sextus

Before the discovery of the Nag Hammadi Library, the *Sentences of Sextus* was known in Latin, Syrian, Armenian, and Georgian translations, but the version in the Nag Hammadi Library is the oldest version now available.

The Sentences represents Wisdom sayings but also contains rather striking high moral values. Some of the material may be from non-Christian sources, but it's hard to avoid the impression that much of the moral guidance here is deeply Christian in tone and tenor.

The "Sentences" isn't Gnostic material, although it shows occasional ascetic tendencies; following are some exemplary quotations from the Sentences of Sextus that show some ascetic, if not outside Gnostic, tendencies:

- ✔ "Do not become guilty of your own death."

- ✔ "Do not be angry at him who will take you out of the body and kill you."

- ✔ "If someone brings the wise man out of the body wickedly he rather does what is good for him, for he has been released from bonds."

- ✔ "The fear of death grieves man because of the ignorance of the soul."

—Sentences 320-322, (tr. Wisse, ed. Robinson, 505)

But these ascetic, antimaterial tendencies are just slight. In fact, the concern for the material and social well-being of others, and the concern for Christians being involved in helping others, is a materially moral tone foreign to much of the deeply Gnostic writings of the Nag Hammadi collection. As you see throughout this chapter, such writings are preoccupied with identifying names and powers of spiritual entities. Here are some of the more striking moral advices in the Sentences that make it clear that this work is definitely not Gnostic:

- ✔ "If you take on the guardianship of orphans, you will be the father of many children and you will be beloved of God." (340)

- ✔ "The love of man is the beginning of godliness." (371)

✔ "He who takes care of men while praying for all of them — this is the truth of God." (372)

✔ "It is God's business to save whom he wants; on the other hand, it is the business of the pious man to beseech God to save everyone." (373)

✔ "It is better for man to be without anything than to have many things while not giving to the needy; so also you, if you pray to God, he will not give to you." (377-378)

✔ "If you, from your whole heart, give your bread to the hungry, the gift is small, but the willingness is great with God." (379)

✔ "May your pious works precede every word about God." (359)

✔ "God does not need anything, but he rejoices over those who give to the needy." (382)

✔ "The faithful does not speak many words, but their works are numerous." (383)

✔ "The philosopher who is an outer body, he is not the one to whom it is fitting to pay respect, but the philosopher according to the inner man." (392)

(all from ed. Robinson, 506-508)

Gnostic legends and tales

These writings from the Nag Hammadi Library (and some known outside of that collection as well) seem to expand on New Testament characters and traditions. Some are written like letters (such as Paul's or John's Epistles in the New Testament) or legends (like the non-canonical *Acts of Andrew* or *Acts of Paul and Thecla*). Not all these writings are clearly Gnostic, but they may have been kept by Gnostic Christians because they could be easily interpreted in a Gnostic manner.

The Prayer of the Apostle Paul

This brief prayer (it's less than one translated page) was in the opening cover of the first group of writings found at Nag Hammadi and isn't especially different from prayers in other books. From around 250–300 CE, it's a joyful request to God to reveal important knowledge: ". . . And the first-born of the pleroma [fullness] of grace — reveal him to my mind!" *(Prayer of the Apostle Paul, tr. Mueller, ed. Robinson, 27-28)*.

The Treatise on Resurrection

An interesting writing addressed to a certain "Rheginos" and addressing the nature of life after death, the *Treatise on Resurrection* (from around 170–200 CE) attempts to reassure the Christian believer about what happens during and after one's mortal demise. It states, "The thought of those who are saved shall not perish. The mind of those who have known him shall not perish" *(Treatise on Resurrection, 46, tr. Peel, ed. Robinson, 55).*

The resurrection is seen as a kind of "completeness" that isn't possible in earthly life, but resurrection already begins with those who have renounced evil during this life. Those who: ". . . flee from the divisions and the fetters . . . already have the resurrection . . ." *(Treatise on Resurrection, 49, ed. Robinson, 56-57).* The idea seems to be that freedom from the chains of this world can begin in this life by knowing and studying Gnostic information.

The Exegesis of the Soul

This roughly 200–230 CE work is among the more interesting of the writings because the story is fairly clear. The *Exegesis of the Soul* is a novelistic story of the soul expressed through the journey of a female being who falls into the material world. Her plunge into the bodily form is described as a descent into prostitution, but she's redeemed by a purer love and then returns to the house of the father.

This work, somewhat unusually, is typified by frequent quotations not only from the Bible but also from Homer's *Odyssey*. Also, marriage and intercourse are used as symbols of becoming reunited with true selves (like the image of the Bridal Chamber in other Gnostic writings like the Gospel of Philip; see that section earlier in this chapter).

The Exegesis, however, doesn't have very many explicitly Christian teachings. However, it does speak in a female voice and use images of falling into abuse before being restored by "despising this life, because it is transitory." The female being learns about her light as "she goes about stripping off this world" (tr. W. Robinson, ed. Robinson, 192–198).

The Apocalypse of Paul

In this roughly 150–200 CE text, Paul meets a child on the road who knows all about Paul and begins to explain spiritual realities to Paul. Immediately following a little lesson from the boy, Paul then goes into various layers of heaven, where he witnesses souls on trial and learns a bit more about the nature of heaven and spiritual reality by ascending upwards into these various layers of heaven.

The Acts of Peter and the Twelve Apostles

Professor Parrott, one of the translators of the *Acts of Peter and the Twelve Apostles* into English, argues that this work from around 100–300 CE isn't necessarily a Gnostic work because the views of Jesus are more or less orthodox. Instead, it may belong to the later Christian "Acts" literature that we examine in Chapter 15. The Acts is a fascinating allegorical tale of the disciples being sent into the world to spread the message of Jesus. In fact, it's a charming story.

When Peter and other disciples decide to set sail on a ship, they find themselves arriving on a strange and otherwise unknown island called "Habitation." Peter decides to help the disciples find a place to stay and goes to the city. There, he happens upon a man crying, "Pearls, Pearls!" But the rich people of the island can't actually see that the man is holding anything, and thus they reject him as a mocker. The poor people of the island, however, are deeply impressed with the man's claims to have pearls and beg to at least see them even though they can't afford to buy any. The man identifies himself as "Lithargoel," and tells Peter that Peter is welcome to come to *his* city, but that the way is hard. One must not carry much of value or even excess food or water because the robbers and animals along the way will take anything of value.

Peter finds the town but is met on the road by a physician and an assistant. The physician reveals himself to be another form of Lithargoel, who then reveals himself to be Jesus! Jesus explains to Peter that he must go through the world with the gospel as a pearl to offer freely to the poor, and Peter must renounce all wealth to make it through the world:

> *. . . the physicians of this world heal what belongs to the world. The physicians of souls, however, heal the heart. Heal the bodies first, therefore, so that through the real powers of healing for their bodies, without medicine of the world, they may believe in you, that you have power to heal the illnesses of the heart also.*
>
> —Acts of Peter and the Twelve Apostles 11 (tr. Parrott, ed. Robinson, 293)

The care for physical needs is uncharacteristic of Gnostic literature, but this story was probably preserved by Gnostics because it could be interpreted in a Gnostic manner. This work is a great example of allegorical tales from the early Christians (like the *Shepherd of Hermas*, the *Acts of Paul and Thecla*, and others).

The Thought of Norea

The roughly 100–250 CE work *The Thought of Norea* consists only of 52 lines of text and appears to be a kind of prayer or praise of Norea, a proposed daughter of Eve. It may be a prayer said in a prelude to some reading of other literature that purports to be from Norea.

The Testimony of Truth

From around 175–250 CE, *The Testimony of Truth* is considered only a partial document, with perhaps as much as half of it missing. Still, you can get an interesting idea of the character of this writing, including its anti-material notions, its anti-Hebrew ideas based on its initial attack on the Mosaic Law, and its take on the idea of procreation:

*The Law commands one to take a husband or to take a wife and to beget,
to multiply like sand of the sea. But passion which is a delight to them
constrains the souls of those who are begotten in this place, those who defile
and those who are defiled in order that the Law might be fulfilled through
them. And they show that they are assisting the world; and they turn away
from the light . . .*

—Testimony of Truth 30 (tr. Pearson, ed. Robinson, 450)

This writing claims that when Jesus was baptized, the Jordan River stopped
flowing. It goes on to explain that because the Jordan River represents the
desire for sexual intercourse, Jesus basically stopped sex! Again you can see
the Gnostic suspicion of any human sensuality.

Furthermore, this writing is more explicit than others about the fallen nature
of the Jewish God. Pointing to a number of admittedly troubling passages in
the Old Testament as evidence (such as God "hardening" Pharaoh's heart
in the Exodus story and God sounding generally vengeful in many Old
Testament passages), the writer claims that this isn't a true God!

The Interpretation of Knowledge

Elaine Pagels, one of the foremost scholars of Gnostic Scriptures, considers
the *Interpretation of Knowledge* to be a "unique opportunity" to see how the
Christian Bible was interpreted and used in Christian Gnostic circles. This
likely second-century CE writing appears to be a series of teachings based
on scripture, but the teachings are given a decidedly Gnostic interpretation.
Pagels seems correct, however, when she emphasizes that this writing also
includes many attempts to settle disputes among the members:

*But is someone making progress in the Word? Do not be hindered by this;
do not say: "Why does he speak while I do not?" for what he says is also
yours, and what which discerns the Word and that which speaks is the
same power . . .*

—Interpretation of Knowledge 16-17 (tr. Pagels, ed. Robinson, 478)

The writer borrows St. Paul's description of the Church like the various
cooperating parts of the human body:

*If they are fit to share in the true harmony, how much the more those who
derive from the single unity? They ought to be reconciled with one another.
Do not accuse your Head because it has not appointed you as an eye but
rather as a finger. And do not be jealous of that which has been put in the
class of an eye or a hand or a foot, but be thankful that you do not exist
outside the body . . .*

—Interpretation of Knowledge 18 (ed. Robinson, 479)

A Valentinian Exposition

Another exposition of Gnostic cosmology, *A Valentinian Exposition* (from around the early second century CE) is similar in some ways to the Tripartite Tractate (refer to that section earlier in this chapter) but has some significant differences of view on many aspects of that cosmology.

As Pagels points out, this work claims that God is originally a single unitary being, whereas the Tripartite Tractate seems to suggest that the original being was a combined being of male and female elements in the single unity. There are three documents that collectively make this "Exposition," including writings on Anointing, Baptism, and Eucharist.

Of particular interest with regard to this work are the ending paragraphs, which may be parts of a Gnostic anointment, baptism, and Eucharistic ritual. Consider this portion of an anointing ritual, perhaps intended for prayers of healing to accompany being anointed with oil. The prayer starts rather nicely:

> *It is fitting for you at this time to send thy Son, Jesus Christ, and anoint us to that we might be able to trample upon the snakes and the heads of the scorpions and all the power of the Devil — since he (that is, Christ) is the shepherd of the seed. Through him we have known thee. And we glorify thee: Glory be to thee, the Father in the Son, the Father in the Son, the Father in the holy Church and in the Holy angels. From now on he abides forever in the perpetuity of the Aeons, forever until the untraceable Aeons of the Aeons. Amen.*

> —On the Anointing (tr. Pagels, ed. Robinson, 487)

The First Thought in Three Forms (Or "Trimorphic Protennoia")

The 100–200 CE work called the *First Thought in Three Forms* consists of a series of "I am" sayings by a being who identifies the nature of true spiritual existence. In general, the First Thought describes the various ways in which light is understood to defeat darkness in the cosmos. Historians consider this work to be Christian only by a few editorial glosses added to the writing; it doesn't directly address issues of the identity and nature of Christian life. Consider a portion:

> *I am the Invisible One within the All. It is I who counsel those who are hidden, since I know the All that exists in it. I am numberless beyond everyone. I am immeasurable, ineffable, yet whenever I wish, I shall reveal myself of my own accord. I am the head of the All. I exist before the All, and I am the All since I exist in everyone . . .*

> —First Thought in Three Forms 1 (tr. Turner, ed. Robinson, 513)

The writing contains some discussions of the Christ, but in esoteric language of Gnostic spirituality:

> *Then the Perfect Son revealed himself to his Aeons who originated through him, and he revealed them and glorified them and gave them thrones and stood in the glory with which he glorified himself. They blessed the Perfect Son, the Christ, the only-begotten God. And they gave glory, saying "He is! He is! The Son of God! The Son of God! It is he who is! The Aeon of Aeons beholding the Aeons which he begot! For thou hast begotten to thine own desire! Therefore we glorify thee . . . [sounds indicated by vowels]."*

—First Thought in Three Forms 38 (ed. Robinson, 513)

The Act of Peter

The Act of Peter is a strange 150–200 CE story purporting to be about Peter's daughter; it reflects Gnostic interest in denying physical sexuality and embracing ascetic denial of the flesh.

As the story begins, a crowd gathers around Peter, and they point out a gross inconsistency: Peter has healed many people of their diseases and afflictions, but Peter's own daughter is paralyzed and can't walk. "Why do you not heal your own daughter?" they ask.

Peter then heals her instantly, proving that God is well able to do it. But he then tells her to return to her place and "become an invalid again." The crowd is horrified, but Peter explains that this is all for the best because she's too beautiful and men might sin because of her! (Nice dad, eh?)

Peter then tells the story of Ptolemy, who was totally captivated by Peter's daughter's beauty when she was only 10 years old. Ptolemy captured her, and just before he tried to have sexual intercourse with her, she became paralyzed. The servant of Ptolemy brought her back to Peter and his wife in this condition.

After this, Ptolemy becomes so overcome with guilt that he goes blind from weeping. Peter calls for him, and Ptolemy is led to Peter's presence. When Peter heals him, the miracle leads to many people becoming Christian. There's a brief suggestion that Ptolemy did many good things during the remainder of his life and in his will left a large amount of money to be given to the poor.

The Act closes with a prayer of thanksgiving from Peter, who distributes bread from the money left by Ptolemy. Of course, we would say that this isn't a very flattering picture of Peter's own family life, nor a very loving attitude toward his daughter!

Gnostic Christianity's Influence on "Orthodox" Christianity

Gnostic Christianity represented a significant alternative form of early Christianity even though it didn't survive the ancient world and therefore ceased exercising much influence on the formation of Christianity in later periods.

Gnostic Christianity helped to create the conditions in which orthodox Christianity began to take shape. To put it another way, what was later (say, after the fifth to sixth centuries CE) recognized as orthodox Christianity took shape precisely by arguing with and reacting to Gnostic Christianity.

Orthodox (remember that in this case, we mean simply "orthodox" in belief, not the later "Eastern Orthodox" churches) Christianity had to reaffirm its commitment to the human Jesus. Orthodox Christians argued about the precise relationship of Jesus as a being that is both human and divine — to deny the human part was to tear away a major part of Christian affirmation of this world as God's good creation and also tear away the importance of the bodily, material world in which people must live and function. Care for the poor and care for the hungry are important "body" issues that orthodox Christianity affirmed against the Gnostic tendencies to deny the importance of this world and human bodies. We take care of each other *because* bodies are important! Furthermore, the physical existence of Jesus as human is a strong basis for arguing such issues as concern for the environment.

Gnosticism also had a tendency to deny the significance of sexuality as among God's gifts to humanity. A strict Gnostic denial of the ultimate importance of physical bodies may be a comfort to those who suffer or are in pain in their bodies in this world, but it also has the unfortunate impact of suggesting that sexuality and family life are somehow bad or impure.

Finally, it's still argued that the debates against the Gnostics also forced the orthodox Christians to clarify which books and writings were acceptable and which were not. Clearly, just because something is written doesn't make it acceptable . . . and the early Church finally had to come to grips with this fact.

Chapter 13

Christian Books That Were Strongly Considered

Sometime after 700 CE in the medieval period, the most popular of the early Christian writings that are *not* in the New Testament began to be gathered together and referred to as "the Apostolic Fathers." (Yes, you read that right: The writings themselves — *not* their authors — were referred to as "the Apostolic Fathers.") Interestingly, some of these books may have been written before some of the books that *are* in the New Testament.

In the early centuries of Christianity, many people believed that the early books were written by students of the first Apostles of Jesus, suggesting a line of tradition that begins with Jesus and proceeds through his disciples (the Apostles), and then to the next generation, the so-called Apostolic Fathers.

In this chapter, we take a closer look at these fascinating writings and note that these are especially important because *some* of these books actually *were* part of some early Christian New Testaments. Remember, the final list of books that are the Christian Bible came out in 367 CE. There was a variety of opinions about certain books. The early Christian books most often mentioned with great appreciation are the books we survey in this chapter.

There's considerable disagreement about these writings, especially on the issue of *when* they're dated. We briefly discuss the debates as we look at each of these famous writings, but one thing is absolutely clear: This chapter discusses the most important Christian writings that are *not* in the New Testament. These really are the "Almost In" books of early Christianity. Therefore, it's an interesting exercise to read through these writings and wonder how any of these books might have changed the modern form of Christianity if they had been included in the New Testament. In some cases, perhaps they wouldn't have caused very much change, but in other cases, they may have changed things for the better. This exercise is part of the fascination with these writings.

The Standard List of the Apostolic Fathers

The following lost books comprise the majority of the commonly accepted list of writings known as the Apostolic Fathers:

- The Shepherd of Hermas
- The Didache (also known as the Teaching of the Twelve Apostles)
- The Epistle of Polycarp
- The Martyrdom of Polycarp
- The Letters of Ignatius
- 1 and 2 Clement
- The Epistle of Barnabas
- The Epistle to Diognetus

One reason these writings were so popular is that they seem to give evidence of the struggles of early orthodox Christianity against rival forms of Christianity. It's now known that there were lots of different kinds of Christianity in the first few centuries, but only some of these forms survived.

The form of Christianity that emerged as orthodox, leading toward the Roman Catholic and Eastern Orthodox traditions, is represented in these early writings, and that's one reason these writings, on occasion, mention early debates between Christian groups. Equally pressing is the state of the Christian movement itself in times of trouble and persecution; some of these writings are quite moving in their concern for the well-being of Christians in various ancient cities and locations.

The Shepherd of Hermas

By far the most impressive, longest, and *strangest* of the early Christian writings that almost made it into the Bible is the collection of various writings known as the *Shepherd of Hermas*.

Essentially, the Shepherd of Hermas is an account of the visions and revelations from angelic figures to the freed slave named Hermas, the recipient and ostensibly the writer of the work. This bizarre collection of materials is a mixed bag of imagery and scenes. At times, it's charming, fascinating, surprising, and a delight to read. There are moments when it even sounds a bit like something from Tolkien (author of *The Lord of the Rings* series, among other works). But there are also passages in the Shepherd of Hermas that are downright disturbing, like the images of the punishment of sinners as sheep being mistreated by mean shepherds called "angels of punishment."

Strange as it may seem to the modern reader, Hermas was a *very* popular early Christian work, and it was printed with the New Testament in some very early handwritten Bibles and collections of Christian writings.

"The Shepherd of Hermas" is a bit of a misnomer, frankly, because the angelic person who communicates with Hermas in the work assumes many identities, including women of varying ages. Although it's an actual shepherd in only part of the book, *The Shepherd of Hermas* is the work's traditional title.

The Shepherd of Hermas can be appreciated as a collection of the kinds of stories, images, and conversations that would have kept early Christians, and perhaps even early Christian young people, entertained for hours. Although they run a bit long at times, many of these stories are still quite entertaining and occasionally profound. In the following sections, we discuss some of the various visions and lessons that are found in the Shepherd of Hermas.

Who was Hermas? Who knows?

It's often suggested that the writing attributed to Hermas is from Rome, but truth be told, no one knows for sure who Hermas is, was, could have been, or wasn't.

In Romans 16:14, Paul writes, "Salute Asyncritus, Phlegon, Hermas, Patrobas, Hermes, and the brethren which are with them." Don't confuse the Hermas mentioned by Paul for the Hermas of the Shepherd of Hermas.

It's possible that "Hermas" is a fictional name given the conventions of writing such apocalyptic books, which often use a pseudonym for the author or source.

The Shepherd of Hermas is assumed to be a second-century work. Origen, the early Christian writer (185–254 CE), mentions it, providing the latest date for its existence, while some estimates for Hermas include even the early decades of the second century CE, circa 100–130 CE. Among the difficulties with dating this work and assigning it to a known area is the fact that it doesn't quote Christian writings very much at all, and it seems entirely removed from some of the debates of the late first and early second century.

Surveying the Shepherd of Hermas

The Shepherd of Hermas was normally divided into three sections, but there weren't clear-cut distinctions among them. Recent editions of this work have redivided this long writing along similar lines but provide chapter breaks for easier reference; the revised organization breaks it down into these three sections:

✔ The Visions: Chapters 1–25

✔ Commandments/Mandates: Chapters 26–49

✔ Parables: Chapters 50–114

Historians usually classify the Shepherd of Hermas as apocalyptic because it involves visions and revelations from angelic figures to the freed slave named Hermas, the recipient and ostensibly the writer of the work.

Lessons from Hermas's visions

In the beginning of the book, Hermas is introduced as the former slave of a Roman noblewoman named Rhoda. The writer (who's understood to be Hermas) explains that he became friends with Rhoda long after he served as her slave and once helped her out of the Tiber River while bathing. Presumably, Hermas saw her naked, but he claims that his thoughts of her were pure: "When I observed her beauty I began reasoning in my heart, 'I would be fortunate to have a wife of such beauty and character.'"

Later, while traveling, he falls asleep only to have a series of very strange dreams. Initially, Rhoda appears to him in his dream, accusing him of impure thoughts. Hermas protests, and the rest of the book consists of lessons revealed to Hermas by various heavenly figures.

The first is a woman who appears to Hermas at different stages of life, suggesting different stages in the life of the Christian Church and even in the life of a Christian. In subsequent visions, a younger woman appears to Hermas and reveals a great tower built of various bricks drawn from different locations. The book later clarifies that the reader is intended to understand this tower as the Christian Church composed of different kinds of people, some considered good and others bad. The different colored bricks that make up the tower are a parable about different kinds of people — those with faith that sustains them, those who give up their faith, and all who have a variety of different experiences.

In fact, three main images run through the book to represent different forms of the same general message about the composition of the Church and different kinds of people. The images are

✔ Different bricks that make up the tower

✔ Different plants that come from seedlings cut from the tree that is the Church

✔ Material drawn from different mountains to build the Church

Although these are the main images, there are other genuinely strange aspects of Hermas's visions, such as his vision of an overnight stay with a group of beautiful virgins (chapters 87–88). Although sexual activity is decidedly denied, the description has an erotic element with which Freud would no doubt have had a field day. Later, the book piously interprets the virgins as holy spirits, but not before the reader's imagination has run wild!

Lessons from the commandments of the Shepherd

Following Hermas's visions, a shepherd is introduced as a kind of angelic companion to Hermas; the Shepherd tells Hermas that he has been assigned to stay with Hermas and instruct him.

In much of the rest of the book, you read about the Shepherd's lessons for Hermas. As you can see from the following list, these commandments include some rather basic ideas (our comments appear in parentheses):

✔ Believe that God is one, who created and completed all things.

✔ Hold on to simplicity and be innocent . . . do not slander others.

✔ Tell the truth always.

✔ Don't allow sexually immoral thoughts to arise within you — think of *your* wife, not others' wives.

✔ Be patient, and resist being irritable and bitter.

✔ Proceed on the Straight Path, and avoid the Crooked Path. (Included is the notion that you can follow one of two angels in your life: a good one or a bad one.)

✔ Obey the Commandments of God, and don't fear Satan.

✔ Refrain from Evil, but don't refrain from doing Good.

✔ Don't be of two minds — be confident in your faith.

✔ Don't be grieved. (Apparently, this means that you shouldn't worry about the concerns of this life.)

✔ Test Prophets for the truth — don't believe in false prophecies.

✔ Clothe yourself with the desire to do good, and avoid evil desires.

Parables to reaffirm the Shepherd's commandments

The last section of the Shepherd of Hermas is the Parables, or stories. Some of these are similar to Jesus's parables (for example, the famous "sower of seeds" parable in Mark 4:3–9 and the "talents" parable in Matthew 25:14–31). The difference is that the parables of the Shepherd of Hermas teach different kinds of lessons; most of these stories reaffirm the same lessons taught by the Shepherd in the Commandments section of the book (see the preceding section).

The Didache: The First Written Catechism

An early teaching tool intended to summarize the moral expectations of Christian faith is *The Didache;* it's also known as the *Teaching of the Twelve Apostles.*

The word "Didache" is taken from the Greek word for "teaching."

The Didache is often dated very early — at the end of the first century CE — which suggests considerable historical value to some of the discussions included. For example, the discussions of fasting, baptism, and Eucharist (Communion) establish that these practices were being regularized in Christian worship at a very early date.

The three main subjects taken up in the Didache, each of which we discuss in this section, are

- ✔ The two ways: Chapters 1–6
- ✔ Church order: Chapters 7–15
- ✔ Church offices: Chapter 16

The two ways

The first section of the Didache presents another version of the famous two paths identified as life and death — a theme that's common to both Christian and Jewish moral instruction.

The path of life is described by the moral principles involved, and the path of death is described by a listing of traits characteristic of this negative direction. The opening sequence of this part of the Didache is short and to the point; it draws directly on the teaching of Jesus: "There are two paths, one of life and one of death . . . this then is the path of life. First, love the God who made you, and second, your neighbor as yourself . . ." (Didache 1).

Although Jesus isn't explicitly quoted here, this section consists largely of quotes from the New Testament strung together in a series, specifically Matthew 22:37–39 and Luke 10:27.

The social conservatism in the Didache is often debated. Just how much did Christians want to change society, for example? In Paul's letter to the Ephesians, Paul famously states that slaves are told to obey masters even as masters are also told never to mistreat slaves (Ephesians 6:5–9). So, some argue that this is evidence that Christians were cautious and didn't seek major social change. But is this really a social conservatism? Other historians argue that the early Christians may not have even been able to conceive of Roman society without slavery, and besides, they didn't make the rules or live in a society in which change could be suggested (Rome was hardly a democracy!). Therefore, the early Christians changed what they could change — their *own* society. Thus, they sought to make the conditions better at least among themselves and even purchased the freedom of Christian slaves on occasion. (Ignatius's *Letter to Polycarp* mentions purchasing freedom for slaves among Christians (4:3), but Ignatius also seems concerned that the churches not use all their money for this purpose!)

Church order

The second section of the Didache takes up instructions for church rituals, such as baptism, fasting, and the "thanksgiving meal," or Eucharist. This section even includes suggested prayers for the observation of these early Christian rituals.

The section is of obvious interest to those who study the history of Christian rituals because it provides a very early account of these practices in the Christian movement. On baptism, for example, the Didache says the following:

> And concerning baptism, baptize this way: Having first said all these things, baptize into the name of the Father, and of the Son, and of the Holy Spirit, in living water. But if you have no living water, baptize into other water; and if you cannot do so in cold water, do so in warm. But if you have neither, pour out water three times upon the head into the name of Father and Son and Holy Spirit. But before the baptism let the baptizer fast, and the baptized, and whoever else can; but you shall order the baptized to fast one or two days before.
>
> —Didache 7

Church offices

The last section of the Didache is a description of various offices in the Christian Church, with particular attention given to the care of Christian prophets. The book warns that there are some who claim to be church leaders and teachers, but there are ways to recognize whether they're genuine or not. The most common test is based on their attitude toward money and whether they hang around and mooch off the church too much! A pretty good indicator of genuineness, eh?

The end of the Didache is a brief apocalyptic description of the end times, but this text doesn't appear to be complete, and many historians suggest that the actual ending has been lost.

The Epistle of Polycarp to the Christians at Philippi

Polycarp was an early church leader in Smyrna, which is today Izmir in modern Turkey. He's singularly unique because so much is known about him thanks to three writings, all of which are part of the Apostolic Fathers. These writings are

- The Epistle of Polycarp to the Christians at Philippi
- An account of Polycarp's death (see the next section "The Martyrdom of Polycarp")
- Ignatius's letter to Polycarp (see the later section "The Letters of Ignatius")

Polycarp's letter to the Christians at Philippi is a general body of advice to all levels and ages of the people in the Church asking them to behave in an appropriate manner and especially to take care of one another. Leaders of the church, for example, are advised to avoid the love of money. (Hmmm, that's a good tip for everyone, we think.)

The letter also cautions against "false teachings" and "false teachers," suggesting that, at the time it was written, the differences in viewpoints among Christians were beginning to bother leaders who considered themselves orthodox in their views.

Polycarp's letter also addresses friction within the Church, but an interesting difference is that Polycarp quotes from the teachings of Jesus (especially sayings that you may know from the books of Matthew and Luke) much more frequently than another Apostolic Father, Ignatius, does.

The Martyrdom of Polycarp

Among the most unusual of the writings known as the Apostolic Fathers is the short account known as the *Martyrdom of Polycarp*. It's a description of precisely that: the events leading up to and then the death of the Church leader, the elder Polycarp, Bishop of Smyrna.

Historians have long noted the similarities between this description and many of the Passion accounts of Jesus given in the Gospels; the parallels are no doubt intentional because the writer of the Martyrdom of Polycarp frequently notes, ". . . for Polycarp waited to be betrayed, as also did the Lord. . . ." Other comparisons are the famous dialogues: In the Gospels, Jesus has interesting dialogues with Pilate and Herod, and in the Martydom of Polycarp, Polycarp engages in dialogue with his adversaries who have the power of his life in their hands. In both cases, Jesus and Polycarp act as if these adversaries are *not* really deserving of much respect!

Scholars date this book anywhere from the 150s to the 170s CE, but most historians prefer the earlier date because the actual death of Polycarp is cited in the early 150s.

The Martyrdom of Polycarp includes rather gruesome descriptions of deaths of Christians by torture and wild animals in public executions. Included in the descriptions of the death of Polycarp are elements typical of other martyr stories, such as the many attempts by Roman officials who try to talk Polycarp out of his own execution: "Take pity on your age!" But the crowd calls for the death of Polycarp and other Christians who are called "atheists" for not "believing in" the Roman gods. The cry of the crowd is reminiscent of the Passion accounts of Jesus, but in this case, it's clear that the crowd is composed of all kinds of people.

According to this writing, Polycarp has visions and dreams about his impending death and therefore knows that his martyrdom is coming. Along the way, the document carefully cautions Christians against actively seeking to be martyred; yet it makes it clear that if Christians are faced with death and martyrdom, they should face it with courage.

Polycarp is offered release if he only confesses "Caesar is Lord," but he refuses. In an act of impressive defiance, he's told to turn to his fellow Christians and say "Away with the atheists," but instead he turns to the Roman officials and crowd and says to *them,* "Away with the atheists!" As in many martyrdom accounts (including the famous discussions between Herod, Pilate, and Jesus in the New Testament, and 2 Maccabees in the Apocryphal books), a long conversation takes place between the Roman official and Polycarp, but Polycarp refuses all attempts to get him to recant his faith.

According to the writing, when the officials try to burn Polycarp alive, a miracle occurs that spares him from the flames even though they keep burning around him. Frustrated that he's not burning up, a Roman soldier stabs him with a lance. At once, a dove emerges from the wound, and the blood that gushes from Polycarp extinguishes the flames. The dove often is considered a manifestation of Polycarp's rising spirit.

After Polycarp's body was successfully burned following the stabbing, Christians considered his bones treasures that should be kept. This reaction points to a very early beginning of the tradition of relics that became so widespread in later Christianity.

The Letters of Ignatius

Ignatius was a leader in Antioch, one of the most important cities for early Christianity. (It's where the word "Christian" was first coined, according the biblical book of Acts.) In the *Letters of Ignatius,* he heads from what's known today as Syria to Rome to his own execution.

Far from avoiding his impending death, however, Ignatius seems to revel in the idea of his own martyrdom. Ignatius travels under guard by land, taking considerable time to get to Rome. Along the way, he receives visitors, sends and receives letters, and interacts with Christian groups.

In this section, we examine the seven letters of Ignatius, which some scholars used to doubt as authentic (and thus, possibly written later) in part because other, clearly later letters were also circulating. But the seven we examine here are considered the real deal!

The messages of the seven letters

Today, seven of the Letters of Ignatius are considered authentic, but for centuries many more than seven letters were in circulation, some in very long versions. Not surprisingly, considerable debate raged about what were the authentic letters even though the seven currently considered authentic were mentioned and quoted in second-century Christian writings. By the seventeenth century, however, the generally recognized seven letters of Ignatius had been agreed upon by historians and leaders of the Christian Church.

It appears that Ignatius was martyred in the time of the Roman Emperor Trajan (98–117), so the seven letters are a very early collection of important Christian letters.

Each of Ignatius's seven letters is addressed to a different group (or individual in the case of the seventh letter). They have some interesting similarities and differences, such as Ignatius's lovely tendency to provide some encouragement at the beginning of his letters, even as he addresses different issues specific to each location. The following list takes a look at each letter one by one:

✔ **To the Ephesians** (the Christians in Ephesus, in modern Turkey)

In this letter, Ignatius reaffirms the reputation of the Church in Ephesus to be strong and compassionate, but he also advises the people to be careful of "false teachers" who would divide the Church against itself. It's evident in this letter that Ignatius is capable of some charming prose: "This is the beginning and end of life: faith is the beginning, love is the end. And the two together in unity are God: all other things that lead to nobility of character follow" (14:1).

✔ **To the Magnesians** (the Christians in Magnesia, in northern Greek territory)

The notable content in this letter is Ignatius's attacks on Judaizers who maintain Jewish traditions. Ignatius wants to maintain the "new" teachings of Jesus.

✔ **To the Trallians** (the Christians in Tralles, now Aydin in modern Turkey)

After his typical encouraging opening, Ignatius warns about theological ideas that he doesn't agree with. In this letter, the imagery gets serious as he attacks those who ". . . mingle Jesus Christ with themselves, as if giving a deadly drug mixed with honeyed wine, which the unsuspecting gladly takes with evil pleasure, but then dies" (6:2). The fact that Ignatius emphasizes in chapter 9 that Jesus really was born, really lived, and really died at the hands of Pilate suggests that the heresy he was fighting against was the idea that Jesus only appeared to be a physical person but really was not. (This is an early heresy known as *docetism,* meaning "to appear.")

✔ **To the Romans**

Ignatius commends the faith of the Roman church but cautions them against taking action to prevent his martyrdom: "I urge you, do not become an untimely kindness to me. Allow me to be bread for the wild beasts; through them I am able to attain to God" (4:1). Interesting, however, he also refers to his Roman guards as "wild beasts" who frequently mistreat him (5).

✔ **To the Philadelphians** (the Christians in Philadelphia, now Alasehir in western Turkey)

Again, Ignatius is concerned about divisions within the Church and urges unity: "For there is one flesh of our Lord Jesus Christ and one cup that brings the unity of his blood, and one altar, as there is one bishop together with the presbytery and the deacons, my fellow slaves"(4). Apparently, there were also those who advised continued observance of Jewish ritual laws, which upset Ignatius immensely (see the letter to the Magnesians earlier in this list). By this time, Christianity and Judaism were going their separate ways, and there was no love lost between them.

Ignatius's letter to the Philadelphians makes an interesting reference to debates about the sayings of Jesus, but Ignatius asserts his own confidence and qualifications to interpret the tradition about Jesus, even if others claim to have a "written record." Ignatius's words suggest that there already may have been disputes about genuine writings — that is, writings that disagree with what Ignatius considers correct belief about Jesus. He writes, "But as for me, Jesus Christ is the ancient records: the sacred ancient records are his cross and death, and his resurrection, and the faith that comes through him" (8).

✔ **To the Smyrneans** (the Christians in Smyrna, now Izmir in Turkey)

In Smyrna, there were disputes about whether Jesus was truly human or only appeared to be. In his letter to the Smyrneans, Ignatius gets a bit testy with folks who argue that Jesus only appeared to be human: "They are the ones who are only an appearance!" (2:1). Ouch. Ignatius cites the post-Resurrection accounts in the Gospels to argue against this tendency to deny the material reality of the human Jesus. He advises Christians in Smyrna to avoid those who argue with them about Jesus's humanity.

✔ **To Polycarp, Bishop of Smyrna**

Ignatius addresses a letter to a fellow church leader, Polycarp, Bishop of Smyrna. Given the divisions Ignatius refers to in his general letter to the Christians in Smyrna (see the preceding bullet), it comes as little surprise that he advises Polycarp to work toward unity and quotes Jesus (Matthew 10:16) to advise Polycarp to be ". . . wise as a serpent in all things and always pure as the dove" (2:2).

Defending Christian orthodoxy

Of particular interest in the letters of Ignatius is his defense of Christian orthodoxy (that is, the "right belief"). It's why these writings have gotten so much attention, especially by historians who wish to better understand the divisions and debates that plagued the early Christian movement. In his letters, Ignatius takes objection to two major heresies: the Judaizers and the Gnostics.

Judging Judaizers

Judaizers (somewhat ironically given that Christianity was, after all, originally a Jewish movement) are Christians who wish to affirm their continued Jewish identity and even insist that a strong adherence to traditional Jewish practices — such as attending synagogue, observing strict food laws, and maintaining ritual purity — ought to be the norm for all Christians, whether Jewish or Gentile.

Why was circumcision so important?

Circumcision, the surgical removal of the fore-skin on the male penis, is a physical act that's usually performed within a month of birth for male children in many religious and cultural traditions around the world.

There's an ongoing debate about whether the practice is rooted in ancient beliefs about health or superstition, but it's clear that it was considered one of the main ritual requirements of Jewish identity and faith in ancient Jewish practice, beginning early in the biblical texts. According to the tradition in the book of Genesis, this physical mark was the sign of the agreement that God made with Abraham and a sign to accompany God's promise that Abraham would have as many descendants as the stars in the sky (Genesis 15 and Genesis 17:11).

When you think about it (after blushing, perhaps), it makes some sense that the physical sign of this nature would involve the male sex organ if the accompanying promise was the promise of descendants. Thus, any sexual act would involve being visually reminded of God's promise to Abraham!

However, circumcision came to have wider symbolic significance as well, and in early Christianity, it was used as a kind of shorthand or code to speak of Jewish ritual observance more generally. Thus, Paul speaks of a kind of spiritual circumcision in his famous letter to the Roman Christians: "For a person is not a Jew who is one outwardly, nor is true circumcision something external and physical. Rather, a person is a Jew who is one inwardly, and real circumcision is a matter of the heart — it is spiritual and not literal. Such a person receives praise not from others but from God" (Romans 2:28–29).

Clearly, the single physical marking has come to represent a spiritual identity that involves observing more than this one act in Jewish tradition. When historians speak of the pro-circumcision arguments in early Christianity, they refer to people who advocated a wide range of Jewish ritual practices, not only this one. However, one can easily understand why new adult male converts to Christianity often found the idea of circumcision to be highly objectionable (and even scary!). It wasn't always just a symbolic objection, nor was it always just a religious issue.

As the Christian movement grew among non-Jews, there was considerable debate about whether Christianity should change its ritual practices to accommodate the increasing non-Jewish population of converts. These folks weren't always attracted to all the ritual requirements of Jewish life — most notably, undergoing circumcision (see the nearby sidebar on this pleasant topic!). In his letter to Christians in Philadelphia, for example, Ignatius calls his Jewish and Christian opponents on this issue "tombs of death" (6:1).

Not buying into Gnosticism

Gnosticism is the idea that humans are spiritual rather than material beings and that the most important reality is spiritual rather than the temporary body that humans occupy. (For more on Gnostic writings, see Chapter 12.) This philosophical set of ideas had a great impact on many Christians.

Gnosticism tends to praise the idea of death as liberating the soul and downgrades the significance of any material issues of life as mere distractions. Furthermore, Christian Gnostics wrote many of their own writings, considering Jesus a true Gnostic teacher when interpreted correctly. However, the Gnostics also wrote their own Gospels complete with highly suspicious quotations from Jesus that rather conveniently supported their own ideas. When in his letter to the Smyrneans Ignatius attacks those who teach that Jesus only "appeared" to suffer but didn't actually suffer (because he didn't have a real body, which would have offended Gnostic ideas about the importance of the spiritual over the material), it seems clear that Ignatius is directing some fire toward Gnostics in the churches (2).

1 Clement

I (Daniel) confess that when asked, "Which of the Apostolic Fathers would you have included in the New Testament?", I usually answer without hesitation: 1 Clement. Why? Because this letter is mostly about people getting along with each other. As I look at the world of Christians squabbling with each other, it seems to me that it surely wouldn't have hurt to have a stronger message of "Peace, brothers and sisters!" over the centuries. And as a wise old friend of mine was fond of saying, "And if it can't hurt, it's gotta help!"

1 Clement is written in standard letter form and now is divided traditionally into 65 chapters. However, this breakdown is misleading because the work isn't as long as you may think; some of the so-called chapters are only five or six verses long. Also, 1 Clement is directed to the Christians in Corinth (yes, the same church addressed by Paul in the New Testament books of 1 and 2 Corinthians . . . apparently a somewhat feisty congregation!).

There's some controversy over whether the writer of 1 Clement really was Clement, the historical leader of the Christians in Rome, and even whether the historical Clement was the second or third Bishop in Rome. Some scholars wonder whether a person of such authority wouldn't have mentioned that he had such authority in the course of the letter. The belief that Clement is the author of this letter is at least as old as the early fourth-century writings of Eusebius, and one Christian writer — Dionysius of Corinth — claims Clement as the author in the second century CE. In any case, it's very possible that this letter dates from the time of Roman Emperor Domitian (81–96 CE), particularly given the argument of some scholars that the letter may be a response to conditions of persecution during Domitian's reign.

Two reasons 1 Clement is important

Professor Bart Ehrman, who has written extensively on early Christian literature, believes that the importance of 1 Clement can be summarized in the following points:

- ✔ The early and heavy use of Hebrew Bible Scripture quotation in Christian letters, pointing to an early tradition of citing treasured religious writings even before there was an official canon
- ✔ The presumed importance of the church in Rome as a source of leadership and influence over other churches

1 Clement begins by praising the reputation of the church in Corinth and expressing the writer's sadness over the disagreements that have arisen — especially disagreements among younger church members over the older leadership that arose because of jealousy. The letter then goes through an interesting series of Hebrew Bible citations of conflicts between characters in the Jewish tradition, pointing out how jealousy ruined their relationships and even endangered lives. The writer follows that up with contemporary examples, one of which is how jealousy led to the killing of Peter and Paul: "Because of jealousy and strife Paul pointed the way to the prize for endurance. Seven times he bore chains; he was sent into exile and stoned, he served as a herald in both the East and the West, and he received the noble reputation for his faith" (5:5–7).

In a particularly moving section, the writer of 1 Clement advises repentance, that is, willingness to admit your mistakes in hopes of reconciling with those you disagree with. 1 Clement reviews another series of episodes of reconciliation in Hebrew history, including Noah, Abraham, Jonah, and finally Jesus.

Clement's message for the ages

What's Clement's message for the ages? Basically, it's "Why can't we all just get along?" It appears in thoughts like these:

- ✔ "We should treat one another kindly, according the compassion and sweet character of the one who made us." (14:3)
- ✔ "Therefore we should cling to those who keep the peace with piety, not those who wish for peace out of hypocrisy." (15:1)

This message is based firmly in the writer's understanding of the example of Jesus. 1 Clement's advice to the leadership is also a strong word of caution, recognizing that the conflict most likely has two sides:

For Christ belongs to those who are humble-minded, not to those who vaunt themselves over his flock. The scepter of God's majesty, the Lord Jesus Christ, did not come with an ostentatious show of arrogance or haughtiness — even though he could have done so — but with a humble mind, just as the Holy Spirit spoke concerning him.

—1 Clement 16:1–2

According to 1 Clement, even the regular patterns of the planets and sun are signs of the harmony and peacefulness of the cosmos; the sun and moon don't interfere with one another (1 Clement 20). Interestingly, the writer even makes reference to the legend of the Phoenix, the bird that's reborn in flames every 500 years! It seems likely that the writer takes this legend quite literally as a natural example of resurrection and new life.

2 Clement

Some scholars have suggested that 2 Clement is the most under-appreciated book of the Apostolic Fathers. Perhaps so. Although it's often called a "letter," it doesn't reveal the standard elements of the letter form and is, in fact, a speech or sermon. It may be the oldest Christian sermon after the preaching that's summarized in the book of Acts in the New Testament. Historians are equally perplexed about the author; it certainly isn't Clement, but nobody knows who else it could be! Finally, no one even knows when 2 Clement was written, although most guesses place it around 120–170 CE.

Questionable interpretations of Scripture

In general, 2 Clement advises moral behavior based on a large number of references to the Hebrew Scriptures and Jesus. However, 2 Clement reveals some interesting techniques for the interpretation of Scripture — and I rather doubt that modern readers of the Bible would be entirely happy with what appears to be somewhat strained interpretations just to make passages relevant for the writer.

Consider the following, which begins with a quotation from the biblical Prophet Isaiah: "Be jubilant, you who are infertile, and who do not bear children! Let your voice burst forth and cry out, you who experience no pains of labor!" (Isaiah 54:1). In Isaiah, this is most likely a call to anticipate renewal and restoration of Israelite peoples after going through difficult times. But the writer of 2 Clement takes it in a completely different direction: "Now, when it says, 'Be Jubilant, you who are infertile and who do not bear children', it is referring to us. For our church was infertile before children were given to it . . ." (2 Clement 2:1).

The writer isn't saying, "That verse *might* be thought to *remind* us of our situation." Oh no. The writer says, "That old verse was *literally* talking about us right now!"

In other words, 2 Clement essentially says that the Hebrew Bible is really a Christian document because it speaks about Christians and the issues that Christians face. This interesting aspect of 2 Clement reveals some of the ways in which Christians made the Hebrew Bible (or Old Testament) into a Christian — and therefore *not* Jewish — book.

A lost teaching of Jesus?

Another fascinating aspect of 2 Clement is that it cites a teaching of Jesus that is unknown in the Gospels but similar to a Gospel version of the teaching. There's the Gospel teaching in which Jesus says, "I send you as sheep among wolves . . ." (Matthew 10:16; Luke 10:3). But 2 Clement records that Peter actually discussed this idea further:

> *But Peter replied to him, "What if the wolves rip apart the sheep?" Jesus said to Peter, "After they are dead, the sheep should fear the wolves no longer. So too you, do not fear those who kill you and then can do nothing more to you; but fear the one who, after you die, has the power to cast your body and soul into the hell of fire."*
>
> —2 Clement 5:2–4

The writing as a whole seems quite obsessed with the notion of repentance and turning away from sin in this world quickly. 2 Clement carries a strong notion about judgment coming soon but also an equally strong sense of the responsibilities of taking care of people in this world. The writer says, "Giving to charity, therefore, is good as a repentance from sin. Fasting is better than prayer, but giving to charity is better than both. Love covers a multitude of sins . . . for giving to charity lightens the load of sin" (16:4).

A final thought on faith and doing the right thing

A final thought comes at the end of this sermon: If repentance is so important, why do the sinners seem to be doing so well? It seems at first that 2 Clement is giving the standard, stereotypical answer: "They'll be paid in heaven," but then the writer concludes with a profound thought, namely that this is a matter of *faith*, not a business transaction! People don't do the right thing merely for instant rewards but rather for the simple fact of doing the right thing! The text is as follows:

But neither should this thought disturb you, that we see the unjust becoming rich while the slaves of God suffer in dire straight. We need to have faith, brothers and sisters! . . . For if God were to reward the upright immediately, we would straightaway be engaged in commerce rather than devotion to God. For we would appear to be upright not for the sake of piety but for a profit.

—2 Clement 20:2–4

The Epistle of Barnabas

The *Epistle of Barnabas* is attributed to a very early Christian leader and preacher who was often associated with Paul but isn't considered a genuine writing of this early Christian. Nevertheless, it's a very popular early work and one of the Apostolic Fathers.

It appears that the Epistle is addressed to Christians (or specifically Jewish-Christians) who wished either to return to Judaism or practice a form of Christianity that continued to embrace much of Jewish traditional practice and ritual.

The writing seems to anticipate the rebuilding of the Temple of Jerusalem, which was destroyed by Romans in 70 CE, and so usually is dated after that event. It's also possible that it dates to the early decades of the second century when there was some speculation of rebuilding the Temple yet again. Some historians speculate that a particular event may have incited the strong anti-Jewish polemics of this writing; possibilities include the Bar Kochba Revolt of 130–132 CE, in which some Jewish-Christians were persecuted by Roman officials for suspicion of being involved in the revolt (and perhaps some were!).

Frankly, historians of Christianity express some relief that the Epistle of Barnabas wasn't accepted into the New Testament canon because it contains a level of anti-Jewish polemics that no doubt would have made Jewish-Christian relations over the years worse than they already were.

Right off the bat, Barnabas attacks traditional Jewish practices

The Epistle begins immediately with an attack on traditional Jewish practices of sacrifice and fasting, declaring both to be empty actions from a Christian perspective. To make this point, the writer even quotes Hebrew prophets who criticize the sacrifice! The Hebrew prophets, like Amos (Amos 5:21–25), were deeply offended by the abuse of the sacrificial system by wealthy persons who simply wanted to cover over their mistreatment of the poor by adding more sacrifices rather than actually changing their behavior.

Barnabas's bizarre interpretation techniques

The Epistle of Barnabas reveals some very strained techniques of interpretation. For example, in the Old Testament, Abraham is told to circumcise 318 people (Genesis 14:14). The Epistle of Barnabas (chapter 9) compares the Greek letters used to write these numbers to the letters used to spell "Jesus," therefore taking this Old Testament passage as a reference to Jesus.

Sometimes these interpretations are quite entertaining (Moses commands humans to not eat pigs because pigs live in luxury and therefore are examples of laziness and gluttony; chapter 10) and other times are downright nasty (Jews are called fools for wanting to rebuild the Temple; chapter 16). This is hardly an acceptable technique for interpretation in modern historical work, but isn't entirely unusual for ancient arguments. Such techniques were well known in other documents, even including early Rabbinic interpretation of Scripture within the context of early Judaism.

For the writer, righteous actions are better than sacrifice, and taking care of the poor is better than fasting (a thought that's already noted by Hebrew prophets like Isaiah 58 and Micah 6:7–8). Thus, the writer wants to argue that God has passed over the Jews in favor of the Christians and attempts to use the Old Testament to argue his point.

Some historians believe that the last portion of the writing, chapters 17–21, may have come from another source because it goes in a radically different direction, taking up the famous "two paths" idea seen in the Didache (see the earlier section) — the path of light versus the path of darkness.

Revisiting the two paths

As in other early Christian writings, the Epistle contains a discussion of the two paths: one of righteousness, and one of evil ("the Dark One"; 20:1). The two are contrasted with all kinds of characteristics of good (be humble, meek, and gentle) and evil (sexual immorality, killing the unborn, greed), in the contrast between light and darkness. This form of teaching that radically contrasts between good and evil, sometimes involving following good angels and bad angels (see the earlier section "Surveying the Shepherd of Hermas"), was a typical teaching style of early Christian and Jewish writings.

The Epistle to Diognetus

The *Epistle to Diognetus* is considered one of the first Christian apologetics, or defense of Christian faith to a person asking for more information. This old and common form of Christian writing may come out of authentic answers to inquiries by real people or simply may be a rhetorical device. This particular work seems to be dated at the latest to the late-second century, but many suggest it's early-second century.

An *apologetic* is a formal defense of a doctrine. The word comes from the Greek word "apologia," which means "in defense of."

The writer of the Epistle begins with an attack on Roman worship of forms, idols, and figures, and also explains why Christians aren't the same as Jews.

The Christian is a sojourner in the world

The most famous exposition in the Epistle to Diognetus is the rather poetic description of Christians as aliens, or *sojourners,* in the world. It's perhaps intended to be an exposition of the famous words of Jesus to be in the world but not "of the world" (John 17). Here's the quote from the Epistle:

> *They live in their respective countries, but only as resident aliens: they participate in all things as citizens, and they endure all things as foreigners. Every foreign territory is a homeland for them, every homeland foreign territory . . . they live on earth but participate in the life of heaven . . . they love everyone and are persecuted by all. They are not understood and they are condemned . . . to put the matter simply, what the soul is in the body, this is what Christians are in the world . . .*

> —Epistle to Diognetus 5:5, 5:9, 6:1

The bottom line: Pay attention to God's creation

The writer of the Epistle defends Christianity as a faith that delivered pagan Greeks and Romans from their former blindness in worshipping empty gods and suggests that the truth of Christianity can be perceived simply by paying attention to the majesty of God's creation. The suggestion that such insights will result in people taking better care of each other is moving. Here's the quote from the Epistle:

> *For whoever takes up the burden of his neighbor, whoever wants to use his own abundance to help someone in need, whoever provides for the destitute from the possessions he has received from God — himself becoming a god to those who receive them — this one is an imitator of God.*

> —Epistle to Diognetus 10:6

Chapter 14

Traditions about St. Paul

. . . .

In This Chapter

▶ Exploring writings attributed to Paul

▶ Following along on Paul's adventures in other writings

. . . .

*W*ithout a doubt, the second most important character in the New Testament after Jesus is Paul of Tarsus, or St. Paul. The two main reasons Paul is so important are:

✔ His influence is felt in virtually all forms of modern Christian expression.

✔ A large portion of the New Testament is influenced by his writings, his work, or his thought.

It comes as no surprise, then, that there are *lots* of writings dealing with Paul — even a few claiming to be written *by* Paul — that didn't make it into the New Testament. In this chapter, we take a look at non-canonical Paul — both the writings that claim Paul as the author and a few legendary accounts of Paul's adventures.

Paul is thought to have written *most* but not *all* of the letters (called *epistles*) attributed to him in the New Testament. Some writings, like Hebrews, may have been included in the New Testament because at one time they were *thought* to be written by Paul, but modern New Testament scholars are quite certain that Hebrews and a few others are definitely *not* from our boy! See the nearby sidebar, "Arguing about Pauline authorship in the New Testament," for more.

So, if letters were written in the name of Paul, but not *by* Paul, and they're in the New Testament anyway, it's hardly surprising that the practice of writing *Pauline books* continued. These writings supposedly by Paul and many *about* Paul continued to be produced in the first 500 years of Christianity.

Arguing about Pauline authorship in the New Testament

As with many influential writers, confusion surrounds Paul's writings. Paul is credited with writing *a lot* of books in the New Testament; virtually all New Testament scholars agree that Paul wrote Romans, 1 Corinthians, 1 Thessalonians, Galatians, Philippians, and Philemon. However, even though all these works are purported to be written by Paul, most New Testament scholars are quite adamant that Paul did *not* write 1 and 2 Timothy, Titus, or 2 Thessalonians; also, he probably (this is less certain) didn't write Ephesians or Colossians.

Some New Testament scholars think that one reason someone would sign another name to a work is to do that person honor; if you think you were influenced by someone important, you may think it's arrogant to sign your own name when you think your ideas are basically from your teacher, so you sign your teacher's name, not yours. It's a perfectly innocent idea but one that's likely to cause problems for later generations who don't agree that accurate authorship isn't important!

Scholars come to these opinions about Paul's writings usually based on arguments of Greek writing style or even content. They argue that subtle but potentially significant differences exist between Colossians, for example, and 1 Corinthians or Romans in terms of religious arguments. Consider the difference between the following two passages:

✔ "Therefore we have been buried with him by baptism into death, so that, just as Christ was raised from the dead by the glory of the Father, so we too might walk in newness of life. For if we have been united with him in a death like his, we will certainly be united with him in a resurrection like his." (Romans 6:4–5)

✔ "When you were buried with him [Jesus] in baptism, you were also raised with him [Jesus] through faith in the power of God, who raised him from the dead." (Colossians 2:12)

Did you catch it? In Romans, Paul talks about how, in the future, we will experience resurrection like Jesus did. Colossians, however, suggests that a Christian, by becoming a Christian, has already experienced a raising! Would Paul have written the Colossians line? Many argue no and say that he may not have entirely approved of this idea of a "present experience" of resurrection, which makes it into a kind of spiritual experience. Paul probably believed in an *actual* resurrection, like Jesus already experienced, but for us it will be *after death and in the future!*

Is this enough to build an argument that Colossians was written by a different author? Maybe so . . . but at least you see how these debates can go.

Paul didn't know Jesus before the crucifixion but rather says that he was called to be an Apostle (an early follower of Jesus) by a startling vision of the risen Jesus while on the road to Damascus. Before this vision, Paul was apparently quite anti-Christian and even presided over persecution of Christians. After his experience, Paul became one of the most dynamic preachers and teachers of Christianity in the entire history of the movement!

Later Non-Biblical Letters and Writings Attributed to Paul

Paul (shown in a mosaic in Figure 14-1) is most famous for his letters in the New Testament. They were addressed mostly to churches but sometimes to an individual (for example, Philemon is in fact a personal letter to an early Christian named Philemon). As we explain earlier, Pauline letters continued to be produced after Paul was long gone. Neat trick, eh?

In this section, we look at some of these later letters that were supposedly written by Paul, even though no one today really believes it. These letters include one that seems to be basically a patchwork from *real* letters, another tradition that consists of correspondence with the Roman philosopher Seneca, and finally another letter to Corinth!

Figure 14-1:
St. Paul.

Scala / Art Resource, NY

The Epistle to the Laodicians

The Epistle to the Laodicians consists largely of sentences from genuine Pauline epistles strung together in a very short letter. It's no surprise, then, that it sounds like Paul because most of it is! Consider the following familiar-sounding phrases:

> *And his mercy will work in you, that you may have the same love and be of one mind. Therefore, beloved, as you have heard in my presence, so hold fast and work in the fear of God, and eternal life will be yours. For it is God who works in you. And do without hesitation what you do. And for the rest, beloved, rejoice in Christ and beware of those who are out for sordid gain. May all your requests be manifest before God and be steadfast in the mind of Christ. And do what is pure, true, proper, just and lovely. And what you have heard and received, hold in your heart, and peace will be with you.*

—Epistle to the Laodicians 9–16 (tr. Elliott)

Still, this letter has been recognized as a later writing by early Church writers.

The Correspondence of Paul and Seneca

The Correspondence of Paul and Seneca is supposed to be an exchange of brief letters between Paul and the famous Roman philosopher Seneca ("The Younger"; 4 BCE–65 CE). However, we have *no* evidence from the known writings of Seneca that he ever carried on such a correspondence, and frankly, very little of any significance is said between them in this writing, other than mutual admiration.

That admiration, in itself, was probably the point; it's possible that the writing was intended to show how even a famous Roman respects Paul. But beyond that, the Correspondence isn't very thrilling. Seneca, for example, applauds Paul's ideas but doesn't say which thoughts he has in mind or why he likes them:

> *These thoughts, I believe, were expressed not by you, but through you; though sometimes they were expressed both by you and through you; for they are so lofty and so brilliant with noble sentiments that in my opinion generations of men could hardly be enough to become established and perfected in them. I wish you good health, brother.*

—Correspondence of Paul and Seneca (tr. Elliott)

Paul, being not terribly modest (an attitude that's occasionally evident in the *real* New Testament Paul), expresses his thanks for the compliments:

. . . you write somewhere that you are pleased with my letter, and I count myself fortunate in the approval of a man who is so great. For you, a critic, a philosopher, the teacher of so great a ruler, nay even of everyone, would not say this unless you speak the truth. I hope that you may long be in good health.

—Correspondence of Paul and Seneca (tr. Elliott)

And it goes on rather like this for about 14 short little letters. (Yawn.)

The Later Corinthian Correspondence

The *Acts of Paul* collections include documents purported to be an exchange of letters between Paul and the Christians in Corinth. Scholars consider these letters, called the *Later Corinthian Correspondence,* an extension of the correspondence in the New Testament — 1 and 2 Corinthians, generally acknowledged to be actual writings of Paul. These letters, however, are latter creations, associated with these later writings about Paul and not written by Paul himself.

This collection of letters begins with a letter to Paul about two visitors who have come to the Corinthian Church teaching ideas that the Corinthians don't think are right:

What they say and teach is as follows: They assert that one must not appeal to the prophets and that God is not almighty, there is no resurrection of the body, man has not been made by God, Christ has neither come in the flesh, nor was he born of Mary, and the world is not the work of God but of angels . . .

—Later Corinthian Correspondence (tr. Elliott)

Most of these ideas are readily identified with the mystical teachings of Gnosticism, which we cover in Chapter 12. So, whatever the source of these purported letters, they're certainly not from Gnostic Christian writers given that the letters strongly attack those views.

Paul replies to this letter at some length, affirming traditional and orthodox views of Jesus being born of Mary, from the line of David, and being raised in the flesh at his resurrection. Paul also affirms the Old Testament traditions, especially the Prophets. In short, Paul summarizes:

Turn away from them and keep aloof from their teaching. And those who say that there is no resurrection of the flesh shall have no resurrection!

—Later Corinthian Correspondence (tr. Elliott)

Paul also refers to Jonah as a symbol of Christ's resurrection (an interpretation of Jonah that was popular in early Christian folklore).

Legends about Paul

In this chapter, we consider a number of stories that later Christians (after the first century) began to write about the first followers of Jesus — the Apostles. But the Apostle Paul is rather special in that he occupies a good deal of attention in the New Testament (more than any other Apostle), so it's hardly surprising that many legends about him arose.

The writings that comprise the Acts of Paul contain numerous themes and ideas similar to the other later Acts (those of Peter, Thomas, and so on), but the strong female figures in the other writings aren't nearly as powerfully portrayed as Thecla in the Acts of Paul (see the next section for her story). These writings have generated a considerable amount of interest because they suggest that there may well have been strong female leaders in the early Christian movement — and perhaps even a *real* Thecla who stands behind the legends (like there's a real Paul who stands behind these legends, as well).

Virtually *all* this material was known by early Christians to be late and unconnected to Paul, with the possible exception of the Paul and Thecla tradition, which a few early Christian writers appear to have taken seriously. Modern historians continue to be fascinated with the *story* of Thecla, as were ancient Christians right into the Middle Ages. However, modern historians are in agreement that this material shouldn't be taken as anything other than interesting indications of what second to fourth century Christians were thinking and reading about.

The Acts of Paul and Thecla

The story of St. Paul and his ministry to, and later with, Thecla is one of the most fascinating pieces of early Acts literature (see Chapter 15 for other Acts of early Apostles). In fact, the female character Thecla was a very important person in later Christian art and legend, but it's unknown if her character in that usage was based on a real person or entirely a matter of folklore.

The *Acts of Paul and Thecla* opens with Paul traveling with two non-Christians, finally arriving in a town where Paul knows a Christian family headed by Onesiphorus, his children Simmias and Zeno, and wife Lectra. Obviously, Lectra hasn't exactly behaved according to Paul's counsel of virginity, but there's no condemnation of them for being a family:

> *. . . after Paul had gone into the house of Onesiphorus there was great joy and bowing of knees and breaking of bread and word of God about abstinence and the resurrection. Paul said, "Blessed are the pure in heart, for they shall see God; blessed are those who have kept the flesh chaste, for they shall become a temple of God; blessed are the continent, for God shall speak with them; blessed are those who have kept aloof from this world, for they shall be pleasing to God; blessed are those who have wives as not having them, for they shall experience God . . ."*

—Acts of Paul and Thecla 5 (tr. Elliott, 365)

Paul's fame becomes a matter of local gossip, and soon many people are coming to hear him preach, including Thecla, a woman from an elite family who's engaged to marry a local nobleman named Thamyris. However, Thecla's mother becomes quite worried about her daughter's interest in the teachings of Paul, and she contacts Thamyris with the bad news: Thecla is talking about remaining unmarried! Oh no! When Thamyris investigates, he finds that Thecla's mother is right, and he's furious. Soon, Paul is arrested and Thamyris is among the accusers:

> *O proconsul, this man — we do not know where he comes from — makes virgins averse to marriage!*

—Acts of Paul and Thecla 16 (tr. Elliott, 367)

And the trial begins. Paul is imprisoned until the local governor can determine what to do with him. Meanwhile, Thecla continues to visit Paul in prison. When she's dragged into the trial, she states publicly that she refuses to marry Thamyris, and her own mother condemns her to die for refusing the marriage! Thecla is condemned to be burned for her refusal, but the attempt to execute her fails:

> *. . . the executioners arranged the wood and told her to go up on the pile. And having made the sign of the cross she went up on the pile. And they lighted the fire. And though a great fire was blazing it did not touch her. For God, having compassion upon her, made an underground rumbling, and a cloud full of water and hail overshadowed the theatre from above, and all its contents were poured out so that many were in danger of death. And the fire was put out and Thecla saved.*

—Acts of Paul and Thecla 22 (tr. Elliott, 368)

In a subsequent episode, Thecla follows Paul to Antioch where a man named Alexander attempts to marry Thecla. But she "tore his cloak and pulled off his crown, and made him a laughing-stock!" Here you see the theme of strong female characters in this later Christian folklore literature. Thecla is not intimidated! For her attack and refusal to marry, she's condemned to be fed to wild beasts in a theatre. Even though she is befriended by a high-placed noblewoman named Queen Tryphaena, Thecla's sentence is still to be carried out.

When Thecla faces the wild beasts, however, the first creature — a lioness — roars out of her cage only to lie at the woman's feet. When next a bear tries to attack her, the lioness kills it. Finally, the lioness confronts a lion, they're both killed, and Thecla mourns the death of her protector, the lioness. She jumps into a pool of water filled with dangerous "seals" in order to baptize herself. Because no animals seem able to kill her, Alexander (the second man she refused to marry) demands that he be allowed to release bulls to kill her. But when Queen Tryphaena faints and people believe she has died, Alexander calls a halt to the event.

The Governor, however, is impressed with all these events and asks Thecla to explain why no animals will touch her. She replies:

> *I am a servant of the living God and, as to what there is about me, I have believed in the Son of God in whom he is well pleased; that is why not one of the beasts touched me. For he alone is the goal of salvation and the basis of immortal life. For he is a refuge to the tempest-tossed, a solace to the afflicted, a shelter to the despairing; in brief, whoever does not believe in him shall not live but be dead forever.*

> —Acts of Paul and Thecla 37 (tr. Elliott, 371)

The Governor releases Thecla to the joyful shouts of many women who came to the theatre in her support. Queen Tryphaena converts to Christianity and takes Thecla home for a rest, and later she heavily supports the poor and the Christian ministry of Thecla. Thecla goes to visit Paul, who's astonished to see her alive and well, but Thecla soon returns to her homeland where she "enlightened many by the word of God" and eventually "rested in a glorious sleep." So ends the story of Paul and Thecla.

Further Acts episodes and travels

Further descriptions of Paul's travels and miracles come after the Thecla material. Included in this material is the *Third Epistle to the Corinthians,* and then the Acts of Paul carry right on! In one fascinating episode, Paul is praying with fellow Christians in Corinth when he hears two prophets who stand and deliver messages. At first, a male prophet announces that Paul is going to be martyred. This news distresses everyone (Paul included!) until a second prophet, a woman named Myrta, rises and assures them all that God has a wonderful plan for Paul in Rome and that many will be saved because of his ministry. At this reassuring word, Paul and others rejoice.

What's fascinating about this episode, of course, is the window it provides into a Christian service where messages from Prophets are part of the gathering — suggesting that this story may be an accurate portrayal of these kinds of early Christian gatherings and the hearing of Prophets among the people.

The Martyrdom of Paul

Among the Acts of Paul literature is a striking description of the last days of Paul in the writing the *Martyrdom of Paul*. Having arrived in Rome, Paul is told of the death of a young man named Patroclus, who was even known to Caesar Nero. Paul leads the Christians in prayer for his life, and the boy rises to life. Nero is stunned to see the boy alive, and the following conversation reveals the strong political orientation of some of this literature:

> *"Patroclus, are you alive?" He answered, I am alive, Caesar. But he said, "Who is he who made you alive?" And the boy, uplifted by the confidence of faith, said, "Christ Jesus, the king of the ages." The emperor asked in dismay, "Is he to be king of the ages and destroy all kingdoms?" Patroclus said to him, "Yes, he destroys all kingdoms under heaven, and he alone shall remain in all eternity, and there will be no kingdom which escapes him." And he [Nero] struck his face and cried out, "Patroclus, are you also fighting for that king?" He answered, "Yes my lord and Caesar, for he has raised me from the dead!"*
>
> —Martyrdom of Paul 2 (tr. Elliott, 386)

Nero is obviously frightened by the power of Paul and the Christians and is horrified to discover that some among his own guard and soldiers have become followers of Jesus. He promptly has them executed, acting in precisely the tyrannical manner that history has judged the real Nero to have lived. Finally, Paul appears before Nero, who condemns Paul to be beheaded (the form of capital punishment for Roman citizens, who weren't crucified or tortured). After Paul is beheaded, however, his spirit is seen praying with other Christians, and more members of Nero's guard become Christians as a result of seeing Paul's spirit. So ends the account.

The Apocalypse of Paul

The *Apocalypse of Paul* is a major writing that's more widely known than another, short apocalyptic writing from the Nag Hammadi Library that's clearly Gnostic (we look at it briefly in Chapter 12). The Apocalypse is quite lengthy, but unlike many apocalyptic writings, it's not terribly difficult to understand. In fact, we sometimes wish that some of it *was* difficult to understand given that the sections of "judgment on sinners" can get both graphic and, well, rather mean-spirited.

Why write an Apocalypse that claims to be from Paul? Because Paul had serious apocalyptic interests (see 1 Corinthians 15, for example) and even refers in the New Testament to a vision that he either learned about or experienced for himself. Consider this excerpt, and note that 2 Corinthians 12:6–7 suggests that Paul is the visionary in question:

It is necessary to boast; nothing is to be gained by it, but I will go on to visions and revelations of the Lord. I know a person in Christ who fourteen years ago was caught up to the third heaven — whether in the body or out of the body I do not know; God knows. And I know that such a person — whether in the body or out of the body I do not know; God knows — was caught up into Paradise and heard things that are not to be told, that no mortal is permitted to repeat.

—2 Corinthians 12:1–4

The Apocalypse of Paul was written with this famous passage from Corinthians firmly in mind. But how early is the Apocalypse writing? In his 1924 edition of English translations of much of the early Christian apocryphal books, Professor James notes that the first *certain* reference to this writing is from St. Augustine (354–430 CE), who dismissed it as a forgery. Apparently, however, it was popular among early monks, which makes sense because their particular lifestyle is praised in many aspects of this writing.

One of the interesting aspects of this writing is that it begins with a later monk (perhaps from the fourth century) having a vision while living in the same house as Paul in Tarsus (modern Turkey). In this vision, the monk is told to tear into the foundation of the house, where he finds a box. He opens the box to reveal a writing left by Paul. Most ancient writings rarely describe their own discovery, so this is a rather interesting beginning (and suggests that the writing can't be later than the fourth century).

God speaks to the sun, moon, stars, and ocean

The writing from Paul is described in great detail, beginning with a series of conversations between God and the sun, moon, stars, and ocean. Each says to God that it's sick and tired of watching humans screw up their lives (and their eternal fate) so badly, and each asks why God doesn't let them use their powers and teach humans a lesson. Each time, God answers in the same way — "I know what they are doing" — but assures the sun, moon, stars, and ocean that God wants to be patient, ". . . until they [humans] are converted and repent" (*Apocalypse of Paul 6,* tr. Duesnsing and Otero, Schneemelcher, II, 717).

The earth explains how it's especially depressing to watch what happens at sunset:

For at that hour all the angels go to the Lord to worship him and bring before him all the deeds of men, whether good or evil, which each of them does from morning until evening. And one angel goes forth rejoicing from the man he indwells but another goes with sad face . . .

—Apocalypse of Paul 7 (ed. Schneemelcher, 718)

This notion that Creation watches the sins of humanity is a rare theme in apocalyptic literature and may well be inspired from Paul's famous words in Romans:

> *For the creation waits with eager longing for the revealing of the children of God; for the creation was subjected to futility, not of its own will but by the will of the one who subjected it, in hope that the creation itself will be set free from its bondage to decay and will obtain the freedom of the glory of the children of God. We know that the whole creation has been groaning in labor pains until now; and not only the creation, but we ourselves, who have the first fruits of the Spirit, groan inwardly while we wait for adoption, the redemption of our bodies.*

> —Romans 8:19–23

As Paul watches, angels come to God with good news about the good people they're in charge of watching over. But after the angels are finished, "other angels who were weeping came into the meeting," and they report the bad news and beg to be released from their duties of watching such sinners! God tells them the same thing that God told the sun, moon, and stars: "You must serve them until they are converted and repent, but if they do not return to me, I shall judge them" (*Apocalypse of Paul 10,* ed. Schneemelcher, 719).

At this point, Paul is escorted to the third part of heaven where he witnesses a group of particularly nasty-looking angels whom he's told are angels of punishment, "appointed for the souls of the wicked" (*Apocalypse of Paul 11,* Schneemelcher, 719). Immediately after this, however, he sees glorious, shining angels and is told: "These are the angels of righteousness: They are sent to lead in the hour of their need the souls of the righteous who believed God was their helper!" (*Apocalypse of Paul 12,* ed. Schneemelcher, 720).

Paul sees the process of judgment

Paul asks to see how the process of judgment actually takes place in an individual case, and he's taken to view a kind of trial (which could have been the inspiration for the Albert Brooks movie *Defending Your Life*):

> *And the angel said to me: This man whom you see is righteous. And again I looked and I saw all his deeds which he had done for the sake of the name of God; and all his desires, which he remembered and which he did not remember, all of them stood before him in the hour of need . . . the wicked found no dwelling in him, but the holy had power over his soul, directing it until it left the body . . .*

> —Apocalypse of Paul 14 (ed. Schneemelcher, 720)

Paul even sees evil angels appear and demand to examine the soul for signs of their evil handiwork! They're anguished, however, that they missed a righteous soul: "How did this soul escape us! It did the will of God on earth!" (*Apocalypse of Paul 14:30,* ed. Schneemelcher, 721).

The next scene is another individual trial, this time of someone who's judged to be unredeemed and evil. The book works like this — contrasting good with evil, light against dark, going back and forth between rewards for the good and punishment for the bad. In this case, Paul is told to watch the trial of:

> . . . *a soul which has provoked the Lord day and night by saying: I know nothing other than this world: I eat and drink and enjoy what is in the world. For who has gone down into the underworld and coming up has told us that there is a judgment there?*

> —Apocalypse of Paul 14–15 (tr. Elliott, 625)

The evil angels relish this trial: "Yes! . . . you belong wholly to us!" (*Apocalypse of Paul 16,* ed. Schneemelcher, 722). When this soul pleads with God, God says: "You showed no mercy in your life, why should I now show mercy to you? Confess your sin!" (*Apocalypse of Paul 17,* ed. Schneemelcher, 723).

The soul makes the mistake of saying that he didn't sin in his life. Oops, that's the wrong thing to say to God in heaven! God replies:

> *Do you think that you are still living in the world where each of you sins and conceals it and hides it from his neighbor? Here, however, nothing is hidden!*

> —Apocalypse of Paul 17 (ed. Schneemelcher, 723)

What's particularly interesting (and frankly, a bit troubling) in this scene is that this evil soul is shown the souls of all the people he wronged during his life! Not a pretty picture.

Paul visits the dwelling places of the righteous and sinners

After the long series of conversations regarding judgment, Paul is escorted to the second heaven (one level down, we suppose). Here, he's shown the dwelling place of the righteous. It's a glorious and shining land, so wonderful that even the good people say, "Why did we utter a word from our mouth to irritate our neighbor for even a single day?" (*Apocalypse of Paul 22,* ed. Schneemelcher, 726). Paul is curious, however, and asks his angelic host to see more.

He's led to Lake Acherusia, where he's shown the City of Christ. Paul gets a tour of the city and sees righteous people and their dwelling places as well as the various features of the surrounding walls and towers. Here, Paul is introduced to famous people of the Bible, such as the Patriarchs of the Old Testament, the Prophets, and even all the infants that King Herod ordered killed (according to Matthew 2:16) when he tried to eliminate the young Jesus. The Apocalypse of Paul describes more of the various sights of the City until Paul's escort takes him to "the other place."

Paul is shown a river of fire: Some people are immersed up to their knees, some up to their navels, others to their lips, and others up to the hair! There follows a gruesome description of the various sins committed by those who have these various "levels" of punishment and suffering. Some are being punished for sexual sins (adultery and fornication figure rather prominently in these descriptions) and others are punished for lack of mercy and compassion on the poor.

Especially interesting, however, are the horrific punishments meted out to Church leaders who didn't properly conduct their offices or their lives even though they were part of the Church. In these descriptions (divided into particular Church offices, such as deacon, elder, and so on), you hear the writer's serious protests against corruption in the Church (according to his view) from the period of the fourth century.

Paul continues his "tour of terror" — the Apocalypse even identifies punishments for somewhat unexpected sins like breaking one's fast before the appointed hour — and you can get a general idea of the narrative from the following:

> *And again I saw there men and women set with lacerated hands and feet and naked in a place of ice and snow, and worms consumed them. And when I saw it I wept and asked: "Who are these, sir?" And he said to me: "They are those who harmed orphans and widows and the poor, and did not hope in the Lord; therefore they pay their own particular penalty unceasingly."*

> —Apocalypse of Paul 39 (ed. Schneemelcher, 732)

All in all, Paul's tour is pretty scary stuff, which is, of course, precisely the point of this kind of literature. Paul's reaction to all he sees is hardly pride or arrogant enjoyment of punishment. In fact, Paul weeps bitterly at the fate of the condemned; he weeps so much that the Angel asks him, "Are you more compassionate than the one who made them? These people chose their fate!" (*Apocalypse of Paul 40,* ed. Schneemelcher, 734).

Paul meets biblical figures

Paul eventually meets more biblical characters, including Mother Mary, whose conversation with Paul in this writing is particularly interesting, given that they never met in real life. Because this story is a vision of the human Paul, Mary advises him to be patient because he will come back to heaven soon enough! Paul then meets and greets a series of biblical characters, including Moses and Adam. The work abruptly ends after the brief encounter with Adam, suggesting to many modern historians that the Apocalypse of Paul is missing its actual ending.

Not much in the Apocalypse of Paul reflects the actual historical Paul, any of his writings, or even much of his life as it's known from his own writings and the biblical *Acts of the Apostles*. Finally, there's no early tradition that Paul wrote such a work; a tradition surely would have arisen very early if Paul did in fact compose such a work. For these reasons, scholars consider it to be clearly a later work of imaginative authors.

Chapter 15

Even More "Acts": Writings of Other Early Christian Leaders

*T*he biblical book of *Acts of the Apostles* is a kind of historical narrative that describes some of the stories of early followers of Jesus *after* the death, resurrection, and ascension of Jesus. But the book of Acts in the Bible is a bit miserly with information about *all* the disciples. It talks some about Stephen, a bit more about Peter, less about James, and a lot about Paul. But the fact that there were other disciples, too, begs the inevitable question: What happened to them?

Among the early Christians were some creative writers who were more than up to the task of answering that question. *Acts of Thomas, Acts of Andrew, Acts of Matthew,* and *Acts of Peter* are their writings about more of Jesus's disciples, and it seems that books may have been written about other disciples as well. There were even further Acts of Paul, but we deal with those in Chapter 14, which focuses on this central early Christian preacher and teacher.

For the most part, these Acts works are rather late — third century and after — which is one reason they wouldn't have been considered for the Bible. However, they may be based on some older legends. Figuring out if any of these stories are based on *actual* events in the lives of the Apostles is tricky business indeed! There may be some genuine memories behind some of the fanciful stories — such as Thomas actually going to India — but beyond that, many of these stories appear to be for pious entertainment and "edification" (a fancy word that basically amounts to calling it "feel good" fiction!).

This chapter provides you with some information on this type of Acts literature and then discusses the various Acts stories that took their lead from the more widely known biblical book Acts of the Apostles.

Getting a Handle on Acts Literature

Clearly modeled on the New Testament book of Acts (also called Acts of the Apostles), these later Acts books share a number of interesting similarities even if they deal with different Apostles. It's a bit of a mystery why these few Apostles were chosen — and perhaps there are others that are now completely lost — but the fact that these Apostles have these Acts books *may* suggest that some stories circulated about these specific Apostles very early on.

Necessary style characteristics of Acts lit

In some ways, Acts books are almost the same thing as a Gospel, except that they aren't about Jesus! Acts aren't really biographies because they don't really talk about birth and development of the Apostles. They aren't really just teaching books, either, because they do tell stories about the adventures of their Apostle subjects. In fact, the closest analogy to these Acts writings are the saint stories in the later Catholic and Orthodox Christian traditions; they're pious stories meant to both entertain and *edify,* or carry spiritual messages for the reader. We think the best way to really appreciate these stories is to imagine a group of young children (probably not *too* young) sitting around an elder Christian man or woman who is telling them stories of the first followers of Jesus. As you read the stories, imagine the eyes of the children getting bigger during the "scary" parts, hear the laughter during the charming parts, and even feel the sadness during the descriptions of courageous death and martyrdom.

Although the Acts writings are certainly innocent enough as a kind of Christian "pious folklore" and entertainment, early heresy hunters like Epiphanius were concerned lest anyone take any of this material too seriously, and therefore the works were condemned.

The criticism and condemnation is no surprise when you take into consideration the Encratitic (see the sidebar, "Encratitic ideas: Going extreme" for more on this concept) and "anti-physical" character of some of the stories. These tendencies would have raised suspicion of even more serious heresy like Gnosticism.

However, we suggest that the Encratitic elements of the stories are really the only jarring aspects of what otherwise can be read with great enjoyment. They're really very entertaining stories, and it's easy to see why they were popular. Some of the events mentioned in these writings even turn up later in medieval religious plays performed for audiences in villages and cities throughout medieval southern Europe (especially France, Spain, and a bit in England).

Encratitic ideas: Going extreme

Encratitic ideas are associated with Christians who believe that any form of sexual activity — even within marriage — is improper. Fun bunch, right? But how early does this strange notion appear? Does 1 Timothy 4:1–5 in the New Testament (often erroneously attributed to St. Paul) already speak of those who deny marriage and sexuality? Does 1 Corinthians 7 suggest that Paul is already facing these ideas at the church in Corinth? Whether or not it's an idea among *very* early Christians, we certainly know that the writings of the Church father Clement of Alexandria (d. 215 CE) begin to speak about an early "heresy" associated with the denial of sexual activity, even for married people.

This way of thinking is often associated with Gnosticism and other movements that denied the goodness of the material world and the physical creations. Sexuality seems to have been a particularly troubling issue for many early Christians who thought that any and all sexual activity was giving in to evil desires and lust. In contrast, Orthodox Christianity affirmed marriage and married sexuality and refused to go along with any condemnation of the physical world as inherently evil.

In its ultimate expression, a Gnostic-type denial of the "redemption" of the physical could amount to a denial that Christ was ever really human because, in their view, if Christ became human (that is, "physical") he would have had an "unholy" involvement with the physical world. The idea that Jesus only appeared to be human, but never was, is known as *docetism.* Orthodox Christianity may have had lots of arguments about *how* Jesus could be fully human and fully God, but it always presumed that he was both, in some mysterious way.

In later Christian history, despite being condemned as heretical, Encratitic ideas occasionally reappear. For example, among the Russian Christian sects known as the Skoptsky (literally, "castrates"), some members actually cut off their sexual organs; less drastic, the Shaker sect of early American history denied sexuality entirely for its members (which eventually led, as you can imagine, to the movement dying out).

Who wrote these stories?

The documents we look at in this chapter have some interesting similarities; they're so similar, in fact, that a tradition arose rather early that one man, Leucius Charinus, wrote them all. Leucius is the original author proposed for all the more famous Apocryphal Acts: *Acts of Paul* (see Chapter 12), *Acts of Peter, Acts of John, Acts of Andrew,* and *Acts of Thomas.* Although not a biblical name, Charinus was associated with John the Apostle as early as the ninth century CE.

Contemporary scholars doubt that one person actually wrote all these works, but interesting parallels between the works make it clear why this idea of a common author arose:

  ✔ All the writings have a strong streak of *Encratitism,* which refers to the tendency to condemn all forms of sexual activity even among married persons. This could have been a tendency among many Christians who went to extremes on this idea, or it could have been the work of a particular early group of Christians who advocated somewhat extreme ideas (Paul dealt with some of these folks in 1 Corinthians 7).

✔ All the stories feature spectacular miracles performed with such ease that they seem almost mundane!

✔ Almost all the stories feature spiritual conflict between the hero of the story and evil opponents (often Roman officials).

The similarities among these works probably result from the fact that they all were written according to an accepted style for these kinds of writings. The style was based very loosely on the style of the biblical (and older) Acts of the Apostles, although these stories exceed the biblical book in drama and impressive accomplishments.

The Acts of Andrew

A variety of texts that feature Andrew as the main character are grouped together in a kind of family of writings. The following works are collectively read together as the *Acts of Andrew:*

✔ The Acts of Andrew

✔ The Acts of Andrew and Matthias

✔ The Acts of Peter and Andrew

✔ The Acts of Andrew and Paul

In this section, we briefly summarize the various stories that make up the Acts of Andrew and touch on various ideas presented in the writings that differ from Orthodox Christianity.

It's difficult to determine which events and which stories in the Acts of Andrew are the oldest. The oldest actual reference to writings now known as the Acts was in the early Church father Eusebius's writings from the fourth century CE. (He makes it very clear that he does *not* like the writings.) For our purposes, however, we summarize the various texts that are collectively read together as the Acts of Andrew without worrying about which stories are older.

Andrew, Stratocles, and Maximilla

In the Acts of Andrew, you're first introduced to Stratocles (pronounced *strat-oh-clees*), the brother of Aegeates (pronounced egg-ee-*ah*-tees), who's married to Maximilla. Stratocles is terribly worried about a servant who has become sick, but Maximilla tells her brother-in-law not to worry because there's a holy man in town (our hero, Andrew!). As Andrew arrives at the villa of the wealthy citizens, he immediately senses a spiritual struggle going on inside:

On entering the gate, Andrew says, "Some force is fighting inside; hurry brothers!" Without asking questions, he bursts inside to find the servant foaming at the mouth, entirely contorted.

Maximilla and her friends tell Stratocles, "Now you're going to see something pretty cool" (our paraphrase, sorry . . .). Andrew demands that the demon leave the servant, and voilá! The demon promptly obeys Andrew's command.

Stratocles is clearly impressed, and Andrew gives a long speech with interesting imagery. Instead of speaking of Stratocles "converting" in conventional terms, Andrew says that there's a new person trying to be born within Stratocles and that Andrew wishes to be a kind of midwife to the birth of a new person (odd language, perhaps, but you get the point). In short, Stratocles becomes a follower of Andrew and a Christian, and the other Christians seem quite pleased with this new convert from the upper class!

The conversion of the upper class wasn't unusual, but it was a cause for some concern among other Romans. It seems they tolerated the religious notions of the slaves, women, and foreigners — but when Christianity began to make inroads in the upper class, it immediately appeared on the radar screen of the elite, and that often meant trouble. In these stories, conversions *and* miracles often stir up the anger of local authorities. It seems that this reaction is a true-to-life theme in these stories.

This idyllic scene is interrupted by the arrival of the evil tyrant Aegeates. He doesn't notice the Christians who have gathered in the villa because it's clear that he has one thing in mind — sleeping with his wife Maximilla! When Aegeates seeks her out, he doesn't realize that she's at prayer:

> *Rescue me at last from Aegeates filthy intercourse and keep me pure and chaste, giving service only to you, my God . . .*

> —Acts of Andrew 14

A tired Aegeates doesn't push the issue and sleeps. Maximilla seeks advice from Andrew, who prays that she be delivered from "this disgusting pollution" of married sex. Maximilla makes a servant girl named Euclia up to look like herself in order to sexually service Aegeates for a number of days. Euclia begins to make demands for money and jewelry, and she brags to other servants. Aegeates finally gets wind of all this and punishes Euclia severely — still wanting to preserve Maximilla's reputation. However, Aegeates is pretty angry about Maximilla's refusal to sleep with him, and he soon discovers that it all traces back to the religious teacher Andrew. Andrew is imprisoned, much to the people's anguish, but the prison gates are miraculously opened when visitors come to see him. Andrew continues to meet with visitors, including Maximilla, but he never actually leaves the prison. The book features Andrew's rather long (and often a bit tedious) speeches telling Maximilla not to succumb to Aegeates's demands to sleep with him.

Throughout these various speeches and prison orations, Andrew seems in perfect control of events and intent on martyrdom. Despite threats from Aegeates, Andrew refuses to encourage Maximilla to sleep with her husband. Aegeates considers his options to kill Andrew (inspired, the writing suggests, by "his father, the Devil!"). Finally, Andrew reveals to his followers that Jesus has shown him that he is to die by impalement on a stake.

The first time that Andrew is taken for execution, Stratocles beats up the armed guards in order to release Andrew! He implies that he would have killed them if Andrew had not stopped him:

> *Thank the blessed one for educating me and teaching me to check my violent temper. Otherwise, I would have demonstrated for you what Stratocles and Aegeates the rogue are capable of!*

> —Acts of Andrew 52–53

Andrew explains that his followers shouldn't be so concerned about his impending death, and he even laughs at Stratocles's lack of understanding. (A common Gnostic theme is derisive laughter when someone doesn't properly understand something.) Andrew then explains that death will be the wonderful release of his soul and insists that his crucifixion proceed.

Andrew's miracles cause social unrest

In another of the Acts of Andrew writings, Andrew heals a soldier of a demon, and the soldier immediately puts away his military clothing and weapons and tells Andrew that he wishes to "acquire the uniform of your God." His fellow soldiers warn him that he'll be punished, but the former soldier and now follower of Andrew tells his mates to consider the power of Andrew:

O ignorant ones, do you not see what kind of man this is? For he has no sword in his hand nor any weapon of war and yet these great miracles are performed by him . . .

—Acts of Andrew (tr. Elliott, 271)

Other stories of Andrew

In addition to individual writings, a summary of other Andrew writings is provided by Gregory of Tours (a Gallo-Roman historian of the sixth century); it summarizes other miracles and adventures in texts that no longer exist.

Among the stories is an interesting piece about Andrew in the town of Thessalonica (the church that received what's known as 1 Thessalonians, the first famous letter from Paul in the New Testament). When soldiers approach Andrew to take him prisoner for preaching against the local temples and idols, one of the soldiers falls dead. Andrew raises him to life again to prove God's power, but the officer in charge isn't impressed. He puts Andrew in a stadium and releases a wild boar to attack him, but the boar doesn't touch Andrew. The soldiers try to whip a bull into killing Andrew, but the bull turns on the soldiers, kills many of them, and then falls dead. Then the proconsul sends a leopard to attack Andrew, but the leopard kills the proconsul's son! Andrew promptly raises the son back to life, at which point the proconsul goes home defeated.

Acts of Andrew and Matthias

In a text among the Andrew traditions, called the *Acts of Andrew and Matthias* (perhaps referring to Matthew), Matthias is sent to a city of cannibals called Myrmidonia. When Matthias is captured, he's fed for 30 days in preparation for being eaten, but then Jesus appears to Andrew and tells him to go save Matthias.

Andrew takes friends and heads out to find a boat to sail to Matthias's rescue. But the hired boat has some rather strange crewmen — it turns out that the captain is Jesus in disguise. He carries on interesting conversations with Andrew along the way. When a storm comes up, the disguised Jesus even tells Andrew to reassure his friends in the boat by telling them stories about Jesus:

If you are indeed a disciple of the one called Jesus, tell your disciples the miracles your teacher did so that their souls may rejoice and that they may forget the terror of the sea . . .

—Acts of Andrew and Matthias 8

Jesus the disguised boatman quizzes Andrew about various stories of Jesus, and there's a delightful scene in which Andrew tells the boatman that if Andrew were to tell the boatman *all* the mysteries that Jesus revealed to Andrew, "you would not be able to endure them!" The irony is rich, and the way in which such stories could be made into Christian folklore plays in later medieval European traditions is patently obvious. There are moments of very impressive storytelling in these narratives.

Andrew arrives in time to free Matthias and over 100 other prisoners that were to be eaten as well, and he foils the townspeople's attempts to kill their victims. Finally, Andrew reveals himself to them, and they torture him horribly. Each time, however, Andrew is healed. Finally, a flood overtakes the city and many people are drowned. In the end, Andrew raises all the victims from the dead, and the entire town converts to Christianity, builds a church, and begs Andrew to stay and teach them.

Acts of Peter and Andrew

In the *Acts of Peter and Andrew,* a rather interesting story takes place where Peter and Andrew are engaged in a kind of debate with a wealthy man named Onesiphorus. When Onesiphorus wants to know the secret of Peter's and Andrew's power, Andrew says that Onesiphorus must abandon his wife and possessions. He's angry at this, and when Peter quotes Jesus to say, "It is easier for a camel to pass through the eye of a needle than for a rich man to enter heaven" (Matthew 19:24), Onesiphorus can't believe his ears! It seems impossible! Here's where the story gets interesting.

Peter gets a needle, places it on the ground, and then commands a camel to walk through the eye of the needle. According to the story, "The eye opened like a gate and the camel passed through; and a second time, at Peter's bidding . . ." *(The Acts of Peter and Andrew 18-19, tr. Elliott, 301)*. Although it's questionable whether this literal interpretation is what Jesus had in mind, the demonstration does make for a great story!

This episode is interesting for another reason: It suggests how some of these legends began as interpretations or parables that arose when discussing and teaching the sayings of Jesus — rather like a sermon illustration in a good Sunday morning sermon!

The Acts of John

The work referred to as the *Acts of John* is a composition of a variety of ancient and medieval texts. When the story opens, John has arrived in Ephesus (the city where very early Christian traditions suggest that the actual Apostle John died). A man identified as a "commander in chief,"

Lycomedes, begs John to heal his wife Cleopatra (not an uncommon name in the ancient world, of course). John goes to heal Cleopatra, but Lycomedes is so overcome with anxiety about his wife that he dies. John brings the raised Cleopatra into the next room and proceeds to raise Lycomedes from the dead! Lycomedes is so overcome with appreciation that he not only supports John's ministry but also hires a painter to produce a painting of the Apostle. When John sees the final portrait, he has the opportunity to make an interesting little speech about Jesus as the great painter:

> *[Jesus] who paints us all for himself, who knows the colors which I bid you use are: belief in God, knowledge, fear of God, love, fellowship, meekness, goodness, brotherly love, chastity, integrity, firmness, fearlessness, cheerfulness, honesty . . .*

—Acts of John 29

But John, who (it says) has never seen an image of himself, says that the real painting is childish and imperfect — a painting that is a "dead picture of what is dead." This is a faintly Gnostic sense of denying the significance of the material world. (Too bad, because otherwise the idea of Jesus as the "great painter of life" is a rather charming idea).

John goes on to preach lengthy sermons in which Gnostic ideas are even more evident. For example, John talks about times when he touched Jesus only to discover that Jesus's body wasn't normal:

> *Sometimes when I meant to touch him, I met a material and solid body; and at other times again when I felt him, the substance was immaterial and bodiless and as if it were not existing at all . . .*

—Acts of John 93

John also describes a strange ritual in which Jesus tells his disciples to make a circle around him as he sings a strange song:

> *Now we give thanks, I say:*
> *I will be loosed, and I will loose. Amen.*
> *I will be pierced, and I will pierce. Amen.*
> *I will be born, and I will bear. Amen.*
> *I will eat, and I will be eaten. Amen. . . . .*
>
> *The whole universe takes part in the dancing. Amen.*
> *He who does not dance, does not know what is being done. Amen.*

—Acts of John 95–96

These lines suggest that Jesus emphasizes the mysterious over the obvious — the spiritual over the material. Gnosticism relished these puzzles that suggest that there's more to life than the obvious, and they enjoyed the test of wits and strange language that's open to mystical interpretations. It may even suggest actual rituals to accompany such language!

The writing then goes into an even longer description of various names for God, Jesus, and references to the cross. Jesus explains that he actually wasn't on the cross:

> *Therefore I have suffered none of the things which they will say of me: that suffering which I showed to you and to the rest in dance, I wish to be called a mystery . . .*

> —Acts of John 101

After these long speeches from John, the stories about him resume (although they too feature speeches!). At Ephesus, which was actually famous for the cult of Artemis, John destroys the Idol of Artemis, and the pagan Temple begins to fall apart, killing a priest inside the grounds. Eventually, John raises the Priest from the dead, and the Priest becomes a disciple of John.

There follows a series of events including an interesting episode when John returns to Ephesus for another visit. John hires a room for himself and the others with him, but the beds are full of bugs! John commands the bugs to "be considerate, and leave your home for this night . . ." and like in a Disney film, they obey and crawl out, only to return when John and his gang leave the room!

Finally, there's a *very* odd episode in which a beautiful woman named Drusiana, wife of Andronicus, dies. John delivers a speech basically saying that she's at rest and no longer in danger of being sexually active! In the meantime, a man named Callimachus, who was aflame with sexual desire for Drusiana, bribes a servant to let him and his servant into her tomb. He prepares to sexually use her corpse, stating that what she refused in life, he can take in death. But both Callimachus and his servant are killed by a snake, and they remain in the tomb for three days. Meanwhile, John and Andronicus go to visit the tomb to pay their respects . . . only to discover that Drusiana's body isn't alone. John raises Drusiana and Callimachus, who confesses his sin. John also raises the servant, who refuses belief in the God of John and eventually dies a horrible death as a sinner! This very bizarre story provides an opportunity for still more long speeches from John about spiritual realities and the true nature of Christian faith.

Professor J. K. Elliott points out in his translation of the Acts of John that an early Christian writer named Nicephorus produced what's called a *stichometry*. A *stich* is a line of writing, so a stichometry amounts to a work in which Nicephorus actually counted lines of text. Because Nicephorus says that the original Acts of John consisted of 2,500 lines, and because that many lines no longer exist for scholars to study, Elliott suggests that about two-thirds of the original work has survived. Over the years, scholars and historians have tried to reproduce the original work, so the work that Elliott translates for modern readers is a composition from a variety of ancient and medieval texts.

The Acts of Peter

It hardly comes as a surprise that early Christians were curious about the *other* main Apostle of the first group: Peter (see Figure 15-1 for just one of many artistic renderings of this great figure in Christianity). So, legends about the famous Peter were also written, gathered together, and passed on. Because Peter later became the basis for the Bishop of Rome (the Pope), stories about Peter are particularly interesting even if they aren't historical. There are longer and shorter works that talk about Peter, and scholars argue which part belongs with which part — but that doesn't really stop us from reading them with great appreciation.

Note: Because there's some discussion about how the Acts of Peter originally read, and because there are various versions of the text, we've chosen to summarize the texts as presented in Professor Elliott's translations.

Figure 15-1:
The Apostle
Peter.

Werner Forman / Art Resource, NY

Peter and his objection to his daughter's sexuality

One of the traditions associated with the Acts of Peter collections is a story about Peter's paralyzed daughter. (A version of this same story appears in the Nag Hammadi Library, which we mention in Chapter 12.)

Peter goes about his work of healing many people, but a few concerned critics ask him why he doesn't heal his own daughter. They question whether or not he can actually do it. Good questions, right?

Peter heals her to demonstrate that he can, after which she reverts to her previous state. Peter then explains the reason his daughter appears crippled and partially paralyzed. When she was only 10, a man named Ptolemy became sexually attracted to her. Before he could act on his desires, however, she was paralyzed. Soon afterward, Ptolemy confessed his sin and lived an exemplary life, leaving his wealth to the poor when he died. The implication of this strange (and frankly somewhat cruel) story is that, from the perspective of the writer, it's better to be crippled than sexually attractive!

Even *worse* is the short story in the Acts of Peter that features a peasant man who asks Peter's advice about how to preserve his daughter's virginity. Peter tells him, "The Lord will bestow upon her what was expedient for her soul" — and she falls dead! Once again, you can identify the Encratitic tendencies of these writings — carried to an extreme degree. The message is that it's better to be crippled or even dead than engage in sex.

Peter and Simon the Magician face off

A major portion of the Acts of Peter tradition introduces Simon, known also as Simon Magus (which means "Simon the Magician") from a biblical story in Acts chapter 8, where a magician named Simon offers to "buy" the ability to perform miracles.

In the Bible, Peter scolds Simon somewhat severely, but then you hear nothing more about him. However, Simon passed into Christian folklore and became a kind of archenemy of early Christians and one responsible for many heresies. Whether blaming Simon for heresies is pure folklore or has any basis in a historical person is now impossible to tell.

The Acts of Peter features a major confrontation between Peter and Simon.

Simon trashes Christianity

God tells Peter to go to Rome to confront Simon, who has apparently been leading many people astray with his attacks on Christianity and his otherwise impressive magical abilities. When Peter arrives in Rome, he's greeted by what remains of the Christian community; they explain that things are worse than Peter may have known!

A former good Christian and elite citizen named Marcellus once heavily supported the poor and widows in Rome and was even known by the Emperor for his good deeds. But Simon has convinced Marcellus that Christianity is false; as a result, Marcellus has housed Simon and turned away from the Christians *and* his service to the poor.

Peter retorts with speeches and minor miracles

When Peter hears of Simon's influence on Marcellus and his overall effect on the Christians in Rome, he goes into a long, angry speech about evil and the work of the devil. The confrontation between Peter and Simon seems inevitable. When Peter then goes to confront Simon and challenge him, Simon refuses to meet Peter. Peter miraculously gives a big dog the power of speech and sends him to confront Simon.

In the meantime, Marcellus is rather impressed with Peter's actions and runs to Peter to confess his failure. Marcellus is received back into fellowship (with accompanying long speeches from Marcellus and Peter, of course). As Peter speaks to a local crowd, a demon-possessed man laughs at Peter and tells him that Simon is still arguing with the talking dog. When Peter drives out the demon, it bursts a statue of Caesar into fragments, after which Peter miraculously reassembles the statue.

Peter's minor miracles (including resurrecting a smoked fish from the market) appear to be building up to the confrontation with Simon. Finally, Jesus appears to Peter to tell him to get ready for the big struggle, and along the way, Jesus tells Peter about some of Simon's trickery in the past.

Simon denies Peter's theology about Jesus

Marcellus describes a very strange dream to Peter about an ugly woman appearing — representing Simon's evil power. In the dream, Marcellus says, Peter told him to take his sword and cut off her head! Marcellus basically says he couldn't hurt a fly, and a heavenly being comes and chops up the woman in his dream. Peter seems encouraged by this grisly dream, thinking it reassures him of defeating Simon.

Everyone comes to an assembly in Rome: senators and prefects, Christians, and onlookers. Peter and Simon stand before the crowds, who demand that Peter prove his miraculous powers. But first, there's a verbal debate. Peter recounts the story from Acts 8 and challenges Simon. Simon denies Peter's theology about Jesus:

> *Men of Rome, is a God born? Is he crucified? Whoever has a master is no God. And when he spoke, many said, "You are right, Simon!" And Peter said, "Cursed be your words against Christ . . ."*

> —Acts of Peter 23

Peter defeats Simon

Peter cites Scripture to support his assessment of Jesus, but then he confronts Simon again, essentially saying that talk is cheap and demanding to see Simon's powers.

The Prefect in charge demands an impartial challenge. He puts one of his slaves in front of the two men and tells Simon to kill him and Peter to revive him. Simon whispers something in the slave's ear, and he falls dead. But just before Peter responds, a prominent woman from the crowd speaks of her dead son, and Peter asks that he be brought to Peter then and there. Simon isn't impressed with all this and returns the crowd's focus to the dead servant.

Simon asks the crowd if they will punish Peter if Simon can also raise the servant. When Simon makes the servant *appear* alive (apparently by moving his head), the crowd goes for Peter. Peter asks them to examine the servant, and they discover that he isn't really alive! The crowd turns on Simon, threatening to burn him — but Peter demands that Simon be spared:

> *If you continue, the boy shall not rise. We have learned not to recompense evil for evil, but we have learned to love our enemies and to pray for those who persecute us. For should even he repent, it is better. For God will not remember the evil. Let him, therefore, come to the light of Christ. If he cannot, let him inherit the portion of his father, the devil. But do not let your hands be contaminated . . .*

> —Acts of Peter 28

Peter raises both the servant and the woman's son, and the woman is so grateful that she gives money to the poor. In the meantime, Simon makes one last great attempt to overcome Peter: He tells everyone that he's going to fly! Amazingly, Simon accomplishes this feat, but Peter strikes him from the sky with his power, and Simon breaks his leg from the fall. In a somewhat perfunctory ending, the story states that Simon eventually dies.

Martyrdom of Peter

The end of the tradition focuses on the martyrdom of Peter. Rather like the stories of Andrew (refer to the earlier section "The Acts of Andrew"), Peter meets his death at the hands of a Roman official who's angry that his wife has become a Christian and thus refuses to sleep with her husband anymore!

The story of Peter's death affirms a tradition that Peter died on a cross, but upside down. In the end, Peter affirms that only the "visible" part of him will die — his soul will live on.

The Acts of Thomas

It's fortunate that most of the *Acts of Thomas* has survived for study. The earliest mention of these traditions is in the writings of the fourth-century "heresy hunter" Epiphanius, but allusions to some of the specific traditions and stories also appear in earlier material.

The opening scene: Thomas gets picked to bring Christianity to India

As the Acts of Thomas begins, the Apostles are casting lots to determine where each Apostle is to go in the world. Jesus's brother Thomas finds out that he's headed to India. He's not terribly excited about this assignment and tries to avoid going, even after Jesus appears to him in the night. So, when a merchant named Abban comes to visit from India, Jesus actually "sells" Thomas to Abban, claiming that Thomas is Jesus's slave. When Thomas discovers that he has been sold, he accepts the inevitable, and in a reconciliation of sorts, Jesus gives the money from the sale back to Thomas to help him on his journey. Abban, on the other hand, is delighted with his purchase, especially when Thomas informs him that he's a carpenter like his brother and father, Joseph.

The belief that Thomas brought Christianity to India is very ancient, and many Indian Christians to this day claim "Apostolic origins" for their Church. The fact that very early traditions suggest an association between Thomas and India is intriguing and may well suggest that Christianity did indeed come to India very early in Christian history. Certainly there were well-traveled trade routes linking Rome, Palestine, and India, and some trade routes went even as far as China!

The second scene: Thomas doesn't build a palace . . . on Earth, that is

In the second scene of the Acts of Thomas, there appears one of the most charming stories of the entire corpus of writings we consider in this chapter.

Abban, the one so overjoyed to have purchased such an accomplished slave, tells King Gungaphorus all about Thomas and his abilities. The King wants to build a great palace and asks if Thomas can do it. Thomas answers:

> *Yes, I shall build it and finish it; for because of this I have come, to build and to do carpenter's work.*

> —Acts of Thomas 17

This comment has a double meaning because Thomas refers to *the* "carpenter's work." The carpenter is clearly Jesus, and so Thomas makes a veiled reference to the fact that he's in India in order to share Jesus's message and spread Christianity. Some traditions even suggest that Thomas was the twin brother of Jesus and therefore that's why Thomas was also a carpenter.

The King sends money to Thomas on a regular basis, which Thomas promptly distributes to the poor of the area. But when the King asks some friends what his new palace looks like, they inform him that Thomas has built no such palace but has given away the King's riches along with healing the sick and performing many miracles.

The King is so angry that he considers ways to kill Thomas. That night the King's brother Gad dies and appears in heaven. When the heavenly attendants show Gad the various places to live in heaven, he sees a magnificent palace and asks to live there! He's told that he can't because, "This palace is the one which that Christian has built for your brother . . ." (*The Acts of Thomas 22, tr. Elliott, 456*).

Gad begs to be allowed to tell his living brother about the glorious palace that Thomas has built by doing good deeds in the name of the King. Returning to life, Gad begs the King to be allowed to live in even a basement room of the magnificent palace in heaven. The King comes to understand how Thomas built his palace in heaven rather than on earth, and the King and his brother then spend the rest of their lives giving to the poor and are eventually *sealed* (anointed with oil) and then baptized as Christians.

Incidentally, one of the interesting aspects of these later Acts writings is the information provided about rituals such as anointing with oil and baptism. The Acts of Thomas, for example, shares ritual words to accompany the anointing that may suggest aspects of the actual sacramental rites of the third to fifth centuries CE. While anointing with oil, Thomas says:

Come, holy name of Christ, which is above every name
Come, power of the Most High, and perfect compassion,
Come, gift most high
Come compassionate mother
Come fellowship of the male
Come revealer of secret mysteries . . .

—Acts of Thomas 27

The third scene: The Garden of Eden's "serpent descendant" obeys Thomas

In the third scene, Thomas sees a great serpent by the road who has attacked a young man. In a long speech, the serpent identifies itself as a descendant of the serpent that tempted Adam and Eve, that hardened Pharaoh's heart against the Israelites, and that's tied to a series of other negative influences in Scriptural tradition. Thomas commands the serpent to heal the boy by sucking out the poison, and the serpent obeys Thomas. Just imagine this scene depicted in medieval plays!

The fourth scene: A colt gives Thomas a ride

In the fourth scene, Thomas converses with a colt that eventually convinces Thomas to ride on his back so that the colt can perform a service to the Apostle. At first, Thomas refuses to mount the animal, but the colt assures him that it would be a blessing. After the colt delivers Thomas to his destination, Thomas tells the colt to return to the wild.

The fifth scene: Thomas banishes an incubus

In the fifth scene, Thomas drives away a demon who has been sleeping with a woman for five years. When Thomas drives away the demon, the demon makes a fascinating speech as he leaves the woman that he has fallen in love with: He comments that Thomas looks like Jesus, who fooled the devil because he didn't look very impressive in his earthly form.

The sixth scene: Thomas rails against "insane intercourse!"

In the sixth scene, a young man who has just committed murder attempts to take the Eucharist with Christians; he's immediately physically deformed for his crime. When he explains what happened, he tells of his passion for a woman who wouldn't sleep with him; he murdered her out of jealousy that she would sleep with anyone else:

> *When the apostle heard this he said, "Oh insane intercourse, how you lead to shamelessness! O unrestrained lust, how have you excited this man to do this!"*

—Acts of Thomas 52

The Apostle Thomas goes to the place where the woman killed lay dead, and together, he and the killer raise her from the dead. She then discusses her vision of visiting various places in hell and tells of the punishments of those who have sinned in this life. Thomas uses the occasion of her explanation of the "other side" to deliver a lengthy sermon on Christianity, emphasizing the judgments that will be given for the sin of adultery and finishing with some thoughts on the meaning of the coming of Jesus.

The seventh and eighth scenes: Thomas banishes more demons

An officer of King Masdaeus encounters Thomas and tells Thomas of the troubles of his wife and daughter, who seemed to have been attacked by demons. Thomas has pity on them, gathers them and a group of friends together for a sermon, and seems to assure them that they will be okay.

The group travels to the home of the officer, and along the way Thomas miraculously tames wild asses to pull the wagon and then dismisses them when the journey is finished. Thomas calls for the daughter and mother to come forward, and he heals them.

The ninth scene: Thomas counsels against marriage and sex

In the most lengthy of the adventures in the Acts of Thomas, the Apostle Thomas encounters Mygdonia, the wife of the elite Charisius. Thomas is preaching about Jesus and the lifestyle of Christians, and many are impressed — especially Mygdonia, who immediately bows before Thomas and asks to be included in this new teaching.

As a result of Thomas's influence, Mygdonia goes home a changed woman who no longer wishes to sleep with her husband because she's now "bound" to someone even greater (Jesus, of course). Charisius, not entirely realizing that he has essentially lost his wife, tells her about a dream:

> *I saw myself at a meal near King Misdaeus, and beside us stood a table fully laden. And I saw an eagle coming down from heaven taking away two partridges from the place before me and the king, which he carried into his nest [Greek: heart]. And he came near again fluttering about us. And the king ordered a bow to be brought to him. The eagle took a dove and a pigeon from the place before us. The king shot an arrow at him which passed through him from one side to the other without hurting him. And he flew to his nest unscathed . . .*

> —Acts of Thomas 91 (tr. Elliott, 482)

This dream essentially summarizes what is about to happen: The eagle (which represents Thomas, Christianity, or Jesus — but is more often an image of political power like Rome, so this is an ironic image for a Roman to imagine!) will take away the wife of Charisius, but the King's wife will also come under the influence of Thomas's teaching. Similar to the other Acts literature we consider in this chapter, Thomas is imprisoned by the angry Charisius and the King for turning their women against them. The preaching of Christianity in some of these early Acts writings actually breaks up some marriages of the elite. Some feminist readers now say that these are acts of liberation because the women were often trapped in unjust and oppressive relationships. This is an interesting idea, of course, but it seems that part of the point here is the avoidance of sexuality as well in a radical definition of purity.

Thomas tells the famous "Hymn of the Pearl" story

While facing prison, Thomas tells his fellow prisoners a story, known as "The Hymn of the Pearl," that's one of the most famous stories in the Acts of Thomas. In this narrative (which may or may not have its origin in this writing), a child is sent on a journey by his parents to find a pearl guarded by a serpent in another world. But the child must leave behind his wealth and riches to go on the journey. Also, because he goes to a different world, he needs to make himself look like the others in that world:

> *I clothed myself in garments like theirs, so that I would not be seen as a stranger*
> *And as one who had come from abroad to take the pearl*
> *Lest the Egyptians might arouse the serpent against me*
> *But somehow they learned that I was not their countryman.*
> *They dealt with me treacherously, and I tasted their food*
> *I no longer recognized that I was a king's son, and I served their king*
> *And I fell into a deep sleep because of the heaviness of their food . . .*

> *. . . The child forgets his true identity, until a letter from the parents wakes him up:*
> *To our son in Egypt, greetings!*
> *Awake, and rise from your sleep*
> *Listen to the words in this letter*
> *Remember you are the son of kings*
> *You have fallen beneath the yoke of slavery*
> *Remember your gold-spangled garment*
> *Recall the pearl for which you were sent to Egypt,*
> *Your name has been called to the book of life . . .*

—Acts of Thomas, "The Hymn of the Pearl" 109, 111

This story is an allegory of the Gnostic belief that persons are from the God of Light; they descend into the world of the material things and forget who they really are — thinking that the material world is all there is. The letter from the child's parents is, then, the Gospel message of the Gnostic Jesus, who reminds people of who they really are:

> *Remember you are the son of kings!*
> *You have fallen beneath the yoke of slavery.*
> *Remember your gold-spangled garment*
> *Recall the pearl for which you were sent to Egypt,*
> *Your name has been called to the book of life!*

—Acts of Thomas 111

The martyrdom of Thomas

Charisius believes that by imprisoning Thomas he has dealt with his problem and his wife will return to his bed (and, he probably thinks, to her senses!). In an interesting conversation, Charisius asks if he's more beautiful than Jesus! After all, didn't Mygdonia once love him? Mygdonia explains how her new faith makes the old "love" pale in comparison:

> *That time was of the earthly life, this of the everlasting. That was of a transient pleasure, this of an everlasting. That was of the day and of the night, this of the day without night. You have seen the wedding which passed over and remains here. This wedding remains in eternity. That communion was of destruction, this is of eternal life . . .*

—Acts of Thomas 124 (tr. Elliott, 495)

Upon hearing this, Charisius is so angry that he goes to King Misdaeus to demand that Thomas be killed to prevent the spreading of such thoughts. The King tells Thomas that if he heals the marriage, then Thomas will go free, but Thomas refuses and isn't impressed with the King's threats. Soon enough, even the King's wife is impressed by Thomas, and the King blames Charisius for ever mentioning Thomas to him! If that isn't bad enough, Vazan, the King's son, takes an interest in Thomas and eventually becomes a follower as well.

Sexuality and liberation in the ancient world

Some scholars have wondered if there isn't more to the frequent theme seen in ancient writings about women giving up sex and even their marriages. Was it merely a form of early Christian spirituality that denied any physical pleasures as always sinful? Some scholars have noticed that there are many *strong* female characters in these writings who

✔ Defy social convention

✔ Act unafraid of their male "superiors"

✔ Often use language suggesting that they no longer feel that they're under male authority

Do these writings reflect an ancient form of women's liberation? Some historians argue that ancient marriage was almost always a relationship in which a male dominated a female, and ancient sexuality was almost always a sign of male dominance over females. If this is presumed in many cases, then one way to have expressed women's liberation in the ancient world was to liberate women from marriage and sexuality entirely — even break up oppressive relationships! On their own, women were then free from earthly domination and free to exercise leadership — precisely what's reflected in these writings!

So, part of the teaching in ancient Christian writings may have been motivated by a disdain for physical participation in sex or other "pleasures of the flesh" (gluttony, drinking, and adultery are frequently mentioned), but another part of the teaching may have been that these writings were trying to express a sort of women's liberation for the third to fifth centuries.

In fact, many social commentators and theologians argue that, in the roughly 1,700 years that have passed, people haven't yet really learned to make marriage and sexuality more liberating — although perhaps people at least understand the importance of equality more now than then, even if they still aren't good at practicing it!

The story continues with the King becoming increasingly determined to kill Thomas and Thomas continuing to minister to those who follow him, seemingly unimpressed with the anger of the King. In the end, the Martyrdom of Thomas is described as being run through with spears by the King's soldiers. When two of Thomas's followers refuse to leave his body, the "resurrection body" of Thomas appears to them and reassures them that Thomas isn't really dead. Charisius and King Misdaeus eventually realize that they'll never have their wives back and allow them to continue in their Christian practices.

A final word and a happy ending

A short narrative ends the Acts of Thomas (it's kind of like an afterword). King Misdaeus has another son who's possessed of a demon, and the King goes to the grave of Thomas. The Apostle's body, however, was taken elsewhere for burial, so the King places dust from the grave on his son's neck and says a prayer begging Jesus to heal his son. When the boy is healed, the King joins the Christian group in his kingdom, and the writing ends on a rejoicing note — an appropriately Hollywood happy ending!

Checking Out Some "Secondary" Acts

More Acts stories and writings continued to be written even into the third to seventh centuries. More stories were added, and older stories were elaborated and drawn out. As we mention earlier, some of these episodes and stories began to turn up after the tenth century in medieval European *Bible plays,* which were performed outside churches and in villages by traveling troupes of actors. (The film *The Reckoning* is an interesting depiction of such traveling groups.)

In the 1924 edition of English translations of many of these non-biblical Acts works, M. R. James speaks of the secondary character of many texts that should be grouped with the older Acts literature that we cover in this chapter.

Both James and Elliott (whose more updated and superior translations we've been mainly using) agree that these texts have minimal theological importance but contain stories and traditions that continued to be of interest to later readers.

Most of these later works don't warrant extensive coverage in this book because they appear long after the canon was established for the Christian Bible. Still, the early Christian folklore is often interesting and always entertaining, and it's interesting to note that such stories of early Christian leaders continued to be written for hundreds of years. In fact, references to such writings continue into the fifth to eighth centuries CE, and many of these stories eventually ended up as themes in medieval religious dramas and plays after about 1100–1200 CE.

In this section, we look briefly at two examples of these later Acts-type writings.

The Acts of Philip

The *Acts of Philip* is divided into separate acts, rather like Thomas (see "The Acts of Thomas" earlier in this chapter). In these short acts, Philip performs a series of miracles.

In one, Greek philosophers call on Jewish Priests from Jerusalem to come and deal with Philip, and there's a rather nasty conflict between the High Priest and his 500 assistants that paints Jewish leaders in a very bad light — another sad example of early Christian anti-Semitic ideas, we fear! Philip eventually impresses the 500, who convert, but the High Priest is sent to hell as an unbeliever.

The angry side of Philip is dealt with at the end of the series of writings. Among the favorite stories in the Acts of Philip is Act VIII, which contains the conversion of a leopard! The leopard attacks a goat-kid, but the goat-kid begs for its life (speaking with a human voice) on account of the arrival of Apostles of God. The leopard visits Philip and takes him to where the goat-kid lay, and Philip heals the animal. The animals fall down in gratitude to Philip and his associates!

In the fascinating concluding acts, Philip and Bartholomew are both in trouble in Hierapolis (in the area of modern Turkey) for preaching the Gospel and converting a large number of people, including Nicanora, the wife of the Roman proconsul. Like many of the other Acts, this conversion leads to her refusing sexual relations, which especially upsets the proconsul, who's described as a "tyrant." Philip and Bartholomew are nailed upside down to the wall of the Temple, but the interesting action begins when Philip curses almost the entire town to destruction — the earth opens up and hundreds of people descend to hell!

Jesus comes to visit Philip and scolds him, and then saves the people:

> *And a voice was heard: "I will have mercy on you in my cross of light . . . and I shall bring back those who have been swallowed up." And he drew a cross in the air, reaching down into the abyss, and it was filled with light, and the cross was like a ladder. And Jesus called the people, and they all came up.*

> —Acts of Philip (tr. Elliott, 517–518)

Jesus determines that Philip should be disciplined for his action, and furthermore, Jesus raises the hundreds that were cast into hell. They all convert, repent of killing Philip, and are received into heaven. The story finishes with Philip's death as a martyr, presumably facing some delay in entering heaven as further discipline from Jesus.

The Passion of Bartholomew

In the *Passion of Bartholomew,* the Apostle Bartholomew is sent to India, where he lives with the poor who congregate at a pagan temple for healing. Demons who live there have been healing people in order to maintain their authority but can no longer do so when Bartholomew arrives. When the local King Polymius hears about this, he tells the Apostle that his daughter is possessed of a demon, and Bartholomew heals her. Bartholomew carries on with his traveling ministry, but the King then packs up a camel with silver and gold and tries to find him, only to be visited in the night by the Apostle who tells him that he doesn't care about such things!

King Polymius enters into an extended discussion with Bartholomew, who speaks of the birth of Jesus to the Virgin Mary — the second virgin in human history! When the King asks who is the first, Bartholomew answers that Adam was born of the virgin earth!

The King seems intrigued but is especially impressed when Bartholomew demands that the demon return to the idol in the Temple and confess to everyone that he, the demon, is a fraud and that the people were made ill in the first place by the devil to fool the people into believing that the idol was healing them. King Polymius is so impressed that he tries to break the Temple apart. When he's unsuccessful, Bartholomew miraculously destroys all the idols.

Meanwhile, pagan priests from a nearby town go to King Astreges (King Polymius's brother, it seems) and complain about the destruction of temples and idols. These other priests cause a stir that leads to Bartholomew's martyrdom. However, in a storybook ending where, you may say, "evil gets its reward," the evil King Astreges dies a horrible death, and King Polymius is made a bishop by his people — all of whom have converted.

Chapter 16

Early Christian Apocalyptic Visions

*T*he word "apocalypse" means "revelation," and biblical historians also use it to refer to a kind of religious literature from the ancient Jews and ancient Christians — *apocalyptic literature.* As you can imagine, these works have to do with visions and revelations experienced by the writers. The most famous example of this apocalyptic style of religious literature is, obviously, the *Apocalypse of John,* the last book of the New Testament; not surprisingly, it's better known as *Revelation.* However, many Christians are surprised to learn that this unusual book isn't really that unusual; it's only considered so because it's the only example of apocalyptic writing that the early Christians chose to include in the New Testament. But they had plenty to choose from!

The ancient Jews wrote apocalyptic books also, as we survey briefly in Chapter 4. Historians know that it was a popular — and very influential — form of religious writing in the ancient world because they literally have dozens of Jewish apocalyptic writings and even quite a few explicitly Christian apocalyptic writings. In some cases, because many of the early Christians were also Jewish, some older Jewish apocalyptic writings were edited by Christians to transform an originally Jewish writing into a Christian work by adding a few important references to Jesus. In other cases, it's more certain that works were entirely Christian compositions. Hardly any of these writings were actually included in the Bible (probably just as well!), but they do occasionally make for some bracing reading.

In this chapter, we first discuss the characteristics necessary for something to be considered an apocalyptic writing. Then we survey a few Christian apocalyptic writings that didn't make it into the Bible. Finally, we survey some works that were originally Jewish but underwent some Christian amendments.

You may be wondering how this genre could be so popular given that the New Testament only ended up with one apocalyptic work. According to Matthew 24, Jesus preached on apocalyptic themes, and the most famous apocalyptic book in Christian history — the *Revelation to John* — stands at the symbolic end of the New Testament. Revelation is a full dose of "Christian apocalyptic" to which few of these other writings really add anything significant. After all, the last judgment is the last judgment . . . and apparently, the New Testament was considered to have enough for the early Christians when they determined the canon of the Bible.

"Apocalypse" is Greek and means "revelation." The actual title of the last book of the New Testament is the *Apocalypse of John,* but it's known by the translated title, the *Revelation to John.*

What Makes an Apocalyptic Writing?

Scholars continue to debate the issue of whether apocalyptic writings are really all that different from prophetic writings given that both claim to provide messages from heaven. But there are some interesting differences, especially in their imagery. Scholars often cite some of the following criteria for apocalyptic writings:

- ✔ The writings often claim to be descriptions of visions — visions of the future *or* visions of visits to heavenly places (particularly different levels or places in heaven or hell).

- ✔ After the vision, the writings often introduce an intermediary, an angel or other heavenly creature, who explains (some of) the symbolism of the vision.

- ✔ They usually deal with judgment, but not always.

- ✔ They often suggest events that are just about to take place — time is short!

- ✔ The writings typically involve bizarre images, like multiheaded beasts or combination beasts (lions with wings, goats with many horns, and so on). In visits to levels of heaven or hell, there are often graphic descriptions of punishment with fewer descriptions of rewards.

- ✔ You get a turbulent sense of impending crisis. (This is never calm literature!)

- ✔ If the writing has a vision of judgment, there's often a brief description of an idyllic age that follows, such as the "New Heaven and New Earth" in Revelation in the New Testament.

- ✔ The visionary is often physically affected by the vision, experiencing weakness, collapse, and so on.

   ✔ It seems that time and history as we know it is coming to an end. A great transition is coming soon.

   ✔ Apocalyptic writings only occasionally dwell on themes of social justice and right living. The Prophets heavily emphasize this, but apocalyptic writing does so only once in a while.

Bizarre visions and beasts

As we've stated, apocalyptic writings claim to narrate a vision experienced by the writer, accompanied by strange and bizarre images such as multi-headed beasts or combination beasts (having features of more than one animal). Consider, for example, the only apocalyptic writing that's in the Old Testament, the second half of the book of Daniel:

> *In the first year of King Belshazzar of Babylon, Daniel had a dream and visions of his head as he lay in bed. Then he wrote down the dream:*
> *I, Daniel, saw in my vision by night the four winds of heaven stirring up the great sea, and four great beasts came up out of the sea, different from one another. The first was like a lion and had eagles' wings. Then, as I watched, its wings were plucked off, and it was lifted up from the ground and made to stand on two feet like a human being; and a human mind was given to it. Another beast appeared, a second one, that looked like a bear. It was raised up on one side, had three tusks in its mouth among its teeth and was told, "Arise, devour many bodies!" . . .*

> —Daniel 7:1-5

After reading Daniel, consider Revelation at the end of the New Testament; in chapter 13, you encounter frightening images that were undoubtedly intended to symbolize the Roman Empire:

> *And I saw a beast rising out of the sea, having ten horns and seven heads; and on its horns were ten diadems, and on its heads were blasphemous names. And the beast that I saw was like a leopard, its feet were like a bear's, and its mouth was like a lion's mouth. And the dragon gave it his power and his throne and great authority. One of its heads seemed to have received a death-blow but its mortal wound had been healed . . .*

> —Revelation 13:1–3

Sound familiar? Hopefully you're beginning to see the interesting similarities in the apocalyptic style. In this typical apocalyptic fare, these visions are considered to be symbolic of

   ✔ Regimes in the world

   ✔ Rulers

   ✔ Spiritual powers active in heaven and on earth

Emphasis on the final judgment of all mankind

Also typical of apocalyptic writings is an emphasis on a final judgment of all humanity by God — a sorting out of the good and evil. Sometimes the judgment is accompanied by rather gruesome descriptions of punishment of the wicked and fanciful descriptions of the wonders and blessings in store for the righteous.

Many historians believe that apocalyptic visions come out of circumstances of persecution or suffering and therefore express outrage and anguish. Think about it: If you're suffering in this world, and especially if you see powerful and corrupt people doing very well while you suffer, this kind of "they will get theirs" message is welcome and perfectly understandable. It's the religious literature of frustration and anger that comes from a people too powerless to take any other kind of action, so they *write* and *pray* their anger!

Christians, especially in the first 300 years of Christianity before it became a "tolerated" religion in the Roman Empire (and eventually become *the* religion of the Roman Empire — and started doing some persecuting of its own), often experienced periods of persecution and oppression. Historians debate just how severe this was, but it's clear that many Christians lost their lives and others lost their homes and possessions as a result of officially sanctioned persecution. It hardly seems surprising, then, that even though they were taught by Jesus (and Paul) to never return evil for evil, some Christians still "got their licks in" by writing visionary works about how evil folks would get their punishments soon enough!

The Apocalypse of Peter

The Apocalypse of Peter is a very early writing that's noted in many early Christian discussions of acceptable and unacceptable literature and is included in some collections of sacred writings. It's clear that the work had considerable influence on later Christian thought, but scholars debate about just how influential it was. The suggested dates for the Apocalypse of Peter vary from 100–150 CE, which is very early indeed, and there's evidence that it was still being recopied by Christian scribes as late as the ninth century CE.

The Apocalypse of Peter discussed in this section has no connection with a work with the same title that appears in the Nag Hammadi Library (and isn't as old as this one). We discuss that other one in Chapter 12! Same name, different books. Isn't this fun?

Anticipating the Day of Judgment

The "launching point" for this writing appears to be the authentic discussions from Jesus as recorded in the Gospel of Matthew:

> *When he was sitting on the Mount of Olives, the disciples came to him privately, saying, "Tell us, when will this be, and what will be the sign of your coming and of the end of the age?" Jesus answered them, "Beware that no one leads you astray. For many will come in my name, saying, 'I am the Messiah!' and they will lead many astray. And you will hear of wars and rumors of wars; see that you are not alarmed; for this must take place, but the end is not yet. For nation will rise against nation, and kingdom against kingdom, and there will be famines and earthquakes in various places: all this is but the beginning of the birth pangs . . ."*

> —Matthew 24:3–25:1

According to Matthew 24, Jesus continues with an extended discussion of very apocalyptic-sounding descriptions of coming trials and travails to face the Christians in the near future. Although scholars debate how much of this Jesus actually said and how much is elaborated by the Gospel writers based on, for example, the devastations of the Roman destruction of Jerusalem in 70 CE, this discussion provides the initial impetus for the elaboration found in the *Apocalypse of Peter.*

As the Apocalypse opens, Jesus tells the brief parable of a fig tree that's removed from a garden because it doesn't bear fruit. The fig tree is the "House of Israel," and being removed is the punishment for those who sin and reject God's commands. While gazing into the hand of Jesus, Peter reports a horrific vision of the Day of Judgment:

> *And this shall come at the day of judgment upon those who have fallen away from faith in God and have committed sin. Cataracts of fire shall be let loose; and darkness and obscurity shall come up and clothe and veil the whole world; and the waters shall be changed and turned into coals of fire, and all that is in them shall burn . . .*

> —Apocalypse of Peter 5 (tr. Elliott, Apocryphal New Testament, 602)

Laying out punishments

After the rather stereotypical description of the horrors of the Day of Judgment's arrival, the writing outlines many of the punishments of different kinds of sinners: punishments for those who blasphemed (hanging by their tongues! Ouch!), those who denied righteousness, and those who committed sexually immoral acts. Here are some notable examples:

> *And the murderers and those who have made common cause with them*
> *shall they cast into the fire, in a place full of venomous beasts, and they*
> *shall be tormented without rest, feeling their pains . . . and the angel Ezrael*
> *shall bring forth the souls of those who have been slain, and they shall*
> *behold the torment of those who slew them and say one to another,*
> *"Righteousness and justice is the judgment of God. For we heard, but we*
> *believed not, that we should come into this place of eternal judgment."*

—Apocalypse of Peter 25 (Akhmim Verses. 25, tr. Elliott, 604)

Early Christians were especially opposed to the common Roman practice of exposing unwanted infants to death by exposure — you know, *leaving them outside to die or be killed by animals!* Thus, this visionary writing includes a horrific punishment for parents who commit such crimes:

> *. . . and their children stand opposite them in a place of delight, and sigh*
> *and cry to God because of their parents saying, "These are they who*
> *despised and cursed and transgressed your commandments and delivered us*
> *to death . . . "*

—Apocalypse of Peter 8 (tr. Elliott, 605)

The rich who don't share their wealth with the poor and those who lend money and charge interest also are punished:

> *And into another place nearby, full of filth, they cast men and women up to*
> *their knees. These are they who lent money and took usury [interest] . . .*

—Apocalypse of Peter 10 (tr. Elliott, 606)

But lest you think that the punishments prescribed aren't so harsh after all, note that these penalties are for "sins" that modern folk certainly aren't as concerned about as people obviously once were. The Apocalypse of Peter also condemns those who engage in sex before marriage, homosexuals, and even servants who don't obey their masters! In such cases, of course, we have to take into consideration the changing notions of personal and social moralities when reading this.

In the end, the sinners beg for mercy, but the angel of Hell taunts them: "*Now* you repent, when it is no longer the time for repentance, and nothing of life remains!" *(The Apocalypse of Peter).* The sinners accept the inevitable — God is just!

Some versions of this work suggest that in the end, Jesus actually responds to Peter's weeping for mercy for sinners and promises that eventually all will be forgiven for their sins and Jesus will have pity on them. This idea that there will eventually be universal forgiveness after a period of suffering for sin is evident in some early Christian writings and is widely debated among modern interpreters of this literature.

The Apocalypse of Thomas

The Apocalypse of Thomas may go back to just before the fifth century CE, but it incorporates elements that are rather typical of apocalyptic literature — namely frightening descriptions of the events of the end of time.

In fact, this brief writing doesn't contain much teaching or many positive messages at all. It's essentially a series of despairing predictions about negative events that are only occasionally punctuated by the predictions of a few good rulers. These positive notes give the distinct impression of being temporary "reprieves" in the downward spiral.

The brief opening suggests that Jesus told these matters to Thomas. It's followed by the list of disasters; here's a good example:

> *The place of holiness shall be corrupted, the priesthood polluted, distress shall increase, virtue shall be overcome, joy perish, and gladness depart. In those days evil shall abound; there shall be respect for no one, hymns shall cease in the house of the Lord, truth shall be no more . . .*
>
> —Apocalypse of Thomas (tr. Elliott, 647)

The Apocalypse makes some predictions about good and evil rulers:

> *After a little space there shall arise a king out of the east, a lover of the law, who shall cause all necessary and good things to abound in the house of the Lord . . .*
>
> —Apocalypse of Thomas (tr. Elliott, 647)

But immediately following a period of good things; then:

> *The kings of the earth and the princes and the captains shall be troubled, and no man shall speak freely. Grey hairs shall be seen upon boys, and the young shall not give place to the aged . . .*
>
> —Apocalypse of Thomas (tr. Elliott, 648)

And then, literally, all hell breaks loose:

> *Then shall all the fountains of waters and wells boil over and be turned into blood. The heaven shall be moved, the stars shall fall upon the earth, the sun shall be cut in half like the moon, and the moon shall not give her light . . .*
>
> —Apocalypse of Thomas (tr. Elliott, 648)

At the end of this writing is an arrangement of the seven days (plus one) of the destruction:

- ✔ The first day brings a cloud of blood from the north.
- ✔ On the second day, the earth will move from its place.
- ✔ On the third day, hell will open up (with the great stench of brimstone).
- ✔ On the fourth day, earthquakes will occur.
- ✔ On the fifth day, darkness will cover the earth.
- ✔ On the sixth day, the heavens will open and angels pour out, and souls will reconnect with their bodies for resurrection of the dead.
- ✔ On the seventh day, a great battle between the forces of good and evil will take place.
- ✔ On the eighth day, there will be victory for the righteous as they "rejoice that the destruction of this world has come."

The Apocalypse of Thomas isn't particularly unique, nor does it have much value as a theological document. However, it's a further example of the apocalyptic style and the ironic popularity of these "lists of events" already in the ancient world. (Even modern writers make these "lists of events" that are popular to this day!)

The Letter of James

The Letter of James claims to be secret revelations given by Jesus to James and Peter. Some scholars (J. K. Elliott, for one, who is a noted New Testament and Apocrypha scholar) disagree with other scholars who would date it earlier, and want to date this work to third century CE. Like other documents that we consider in other chapters (especially the Nag Hammadi writings, which we cover in Chapter 12), the Letter is written in the *dialogue* format, with a person asking questions and Jesus answering them. The subject, however, is clearly apocalyptic in tone, although the final judgment is only vaguely hinted at in the context of "attaining salvation."

In the beginning dialogues, Jesus tells Peter and James that they must be "full" so that they aren't "lacking." But what they should be full of isn't clear, and Jesus doesn't ever quite make it clear. He launches into a different discussion immediately following another question about resisting the power of evil. Jesus replies that Satan will try to win them over, and so they must resist. The best way to do that is to resist the enticements of the flesh. Jesus concludes this little speech with these words: "Remember my cross and my death, and you will live!" (*Letter of James 5:30–35*). But James and Peter don't really like that answer — they don't want to face death like Jesus did!

Jesus then counsels them that they must not fear death, because "the kingdom of God belongs to those who are dead" (*Letter of James 6:15–16*). There follows a few more strange discussions about the "head of prophecy" being cut off when John was killed (*Letter of James 6:30;* compare to Matthew 14:8–10), but then Jesus tells Peter and James not to allow the kingdom of heaven to wither away. In a parable-like comparison, Jesus says that the kingdom of God is like a date palm whose fruits provide for many, and Jesus tells Peter and James to continue to provide "good fruit" like the tree.

In one of the most interesting portions of the Letter, Jesus says that Peter and James should be eager for instruction, from which comes life. Again, it's the Gnostic theme that salvation comes from information! But still, Jesus says in this writing that the prerequisites for such instruction are

- ✔ Faith
- ✔ Love
- ✔ Works

Jesus compares instruction to sowing grain: When you plant it, you have faith; when it sprouts, you love it; and you then do the work of using it for the food it provides, putting some in storage to be planted in the future. So, Jesus says:

> . . . *receive for yourselves the Kingdom of Heaven: unless you receive it through knowledge, you will not be able to discover it.*

> —Letter of James 8:25

The Gnostic character of many of the sayings in the Letter of James, and elsewhere in Gnostic writings, is readily apparent. For example, the concept of salvation through knowledge is Gnostic, as is the changing moods of Jesus. (For more on Gnosticism, turn to Chapter 12.) In the following sequence, Jesus's mood turns a bit ugly, and he scolds James and Peter, telling them that their salvation is up to their own behavior and understanding, so they had better not mess it up! Then just as quickly, Jesus speaks about how he will forgive much and leaves them to "plead for you with the Father." One can only sympathize with Peter's confusion at these seemingly contrary words from Jesus, first encouraging and then discouraging:

> *Sometimes you urge us on toward the kingdom of heaven, yet other times you turn us away, Lord. Sometimes you make appeals, draw us toward faith, and promise us life, yet other times you drive us away from the kingdom of heaven . . .*

> —Letter of James 13:25

In the end, Jesus is more positive and is encouraging just before he ascends back into heaven.

"Christianized" Hebrew Apocalyptic Writings

The series of works identified as Christianized Hebrew apocalyptic writings are basically Jewish in tone and imagery, but they're also supplemented with Christian images and ideas. Some scholars argue that they were written this way (with the Christian characteristics) to begin with but simply were written by Jewish-Christians with naturally strong Hebrew influences, using Old Testament themes and images. We address some of these writings in Chapter 4; in the context of this chapter, we look at some of them as specifically Christian apocalyptic works.

Christian additions to the Sibylline Oracles

The *Sibyls* were female seers and diviners of the ancient world, famous for their predictions and oracles of fate. Many ancient cities had Sibyls who drew people from miles around to come and consult them. They weren't originally a Jewish or Christian phenomenon but rather pagan. However, already in the centuries just before Jesus, Jewish writers were borrowing the form of the *Sibylline Oracle* to construct religious writings that "borrowed" the authority of a Sibyl. Among these Jewish compositions are also inserted sections that are Christian in origin, suggesting that Christians at least edited some of the compositions and may have also written whole sections.

The *Sibylline Oracles* deal with somewhat vague predictions of what's coming in world politics, but they were transformed into apocalyptic writings about the end times by both Jewish and Christian writers. More than a dozen books are recognized as collections of Jewish and/or Christian Sibylline Oracles. Among them are a few good examples of likely Christian insertions or editing.

In Book One, you find the following interesting insertion of Christian themes after a sequence of dividing world history into separate sections (dealing mostly with Old Testament times and characters such as the Flood and King David):

> *Then indeed the son of the great God will come,*
> *Incarnate, likened to mortal men on earth,*
> *Bearing four vowels, and the consonants in him are two.*
> *I will state explicitly the entire number for you . . .*
> *Priests will bring gifts to him, bringing forward gold,*
> *Myrrh, and incense. For he will also do all these things.*

—Sibylline Oracles 1:324

Included in this section is an affirmation that Gentiles will be brought under Christ's leadership because they will begin to recognize God's rule. The text that follows plainly shows rather strong anti-Jewish sentiment, blaming Jews for not receiving Christ and not accepting his status from God. It's followed by a rather poetic rendition of the crucifixion of Jesus as drawn from the Passion accounts of the Gospels.

In Book Two, the judgment led by God in the final days is described, in somewhat standard terms. In this description, Christ makes an appearance:

> *Christ, imperishable himself, will come in glory on a cloud*
> *Toward the imperishable one with the blameless angels.*
> *He will sit on the right of the Great One, judging at the tribunal*
> *The life of pious men and the way of impious men . . .*

> —Sibylline Oracles 2:241–242

Professor John J. Collins, one of the world's authorities on this literature, calls Book Six of the Sibylline Oracles a "hymn to Christ." This very short writing speaks of the coming of Christ to heal and to teach wisdom and finishes with a word spoken to the cross itself:

> *O wood, o most blessed, on which God was stretched out;*
> *Earth will not contain you, but you will see heaven as home*
> *When your fiery eye, o God, flashes like lightning.*

> —Sibylline Oracles 6

In Book Eight, you find an even more powerful presentation of the life of Jesus just before a description of the upheavals of God's judgment at the end of time.

Christian additions to the Fourth Book of Ezra

In *The Fourth Book of Ezra,* an originally Jewish writing appears to have been "framed" with Christian chapters at the beginning and end. The main, "Jewish" body of the book consists of revelations to the biblical figure Ezra, a Priest in the Persian Period (who lived roughly around 450 BCE); this writing is normally dated first century CE in the present form.

The Christian additions to this work are the first two chapters and the final two chapters (15–16), which consist of further descriptions of final judgment and the end of the age. In the first chapters, however, Ezra is shown a vision of the history of Israel as well as a move by God to save the Gentiles. Ezra sees a vast multitude determined to worship the true God, and before the older Jewish section of the work begins, Ezra sees a vision of a man "crowning" the multitudes with a crown of faith:

> *Then I said to the angel, "Who is that young man who places crowns on them and puts palms in their hands?" He answered and said to me, "He is the Son of God, whom they confessed in the world." So I began to praise those who had stood valiantly for the name of the Lord . . .*

—Fourth Book of Ezra 2:42–48

Christian additions to the Apocalypse of Elijah

The Apocalypse of Elijah, which purports to be additional visions of the end times given to the Prophet Elijah, also features Christian additions that are usually quite obvious. For example, when God's intention to judge between good and evil is described in the opening section, just after the affirmation of the power of the Devil in the world, it says:

> *Therefore, on account of this, the God of glory had mercy upon us, and he sent his son to the world so that he might save us from the captivity . . .*

—Apocalypse of Elijah 5

You also get this interesting passage about the return of Christ:

> *When the Christ comes, he will come in the manner of a covey of doves with the crown of doves surrounding him. He will walk upon the heaven's vaults with the sign of the cross leading him. The whole world will behold him like the sun which shines from the eastern horizon to the western. This is how he will come, with all his angels surrounding him . . .*

—Apocalypse of Elijah 3:2–4

The Apocalypse goes on with a startling description of the "son of lawlessness," a kind of anti-Christ figure who can do everything that Jesus did on earth except raise the dead — and by that inability he will be "found out" by the faithful. Finally, the writing announces that Christ will inaugurate his reign of 1,000 years and create a New Heaven and New Earth — images borrowed from the New Testament's *Revelation to John.*

The Apocalypse writings that feature Christian "inserts" show not only how early Christians made use of these writings but also the freedom that Christian copyists felt to simply edit in sections that honored their own traditions! There was apparently a strong sense of malleability in working with these writings — that is, they weren't considered sacred or untouchable at all!

Judging from the fact that stories of final judgment, the sufferings of hell, and the glories of heaven continued to be riveting subjects to Christian audiences right up to their appearance as themes in European medieval religious drama from 1200 to the 1500s, apocalyptic themes were constant favorites. People wanted reassurances about their spiritual futures as well as assurance that evildoers would "get theirs in the end." It seems that both were popular and comforting messages.

Part V
The Part of Tens

The 5th Wave

By Rich Tennant

"What makes me question its authenticity as a lost book of the Bible is the last section labeled, '25 Crowd Pleasing Recipes for the Apocalypse.'"

In this part . . .

You want a quick summary, you say? Just give me the basics, you say? A "bottom line" kind of person, are you? Then this part is for you. Here, we summarize a series of "Top Ten" lists that you'll never hear from David Letterman! You get the ten weirdest books written by early Jews as well as ten from Christian writers. You also get our recommendation of ten books that every serious student of the Bible should read. Finally, we consider ten "sayings of Jesus" that are reported in sources outside the New Testament and take a moment to consider the provocative question, "Does it sound like him, or not?"

Chapter 17

Ten Weirdest Jewish Lost Books

In This Chapter

▶ Browsing the Book of Enoch

▶ Exploring documents found with the Dead Sea Scrolls

▶ Reading a few documents with religious "nasty streaks"

▶ Telling stories and glimpsing the possible future

*W*hen we say a lost book is "weird," we mean that it contains any of the following, and in many cases, *all* of the following:

✔ Odd, surreal imagery

✔ Arguments that either don't make sense (to us!) or are contrary to traditional canonical themes found in the Bible

✔ Narrative elements that fly in the face of what the traditions appear to be in the canonical writings eventually endorsed by either the Church for Christians, or the Rabbis for Judaism

These factors contributed to the rejection of these lost books for canonical inclusion, but they certainly make for interesting reading nonetheless!

The criteria we use for selecting "weird" writings for this chapter apply to both the Jewish lost books discussed here and the Christian lost books that we cover in Chapter 18. Now, this "weird" business is, of course, a *huge* matter of opinion. Some folks think that some of the writings that *are* in the Bible inch toward the edge of the "weird" category, if they haven't fallen in! Still, it's interesting to propose reasons why some of these books didn't make the cut for either Judaism or Christianity (now see . . . they *did* agree on *some* things!).

1 Enoch

Several books are attributed to Enoch, but here we're addressing "numero uno" — the book often called simply "Enoch" but better identified as 1 Enoch. In fact, 1 Enoch (see Chapter 6 for a full discussion of this book) makes two of our Part of Tens lists because, even though we consider it to be required reading for anyone interested in biblical studies (see Chapter 20), at the same time it's decidedly weird.

Written most likely between 300–100 BCE, 1 Enoch is a lengthy apocalyptic work; in fact, it's probably the oldest example of this genre of religious writing that exists today.

So why is Enoch in the "weird" category? Apocalyptic literature is already a strange form of writing in that it uses bizarre images, features angelic visitors, involves dreams and visions, and so on. But Enoch really pushes the envelope. It's supposedly written by a human (Enoch) who's taken directly into God's realm (Genesis 5:24) and given a tour of the various places in heaven, including the locations where God keeps rain and snow and wind. Enoch is given lists of names of fallen angels, and he sees mountains of different metals and scenes where judgment is to take place. Then suddenly, the story changes into a detailed discussion of the moral lessons of watching the precise movement of the stars, moon, and sun. Then you read of dreams of cows and falling stars . . . and then there's a retelling of the entire history of ancient Israel as an allegory about sheep. Check out this description of the rise of King David:

> *Now the dogs, foxes, and the wild boars began to devour those sheep till the Lord of the sheep raised up another sheep, one from among them — a ram which would lead them. That ram began to fight on all sides those dogs, foxes, and wild boars . . .*
>
> —1 Enoch 89:42–44 (tr. E. Isaac, in Charlesworth, Vol. 1, 69)

So, if 1 Enoch is so strange, why is it also a critically important work? It's important because there are many sections of 1 Enoch — including a lengthy series of discussions about the "chosen one" of God who will assist in judgment in the end times — that were either later Christian additions to the work *or* represent pre-Christian Jewish ideas quite clearly compatible with later Christian discussions of Jesus! If these are, in fact, pre-Christian sections of Enoch, then they're clearly ideas that would have influenced later Christian reflection on Jesus. Another famous aspect of Enoch: It contains the oldest account of the origin of Satan as a "fallen angel" — an idea that went on to be very influential; it's cited in early Christian literature, and known by many Christians to this very day (even though most Christians don't know anything about the book of Enoch!). Because there's very *little* discussion of Satan in the Hebrew Bible, the prominence of the "fallen angels" in Enoch is all the more interesting.

The War Scroll (From the Dead Sea Scrolls)

The Dead Sea Scrolls contain several writings that were important to the Qumran community — the folks who hid the scrolls in the first place (for a fuller discussion of the Dead Sea Scrolls, head to Chapter 5). They had their own literature, and the *War Scroll* is an apocalyptic vision of the end times when the "sons of light" (obviously the community and their angelic allies) would go to war against the "sons of darkness" (and *their* angelic allies) to retake and purify the Holy Temple of Jerusalem and inaugurate the future. In the end, all darkness is destroyed and light lives on.

This strange vision can get quite graphic and gruesome in its descriptions of spiritual battle. For example:

> *For the battle is yours!*
> *With the might of your hand*
> *Their corpses have been torn to pieces*
> *With no-one to bury them!*

—War Scroll 1 QM Col. XI

> *Place your hand on the neck of your foes*
> *And your foot on the piles of the dead!*
> *Strike the nations, your foes!*

—War Scroll, 1 QM Col. XII

The War Scroll also describes the banners to be carried into battle (including what they will say) and seems to describe certain kinds of troop movements for the angelic, apocalyptic battle. Clearly the Qumran community consisted of some angry and vindictive folks . . . but the interesting bit is that this was to be a spiritual battle fought with angels and men together.

Psalms of Exorcism (From the Dead Sea Scrolls)

Among the weird and interesting writings in the Dead Sea material not found anywhere in the Bible are exorcisms against Satan and evil spirits. Members of the Qumran community were taught to repeat certain prayers when they felt that they were confronted with evil spirits. Here's one such prayer:

When Belial comes upon you, you shall say to him: Who are you, accursed amongst men and amongst the seed of the holy ones? Your face is a face of futility and your horns are horns of a wretch. You are darkness and not light . . . Yahweh will shut you in the deepest Sheol . . .

—11Q Apocryphal Psalms Col. IV

It's odd to think that hurling a series of insults is intended to drive away an evil spirit, but there you are. Maybe all those people swearing on the freeway are really trying to drive out evil spirits. . . .

The Pesher Literature (From the Dead Sea Scrolls)

Pesherim (meaning "interpretations"; "pesher" is the singular form) are writings from the Dead Sea Scrolls that involve biblical material. These are "interpretations" of biblical books, mostly the Prophets. But the style is quite strange and unfamiliar to modern readers. Often, the biblical Prophet (such as Habakkuk, in one of the more famous scrolls) is quoted verse by verse, followed by the phrase, "The Interpretation is . . ." and a very brief explanation. Consider the following example from the Prophet Habakkuk; the actual biblical text refers to judgment against rulers who conquer others mercilessly and build empires:

Alas for you who build a town by bloodshed, and found a city on iniquity!

—Habakkuk 2:12

But the Pesher interpretation transforms this verse into a condemnation of the Priests in Jerusalem that the Dead Sea community members despise (its references to building a city and erecting a community refer to the Jerusalem Temple and its priestly staff):

The interpretation of the word concerns the Spreader of Deceit, who has misdirected many, building a useless city with blood and erecting a community by subterfuge.

—1QpHab (tr. Martinez, 201)

The free manner in which the verses are interpreted and the fact that some of these scrolls specifically mention events that occurred in the first century BCE (instead of the time of the Prophet being quoted) shows that biblical interpretation and proof-texting go way back. Many of the interpretations derived from this verse-by-verse exposition, however, earn these writings a clear place on the "weird" list!

Proof-texting is the practice of using quotations from a document out of context to support an ideological point. Often, when read in context, the quote actually doesn't support the alleged contention.

The Life of Adam and Eve

The Life of Adam and Eve (first century CE) is an example of the late Jewish fondness for legendary "expansions" of the biblical stories, this time dealing with Adam and Eve. Of the two rather different versions of this work, one has more apocalyptic-like elements than the other, but they both follow the same general lines.

After being thrown out of Eden, Adam gets the great idea to stand in the middle of the Jordan River, and he sends Eve to stand in the middle of the Tigris River until God relents and has compassion on the two humans. It sort of goes without saying why this work finds a place on the "weirdest" list. Consider this excerpt:

> And Adam said, "I tell you, water of the Jordan, mourn with me and gather to me all swimming creatures which are in you and let them surround me and so lament together with me. Let them not mourn for themselves, but rather for me, because it is not they who have sinned, but I."

> —Life of Adam and Eve 8

Soon, fish and marine animals gather with Adam and Eve, and they actually stop up the river! Satan, however, tricks Eve into stopping her fast by pretending to be an angel of God who has heard her prayers.

It isn't immediately obvious why stopping up rivers will impress God (or Satan, for that matter). Furthermore, Satan complains to Adam that the reason Satan was expelled from heaven was because he wasn't terribly impressed with God's creation of humanity. It's not exactly the most profound explanation of the origins of evil, but it's certainly entertaining.

The History of the Rechabites

In the *History of the Rechabites,* a pious man named Zosimus is fasting in the wilderness in hopes that God will show him where the "Blessed Ones" dwell. There's no explanation of who these Blessed Ones are until later in the writing. An angel who seems to change shape into a strange animal brings Zosimus to a beautiful island.

One of the unique aspects of this work is that instead of being transported to heaven or hell, Zosimus is taken to a different *geographical* location. When Zosimus finally meets one of the Blessed Ones (who appears to him to be like an angel), he's taken to their gathering. The gathered Blessed Ones ask God why this person is visiting and if it means that the end of the world has come. God says that it isn't the end of the world and that Zosimus should be told who the Blessed Ones are for seven days, after which he'll be returned to his world. The book describes a number of such conversations about these Blessed Ones — how they live, why they live the way they do, and what lessons may be learned from their lives.

This writing is a vision of a geographical apocalypse rather than a future apocalypse. Normally, apocalyptic writings are about events that are about to happen; they describe changes in time. This work, however, describes an idyllic place rather than an idyllic time. This detail makes this writing among the more unusual of the apocalyptic Jewish writings surveyed in this book — not an easy feat to accomplish!

The Sibylline Oracles

In the ancient Greek world (and far beyond it!), there was a legendary *seer*, often described as an old woman, who could peer into the unknown and give reports (called *oracles*) of what she saw. The seer was called a *Sibyl*. No one knows if there ever was a real Sibyl who started all this legendary stuff, but references to her crop up as early as the fifth century BCE.

It appears that it wasn't long before some Jewish writers decided that they liked this Sibyl stuff and therefore started using this style of writing. The result is a rather large collection of writings called *The Sibylline Oracles* (see Chapter 7), or *Books 1–14*. Like other lost book writings, many of the collections are fragmented. The dates of this material begin as early as the third to second centuries BCE, and they continued to be produced and added to after the seventh to eighth centuries CE.

Typical of all the Sibylline Oracles are somewhat vague "predictions" of the rise and fall of empires and individual rulers as well as accounts of palace intrigue (often important for modern historians trying to identify a specific historic ruler).

Part of the fame and attraction of the Sibylline literature are the difficult and puzzling passages that lend themselves to multiple interpretations and meanings. Consider one of these odd and even troubling descriptions of events to come; it's specific enough to be frightening but vague enough to apply to just about anything:

> *But when on earth there are raging earthquakes*
> *And thunderbolts, thunders, lightnings . . . and the mildew of the land*
> *And frenzy of jackals and wolves, and slaughters*
> *And destruction of men and bellowing oxen.*
> *Four footed cattle and laboring mules*
> *And goats and sheep, then much farmland*
> *Will be left barren through neglect*
> *And fruits will fail. Selling of free men into slavery*
> *Will be practiced among very many people, and robbing of temples.*
> *Then indeed the tenth generation of men will also appear*
> *After these things, when the earth-shaking lightning-giver*
> *Will break the glory of idols and shake the people of*
> *Seven-hilled Rome. Great wealth will perish . . .*

—Sibylline Oracles, 2:5–17

Or check out the following, from later in the same section:

> *But whenever this sign appears throughout the world,*
> *Children born with gray temples from birth*
> *Afflictions of men, famines, pestilence, and wars*
> *Change of times, lamentations, many tears;*
> *Alas, how many people's children in the countries will feed*
> *On their parents, with piteous lamentations. They will place*
> *Their flesh in cloaks and bury them in the ground, mother of peoples,*
> *Defiled with blood and lust . . .*

—Sibylline Oracles, 2:153–162

The Treatise of Shem

The Treatise of Shem (see Chapter 7 for details), which historians date to no later than 31–20 BCE, is quite significant for one essential reason: It proves ancient Jewish interest in the zodiac signs and thus at least some Jewish interest in the entire realm of astrology. The interest was probably strongest among Jews living in the Diaspora especially, where they would have had more contact with astrological lore than other Jews back in the homeland.

So what's so weird about this writing? Precisely the astrology! The Old Testament is rather clearly opposed to anything that smacks of "worshipping" the stars (check out Deuteronomy 4:19 and 2 Kings 23:5 in particular), and most historians take this to be a not-too-subtle condemnation of any kind of astrological speculation. As well, both mainline Jewish and Orthodox Christian traditions later condemned any kind of astrology as contrary to a belief in God's ultimate control of the universe. So, you can see why a document like the Treatise would be controversial. It shows the wide variety of ideas among Jews and Christians in the days before "correct thinking" tended to weed out unapproved interests.

As a writing, the Treatise of Shem gives clear astrological guidance in the general terms familiar to those who are into this kind of stuff, but the guidance is vague enough to be impressive at many different times (such as, "You will walk through a door today"). Consider this example:

> *If the year begins in Aries: The Year will be lean. Even its four-footed [animals] will die and many clouds will neither be visible nor appear . . ."*

—Treatise of Shem 1

Not so strange perhaps, but such predictions get rather odd:

> *And oil will be valued in Africa; but wheat will be reduced in value in Damascus and Hauran, but in Palestine it will be valued. And (in that region there will be) various diseases, and sicknesses, even fighting will occur in it. But it will be allowed to escape from it and be delivered.*

—Treatise of Shem 1

The real oddity of the Treatise is precisely the notion that "fates" are embedded in the cosmos in the astrological sense, that things happen because of planetary alignments, signs, and signals; this is contrary to the idea of a personal God who's in control of all events. And such astrological thinking certainly goes against accepted biblical teachings!

The Apocalypse of Zephaniah

The Apocalypse of Zephaniah is a work named for the Prophet Zephaniah of the Bible only because the visionary says in the writing, "I, Zephaniah, saw these things in my vision. . . ."

Of course, the Apocalypse was written many centuries after the traditional time of the Prophet Zephaniah, and thus it was written under a pseudonym borrowed from the earlier history of ancient Israel. Zephaniah was a biblical Prophet from the sixth century BCE. The book in the Bible that contains some of his speeches, what's known as the biblical book of Zephaniah, is already interestingly unique because it features visions that were somewhat unusual for biblical prophets. Some historians suspect that the biblical book of Zephaniah is a writing that's already moving in the direction of apocalyptic-like visions that were definitely more common in the later period, beginning in the fourth to third centuries BCE.

This work features notably weird themes that are familiar to readers of the book of Revelation in the New Testament: for example, angels that blow on trumpets and descriptive passages where the visionary talks about seeing people being punished in judgment.

Like other equally weird apocalyptic works, the Apocalypse reads almost like you, the reader, are walking around the outside of an old downtown department store that's famous for its picture windows. As you walk around gazing at the different windows (which are the scenes in the story), you become increasingly alarmed at the scenes of suffering, punishment, and lamentation. Certainly not the kind of store you want to shop in!

As you can imagine, then, this vision has a very personal impact on the visionary, Zephaniah. For example, in one window (that is, scene) Zephaniah sees people being punished in Hades by horrible-looking creatures, and he wonders what they are. Zephaniah is told about these ugly angels who carry off the bad people:

> He said to me: "These are the servants of all creation who come to the souls of ungodly men and bring them and leave them in this place. They spend three days going around with them in the air before they bring them and cast them into their eternal punishment.
>
> I said, "I beseech you, O Lord, don't give them authority to come to me." The Angel said, "Don't fear. I will not permit them to come to you because you are pure before the Lord."
>
> —Apocalypse of Zephaniah 4

The notion that sins are kept track of in heaven in a kind of holy ledger is affirmed in this writing:

> Then I looked, and I saw him with a manuscript in his hand. He began to unroll it. Now after he spread it out, I read it in my own language. I found that all my sins which I had done were written in it, those which I had done from my youth until this day. They were all written upon that manuscript of mine with there being a false word in them. If I did not go visit a sick man or a widow, I found it written down as a shortcoming upon my manuscript . . .
>
> —Apocalypse of Zephaniah 7

By the ninth chapter, Zephaniah gets good news: "Be courageous! . . . Your name is written in the Book of the Living!" So, in the end, the work encourages the reader to work so that his or her life is listed in the right book!

The Apocalypse of Adam (From the Nag Hammadi Library)

The Apocalypse of Adam is a Gnostic writing found among the Nag Hammadi manuscripts discovered in Egypt in the mid-20th century (see Chapter 12 for more on the Nag Hammadi manuscripts). The son of Adam, named Seth, was very important in some subsects of Gnostic belief because he was supposed to be the one to whom Adam revealed many secrets. Seth passed the secrets on to the people who called themselves *Gnostics*.

There were many Christian Gnostic writings, but the Apocalypse of Adam appears to be a Gnostic Jewish writing — that is, a work that draws on the *Jewish* rather than the *Christian* tradition to argue Gnostic beliefs.

The Gnostics were a strange group to begin with. They believed that the material world wasn't "real" in any profound sense and the only "reality" was spiritual. They also thought that the "God" of the Hebrews, the creator of this world, was an evil god who tries to cover up the truth about the Higher God, the God of Light and Truth. Thus, in other Gnostic writings (which, not surprisingly, are quite strange as well), the Hebrew biblical narrative is typically told as a narrative of enslavement to an evil god who doesn't want humans to know the truth.

The Apocalypse of Adam speaks of Adam and Eve originally knowing that they were superior to the god that made them because they were partly formed from the light of the *higher* God. Eventually, however, they "fell" and lost their knowledge of this higher God. Here, Adam and Eve become "enslaved" to the lesser god:

> *Next, we became acquainted with the god that made us. For we were not alien to his powers. And we served him in fear and servility. And after this, we became dark in our hearts and I, for my part, was asleep in the thinking of my heart.*

> —Apocalypse of Adam 1–2

But, according to the writing, an "Illuminator" will come with the truth. A long poetic sequence describes aspects of this Illuminator as one who was carefully chosen and cared for by the angels of the Higher God; each section of the sequence ends with the phrase, "thus, he came to the water." This person eventually reveals the truth to humanity, which is the knowledge now being passed to the safekeeping of Seth, according to this writing. It seems possible that this writing had something to do with a kind of water ritual (perhaps a sort of baptism or a Jewish "Mikvah") of entry into a Gnostic sect because water and "coming to the water" are themes throughout the entire work.

Although most of the surviving Gnostic writings are Christian, the Apocalypse of Adam stands out as one that appears to have no specifically Christian elements at all, suggesting the wide range of religious themes and sources that Gnostic religious writers could use in the ancient world. Whereas the Christian Gnostics emphasized the coming of Jesus to bring the true knowledge of the higher God of Light, in the Apocalypse of Adam, a Hebrew story (Creation) is used to express some of the same Gnostic themes. The book makes the "weird" list mainly because of the boldness of *changing* the biblical tradition in order to argue *against* the biblical tradition!

Chapter 18

Ten Weirdest Christian Lost Books

* *

In This Chapter

▶ Exploring unusual imagery and miracles

▶ Looking at Jesus from different perspectives

▶ Touching on some really cryptic writings

* *

"**W**eirdness," of course, is in the eye of the beholder. We can already hear many of our colleagues in historical studies and biblical studies bemoaning our selections for weird lost books and e-mailing us to say, "How can you guys call *that* weird!?? It's terribly important!!"

Well, weird doesn't necessarily mean "unimportant," but it does mean (to us, anyway) that these writings include one or more of the following:

✔ Strange images

✔ Arguments that don't appear rational or even sensible

✔ Ideas that strike modern readers as quite contrary to the spirit of the Bible (for example, violent images used in relation to Jesus)

In this chapter, weirdness abounds (always an appealing notion, right?) as we share with you our list of the ten weirdest Christian lost books. (You can find our ten weirdest Jewish lost books in Chapter 17.)

The Shepherd of Hermas

The *Shepherd of Hermas* is a book filled with strange visions that a certain early Christian perceived and then wrote about in this work. It's a bit long and can get a bit tedious, but it was *very* popular among early Christians. Some Christians even grouped it with other books that became the New Testament! The Shepherd of Hermas didn't make the final cut, of course, but it deserves recognition as the kind of "Christian folklore" that was once very popular reading indeed.

In the parables, the largest section of the work, there are three main images that represent different forms of the same general message about the composition of the church and different kinds of people in it. The images are as follows:

- ✔ The different kinds of Christians represented by different bricks that make up the "tower" of the Church
- ✔ Different plants that are seedlings cut from the "tree" that is the Church
- ✔ Material drawn from different "mountains" to build the Church

The parables are sometimes quite clear, but the tone taken in the Shepherd's conversations with Hermas is very odd. For example, after telling Hermas a parable, Hermas quite rationally asks to have it explained:

> *I begged him fervently to explain to me the parable of the field, the master, the vineyard, and the slave who built a fence around the vineyard . . . he answered me, "You are extremely brazen in your requests. You should ask nothing at all, for if anything needs to be explained to you, it will be." I said to him, "Lord there is no point in showing me something that you do not explain, when I do not know what it is."*
>
> —Shepherd of Hermas (Visions, 11:1–2)

The Shepherd tells Hermas that he's brazen and shouldn't ask so many questions . . . but then proceeds to tell him that because Hermas is persistent, the Shepherd *will* explain the parables to him.

Hermas strikes us as entirely reasonable in his requests and the Shepherd as impatient and callous! If we spoke to any of *our* students that way, neither of us would be teaching much longer!

In general, we think this book is strange because it seems to actually delight in its mystery and puzzles. The visions, when explained, seem sensible enough — so why not just get to the point? Why the puzzles, visions, imagery, and impatient questions? Are these elements used simply because they're entertaining, or perhaps because "visions" have their own kind of authority that demands attention? Hmm . . . maybe we should say, "I had this vision . . ." more often than, "I had an idea the other day. . . ." It does have a certain ring to it, eh?

The Gospel of Peter

One of the famous so-called lost Gospels is the *Gospel of Peter*. In this Gospel, the Resurrection of Jesus is portrayed in grand fashion: It features a description of how God sent down two angels to open the tomb of Jesus and how the soldiers guarding the tomb saw it all. At that point, however, things start to get a bit strange; consider this passage:

> . . . [The soldiers] saw three men come out from the sepulcher, two of them supporting the other and a cross following them and the heads of the two reaching to heaven, but that of him who was being led reached beyond the heavens. And they heard a voice out of the heavens crying, "Have you preached to those who sleep?" and from the cross there was heard the answer, "Yes."
>
> —Gospel of Peter, lines 39–42

Essentially, the Gospel claims that Jesus and the angels walk out of the tomb followed by a walking and talking wooden cross. The idea of the "talking cross" has especially fascinated modern scholars, who wonder what this image is intended to communicate.

Symbolic scenes figure prominently in some Gnostic circles and certainly in apocalyptic visions, so either tradition could have influenced the presentation here. However, we categorize this early Christian writing in this "weird" list because it's difficult to understand, particularly why it was considered important or even inspiring to have the cross speak. (What may be even weirder is that early readers were impressed with this notion!)

The Martyrdom of Polycarp

Given that early Christianity faced a series of horrendous persecutions, it's hardly surprising that stories of the courageous martyrdom of early Church leaders became an important form of early Christian literature.

The *Martyrdom of Polycarp* is a very early example of this kind of Christian literature that also happens to feature some unusual miracles along the way, which is why this work is part of the list in this chapter.

Polycarp was an early Bishop in Smyrna (today it's Izmir in Turkey). It's interesting to note that during his persecution, Polycarp was offered release if he only confessed, "Caesar is Lord," but he refused. In an act of impressive defiance, he was told to turn to his fellow Christians and say "Away with the atheists," but instead, he turned to the Roman officials and crowds and said to *them,* "Away with the atheists!" This kind of early Christian brassy and nonviolent courage is quite admirable, in our opinion!

But as we said earlier, some of the miracles described in this work are a bit strange. As in many martyrdom accounts, there are interesting miracles associated with the death. When the officials try to burn Polycarp alive, a miracle occurs that spares him from the flames, but then a Roman soldier stabs him with a lance. At once, a dove emerges (perhaps it's his rising spirit), and the gushing blood extinguishes the flames. Of course, martyrs couldn't always count on miracles to save them, and often the miracles described in early

Christian literature accompany the martyrs' deaths rather than prevent them, but these unusual events suggest a power greater than the power that executes the believers!

The weirdness of the Martyrdom of Polycarp comes partly from the notion that early Christians actually treasured stories of their leaders being executed. This is hardly a modern idea of inspiring literature, and it forces readers to recognize that early Christians lived in quite different circumstances, where accepting the possibility of execution for their beliefs was a sign of strength, not weakness.

The Epistle of Barnabas

We list the *Epistle of Barnabas* in the "weird" category, but we'd also list it in the "dangerous" category, if there was one!

The Epistle, which is not believed to have been written by the famous companion of Paul (refer to Acts 4:26, 9:27, and elsewhere), is a letter that sadly reveals the extent of anger and argument between early Christians and Jews in the first two centuries of Christianity. Because of a reference to possibly "rebuilding" the Temple (destroyed by Roman soldiers in 70 CE), this work is clearly written after 70 CE. Also, you should keep in mind that there's a *much* later writing (which comes after the time of Muhammad and the beginnings of Islam in the seventh century CE) called the *Gospel of Barnabas* that isn't related to the Epistle of Barnabas, which is much older.

The Epistle is a sustained attack on Jewish tradition, probably directed against Jewish-Christians who continued to practice their Jewish religious and ritual life while accepting the identity of Jesus as the promised Messiah. This particular form of early Christianity, often identified as *Jewish-Christianity,* died out by the fifth to sixth centuries CE. After reading *The Epistle of Barnabas,* one hardly wonders why!

While it's true that the Epistle of Barnabas is not *all* negative (some of it is actually quite nice), we think we can live without a Christian calling Jews "wretches":

> *I will also speak to you about the Temple, since those wretches were misguided in hoping in the building rather than in their God who made them, as if the Temple were actually the house of God . . .*

—Epistle of Barnabas 16:1

The general tone of the Epistle is that the promises of the Hebrew Scriptures to the Jews were really about Christians — and Christians replace the Jews as the true people of God. Such arguments aren't unique to this writing, of course, but they become especially problematic in writings that were as widely read as the Epistle of Barnabas. A good antidote to Barnabas, incidentally, is Paul's *Epistle to Romans* in the New Testament, which clearly teaches that God is *not* "finished" with Jews and Judaism!

Anti-Semitism has been a horrendous legacy of some forms of Christianity, and the Epistle reveals how nasty this attitude could be already in the early centuries of Christianity. Hopefully, reading it will remind modern audiences to be much more vigilant about the dangers of hateful or dismissive speech!

The Infancy Gospel of Thomas

If you're intrigued rather than repulsed by the idea of Jesus being a naughty little boy before he "matured" into understanding his identity as the Messiah, then the *Infancy Gospel of Thomas* is the book for you.

The young Jesus is portrayed in the early part of this writing as a mouthy, bratty, headstrong kid who "zaps" other kids dead on the spot for messing with his playtime or for bumping into him. Later versions of these legends try hard to portray the events in a more positive light (the boy who bumped him was a bully, and so on), but this does little to remove the initial shock of reading the Infancy Gospel. When Mary and Joseph's neighbors complain, they're struck blind by Jesus.

The point of this writing seems to be that Jesus eventually grows up and gets it. By the age of 12, he realizes what he's called to do — preach compassion and engage in healing. But the opening sequences are a bit startling for modern Christians who aren't used to thinking of Jesus as a troubled kid!

Unless you have a bratty kid who you hope will grow up to be great some day, this story may leave you with the question, "Why did any early Christians find these stories inspiring?"

One likely answer is this: If the young Jesus had a few things to learn, like *real* humans inevitably do, the story is an effective way of arguing that Jesus *was* fully human in all ways as well as the "Son of God" and Messiah. It's always hard to relate to someone who's perfect in every way. Historians know that the identity of Jesus as *both* "human" and "divine" was a subject of constant

Christian debate, and the Infancy Gospel of Thomas is one interesting — although certainly unconventional — way to argue the "humanness" of Jesus by arguing that as a youth, he experienced the need to mature and grow in wisdom like humans do. After all, Luke 2:52 says that Jesus "grew in wisdom," suggesting that Jesus didn't know *everything* from birth!

Valentinus: On Jesus's Digestive System

One of the most important Gnostic leaders, Valentinus (100–170 CE), is quoted by an early Christian writer named St. Clement of Alexandria. In this otherwise lost work, Valentinus comments on Jesus's digestive system because he was determined to deny that Jesus was a normal human being like others. The full humanity of Jesus is affirmed by most Orthodox Christians. Consider Valentinus's argument:

> *He was continent, enduring all things. Jesus digested divinity: he ate and drank in a special way, without excreting his solids. He had such a great capacity for continence that the nourishment within him was not corrupted, for he did not experience corruption.*

> —Epistle of Valentinus to Agathopous
> (quoted in St. Clement of Alexandria, tr. Layton, 238)

Maybe it's a good thing that this Epistle from Valentinus is still lost, eh? It shows you the extent to which ancients tried to debate the exact relationship between the physical and spiritual natures of Jesus (human and God). This argument raged for centuries, incidentally, and was the subject of major church gatherings in the first six centuries of Christianity.

The Gospel of Truth (From the Nag Hammadi Library)

One of the most important writings from Valentinus (see the previous section), the *Gospel of Truth*, was found among the Nag Hammadi materials. It's among the clearer Gnostic writings and at times is quite moving. One can begin to actually see the attraction that Gnostic interpretations of Jesus must have had for those with a certain attraction to the mystical. (See Chapter 12 for an in-depth discussion of Gnosticism and Gnostic writings.)

In the following passage from the Gospel of Truth, Jesus becoming humanlike is explained as an act of God's compassion to be more easily known to humans. However, even as the general idea comes across, the imagery maintains its Gnostic "foreignness":

> *Acquaintance from the father and the appearance of his son gave them a means to comprehend. For when they saw and heard him, he let them taste and smell of himself and touch the beloved son, after he had appeared to tell them about the father, the uncontained, and had breathed into them what was in the thought (of the father) doing his will. When many had received the light, they converted to him, for they were strangers and did not see his image and had not recognized him.*
>
> —Gospel of Truth 5:23–36 (tr. Layton, 259)

Calling the higher God the "uncontained" one, calling the divine within humans part of the "thought" of the Father that was "breathed" into them, and referring to Christian conversion as acquiring knowledge (rather than acknowledging God's actions in the world through Jesus) are all rather strange notions that are typical of Gnostic Christianity. There's little emphasis on the material, the world, and the humanness of Jesus; in some ways the Gospel of Truth is the *opposite* of the Infancy Gospel of Thomas, which depicts Jesus as perhaps a bit *too* human (see the "Infancy Gospel of Thomas" section earlier in this chapter).

The Acts of Andrew

You may have guessed that we really like the early Christian folklore that's featured in these various "Acts of . . ." books that tell strange and wonderful stories of early Apostles like Thomas, Peter, Paul, and this one dealing with Andrew. (Chapter 15 describes many of these early Acts stories.)

However, as this is the "weirdest" category, we confess that the *Acts of Andrew* is our *least* favorite of this genre because it seems that Andrew is most concerned with keeping people pure from engaging in sex — *any* sex — whether it's between married or unmarried people!

The attitude in this book reveals that there were early groups of Christians who thought that *all* sexuality was evil, despite Paul's advice to people who want to get married that they *should* get married *and* sleep together! (If you don't believe us, read 1 Corinthians 7.) Despite its bad rap, Christianity is not "anti-sex," so this work goes completely against what's taught in the Bible with ideas like the following passage, in which Andrew counsels a female convert who's resisting all sexual intercourse with her husband, Aegeates:

"O Maximilla, my child," Andrew replied, "I know that you have been moved to resist any proposition of sexual intercourse and wish to be dissociated from a foul and filthy way of life . . . Maximilla, do not commit this act! Do not submit to Aegeates' threat. Do not be moved by his speech."

—Acts of Andrew 37 (tr. Elliott, 256)

Even at the end, the Acts of Andrew confirms its "anti-material" attitude by teaching that the body is not important; Andrew's death isn't even very important to him because it's the soul that's truly "real."

The First Thought in Three Forms (From the Nag Hammadi Library)

Try this one on for size:

It is I who am the sound that exists
Bestowing sound upon everyone;
And they recognize that a posterity exists within [me]
It is I who am the parent's thinking;
And from me emanated sound, that is acquaintance with the infinites:
I exist as the thinking of the entirety
Being joined to unrecognizable and incomprehensible thinking
I personally showed myself forth among all those that had recognized me.

—First Thought in Three Forms, 36:14–22 (tr. Layton, 90)

If your reaction to this excerpt from the Gnostic *First Thought in Three Forms* is some version of, "Um, could you run that by me again, please?" then we all agree that this is mighty strange stuff. Imagine sitting in a meeting where this is read out loud . . . and people around you are nodding their heads and saying, "Oh yes!" "Amen," and "That's right!" Frankly, we would wonder what we were missing.

Gnostic literature attempts to explain the origins of beings, often suggesting that beings other than the original God came into existence by first being "thoughts" of the original God. Those thoughts then take on life on their own and then get into conflicts. The literature eventually explains that humanity gets caught in the midst of these spiritual, ethereal conflicts. *Some* people found these writings inspirational and informative . . . and we find that about as disturbing as the writings themselves, but perhaps we need to be more open-minded . . .

The Reality of the Rulers (From the Nag Hammadi Library)

As with the preceding section, we can barely make sense of this work either. The *Reality of the Rulers* is another good example (we suppose . . .) of Gnostic spirituality at its *best* (or *worst*). Hard to read, hard to understand, and filled with obscure references. As we say about the First Thought in Three Forms, the amazing thing about some of these writings is that *some* early Christians actually *liked* this stuff and were able to make sense of it. Our opinion is that something was in their brownies, but don't take our word for it . . . have a little sample (of the book, that is, not the brownies):

> *This Ruler, by being androgynous, made itself a vast realm, an extent without limit. And it contemplated creating offspring for itself, and created for itself seven offspring, androgynous just like their parent. And it said to its offspring, "It is I who am the god of the entirety."*

—Reality of the Rulers 94–95

Scholars can discern that this work is mostly about the Creation accounts, but the specific details are elusive, to say the least. Furthermore, we're generally nervous about writings that are so vague that anyone can read just about anything they want into them. We have a bad enough time with the real New Testament . . . we hardly need *more* confusion, now, do we?

Still, it's important to be as respectful as possible. A large number of Gnostic Christians suffered some severe abuse (at the least) and persecutions (at worst) for treasuring this kind of writing. Just because today's readers think it odd doesn't mean for a split second that those who *did* love this stuff deserved anything worse than a respectful debate!

Chapter 19

Ten Sayings of Jesus You Won't Find in the Bible

Some early sayings of Jesus are quite different from the four "canonical" Gospels. Although these utterances don't abound, they *are* out there and deserve some attention. We look at ten of them in this chapter and tell you why they're noteworthy.

The most important early source of such sayings is the Gospel of Thomas from the second century CE, but Jesus's quotes also appear in the works of early Christian writers like Origen, Tertullian, and Jerome. (It seems that these guys had access to writings that are now lost.) Many scholars have gathered up most of these sayings and then asked themselves, "Do any of these sound genuine?" This study raises interesting questions, like whether these "sayings" sound like other known Jesus sayings or even sound like a first century Jewish teacher! And the answers are sometimes yes, sometimes no.

We're not just interested in those sayings that are *the most likely to really be Jesus.* We're also interested in sayings that seem to accurately portray the historical Jesus — in other words, statements that are very close to the spirit of Jesus. So, as a Quaker biblical scholar, I (Daniel) understand the historical Jesus to be, at the very least, a profoundly revolutionary teacher who taught about social as well as spiritual change and justice and who also advocated nonviolence over violence as the means to work for that change.

Therefore, my selection of "top ten" sayings of Jesus *not* in the Gospels is influenced by my own background. Others would choose differently, and from different sources. But then again, that's part of the fun of being different kinds of people, right?

Take Care of Your Brothers

Source: The Gospel of the Hebrews/Nazarenes, a lost Gospel only rarely quoted in Pseudo-Origen (possibly after 250 CE); and other early Christian writings

> *Another rich man said to him, "Master, what good things shall I do to live?" He said to him, "O man, fulfill the law and the prophets." He replied, "I have done that." He said to him, "Go, sell all that you possess and distribute it to the poor, and come, follow me." But the rich man began to scratch his head and it did not please him. And the Lord said to him, "How can you say, 'I have fulfilled the law and the prophets' since it is written in the law: You shall love your neighbor as yourself, and lo! Many of your brethren, sons of Abraham, are clothed in filth, dying of hunger, and your house is full of many goods, and nothing at all goes out of it to them." And returning to Simon, his disciple, who was sitting by him, he said, "Simon, son of Jonas, it is easier for a camel to enter the eye of a needle than for a rich man (to enter) the kingdom of heaven."*

—Gospel of the Nazarenes

Many will recognize that, according to The Gospel of Matthew, Jesus said something very much like this already. Following is an excerpt from the Gospel of Matthew:

> *The young man said to him, "I have kept all these; what do I still lack?" Jesus said to him, "If you wish to be perfect, go, sell your possessions, and give the money to the poor, and you will have treasure in heaven; then come, follow me." When the young man heard this word, he went away grieving, for he had many possessions. Then Jesus said to his disciples, "Truly I tell you, it will be hard for a rich person to enter the kingdom of heaven. Again I tell you, it is easier for a camel to go through the eye of a needle than for someone who is rich to enter the kingdom of God." When the disciples heard this, they were greatly astounded and said, "Then who can be saved?" But Jesus looked at them and said, "For mortals it is impossible, but for God all things are possible."*

—Matthew 19:20–26

When you compare the Gospel of Matthew to the Gospel of the Nazarenes, you see that the Gospel of the Nazarenes has Jesus going into much greater detail about the social expectations of what it means to share with each other and take responsibility for each other. So, for some readers, the Nazarene version seems to be more Jewish in its social concerns for others.

Near the Fire

Source: Origen, an early Christian theologian (185–254 CE); the Gospel of Thomas (second century CE)

In his work entitled *Sermons on Jeremiah,* Origen refers to a quote from Jesus that he's not sure is genuine; modern New Testament scholars are more convinced of the source because the quote also occurs in the Gospel of Thomas:

> *He who is near me is near the fire. He who is far from me is far from the kingdom.*

This saying isn't so different from the strong self-identification statements that Jesus makes in the Gospel of John, but it combines this idea with the strong teachings of Jesus on the "Kingdom of God" more typical of the Gospel of Mark.

More on Fire!

Source: Gospel of Thomas (second century CE)

The really interesting thing about this saying is that it seems related to the previous saying from Origen in that Jesus is talking about the Kingdom of God with the element of "fire." This use of fire in a positive sense seems typical of Jesus and his use of somewhat shocking images, such as serpents. In short, it *does* sound like him!

> *Jesus said, "I have cast fire on the world, and behold, I guard it until it blazes."*

John the Baptist talks of Jesus baptizing with fire (Luke 3:16), and Jesus describes his work as "bringing fire":

> *I came to bring fire to the earth, and how I wish it were already kindled!*
>
> —Luke 12:49

Make Your Enemies into Comrades

Source: Oxyrhynchus Papyrus 1224, an early Greek fragment from the third to fourth centuries CE

> *And pray for your enemies. For he who is not against is with you. He who today is far-off — tomorrow will near to you. . . .*

This quote is a clear combination of two otherwise well-known sayings of Jesus:

> *John answered, "Master, we saw someone casting out demons in your name, and we tried to stop him, because he does not follow with us." But Jesus said to him, "Do not stop him; for whoever is not against you is for you."*
>
> —Luke 9:49–50

> *You have heard that it was said, 'You shall love your neighbor and hate your enemy.' But I say to you, Love your enemies and pray for those who persecute you . . .*
>
> —Matthew 5:43–44

One can argue that Jesus *could* have said the words from Oxyrhynchus Papyrus 1224 precisely because he *definitely* said things just like it! But the combination in the Greek fragment puts a much stronger emphasis on the positive results that can come from "loving enemies" — one of the most difficult sayings of Jesus. Here you see Jesus as a practical teacher of diplomacy and peacemaking — and the potential results.

The Importance of Making Peace

Source: Gospel of Thomas (second century CE)

> *Jesus said, "If two make peace with one another in the same house, they will say to the mountain, 'Be moved!' and it will be moved."*
>
> —Gospel of Thomas 48

This is an adaptation of Jesus's teaching on moving mountains already known in the Gospel tradition, although in Thomas, the emphasis is on the relationship of people. In Mark and Matthew, the emphasis is on faith in God; here's an example from Mark:

> *Jesus answered them, "Have faith in God. Truly I tell you, if you say to this mountain, 'Be taken up and thrown into the sea,' and if you do not doubt in your heart, but believe that what you say will come to pass, it will be done for you . . ."*
>
> —Mark 11:22–23

Care for Your Brother!

Source: Jerome's (347–420 CE) "Commentaries on Ephesians," and "Ezekiel"

> *The Lord said to his disciples: And never be joyful, save when you behold your brother with love.*

This quote is similar to another saying that Jerome quotes from this same alleged source (now lost); Jerome writes:

> *In the Gospel According to the Hebrews, which the Nazarenes read, there is counted among the most grievous offences: '. . . He that has grieved the spirit of his brother . . .'*

These quotes are arguably "more Jewish" in that they're strongly ethical, not only "spiritual" — that is, they're connected to issues in the world (like people taking care of each other) and not just issues of spiritual significance. In short, they're political as well as spiritual!

The Upside-Down Kingdom

Source: The Gospel of Thomas (second century CE)

> *Jesus said, "The man advanced in days will not hesitate to ask an infant of seven days about the place of life, and he shall live. For many who are first will be last . . ."*

In this phrase, the Gospel of Thomas has combined in a tighter saying what may have been *implied* in the context in Mark 9. Note the connection between receiving children and Jesus's famous phrase about role reversal (social reversal) in the Kingdom of God:

> *He sat down, called the twelve, and said to them, "Whoever wants to be first must be last of all and servant of all." Then he took a little child and put it among them; and taking it in his arms, he said to them, "Whoever welcomes one such child in my name welcomes me, and whoever welcomes me welcomes not me but the one who sent me."*
>
> —Mark 9:35–37

The Empty Jar of Meal

Source: The Gospel of Thomas (second century CE)

> *Jesus said, "The Kingdom of the Father is like a woman who was carrying a jar which was full of meal. While she was walking on a long road the handle of the jar broke; the meal spilled out behind her on the road. She did not notice it; she was unaware of the accident. When she came to her house she put the jar down and found it was empty . . ."*

This short parable has no parallel in the Gospel accounts, but it seems similar to the spirit of Jesus when he talks about *unintentional* goodness — going about your life doing the right thing without seeking publicity and attention so that others will see that your good life has an impact on the world. This is the opposite spirit to spin doctors and publicity agents, to put it in modern terms. Here's an example from Matthew:

> *But when you give alms, do not let your left hand know what your right hand is doing, so that your alms may be done in secret; and your Father who sees in secret will reward you.*

—Matthew 6:3–4

The Muslim Jesus?

Source: Exterior mosque carving; also found in "Abdallah ibn Qutayba" (ninth century CE)

On the South Wall of the Great Mosque at Fathpur Sikri (in India), there's a fascinating quote attributed to Jesus. This city was built by the famous Indian monarch, Akbar, in the 16th century but was in use only ten years. By 1605, it was largely deserted because of the inadequate water supply. Carved on the Buland Darwaza (Gate of Victory) is the following saying:

> *Jesus, on whom be peace, has said: "The world is a bridge. Go over it, but do not build a house upon it!"*

This saying, as well as the one covered in the next section, comes from Islamic tradition; we chose to include them in this list to illustrate that Islam, of course, also honors a rich tradition of Jesus sayings. They all came late in the game, of course, as Islam began 600 years after the time of Jesus. But they're still fascinating and occasionally quite moving. In this saying, Jesus advises one to not become too attached to the things of this world — like riches, fame, and power — but keep one's mind on the values of God! Of course, the saying expresses this message with much more poetic grace and the kind of memorable images so typical of Jesus.

The Greater Spirituality

Source: Abdallah ibn Qutayba (ninth century CE)

> *Jesus met a man and asked him, "What are you doing?" "I am devoting myself to God," the man replied. Jesus asked, "Who is caring for you?" "My brother," replied the man. Jesus said, "Your brother is more devoted to God than you are."*

I (Daniel) confess that I love this last one. Tarif Khalidi cites it in his wonderful book, *The Muslim Jesus;* Khalidi uses it as quoted by an early Islamic theologian who died in 884 CE. Islam, of course, honors the teaching and legacy of Jesus very highly, although not as a human embodiment of God as most Christian traditions do.

It's not surprising, then, that Islam maintains a large number of teachings associated with Jesus, some of them clearly based on the known Gospels but others very much in the *spirit* of Jesus, like this gem. This saying reveals clear emphasis on the *practical* spirituality of Jesus — a spirituality that stresses the importance of people taking care of each other!

Chapter 20

Top Ten "Lost" Books Every Student of the Bible Should Read

In This Chapter

▶ Exploring works that expand upon biblical material

▶ Comparing what Jesus said with what he may have said

▶ Appreciating the diversity of views and creative expressions in both Christianity and early Judaism

*T*hey may not have made it into the Bible, but their historical, doctrinal, narrative, and spiritual significance make these ten books "must reads" for serious students of the Bible.

All the works that we address in this chapter are available in books or online and are well worth your time. Experiencing these lost books will enhance your understanding and appreciation of the Bible as it's known today.

The Gospel of Thomas

The Gospel of Thomas is a very early collection of sayings of Jesus arranged in a list without the normal narrative or description of the events in the life of Jesus that you read in the Gospels of the New Testament. It has been dated as early as the late first century or early second century CE.

Many of the alleged sayings of Jesus in the Gospel of Thomas are clearly influenced by the early Christian "heresy" (or should we say "disagreement") known as *Gnosticism,* which emphasized "secret knowledge" as the way to salvation. This knowledge was also characterized by a definite downgrading of the physical world and physical bodies as less important — and even something to be "denied" — as a way to develop the soul or spirit, which was considered far more important. We devote Chapter 12 to Gnosticism and Gnostic Christian writings.

New Testament scholars have been taking the Gospel of Thomas increasingly seriously as a very important non-canonical series of teachings of Jesus. Does it contain some "lost" sayings of Jesus? Maybe, but the whole thing makes fascinating reading regardless.

Some of the sayings attributed to Jesus in the Gospel of Thomas are rather questionable, have Gnostic tendencies, and are dismissed by New Testament scholars as contrary to known sayings of Jesus. However, *some* of the sayings in Thomas are eerily familiar; they sound so much like Jesus that they may well be his and simply weren't preserved in the Gospels of the New Testament.

Another really important reason to know about Thomas actually has to do with the books of Luke and Matthew. One of the most important theories about the origins of Luke and Matthew is called the *two source theory*. This theory suggests that the writers of Luke and Matthew used two books, or "sources," to help them write their Gospels — especially those parts in Luke and Matthew that are virtually the same. The theory also suggests that the writers copied some parts of their works from older sources. One source is definitely the Gospel of Mark, thought to be the oldest Gospel. The other source is called "Q" for the German word "quelle," which means "source." This was a theorized collection of Jesus sayings that may have circulated before the Gospels were written. Such a collection of sayings was disputed by many . . . until Thomas was discovered and proved that such "collections of sayings" did in fact exist as a form of early Christian literature. Thomas isn't "Q," but it shows that there were writings that simply listed sayings — much like "Q" was supposed to be.

1 Enoch

1 Enoch is a long book that claims to be a record of the experiences of the enigmatic figure known as Enoch in the book of Genesis 5:24. That verse suggests that Enoch was taken up into heaven without dying, so the *book* called 1 Enoch is a report that he made to his son after he came back to earth and described his journeys in heaven. The only full version of 1 Enoch is in Ethiopic because it was preserved for centuries by the Ethiopian Christians, who revered it as virtually "Sacred Scripture." The work was rediscovered by westerners in the 18th century.

1 Enoch is weird (see its inclusion in Chapter 17), but it's also terribly important and at times downright fascinating (especially the long allegorical section that describes Old Testament history as adventures of sheep, goats, wolves, and other four-legged friends!). 1 Enoch helps you understand the development of Jewish writing about "end times," commonly called

apocalyptic writing. Presently, 1 Enoch is the oldest example of this style of writing that exists. Pieces of it were found in the Dead Sea material, dated as early as 300–200 BCE.

It's clear that 1 Enoch was terribly important to many people and was widely read by Jews and Christians — it is even quoted in Jude in the New Testament. Furthermore, 1 Enoch proves that there were many different kinds of Jewish belief in the centuries before Christianity, and it establishes that at least *some* Jews were expecting a Messiah very similar to what Jesus later was!

1 Clement

We're often asked if there are any early Christian writings that we would have included in the New Testament if it had been up to us. Frankly, that's a dangerous question, because if it were up to modern readers, the Bible might be twice its existing length for some or half as long for others! But if *we* were asked, we think we have a pretty good answer: We would have been open to including *1 Clement*.

1 Clement praises peace and harmony between Christians, and in our opinion, Christians could use a *lot* more peace and harmony! The letter from Clement (and there's little doubt that it's written in standard letter form) is now traditionally divided into 65 chapters, but the work isn't as long as you may think because some of the chapters are only five or six verses long.

Even though 1 Clement was actually part of some early collections of the so-called important Christian writings that eventually led to the final version of the New Testament, the work has gotten a bad rap in some circles because the writer wants to restore some leaders in a church in which the older leaders have been deposed. So 1 Clement is often read as a kind of conservative call to keep the old guard in power and sometimes is used to defend the status quo! We doubt that the book is that conservative, and moreover, the conservatism is not a *major* part of 1 Clement. Most of the book is a compassionate and concerned pleading from an early Christian leader to other Christians that asks, to quote Rodney King, "Can't we all just get along?"

Joseph and Asenath

Joseph and Asenath is an excellent example of ancient Jewish pious storytelling at its best — charming, entertaining, and at times actually quite moving. It's an example of the kind of writings that use the Bible as the basis for spinning out further elaborations, and some of these elaborations reveal more about the later times than those times in the story itself. In this case, the conversion of Asenath in order to marry Joseph raises interesting questions about conversions to Judaism in the Greek and Roman period, but not the actual "time" of Joseph. Possibly written before Christianity in the first century BCE, this story tells a much-expanded version of the tales of Joseph in Egypt and goes far beyond the material in the closing chapters of the book of Genesis.

Often referred to as a "biblical romance," the story features Joseph working as an official under Pharaoh and falling in love with a beautiful but very headstrong Egyptian woman. She eventually converts to Judaism and becomes Joseph's wife (or we should say that she first falls for *him*, but we don't want to give away too much of a great story!).

Of course, this writing addresses some serious subjects. It may well have featured in debates among Jews with regard to the permissibility of marriage with non-Jews and under which conditions this was acceptable. Furthermore, the more positive statements about Jews living in Egypt may have reflected Jewish life in the Egyptian diaspora in the centuries just before Christianity, especially the large Jewish community in the coastal city of Alexandria — once a very prominent Jewish and later Christian community.

The Odes of Solomon

One day, British Quaker scholar of ancient manuscripts J. Rendal Harris found a book left in his office in Birmingham, England. It turned out to be *The Odes of Solomon!* Although other versions of the Odes have now been identified, we confess that we love this story of discovery — an important ancient writing cannot only be discovered after a search or discovered accidentally, but in this case, it can even be mysteriously delivered to your door!

Not only is the story of how one of the old versions of the Odes of Solomon turned up a charming tale, the book itself is nothing short of beautiful. The sheer beauty of the language and the joyful expressions of faith would have made this, in our opinion, a welcome addition to the Christian Bible. Moreover, in the poems that make up the Odes, you hear something of the spirituality of early Jewish Christians. (The general consensus, although occasionally disputed, is that this is a Christian work deeply influenced by Jewish ideas, and thus perhaps it was an early "Jewish-Christian" writing.) Though the book has some rather odd turns of phrase and even some images that are a bit unorthodox, on the whole it's quite moving. For example, the notion that Jesus didn't really die raises some theological questions — but on the other hand, it may just be a poetic way of speaking of the Resurrection, or it may be a quite unorthodox statement that Jesus wasn't actually fully human and therefore only *appeared* to die. The latter is an idea that Christians argued about rather vehemently in the early centuries!

Still, despite these occasional doctrinal hiccups (which were sufficient, however, to keep the work out of the Christian Bible), we find much of the poetic imagery of the Odes to be as moving as much of the biblical Psalms.

3 Maccabees

3 Maccabees takes place during the reign of Ptolemy IV, whose throne name was "Philopator" (he reigned around 221–205 BCE). It's impossible to know the precise date of this work (long after Ptolemy IV's reign, of course), and some scholars even argue that it may be a veiled reference to *much* later persecutions of Jews, such as in the time of Roman Emperor Augustus, who started to register Jewish subjects and charge a poll tax sometime around 24 BCE.

In 3 Maccabees, Ptolemy determines to exterminate the Jews of Alexandria because he's angry at his reception in Jerusalem when he tries to enter the Temple, which is forbidden to non-Jews. He orders that the Jews be rounded up in a large coliseum and trampled by elephants. But on the first try, the king oversleeps and doesn't give the actual order. On the second try, the king completely forgets about his order and even acts surprised that he would suggest such a thing! When he recovers his anger in the third attempt, angels appear and drive the elephants back toward the king's officials! In the end, the king repents of his attempts and recognizes the loyalty of his Jewish subjects.

3 Maccabees almost has the air of dark comedy. It seems that the stories are told for pious entertainment, but they also feature an interesting assumption that even nonviolent resistance will be honored by God through God's miraculous intervention. (This is a reminder of the stories of Daniel, particularly the story of Daniel in the lion's den and the story in which God miraculously prevents Jewish martyrs from burning in the fiery furnace.) The historical reality of the stories of 3 Maccabees is widely doubted, but the stories are definitely entertaining.

Yet on a more somber note, the stories point to a reality of fearful existence for Jewish subjects of Greek and Roman Imperial rule. Thus, the stories may not be literal history, but speaking of severe persecution was definitely based on the experience of fear and persecution that was only too real for many of the Jewish communities throughout the centuries before and after the rise of Christianity.

The Acts of Peter and the Twelve Apostles

The Nag Hammadi Library, a collection of 13 bundles of written works discovered in 1945 in Egypt, ranks among the most spectacular discoveries of ancient Christian texts in the 20th century.

Although virtually all these works are Gnostic in character and therefore considered outside the "main" tradition that became Orthodox Christianity, some of these writings are real treasures — and we consider *The Acts of Peter and the Twelve Apostles* to be one of those treasures.

Unlike the esoteric and strange writings that compose *most* of the Nag Hammadi Library, the Acts story is a charming tale of the early Christian followers of Jesus encountering Jesus in various disguises as they travel on a fantasy-like journey on an unknown island. The story is filled with allegory and metaphor about the Gospel message and would make a charming children's tale (well, most of it would anyway . . .).

If you like C.S. Lewis and "Christian fantasy" literature, you'll be thrilled to discover that such fantasy literature is among the early, and favorite, styles of early Christian writing. Themes of the righteousness of the poor, the arrogance of the rich and powerful, and the miracle of faith in Jesus are all expressed in powerful terms in this story.

The Acts of Thomas

The Acts of Thomas features one early Christian tale that's worth the price of admission (and worth much of the strange stuff in the rest of the book).

In this early Christian legend, the Apostle Thomas is sent to India and employed by a king to build him a palace. The king regularly sends Thomas money, thinking Thomas is hard at work. But Thomas is actually giving all the money to the poor and starving. The king finds out, and plans to have Thomas killed! But just then, the king's brother dies and his spirit goes to heaven, where he's shown a magnificent palace — a palace that Thomas has been "building" for the king *in heaven* with Thomas's good deeds!

The king's brother is allowed to return to earth briefly to beg the king to allow him to live in even a basement closet of his magnificent heavenly palace! The king understands the message and becomes a devoted follower of Jesus.

The Acts of Paul and Thecla

The story of St. Paul and his ministry to (and later with) Thecla is one of the most fascinating of the early Acts literature. In this series of legends that comprises *The Acts of Paul and Thecla,* Thecla becomes a major female Christian leader after being converted by listening to Paul. In fact, Thecla went on to become a very important person in later Christian art and legend, but we have no idea if the character was based on a real person or entirely a matter of folklore. But even if her story is folklore . . . it's mighty *good* folklore!

When Thecla is threatened with death because she refuses to marry a local nobleman, the attempt to execute her by burning her at the stake fails because of miraculous intervention. Attempts made to feed her to wild animals are also miraculously stopped. The local official who tried to feed her to the lions is convinced by Thecla's courage, and Thecla goes on to become a local Church leader whose preaching converts many.

The big question is why a widely popular Christian legend would feature a *female* preacher and leader if women weren't preachers or leaders in early Christianity. In short, even if Thecla is a legend, she may well be based on *real* female leaders in early Christianity, and that would be good news indeed.

Testaments of the Twelve Patriarchs

Like the story of Joseph and Asenath, the *Testaments of the Twelve Patriarchs* is another expansion of the biblical tradition written by a Jewish writer in the years just before Christianity.

The story is based on Jacob's blessings of his sons in Genesis 48–49. Unlike the book of Genesis, in the Testaments each of the 12 sons of Jacob do the talking, often beginning with a confession of his particular sins and then giving advice to "my children" — the presumed readers of the testaments. One of the reasons that this particular writing was popular — and continues to be read with great appreciation — is the profound ethical advice that many of the brothers give to their readers. In many of these speeches, you see a striking peacefulness precisely at a time when violent events were rocking the Jewish communities (in the second century BCE through to the first century CE).

Much of the teaching in this writing seems to build toward a picture of Joseph, whose compassion for his brothers in Egypt in Genesis is seen as a model of patience and long-suffering. In fact, when you arrive at the *Testament of Joseph,* a section suggests that Joseph's attempts to live a good life parallel the teaching of Jesus rather dramatically. This is either a Christian insertion into the work or a rather dramatic anticipation of Jesus's teachings in Matthew 25:31–46.

Appendix

Resources for Those Who Are Really into This "Lost Books" Thing

● ●

*W*e hope that you've read some (or all!) of the *Lost Books of the Bible For Dummies,* made lots of notes in the margins (yes, we write in our books sometimes!) like "Must read this" or "Wow! Really??" and now you want to head off to the library or bookstore and start your engines! This appendix provides a list of the books *we* recommend to help you on your way. We've included some of the best discussions and best translations of these writings in English. Enjoy your journey, and maybe we'll see you in the aisles of the library (shhhhhhh . . .!).

✔ *Apocryphal Gospels: An Introduction* by Hans-Josef Klauck, translated by Brian McNeil (Continuum, 2003)

This interesting book contains translations of only the materials about Jesus — not other early Christian literature — and some good notes from Professor Klauck.

✔ *The Apocryphal New Testament: Being the Apocryphal Gospels, Acts, Epistles, and Apocalypses* by Montague Rhodes (Clarendon Press, 1924)

If you find this book, buy it (and if you find two, send me one!). This was the standard edition of many of the early Christian writings translated into English and has since been replaced by the next book in this list, the masterful translation by J. K. Elliott.

✔ *The Apocryphal New Testament: A Collection of Apocryphal Christian Literature in an English Translation* by J. K. Elliott (Clarendon Press, 1993)

This is it, folks — the main collection of early Christian non-canonical writings all in one handy volume. It isn't the cheapest book you'll ever buy, but it certainly is one of the most interesting! Professor Elliott is one of the most knowledgeable scholars working in this field, and his translations are not only readable but downright elegant!

✔ *The Cambridge History of Early Christian Literature* edited by Frances Young, Lewis Ayres, and Andrew Louth (Cambridge University Press, 2004)

If you want a little more historical background about the entire world of early Christian writings, including early Christian theologians, this is a very helpful collection of articles. It's a bit academic, but definitely readable.

✔ *Constantine's Bible: Politics and the Making of the New Testament* by David L. Dungan (Fortress Press, 2007)

David Dungan has some really fascinating ideas about how Constantine the Emperor may have intervened in the decisions about what books are in the Bible and what books aren't in the Bible. This clearly written resource makes a compelling argument!

✔ *A Feminist Companion to the New Testament Apocrypha* edited by Amy-Jill Levine (Continuum, 2006)

There are lots of materials in the lost books category that relate to issues dealing with women in early Christianity. If these issues matter to you (and they should matter to all of us, really), then the scholars who contributed to this resource have provided some helpful notes to many early Christian lost books.

✔ *The Five Gospels: What did Jesus Really Say?* by Robert W. Funk, Roy W. Hoover, and The Jesus Seminar (Polebridge/Macmillan Publishing Company, 1993)

This is the famous book that came from the "Jesus Seminar," a gathering of New Testament scholars who tried to come to agreement on which New Testament sayings are definitely from Jesus. This book includes a survey of the sayings of Jesus in the Gospel of Thomas.

✔ *The Formation of the Christian Biblical Canon* by Lee M. McDonald (Hendrickson, 1995)

This is one of the best, clearest, and most thorough presentations of the whole issue of how the canon of the Bible (Old Testament and New Testament) developed in history. McDonald has written a number of works on this topic, but this is the best of the lot.

✔ *The Gnostic Discoveries: The Impact of the Nag Hammadi Library* by Marvin Meyer (HarperCollins, 2005)

This is an interesting book about the Nag Hammadi library and early Christian Gnosticism, but be aware that it's not a collection of translations.

✔ *The Gnostic Gospels* by Elaine Pagels (Vintage, 1989)

Professor Pagels is one of the best known and most widely appreciated scholars of Gnostic Christianity. Always provocative and interesting, she's justly noted for her scholarship on this subject, and in this book, she pays particular attention to the role of female characters in Gnostic texts.

✔ *The Gnostic Scriptures* by Bentley Layton (Doubleday & Co., 1987)

This is probably the most popular translation of the Nag Hammadi (and other) Christian Gnostic writings. Professor Layton has worked hard to make very difficult writings a bit easier to read and perhaps understand. He also provides very helpful discussions and notes with the translations.

✔ *Holy Writings, Sacred Text: The Canon of Early Christianity* by John Barton (Westminster/John Knox, 1997)

This is a very interesting work that deals with some of the more difficult questions about the formation of the early canons of the Bible. If you're fascinated with the process of determining the Bible contents, this book is required reading!

✔ *How the Bible Came to Be* by John Barton (Westminster/John Knox, 1998)

Here, the Oxford scholar John Barton takes up the general question of the emergence of the Bible in a straightforward and learned manner. We highly recommend this resource.

✔ *An Introduction to the New Testament Apocrypha* by F. Lapham (T&T Clark/ Continuum, 2003)

This is a very interesting work that discusses the geography of the early non-biblical materials and how their location may have influenced the kind of writings from that area.

✔ *Lost Christianities: The Battles for Scripture and the Faiths We Never Knew* by Bart D. Ehrman (Oxford University Press, 2003)

Bart Ehrman is one of the most important scholars working in the field of non-canonical literature (having translated an entire edition of the Apostolic Fathers), and his work is well worth a read!

✔ *Lost Scriptures: Books That Did Not Make It Into The New Testament* by Bart D. Ehrman (Oxford University Press, 2003)

Again, Bart Ehrman is one of the best authorities in this field, and this book is a collection of translations of excerpts from some of the writings we discuss in this book. (A full collection, however, can be found in Elliott and the older work by Rhodes, both of which appear earlier in this list.)

✔ *The Old Testament Pseudepigrapha, Volumes 1 and 2* edited by James H. Charlesworth (Doubleday & Co., 1985)

This is the standard translation of the Jewish and Old Testament writings — that is, writings dealing with Old Testament themes, even if written by early Christians. Each translation, by many different scholars, includes an excellent introduction summarizing what scholars think about each writing.

✔ *1 Enoch 1: A Commentary on the Book of 1 Enoch Chapters 1–36, 81–108 (Hermeneia: A Critical and Historical Commentary on the Bible)* by George W.E. Nickelsburg (Fortress Press, 2001)

George Nickelsburg is one of the world's authorities on Enoch literature, and this is the first volume of his wonderfully detailed commentary on the Book of Enoch (also known as 1 Enoch). If you're curious about Enoch, this resource is the place to start!

✔ *Other Early Christian Gospels: A Critical Edition of the Surviving Greek Manuscripts* by Andrew E. Bernhard (T&T Clark/Continuum, 2006)

This is another excellent overview of the non-biblical materials dealing with Jesus, especially for those interested in reading the Greek texts.

✔ *The Nag Hammadi Library* edited by James M. Robinson (Harper and Row, 1988)

This is one of the main and the only comprehensive translations of the Nag Hammadi materials in English. You'll find good notes at the beginning of each translated work.

✔ *New Testament Apocrypha, Volumes 1 and 2* edited by Wilhelm Schneemelcher (Westminster/John Knox Press, 1992)

This wonderful collection of two volumes of translations into English of Christian non-canonical writings covers much of the same ground as Elliott's translation but also contains further scholarly notes. (We used this work particularly for our chapter on non-canonical Pauline writings.)

✔ *A Synopsis of the Apocryphal Nativity and Infancy Narratives* by J. K. Elliott (Brill, 2006)

In this wonderful work, Professor Elliott has arranged all the early Infancy writings about Jesus into a "parallel," which means you can read and compare each of them as you go because he divides them into similar scenes and episodes. Typically brilliant work by Professor Elliott!

Index